FUNDAMENTALS OF
FORTRAN PROGRAMMING

FUNDAMENTALS OF FORTRAN PROGRAMMING

Second Edition

Robert C. Nickerson
San Francisco State University

WINTHROP PUBLISHERS, INC.
Cambridge, Massachusetts

Library of Congress Cataloging in Publication Data

Nickerson, Robert C.
    Fundamentals of FORTRAN programming.

    Includes index.
    1. FORTRAN (Computer program language) I. Title.
QA76.73.F25N49 1979   001.6'424   79-19423
ISBN 0-87626-301-5

© 1980, 1975 by Winthrop Publishers, Inc.
    17 Dunster Street, Cambridge, Massachusetts   02138

10 9 8 7 6 5 4

CONTENTS

PREFACE

The major objective of the second edition of this text remains the same as that of the first edition; that is, to provide a carefully paced introduction to computer programming and the FORTRAN language for students with only a minimal mathematical background. However, with this edition much of the material has been updated to reflect changes in the FORTRAN language and to incorporate current thinking on programming methodology. The revised text covers not only the 1966 versions of ANS FORTRAN but also additional features of FORTRAN 77 (the 1978 version of ANS FORTRAN) and some features of WATFIV-S. This new material has been presented in such a way that it may be covered or omitted at the discretion of the instructor. These topics include format-free I/O, block IF statements, WHILE loops, character data processing, and other features.

In addition to the new language elements, structured programming methodology has been incorporated into the text. The problem-solving process is emphasized from the beginning. Basic program structure is discussed early with complete chapters devoted to decision logic (Chapter 5) and loop control (Chapter 6). The programming process is discussed in detail in Chapter 8 where program development, structure, style, testing, and documentation are examined. The use of subprograms in developing large programs is explained in Chapter 12. The overall approach is to develop in the student the ability to think systematically through the solution to a problem and to implement the solution correctly and understandably in FORTRAN.

A number of other features of the text have been added or revised with this edition. These include the following:

- Both batch and interactive (time-sharing) systems and programming features are discussed. This facilitates the use of the text with either type of system.
- Chapter 3 covers both formatted and format-free I/O. The instructor need only select those sections that apply to the I/O system being used. In general, subsequent chapters are not dependent upon a knowledge of one or the other system.

- The basic I/O discussed in Chapter 3 is the minimum that is necessary for simple numeric input and output. Additional features, including nonnumeric I/O, are presented in a later chapter (Chapter 7), which may be covered at any time after Chapter 3.

- More examples and illustrative programs are included in this edition. As with the first edition, the examples are nonmathematical in nature and are oriented toward applications that the students can readily understand.

- Additional algorithms are discussed including algorithms for logical and character data processing and for array manipulation (e.g., searching and sorting).

- The number of programming problems has been substantially increased. Most problems still require only a minimal mathematical background and emphasize nontechnical areas including business and social science. In addition, a number of problems have been added that will be of interest to math, science, and engineering students.

- Flowcharting is now covered in an appendix rather than in the main text. This allows the instructor to discuss this material at the time that he or she feels is most appropriate. All flowcharts are keyed to programs in the text.

The text is organized into three parts. The first part, consisting of Chapters 1 and 2, introduces the background material necessary to understand programming and FORTRAN. Chapters 3 through 8, comprising the second part, present the fundamental elements of FORTRAN and develop basic programming methodology. Advanced FORTRAN features and programming are discussed in the third part, which consists of Chapters 9 through 13. The five appendices cover differences between various versions of FORTRAN, FORTRAN-supplied functions, the operation of the IBM 029 keypunch, exponential forms, and flowcharting.

Chapters 1, 2, and 13 contain review questions and computer exercises that emphasize important topics in these chapters. Programming problems are provided at the end of Chapter 3 through 12. The problems range in difficulty from relatively easy to very difficult and challenging. Test data is provided with most problems. An instructor's manual is available that contains teaching suggestions, alternative course schedules, answers to review questions, test questions and answers, and overhead transparency masters for a number of illustrations from the text.

Many of the ideas for the revisions in the text came from reviews by users of the first edition. I am grateful for their thoughtful comments and suggestions. I would also like to acknowledge the contribution of my students who provided much feedback as I class-tested the text material.

Finally, I would like to thank my wife, Betsy. Not only did she turn my often illegible scratchings into a typed manuscript, but she also served as editor, critic, and friend throughout the long writing process.

R. C. N.

FUNDAMENTALS OF
FORTRAN PROGRAMMING

Chapter 1

COMPUTERS, PROGRAMS, AND DATA

Computers are devices that are used to solve problems. The process that people go through to prepare a computer to solve a problem is called programming. In this book we explain a particular type of computer programming. However, before we can understand the programming process in detail we must be familiar with a few background ideas. In this chapter we discuss the basic concepts that are necessary to begin studying programming.

1-1. COMPUTERS

We can call any calculating device a "computer." For example, adding machines, slide rules, and pocket calculators are all "computers" because each calculates or computes. However, we usually do not use the word "computer" for these devices. Instead we call something a *computer* if it has three distinguishing characteristics.

First, a computer is electronic; that is, it calculates by electrical means. We aren't concerned with how this is done in this book but there is an important consequence of this characteristic. Because computers calculate by electrical means, they can perform their calculations at a very high speed. Thus, modern computers are able to do hundreds of thousands of operations (such as additions and subtractions) in a second.

The second distinguishing characteristic of computers is that they have the ability to "remember" things. We call the things that a computer can remember *data*. Data[†] is facts, figures, numbers, and words that are important to the problem being solved by the computer. A computer can remember, or, more correctly, *store* data for immediate use or for use in the future.

The final characteristic that distinguishes a computer from other calculating devices is its ability to receive and follow a set of instructions that tells it how to solve a problem. Such a set of instructions is called a *program*. The program is prepared by a person, called a *programmer*, who is familiar with the different things that a computer can do. Once the program is prepared it is given to the computer in a form that the computer can understand and *stored* along with the data to be used by the program. Then the instructions in the program are performed, or *executed*, automatically by the computer.

In this book we are concerned with the process of preparing computer programs. The preparation process is called *programming* and this book explains one commonly used way of programming computers. However, before we can describe programming in detail we need to have an understanding of the physical organization of a computer.

1-2. ORGANIZATION OF A COMPUTER

As we have seen, computers are distinguished from other calculating devices by the electronic, data storage, and stored program characteristics explained in the previous section. However, the physical organization of a computer is more complex than we might think from this discussion. One way of viewing the organization of a computer is shown in Fig. 1-1. In this diagram, boxes represent different components of the computer and lines with arrowheads show the paths that data and instructions can take within the computer. In this section we describe each of the computer components shown in Fig. 1-1. Figures 1-2 and 1-3 show actual computers with many of the components discussed in this section.

There are three basic parts to any computer — an input device, a central processing unit, and an output device. An *input device* is a mechanism that accepts data in some form from outside of the computer and transforms the data into an electronic form that is understandable to the computer. The data that is accepted is called *input data*, or simply *input*. For example, one of the most common forms for conveying input data to a computer is punched cards. An example

---

[†]The word *data* is most correctly used as a plural noun. The singular of data is *datum*. However, people commonly use the word data in a singular rather than plural sense. We will usually follow the common practice in this book.

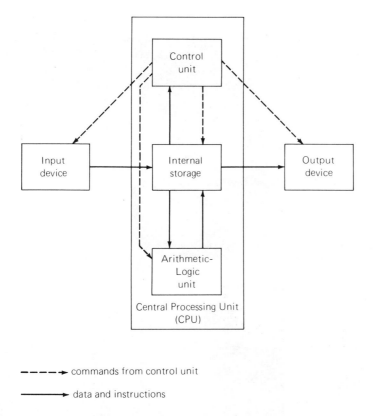

FIGURE 1-1 Organization of a computer.

of a punched card is shown in Fig. 1–4. Data is recorded on the card by punching various patterns of holes in the cards. (We will describe punched card data in detail in a later section of this chapter.) An input device for punched cards is designed to recognize what data is represented by the patterns of holes in a card and to transform the data into an electronic representation understandable to the central processing unit. Such a device is called a *card reader*. (See Fig. 1-2.)

An *output device* performs the opposite function of an input device. An output device receives data in an electronic form from the central processing unit and then transforms the data into a form that can be used outside of the computer. The resulting data is the *output data*, or simply the *output*, from the computer. For example, one common form of output is a printed document or report. Figure 1–5 shows an example of such printed output. Data from the central processing unit is transmitted electronically to a device called a *printer*. (See Fig. 1-2.) In the printer, the data is transformed into printed symbols and a paper copy of the output data is produced.

Instead of punching input data into cards and reading the data with

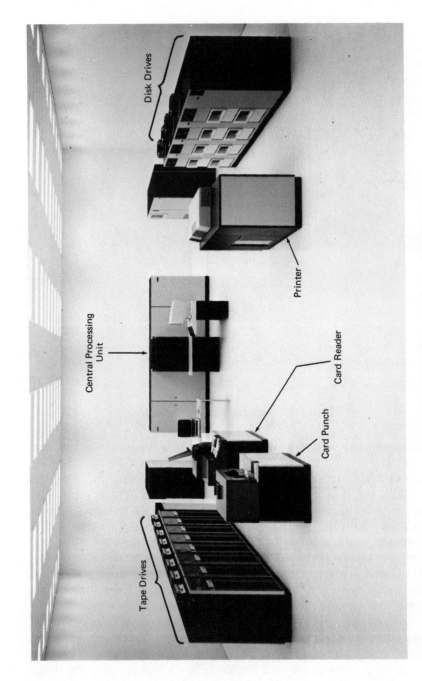

FIGURE 1-2 A typical batch computer system. This is an IBM System/370. (Courtesy of IBM Corp.)

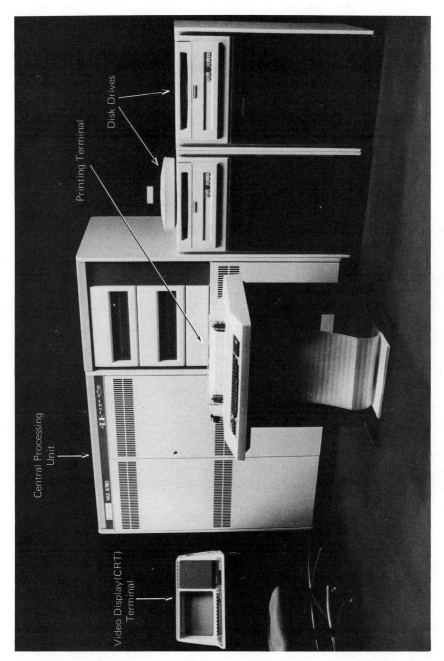

FIGURE 1-3 A typical interactive (time-sharing) computer system. This is a DEC VAX 11/780. (Courtesy of Digital Equipment Corp.)

5

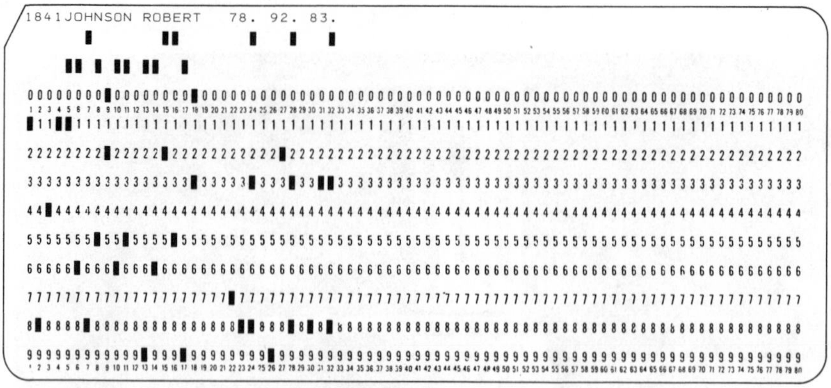

FIGURE 1–4   Punched card data.

a card reader, input is sometimes typed directly into the computer using a typewriter-like keyboard. Often a printing mechanism is attached to the keyboard and the computer uses this to print the output. Such a combined input/output (or *I/O*) device is commonly called a *terminal*. Figure 1–3 shows an example of a printing terminal. Another type of terminal combines a keyboard with a TV-like screen on which the output is displayed. Such a video display terminal is also shown in Fig. 1–3. This type of terminal is sometimes called a *CRT*, for cathode ray tube (another name for a TV tube).

Between the input device and the output device is the component of the computer that does the actual computing or processing. This is the *central processing unit* or *CPU*. (Refer to Fig. 1–1.) Input data is transformed into an electronic form by the input device and sent to the central processing unit. In the CPU the input data is stored and used in calculations or other types of data processing to produce the solution to the desired problem. After processing is completed, the results are sent to the output device where the data is transformed into the final output.

In the central processing unit are three basic units that work to-

TEST SCORE ANALYSIS

NUMBER	STUDENT NAME	TEST 1	TEST 2	TEST 3	TOTAL	AVERAGE
1841	JOHNSON ROBERT	78.	92.	83.	253.	84.3
1906	SMITH MARY	100.	95.	97.	292.	97.3
2133	ANDERSON RICHARD	65.	72.	57.	194.	64.7
2784	WILSON ALEX	73.	69.	78.	220.	73.3
2895	BOYD DEAN	42.	56.	47.	145.	48.3
3047	EMERY ELIZABETH	91.	100.	92.	283.	94.3
3260	COLE JAMES	75.	78.	73.	226.	75.3
3335	GUINN DOROTHY	86.	82.	74.	242.	80.7
3819	JONES ED	71.	85.	78.	234.	78.0

FIGURE 1–5   Printed output.

gether to perform the functions of the CPU. These are the internal storage, the arithmetic-logic unit, and the control unit.

The *internal storage* is the "memory" of the computer. It is in this device that data for processing is stored. In addition, instructions that make up the program are stored in the internal storage. The internal storage of a computer is not the same as human memory. However, like human memory, data can be put into the computer's internal storage and then recalled at some time in the future.

The *arithmetic-logic unit* performs arithmetic and logical operations. Computers can do the basic arithmetic tasks that a human can do. That is, a computer can add, subtract, multiply, and divide. However, more complicated calculations, such as finding the square root of a number, usually are not built into the computer. Instead, such complex processing must be performed by an appropriate sequence of basic arithmetic operations. The logical operations that a computer can do usually are limited to comparing two numbers to determine if they are equal or if one is greater than or less than the other. Complex logical processing, as is required in a computer that plays a game such as chess, is accomplished by long sequences of these simple operations.

The final unit in the CPU is the *control unit*. The function of the control unit is to tell the other units in the computer what to do. It does this by following the instructions in the program. The program, as we have seen, is kept in the computer's internal storage. During processing, each instruction in the program is brought from the internal storage to the control unit. The control unit analyzes the instruction, then gives commands to the other units based on what the instruction tells the control unit to do. The execution of one instruction may involve actions in any of the other components of the computer. (See Fig. 1-1.) After executing an instruction, the next instruction in the programmed sequence is brought to the control unit and executed. This continues until all the instructions in the program have been executed.

As an example of a simple computer program, let's assume that we wish to solve the problem of finding the sum of two numbers using a computer. To do this the computer must get the two numbers to be added from the input device, then the numbers must be added using the arithmetic-logic unit, and finally the sum must be sent to the output device so that we can see the result. Thus, a computer program to solve this problem would involve three instructions:

1. Read two numbers.
2. Add the numbers.
3. Write the result.

The programmer would enter these instructions into the computer using the computer's input device. For example, the instructions may be punched in cards just as input data is punched in cards and read with a card reader. Or the instructions could be keyed into a terminal. The input device would then transfer the instructions to the computer's internal storage.

On a signal to start (perhaps from the person operating the computer) the first instruction in the program would be brought from the internal storage to the control unit. Execution of the instructions would then proceed as follows:

1. Read two numbers. The control unit examines this instruction and issues commands to the other units that cause the instruction to be executed. For this instruction, the control unit issues a command to the input device that causes the two numbers to be transferred from the input device to the internal storage. The second instruction is then brought to the control unit.

2. Add the numbers. This instruction causes the control unit to issue three commands. The first, to the internal storage, causes the two numbers to be sent to the arithmetic-logic unit. Then a command is given to the arithmetic-logic unit to add the two numbers. Finally, the arithmetic-logic unit is commanded to return the result to the internal storage. The last instruction is then brought to the control unit.

3. Write the result. This instruction causes the control unit to issue a command to the internal storage to send the result to the output device. Then a command is given to the output device to write the result.

So far the only input/output devices that we have described are card readers, printers, and terminals. Many computers use other types of I/O devices. Usually several input devices and several output devices are attached to the computer at one time.

A common output device is the *card punch*. (See Fig. 1–2.) When this unit is used for output, the results from computer processing are punched into cards. The punched card output might then be used for input to another program.

Other forms of input and output are magnetic tape and magnetic disk. *Magnetic tape* is much like tape recorder tape; data is recorded on the surface of the tape by patterns of magnetic spots. A *magnetic tape drive* is a device that records data on magnetic tape and also retrieves data from the tape (Fig. 1–2). A *magnetic disk* resembles a phonograph record. However, like tape, the disk surface records data by magnetic spot patterns. A *magnetic disk drive* is a device for recording data on magnetic disks and for retrieving data from disks. (See Figs. 1–2 and 1–3.)

Tape and disk drives are both input and output devices; that is, they can both retrieve input data and record output data. Card readers and keyboards can be used only as input devices; printers, card punches, and video screens (CRTs) are used only as output devices. No matter what device is used, we will always say that the input device *reads* input data and the output device *writes* the output.

Figures 1-2 and 1-3 illustrate typical computers with most of the components described in this section. The computer in Fig. 1-2 has a card reader, a card punch, a printer, and a number of magnetic tape drives and disk drives. Figure 1-3 shows a computer with two terminals and several disk drives. (Usually there are more than two terminals.) Other types of computers have different configurations of I/O devices. The central processing units of different computers also vary, especially in their speed, size, and cost.

As we have seen in this section, a computer system is composed of a number of pieces of equipment. The general term for the equipment that makes up a computer system is *hardware*. Hardware consists of card readers, printers, terminals, CPUs, tape drives, disk drives, and other pieces of computer equipment. Also, as we have seen, a computer system is controlled through a set of instructions called a program. In general, programs are referred to as *software*. The software for a computer is any computer program used with the computer. A computer cannot operate without software. Thus, the computing environment consists of hardware (equipment) *and* software (programs).

1-3. MODES OF PROCESSING

There are two basic ways, or modes, of processing data on a computer: batch processing and interactive processing.

In *batch processing*, all of the data that is to be processed is prepared in some form understandable to the computer prior to the actual processing. For example, all of the data may be punched in cards. Then the batch of data is processed by the computer and the resulting output is received in a batch. An example of batch processing is the preparation of the weekly payroll for a business. At the end of the week each employee turns in a time sheet. The information from each sheet is punched into one or more cards. Once all of the cards are punched, the data is processed by a payroll program to produce the paychecks and other payroll information.

With *interactive processing* a human must interact with the computer at the time that the processing is done. Each set of data is entered directly into the computer, processed, and the output is received before the next input data is supplied. An airline reservation system is an example of this type of processing. When a customer requests a ticket for a particular flight, the reservation clerk enters the information directly into the computer using a terminal. The computer processing involves determining if there is a seat available on the requested flight. The output comes back immediately to the terminal so that the customer will know whether or not the reservation is confirmed.

Sometimes the word *time-sharing* is heard instead of interactive processing. In fact, time-sharing is a mechanism used by a computer to interact with several different computer users at one time. With time-sharing the computer allows each user a small amount of time for data processing before going on to the next user. In effect, the computer "shares its time" among the people trying to interact with it. With time-sharing it is possible for many people to interact with the computer at one time.

Computers that are designed for batch processing often have punched card input and high-speed printer output. The computer in Fig. 1-2 is such a system. When a computer is to be used for interactive processing, input and output is usually through terminals. Figure 1-3 shows an interactive computer system. Usually such a computer has many terminals so that a number of people can interact with the computer.

The type of programming discussed in this book may be used for both batch processing and interactive processing. However, the examples mainly emphasize batch processing using punched card input and producing printed output. Nevertheless, the techniques and concepts are applicable to interactive processing.

1-4. COMPUTER LANGUAGES

In Section 1-2 we saw how a computer solves a problem by following the instructions in a program. The program must describe precisely every thing that the computer has to do to solve the problem. The instructions in the program must be prepared in a form that the computer can understand and interpret. Every instruction must be prepared according to specific rules. If the rules are not followed, then the computer will not be able to understand the instructions in the program.

When we program a computer we are communicating with a machine. In general, when we want to communicate with someone or something we use a *language*. For human communication we use *natural languages* such as English or Spanish. When we want to communicate with a computer we use a computer language.

To write a sentence in a natural human language we form words and phrases from letters and other symbols. The way that we put together the sentence is determined by the grammar rules of the language.

Depending on what words are used and how they are organized, the sentence has some meaning associated with it. With a computer language, the rules that describe how we can combine various symbols into recognizable patterns are called the *syntax* of the language. The meanings associated with different patterns of symbols are called the *semantics* of the language. For example, the *syntax* of a particular computer language may say that one type of instruction has the following form:

variable name = arithmetic expression

That is, the instruction consists of a *variable name* followed by an equal sign followed by an *arithmetic expression.* (Of course, we must know what a variable name and an arithmetic expression are in order to complete the instruction.) The *semantics* of the language tells us that this instruction means that the value of the arithmetic expression on the right of the equal sign is to be assigned to the variable name on the left. (In Chapter 4 we will study this instruction in detail.)

In this book we describe the syntax and semantics of the FORTRAN language. FORTRAN is just one of many computer languages. In fact, there are several groups of languages and many different languages in each group.

One group of languages is called *machine language.* Machine language is the language in which a computer actually does its processing. To a computer, this type of language is a series of electronic impulses. A programmer expresses this language using binary numbers, that is, using a series of 1's and 0's. Each type of computer has its own machine language and since there are many different types of computers, there are many machine languages. However, the most important characteristic of machine language is that, for any particular computer, the machine language for that computer is the *only language that it can understand. Every program for that computer must either be written in its machine language or written in another language, and then translated into its machine language.*

We think of machine language as a low-level language because it is the basic language of a computer. Several higher levels of computer languages exist. These languages are called "high-level" because they are closer to natural human or mathematical language than to machine language. While there are many high-level languages, all high-level languages have one characteristic in common — any program that is written in a high-level language must first be translated into machine language before it can take control of the computer. The translation process differs for each language, but fortunately for the programmer it can be done automatically by the computer. (We will discuss the translation process in more detail in the next section.)

Another characteristic common to many, but not all, high-level languages is that they are independent of the computer being used. That is, a program written in a high-level, *machine-independent* language can ordinarily be used on a wide variety of computers. However, it is still true that for any *specific* computer a program in a high-level language must *first* be translated into the machine language of that particular computer. The same high-level program can be processed on a different type of computer by first translating it into the machine language of that computer.

One of the most widely used machine-independent, high-level languages is called *FORTRAN*. FORTRAN stands for FORmula TRANslation. This language was originally designed to make it easy to solve problems involving many mathematical formulas. Its popularity and ease of use has resulted in its being applied to a wide variety of computer problem-solving situations.

FORTRAN was one of the first high-level languages. Developed originally in the mid-1950's, it has undergone several modifications and improvements. In Appendix A we give a brief history of the development of the FORTRAN language.

Actually, there are many different "dialects" or *versions* of the FORTRAN language. The different versions are very similar but there are features that are acceptable in some versions that are not allowed in others. The differences exist primarily because each computer manufacturer designs a slightly different form of the language for its computers. Sometimes the differences are slight but at other times the differences may be quite significant. In any case, a FORTRAN program that is prepared for one computer cannot usually be processed on a different computer without some modification.

In this book we describe the features that are found in most versions of FORTRAN. If a particular feature or rule does not apply to all versions of FORTRAN, we indicate this in the text. In Appendix A we summarize the differences between several common versions of FORTRAN. Any language characteristic in question should be located in Appendix A so that the rule for the particular version of FORTRAN of interest can be applied.

1-5. PROGRAM COMPILATION AND EXECUTION

As we have seen, a program written in a high-level language must be translated into machine language before it can take control of the computer. For FORTRAN, as well as for most other high-level languages, this translation process is called *compilation*. The translation is performed by a special machine-language program called a *compiler program*, or simply a *compiler*. First a program is written in FORTRAN. Then the FORTRAN program is translated into an equivalent machine-language program by the FORTRAN compiler. Finally the machine-language program is executed by the computer.

As a simple analogy, assume that we have a business with one employee who only speaks Spanish and that we only speak English. Each day when the employee comes to work we must give him or her a list of what we want done during the day. Since we only speak English we have to prepare the list in English and then have it translated into Spanish. For this purpose we hire an English-to-Spanish translator. This person speaks Spanish but also has an English-to-Spanish dictionary and a grammar book for English. With this information the translator is able to take our list of English-language instructions for the day's work and translate it into an equivalent list in Spanish. Then our Spanish-speaking employee can follow the instructions in the list, performing the tasks that we want done. This process is illustrated in Fig. 1-6.

This is basically the same idea behind the compilation and execution of a FORTRAN program. The steps are shown in Fig. 1-7. The program that is prepared by the programmer is called the *source pro-*

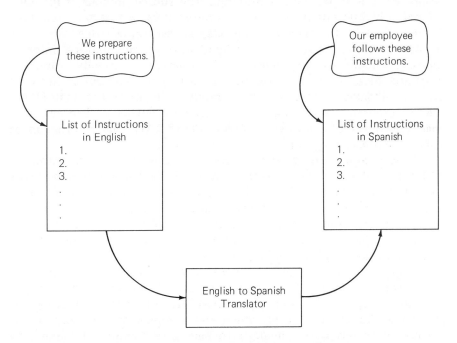

FIGURE 1-6   English-to-Spanish translation.

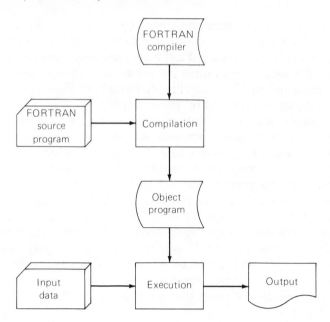

FIGURE 1-7   FORTRAN compilation and execution.

gram. Usually it is punched into cards so that it can be read by a card reader or it is typed into a terminal. The source program is in FOR-TRAN, a high-level language, and therefore it cannot be executed until it is translated into machine language. To accomplish this, the FOR-TRAN compiler program is brought into the computer's internal storage. Outside of the computer the compiler is usually stored on magnetic disk. After the compiler is put in the computer's internal storage, it takes control of the computer and reads the FORTRAN source program, translating it into machine language. The resulting machine-language equivalent of the FORTRAN source program is called the *object program.*

After compilation, the object program is usually stored on magnetic disk. The object program can be retained for future processing or executed immediately. When the program is to be executed, it is first placed in the computer's internal storage. The program then takes control of the computer and performs the tasks specified by the programmer. This often involves reading input data, using this data in calculations and decision-making, and producing output.

For each computer on which we wish to use the FORTRAN language we must have a FORTRAN compiler. The compiler must translate any acceptable FORTRAN program into the machine language of the particular computer for which the compiler is designed. This is equivalent in our simple analogy to having two employees, one who speaks only Spanish and the other who speaks only French. Then we need two translators, one for English to Spanish and another for English to French.

Although the translation of a FORTRAN program into an object program may seem complicated, it is handled to a large extent automatically by the computer. Most programmers need never see their object programs. Instead, the programmer prepares the FORTRAN source program and the data, and everything else is handled automatically by the computer. However, it is important to remember that it is not the source program that is executed; rather, it is the object program that results from the compilation process that is executed.

1-6. PUNCHED CARD INPUT

One of the most common ways of conveying data and programs to a computer is by using *punched cards.* In this section we describe the important characteristics of punched cards and see how information is recorded on cards.

There are several different types of punched cards; Fig. 1-8 shows one of the most common types. This card is made of high-quality paper to resist moisture and comes in a standard size. Its four corners may be square, cut, or rounded and it may be any color. The card is divided vertically into 80 *columns* numbered 1 to 80 beginning at the left. In each column we can punch a pattern of rectangular holes to represent a letter, number, or special character. Because there are 80 columns, the card has a maximum capacity of 80 characters.

The punched card is divided horizontally into 12 *rows* or *punch positions.* The top row is called the 12-row. The next row down is the 11-row. Then comes the 0-row, the 1-row, and so forth until the bottom

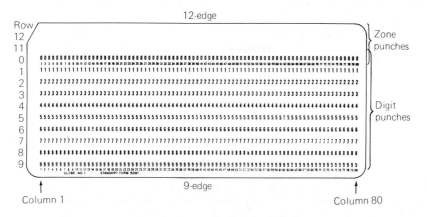

FIGURE 1-8   The punched card.

row which is the 9-row. Notice in Fig. 1–8 that the 0- through 9-rows are numbered on the card while the 12- and 11-rows are not. Punches can be made in the card at the intersection of any row and any column. For example, the card in Fig. 1–9 has a punch in the 3-row of column 8. We call this a "3-punch" in column 8. Similarly, a punch in the 12-row is called a "12-punch" and a punch in the 0-row is a "0-punch." A punch in one of the top three rows (12, 11, or 0) is called a *zone punch* while a punch in the 0- through 9-row is called a *digit punch*. Notice that a 0-punch is both a zone punch and a digit punch.

The top edge of the typical punched card is called the *12-edge;* the bottom edge is the *9-edge.* Again, these are shown in Fig. 1–8. The front of the card is called the *face* of the card. These terms are important because all of the cards in a deck must be oriented in the same way. Instructions on how to orient the cards are usually expressed in these terms. For example, instructions for inserting cards into a particular type of card reader may say "9-edge first, face down." This means that all cards must be inserted into the machine with the bottom edge first and the front of the card facing down. If this is not done correctly, the data will not be read properly by the machine.

Data is recorded in a card using a special code known as the *Hollerith code* after Dr. Herman Hollerith, the inventor of the punched card. It is not necessary to memorize this code because it is recorded automatically when the card is punched with a *keypunch* machine. However, it is useful to be familiar with the general idea of the Hollerith code. (See Appendix C for keypunch operating instructions.)

The basic principle of the Hollerith code is that any character — that is, any number, letter, or special symbol — can be recorded in any of the 80 columns of a card by a unique combination of punches. (See Fig. 1–9.) Numbers, or more correctly *numeric characters* or *digits*, are recorded by a single-digit punch in the row that corresponds to the

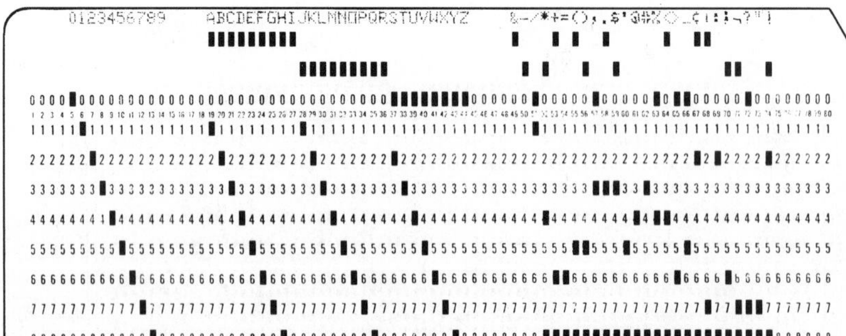

FIGURE 1–9   Punched card data.

character. For example, the numeric character 5 is a 5-punch; the digit 0 is a 0-punch.

An *alphabetic character* (letter) requires two punches in a column, one zone punch and one digit punch. The letter A is a 12-punch and a 1-punch; B is a 12-punch and a 2-punch; P is an 11-punch and a 7-punch; U is a 0-punch and a 4-punch. As we can see in Fig. 1–9, the code for the alphabetic characters follows a clear logical pattern. Notice that there are only capital letters shown; lower-case letters are not usually used on punched cards.

The coding of *special characters* does not follow an easy pattern like numeric and alphabetic characters. A special character can be coded with one, two, or three punches or even no punches. No punches in a column stands for a *blank* or *space* which is a valid and often important special character in computer programming. A single 12-punch signifies the ampersand (&) while a single 11-punch stands for the minus sign. As we see in Fig. 1–9, other special characters require two or three punches.

Notice that each character that is punched in a column of the card is printed at the top of the column. These printed characters are there only for the benefit of the person using the card; they cannot be read by the computer.

The 80-column card is probably the most commonly used punch card. Another card that is sometimes used is shown in Fig. 1–10. This card is smaller than the 80-column card. However, it is organized into 96 columns and thus has a maximum capacity of 96 characters. The columns are arranged in three tiers of 32 columns each. There are 6 rows, and round holes are used instead of rectangular holes. The coding system is different from the Hollerith code. Although the 96-column card has a number of different characteristics, it is used for data and program input in much the same way as the 80-column card.

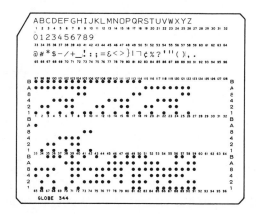

FIGURE 1–10 The 96–column punched card.

1-7. TERMINAL INPUT

Punched cards are often used for input with a batch processing system. For interactive processing input data and programs are usually typed directly into the computer through the keyboard on a terminal. When this is done, each line that is typed can be thought of as representing one punched card. Thus the way data is entered using a terminal is very similar to the way it is punched on a card.

A typed line is organized into typing positions which can be thought of as columns just as we think of the character positions on a card as columns. The maximum number of columns for a terminal depends on what type of device is being used but usually the limit is about eighty. Each time a key is pressed a character is entered into a particular column. Numeric, alphabetic, and special characters can all be typed. The character is also printed, if the terminal is the printing type, or displayed on a screen, if it is a CRT. The space bar is used to enter a blank character. In effect, the space bar advances without printing just as with a typewriter. Since there are no column numbers showing, the programmer must keep track of the columns by counting. At the end of a line, a special key that is usually marked RETURN is pressed. This indicates the end of the line to the computer.

In this book we use a batch processing system with card input and printer output for most examples. However, the principles also apply to an interactive system. Thus, whenever we mention a particular column of a punched card, and an interactive rather than a batch processing system is being used, then the equivalent column or typing position should be used on the terminal. Keeping this in mind, the reader who is using an interactive system shouldn't have any difficulty understanding and using the material in this book.

1-8. DATA ORGANIZATION

So far we have only considered how individual characters are coded on a punched card or typed at a terminal. Although a single character can represent data, more often we group characters together to convey information. Such a related group of characters is called a *field.* For example, a person's name is a field; it is a group of characters that conveys specific information. A social security number is also a field. When data is recorded in a punched card, the columns of the card are grouped together to form fields. For example, Fig. 1-11 shows one way that a card containing information about a student in a college could be divided into fields. In this card the student's identification number is punched in columns 1 through 5, his or her name appears in

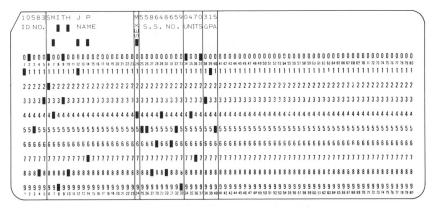

FIGURE 1-11   Card data organization.

columns 6 through 23, and so forth. Notice that a field may be only one column if necessary. For example, the student's sex on the card in Figure 1-11 is punched in column 24. If this information were entered through a terminal, it would be typed in the positions that correspond with the columns on the card. The typing positions would be grouped to form fields just as groups of card columns are fields.

For a particular problem, all cards or typed input lines with the same type of data are usually organized in the same manner. Thus, the student-name field is in the same columns on all cards of the type shown in Fig. 1-11. However, for a different problem, the name field may appear in different columns.

Fields are grouped together to provide information about a single unit such as a person or event. Such a related group of fields is called a *record*. For example, the fields in the card shown in Fig. 1-11 form a record of information about one student. An input line typed into a terminal also forms a record. Finally, all of the records that are used together for one purpose are called a *file*. Thus all of the records of the students in one college form the college's student data file.

Punched cards and typed lines are ways of recording information. Other forms such as printed or CRT output, magnetic tape, and magnetic disk may also be used for information files. With printed or CRT output each line is divided into positions in which characters may be recorded. On cards and terminal input lines we call these positions columns while on printed or CRT output we refer to them as *print positions*. The maximum number of print positions depends on the device being used but typical limits are 80, 120, 132, and 144 print positions per line. When we wish to print or display output we group the print positions into fields just as we group columns to form fields. Then each line becomes a record and all of the printed or displayed output from the program forms the output file.

When a programmer is preparing a program he or she must know how the data in the input and output files are organized. Usually this involves knowing the arrangement or *layout* of the fields in the records of the files. For card or terminal input, the columns of the input fields must be known; with printed or CRT output the programmer must know the print positions of the output fields. Sometimes these layouts are given to the programmer by the person who requires the program. At other times, it is the programmer's responsibility to design his or her own layouts.

In summary, we have seen in this section how individual characters are organized to represent information. Groups of characters, whether punched in cards, typed in a line, printed on paper, displayed on a CRT, or recorded in some other manner, are called fields. Records are groups of fields and a file is a group of records.

REVIEW QUESTIONS

1. What are three characteristics that distinguish computers from other calculating devices?

2. What is a computer program?

3. Data to be processed by a computer is called _____ .

4. The result produced by a computer is called _____ .

5. One of the most common forms for transmitting data and instructions to a computer is _____ .

6. One of the most common output devices for a computer is a

_____ .

7. A video display terminal uses a _____ for input and a _____ for output.

8. The unit of a computer that does the actual computing or processing is the _____ .

9. What are the three units found in the CPU?

10. What happens during the execution of a program? Explain in terms of the units in the CPU.

11. Name two common magnetic devices that can be used for both input and output.

12. What is the difference between computer hardware and software?

13. Explain the difference between batch processing and interactive processing. Give an example of each.

14. The rules that describe how the instructions of a computer language are formed are called the _____ of the language.

15. The meanings of the patterns of symbols in a computer language are called the _____ of the language.

16. What is the difference between machine language and high-level languages?

17. Can a program that is written in FORTRAN be processed on different types of computers? Explain.

18. Translation of a program written in a high-level language into machine language is called _____ .

19. What is the difference between a source program and an object program?

20. How many columns are there on a typical punched card?

21. What are the zone punches and what are the digit punches of a punched card?

22. What device is used to punch data into punched cards?

23. What card code is used for the digit 7, for the letter K, for a comma?

24. Explain the difference between fields, records, and files.

COMPUTER EXERCISE

   Investigate the computer that will be used to process programs that you will prepare. Who manufactured the computer and what is its model number? What input and output devices are available? Is it a batch processing system or an interactive system? (Some computers process in both a batch mode and an interactive mode.) What version of FORTRAN will you be using? What computer languages other than FORTRAN are available on the computer? Find out how to operate a keypunch or a terminal.

Chapter 2

INTRODUCTION
TO FORTRAN

The background concepts that we discussed in Chapter 1 provide a foundation for understanding computer programming. Most of these concepts apply to all computer languages. In this chapter we present an overview of the FORTRAN language without going into detail about how to prepare programs. In later chapters we will explain the specific requirements of FORTRAN.

2-1. BASIC FORTRAN CONCEPTS

Figure 2-1 shows a sample FORTRAN program as it would be prepared by the programmer. This program performs a simple calculation to find the total and average of three numbers. In the next section we will explain how this program works. But for now we are only interested in the FORTRAN concepts that are illustrated by this program.

Coding

When a programmer prepares a program he or she writes on paper the words and symbols that make up the instructions in the program. This process of writing down the program is called *coding*. Coding is usually done on special sheets of paper called *coding forms*. The program shown in Fig. 2-1 is coded on such forms.

Notice that the coding form is divided into a number of lines and that each line has 80 spaces. These spaces correspond to the 80 columns

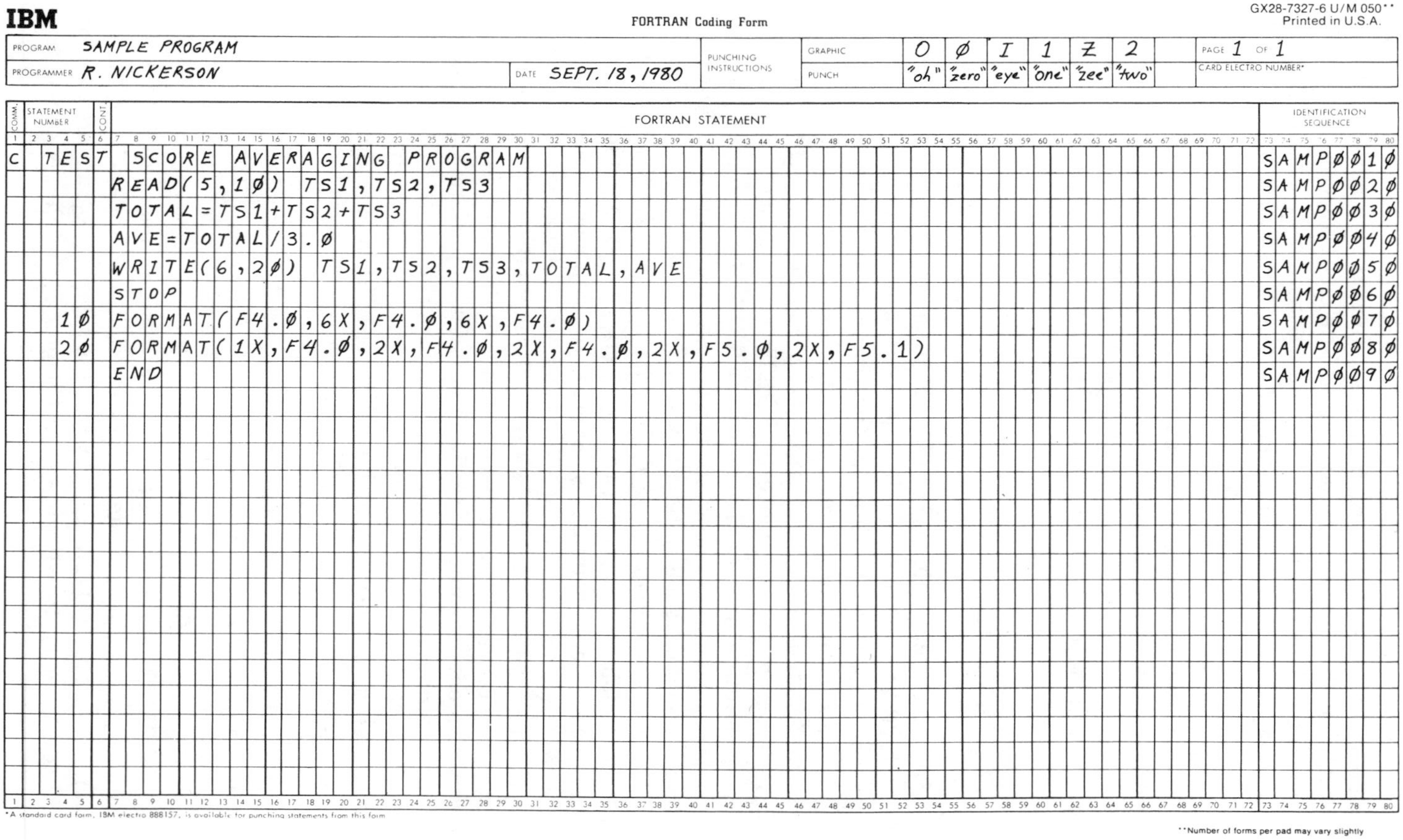

IBM

FORTRAN Coding Form

PROGRAM	SAMPLE PROGRAM				
PROGRAMMER	R. NICKERSON	DATE SEPT. 18, 1980		PAGE 1 OF 1	GX28-7327-6 U/M 050** Printed in U.S.A.

PUNCHING INSTRUCTIONS — GRAPHIC | PUNCH

O	Ø	I	1	Z	2
"oh"	"zero"	"eye"	"one"	"zee"	"two"

FORTRAN STATEMENT

```
C   TEST SCORE AVERAGING PROGRAM
        READ(5,10) TS1,TS2,TS3
        TOTAL=TS1+TS2+TS3
        AVE=TOTAL/3.0
        WRITE(6,20) TS1,TS2,TS3,TOTAL,AVE
        STOP
10      FORMAT(F4.0,6X,F4.0)
20      FORMAT(1X,F4.0,2X,F4.0,2X,F5.0,2X,F5.1)
        END
```

IDENTIFICATION / SEQUENCE:
SAMP0010
SAMP0020
SAMP0030
SAMP0040
SAMP0050
SAMP0060
SAMP0070
SAMP0080
SAMP0090

*A standard card form, IBM electro 888157, is available for punching statements from this form.

**Number of forms per pad may vary slightly

FIGURE 2-1 Coding for a sample FORTRAN program.

23

of a punched card. In FORTRAN coding, the spaces in a line are called columns. As we shall see, each line is punched in a card so that the program can be read by the computer. The characters are punched in the same columns of a card as they are written on the coding form. (If a terminal is used for program input, then each line is typed exactly as it is coded on the coding form.)

When coding a program it is important to distinguish between easily confused characters. For example, the letter O and the number 0 are often indistinguishable when hand-written. To separate these and other characters the sample program in Fig. 2-1 uses the conventions shown on the top right-hand part of the form.

FORTRAN Statements

Each instruction in a FORTRAN program is called a *statement*. A FORTRAN statement tells the computer something about the processing that is to be done in the program. In the sample program in Fig. 2-1 each line (except the first) is a statement. (We will see later that statements can be more than one line in length.) A FORTRAN *program* is a sequence of FORTRAN statements that describe some computing process. To prepare a FORTRAN program, the programmer must know how to form statements in the FORTRAN language and what each statement means.

There are many types of statements in FORTRAN. However, all statements fall into one of two broad classes — executable statements and nonexecutable statements. *Executable* statements cause the computer to perform some action. For example, a statement that tells the computer to get some input data from the input device is an executable statement because it causes the computer to do something. *Nonexecutable* statements do not cause the computer to perform an action but rather describe some characteristic of the program or of the input or output data. For example, a statement that describes the fields in an input record is a nonexecutable statement. In later chapters we will explain the various FORTRAN statements; some will be executable and some will be nonexecutable.

All FORTRAN statements are composed of words and symbols. Some words have special meaning in the language. These are called *keywords* and can only be used in certain places in the program. For example, in the sample program in Fig. 2-1 the words READ, WRITE, and FORMAT are keywords. Other words are made up by the programmer to be used as names for data that are processed by the program. The words TOTAL and AVE in the sample program are examples of this. (Actually, as we will see in Chapter 3, these types of words are called variable names.)

The symbols that are used in the program and that make up the words in the language must come from a set of characters that are acceptable in the language. For FORTRAN, the character set consists of 49 characters. These are the 26 alphabetic characters, the 10 numeric characters, and 13 special characters. (Some versions of FORTRAN do not allow all 13 special characters.) The complete FORTRAN character set is listed in Fig. 2-2.

In summary, the basic units from which we build a FORTRAN program are characters. The group of acceptable characters in the language is called the character set. We form other units in the language, such as keywords, from characters in the character set. We combine keywords, other types of words, and other symbols to form the basic instructions of FORTRAN which are called statements. Then a sequence of statements forms a program.

The Coding Format

When we code a FORTRAN program, each statement is written on the coding form in a special format. Recall that a line on the coding form is divided into eighty spaces called columns. These correspond to the eighty columns of a punched card or the eighty columns (that is,

Alphabetic characters (letters):
ABCDEFGHIJKLMNOPQRSTUVWXYZ

Numeric characters (digits):
0123456789

Special characters:
Blank (space)
= Equals
+ Plus
− Minus
* Asterisk
/ Slash
(Left parenthesis
) Right parenthesis
, Comma
. Decimal point
$ Currency symbol*
' Apostrophe*
: Colon*

*These symbols are not used in all versions of FORTRAN. (See Appendix A.)

FIGURE 2-2 The FORTRAN character set.

typing positions) on a terminal. The rules that describe the coding format specify in which columns the statements of the program may appear.

Each FORTRAN statement must be coded between columns 7 and 72 of the coding form. A statement must not begin before column 7 and must not extend beyond column 72. The statement may start in column 7 or it may be indented. We will see in later chapters that indenting statements can sometimes make the program easier to read. Blank spaces may be used freely to spread out the parts of the statement. This is often done to improve the readability of the program.

No part of a statement may go beyond column 72. If a statement is too long to fit on one line, it must be continued onto the next line. The continued part must also be written between columns 7 and 72. There may be as many as nineteen continuation lines beyond the initial line of a statement. (Some versions of FORTRAN have a different limit on the number of continuation lines.) For each continuation line we must put a character in column 6. The character that is used may be any symbol in the character set except a blank or a zero. For example, Fig. 2-3 shows a FORTRAN statement that requires three lines. The first line of the statement does not have a character in column 6 (or a zero may be used for this initial line). The first continuation line has the digit 1 in column 6 and the second continuation line has a 2 in column 6. Any character other than a zero or blank may be used to indicate continuation but a common practice is to number the continuation lines. Notice in Fig. 2-3 that the coding on each line does not extend all of the way to column 72. A statement may be broken at almost any point and continued on the next line or it may be written out to column 72 before continuing.

Any statement in a program may be given a number between 1 and 99999. (With some versions of FORTRAN the maximum statement number is less than 99999.) If a statement is numbered, the number must appear in columns 1 through 5. For example, in the sample program in Fig. 2-1 two statements are numbered. These are the statements with the numbers 10 and 20. Although any statement in the program may be numbered, unnecessary statement numbers can make the program less efficient. However, as we will see certain statements must be numbered. Statement numbers need not be in sequence. However, no two statements can have the same number.

In addition to statements, we can put explanatory comments in a program. These are often used to describe the processing done in the program so that the program will be easier to understand. To put a comment in a program, the letter C is written in column 1. Then the programmer may write anything that he or she wishes on the line with the C. The computer treats any line with a C in column 1 as a comment and not as a statement. Comments may appear anywhere

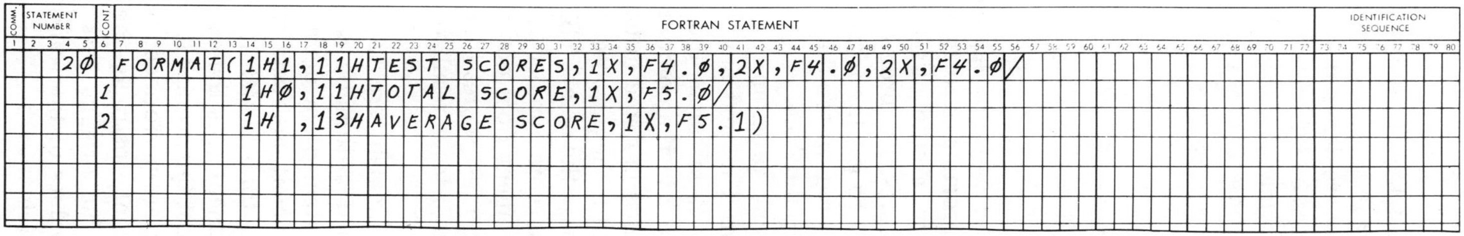

FORTRAN STATEMENT

```
 C STATEMENT  CONT.        FORTRAN STATEMENT
   NUMBER
   20          FORMAT(1H1,11HTEST  SCORES,1X,F4.0,2X,F4.0,2X,F4.0/
               1      1H0,11HTOTAL SCORE,1X,F5.0/
               2      1H ,13HAVERAGE SCORE,1X,F5.1)
```

FIGURE 2-3   Continuing a statement.

in the program before the last line. In the sample program in Fig. 2–1, the first line is a comment.

Columns 73 through 80 are ignored by the computer and may contain any characters or may be left blank. Most often these columns are used for identifying information about the program or to number the lines for sequencing purposes. However, their use is optional. The sample program in Fig. 2–1 shows how these columns can be used to identify and sequence a program.

2-2. A SAMPLE PROGRAM

We can now begin to consider what the sample program in Figure 2–1 does. The purpose of this program is to find the total and average of three numbers that represent a student's scores on three tests. The input data is the three test scores. The program reads the scores from an input device, adds the scores to get the total, calculates the average by dividing the total by three, and writes the test scores and the results of the calculations on an output device.

The first line of the sample program is a comment which explains the purpose of the program. The next line is a FORTRAN statement called a READ statement. It instructs the computer to read three values and to store the values in the computer's internal storage. (We will describe READ statements in detail in Chapter 3.) This statement also tells the computer that for the purposes of the program, the values that are read are referred to by the names TS1, TS2, and TS3 (standing for test score number 1, test score number 2, and test score number 3). Notice that the READ statement does not give the actual values that are read. These values are the test scores that are to be averaged; they are input data and are read in as a result of execution of the READ statement.

Following the READ statement are two statements that perform calculations. These are called arithmetic assignment statements. (We will discuss this type of statement in detail in Chapter 4.) The first arithmetic assignment statement instructs the computer to add the three test scores to find the total (which is called TOTAL in the program). Then the next statement tells the computer to divide the just-calculated total by three to get the average (called AVE).

After these calculations are performed, the next statement, which is called a WRITE statement, instructs the computer to write the results of the processing. The original test scores are written along with the newly calculated values of the total and average. (In Chapter 3 we will discuss WRITE statements.)

Following the WRITE statement is a statement consisting solely of the word STOP. This statement tells the computer to stop executing the program.

All of the statements up to the STOP statement are executable statements. That is, each of these causes the computer to perform some action, either reading or writing data, calculating, or, in the case of the STOP statement, stopping execution of the program. The two statements following the STOP statement are nonexecutable statements. These are called FORMAT statements and they are used to tell the computer the arrangement or format of the input and output data. The first FORMAT statement (numbered 10) describes how the input data appears. The second FORMAT statement (numbered 20) gives the format of the output. (FORMAT statements are explained in Chapter 3.)

The last line of the program is an END statement. This statement consists only of the word END. It indicates that there are no more statements in the program.

These statements make up a complete FORTRAN program. The executable statements are performed in the order in which they are written. Thus, it is important that these statements be written in a logical order. For example, the order of the two arithmetic assignment statements cannot be reversed because the total is used in the calculation of the average and therefore must be calculated first.

Notice that most of the statements in the program are fairly easy to understand. This is especially true of the arithmetic assignment statements which are written very much like mathematical formulas. Beginning with Chapter 3 we will explain in detail how to code different types of FORTRAN statements.

2-3. RUNNING A COMPUTER PROGRAM

The program coded in Fig. 2-1 is a FORTRAN source program. In order to be processed by a computer it must be put into the computer along with special control information and provided with input data. When a program is processed on a computer we say that we *run* the program on the computer. This section describes how a FORTRAN program is run on a computer.

Batch Processing

In a batch processing system the source program is usually converted to a form that the computer can read by punching one card for each line on the coding sheet. The program must be punched

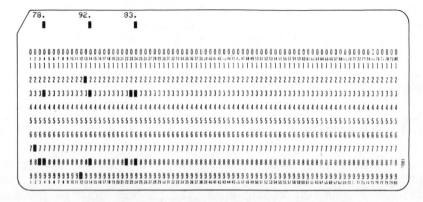

```
END                                                          SAMP0090
20 FORMAT(1X,F4.0,2X,F4.0,2X,F4.0,2X,F5.0,2X,F5.1)           SAMP0080
10 FORMAT(F4.0,6X,F4.0,6X,F4.0)                              SAMP0070
STOP                                                         SAMP0060
WRITE(6,20) TS1,TS2,TS3,TOTAL,AVE                            SAMP0050
AVE=TOTAL/3.0                                                SAMP0040
TOTAL=TS1+TS2+TS3                                            SAMP0030
READ(5,10) TS1,TS2,TS3                                       SAMP0020
C TEST SCORE AVERAGING PROGRAM                               SAMP0010
```

FIGURE 2-4 The source program deck for the sample program.

column-for-column exactly as it is coded. Any punching errors must be corrected before processing the program with the computer. The cards must be kept in the same order as the coded program. The program punched into cards is often called the *source deck*. Figure 2-4 shows the source deck for the sample program.

In addition to the source deck, an *input data deck* must be punched. Initially, input data that tests the program must be designed and punched into cards. This input data must be punched in the layout prescribed for the program. Figure 2-5 shows an input data card for the sample program. This program requires only one input card; however, most programs process many data cards.

FIGURE 2-5 Input data for the sample program.

Finally, the source deck and the input deck must be combined with special cards called *control records*. These records vary from one type of computer to another and are not part of the FORTRAN language. Their purpose is to control the processing of the program on a particular computer. Usually there is a group of control records at the beginning, then the source deck, then another group of control records, then the input data deck, and then a final group of control records. (See Fig. 2-6.) The entire combination of control records, source deck, and input data deck is called a *job* and can be run on the computer.

The function of the control records is linked to the way in which a job is processed. Recall from Section 1-5 that a program goes through two phases — compilation and execution — when processed on a computer. During the first phase the source program is translated into machine language to produce the object program; in the second phase, the object program is executed. The control records arrange the sequencing of these two phases.

Usually the first group of control records informs the computer that a FORTRAN source program follows and instructs the computer to get the FORTRAN compiler program. The compiler program is brought to the computer's internal storage unit. Then the compiler begins reading the source deck. As the compiler does this, it translates the source program into machine language. The compiler program stops processing when it reaches the end of the source program. Now the object program is ready to execute.

During compilation, the source program is printed by the printer. This printed copy of the program is called the *source program listing*. Figure 2-7(a) shows the source program listing for the sample program.

The next group of control records instructs the computer to bring the object program into the internal storage and begin execution. During execution of the object program the various instructions in the program are performed. Some of the instructions that are executed cause input data to be read. Hence, the next group of cards in the job

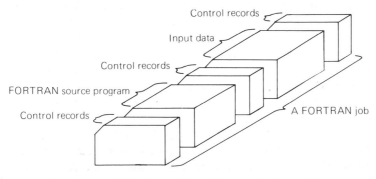

FIGURE 2-6 Deck setup for running a FORTRAN program on a batch processing system.

```
C TEST SCORE AVERAGING PROGRAM                                   SAMP0010
      READ(5,10) TS1,TS2,TS3                                     SAMP0020
      TOTAL=TS1+TS2+TS3                                          SAMP0030
      AVE=TOTAL/3.0                                              SAMP0040
      WRITE(6,20) TS1,TS2,TS3,TOTAL,AVE                          SAMP0050
      STOP                                                       SAMP0060
   10 FORMAT(F4.0,6X,F4.0,6X,F4.0)                               SAMP0070
   20 FORMAT(1X,F4.0,2X,F4.0,2X,F4.0,2X,F5.0,2X,F5.1)            SAMP0080
      END                                                        SAMP0090
```

(a)

```
78.   92.   83.   253.   84.3
```

(b)

FIGURE 2-7   The sample program run on a batch proc-
             essing system: (a) the source program listing;
             (b) the output.

must be the input data deck. In addition, some instructions cause the
results of processing to be printed. This is the actual output from the
program. Figure 2-7(b) shows the output from the sample program.

When execution of the program is completed, the final group of
control records tells the computer that the job is finished and instructs
the computer to go to the next job.

Control records are vital to the proper processing of a job on the
computer. Although the actual organization of the control records
varies with different computers, their basic functions are the same.
They are not related to the FORTRAN language, but are required if
a program is to be run on a computer.

Interactive Processing

If the program is to be run using an interactive processing system
then the source program must be keyed in using a terminal. First the
programmer must connect the terminal to the computer through a
procedure that is usually called "logging on." The actual procedure
that is used depends on the computer. After the programmer has
logged on he or she indicates to the computer what is to be done by
typing various *system commands.* System commands vary from one
type of computer to another and are not part of the FORTRAN
language.

Usually the first system command that is typed indicates that
a FORTRAN program is to be entered. Sometimes this command is
just the word FORTRAN. Following this, the source program is entered,
one line at a time just as it is written on the coding form. The RETURN

key must be pressed after each line is typed. Often it is required that each line have a unique line number and that the line numbers be in ascending (increasing) order. These numbers are not statement numbers and if a statement has a number it must be typed in addition to the line number. Figure 2-8(a) shows the sample program that has been entered in this manner. (We have not included the identifying and sequencing information in this program because the terminal line is not long enough.) One reason why line numbers are used is that a statement can be changed by typing the line number and a new statement. The computer then inserts the line in the appropriate place in the program, deleting the old line.

In order to get a copy of the program printed on the terminal (that is, a *source program listing*) the system command LIST is usually used. This causes the computer to list the program in its entirety. Any corrections that have been made while typing in the program will show in the listing.

After the program has been entered it can be processed by the computer. Recall from Section 1-5 that processing involves two phases— compilation and execution. During the first phase the source program is translated into machine language, creating the object program. Then the object program is executed in the second phase. On an interactive system these two phases are usually initiated by a single command. Often this command is just the word RUN, meaning "run the program."

After the program is compiled, execution begins. During the

```
00100C TEST SCORE AVERAGING PROGRAM
00110     READ(8,10) TS1,TS2,TS3
00120     TOTAL=TS1+TS2+TS3
00130     AVE=TOTAL/3.0
00140     WRITE(9,20) TS1,TS2,TS3,TOTAL,AVE
00150     STOP
00160  10 FORMAT(F4.0,6X,F4.0,6X,F4.0)
00170  20 FORMAT(1X,F4.0,2X,F4.0,2X,F4.0,2X,F5.0,2X,F5.1)
00180     END
```

(a)

```
?  78.        92.        83.
```

(b)

```
78.   92.   83.   253,   84.3
```

(c)

FIGURE 2-8 The sample program run on an interactive
            system: (a) the source program listing; (b)
            the input data; (c) the output.

execution of the program input data must be supplied. When a READ statement is executed the computer prints a question mark on the terminal and stops. This indicates that input data must be entered. The data must be typed exactly as it would be punched on a card. Figure 2-8(b) shows how the input would be entered for the sample program. The spacing must be the same as on the punched card in Fig. 2-5. After the data is typed the programmer presses the RETURN key on the terminal and the program continues to execute. For the sample program this involves calculating a total and average, and printing the results. The output is printed or displayed on the terminal as shown in Fig. 2-8(c).

2-4. ERROR DETECTION

In describing the processing of a FORTRAN program we have assumed that the program contains no errors. In fact, one of the biggest problems that a programmer faces is the detection and correction of errors. More often than not, the program does not complete its run successfully. It is the programmer's responsibility to locate and correct any errors in the program.

There are three times that errors may be detected in the processing of the program—during compilation, during execution, and after execution. The computer can detect errors that occur during the first two times, but the programmer must detect any errors in the third category.

Compilation errors are discovered by the computer during the compilation of the programs. These are usually errors that the programmer has made in the use of the language and are called *syntax errors*. For example, spelling a keyword incorrectly is a syntax error. When the compiler program detects a compilation error, it prints a message that describes the error and where in the program it is located. Even though the compiler has located an error, it usually cannot correct the error and the program is not executed. The programmer must correct any compilation errors that are detected.

If the program has no compilation errors, it is executed by the computer. During execution, other errors may appear. These are called *execution errors*. For example, attempting to divide a number by zero is an execution error. Detection of such an error causes the computer to print an error code or message and to stop executing the program.

The final type of error is detected only after successful compilation and execution of the program. If the output from the program does not agree with what is expected, there is a *logic error* in the program. For example, in the sample program, if the first arithmetic assignment statement had been incorrectly coded as

$$TOTAL=TS1-TS2-TS3$$

then no compilation or execution error would be detected. However, the final output would be incorrect since the total of three numbers is found by adding the numbers, not by subtracting them. This error is in the logic of the program. The computer cannot detect such an error since it cannot understand the logic of the program. It is the programmer's responsibility to check the results of processing and to correct any logic error that may be found.

An error in a computer program is called a *bug*. The process of locating and correcting bugs in a program is called *debugging*. Only after a program has been completely debugged can the programmer be reasonably sure that the program is correct.

2-5. A PREVIEW OF THE PROGRAMMING PROCESS

In the process of preparing a computer program to solve a particular problem the programmer performs a number of tasks. One thing that must be done is to code the program. As we have seen this involves writing the instructions in the program. However, before coding can begin the programmer must understand the problem to be solved and plan the solution procedure.

Understanding the problem involves determining the requirements of the problem and how these requirements can be met. The programmer must know what the program is required to do. This usually involves understanding what output must be produced by the program and its layout and what computations must be performed. In addition, the programmer must determine what resources are available to meet these requirements. This includes determining the available input and its format.

With an understanding of the problem the programmer can begin to design a program to solve the problem. The sequence of steps that is necessary to solve the problem must be carefully planned. This program-designing activity does *not* involve coding the program. Before coding can start the programmer must think through the solution procedure completely. The programmer sometimes writes down the solution procedure in rough notes in English or draws a diagram that represents the solution graphically. In Appendix E we discuss a tool that is sometimes used for developing programs.

After the solution to the problem has been planned the program can be coded. The programmer uses his or her knowledge of the computer language, an understanding of the problem to be solved, and the program design determined previously. With this background the programmer writes the program to solve the problem.

The next step is to test the program by running the program on the computer with test data. The output produced by the program is then compared with the expected output — any discrepancy indicates an error. Testing the program in this manner will not necessarily reveal all errors but usually will point out any serious problems with the program. The actual process of determining the correctness of a program involves much more than just testing the program on a computer. A program is correct because it makes sense logically. The programmer makes sure of this as he or she plans and codes the program.

Finally, the programming process is completed by bringing together all material that describes the program. This is called *documenting* the program and the result of this activity is the program's *documentation*. Included in the documentation is the source program listing and a description of the input and output data. The reason for having documentation is so that other programmers will be able to understand how the program functions. Often it is necessary to return to the program after a period of time and make corrections or changes in the program. With adequate documentation it is much easier to understand how a program operates.

Throughout most of this book we will be discussing the coding activity of the programming process. However, it must be kept in mind that this is only part of the entire process. In Chapter 8 we will return to the other activities and discuss them in more detail.

REVIEW QUESTIONS

1. The process of writing on paper the instructions in a program is called_____ .

2. Each instruction in a FORTRAN program is called a_____ .

3. What is the difference between executable statements and non-executable statements?

4. What are keywords?

5. List the special characters in the FORTRAN character set.

6. Must every statement in a FORTRAN program have a number?

7. How are comments placed in a program?

8. How is a statement that is longer than one line coded in FOR-TRAN?

9. What is the purpose of columns 73 to 80 on the coding form?

10. When running a program on a computer, what must the computer have first, the program or the input data?

11. When a program is punched from the coding on a coding form, how many cards are punched for each line on the coding form?

12. What is the function of control records in a batch processing system? Are they part of the FORTRAN language?

13. What is the function of system commands in an interactive processing system? Are they part of the FORTRAN language?

14. Explain the difference between compilation errors, execution errors, and logic errors.

15. Removing errors from a program is called_____.

16. What are the five steps in the programming process?

COMPUTER EXERCISE

The program shown in Fig. 2-1 is complete and can be run on a computer. In order to become familiar with the structure of FORTRAN, the coding format, control records (or system commands), and other aspects of running a program, this program should be processed on an actual computer. (Slight modification in the READ and WRITE statements may be necessary, depending on what type of computer is used to run the program. In addition, the FORMAT statement shown in Fig. 2-3 may be substituted for statement 20 in the program. This will produce more readable output.)

If a batch processing system is being used, punch the program into cards exactly as it is coded in Fig. 2-1. The resulting source deck should appear as in Fig. 2-4. Punch an input data card exactly as shown in Fig. 2-5. Combine the source deck and the data card with the proper control records. The general deck setup is shown in Fig. 2-6 but the specific control records depend on the computer that is used. Run the program on the computer and get the printed output. Any errors that occur are the result of keypunching mistakes. Correct any errors and rerun the program until the program is error-free. The source program listing should appear as in Fig. 2-7(a). Check the output to be sure that it is the same as Fig. 2-7(b).

With an interactive system, the program is entered through a terminal. Key in the program exactly as it is coded in Fig. 2-1. List the program to get a source program listing as shown in Fig. 2-8(a). Then run the program. If any compilation errors occur, they are the result of typing mistakes. Correct any errors and rerun the program. During execution of the program input data must be entered. Type the input data exactly as shown in Fig. 2-8(b). The data must be spaced the same as it is on the punched card in Fig. 2-5. Check the output to be sure that it is the same as in Fig. 2-8(c).

Chapter 3

BASIC INPUT AND
OUTPUT PROGRAMMING

When we write a computer program to solve a problem we prepare a sequence of instructions for the computer to follow. There are many different sequences that can be used, depending on the problem to be solved. However, one *pattern* appears over and over again. This pattern is simply:

$$\text{input} \longrightarrow \text{process} \longrightarrow \text{output}$$

That is, first we instruct the computer to read some input data to be used in the problem solution. Then we do the processing and computation necessary to solve the problem using the input data. Finally, we write the output data that represents the results of the processing.

For example, in Chapter 2 we saw a sample program that computes the total and average of three test scores. The first step in this program was to read the three test scores as input data. Then the processing involved calculating the total and average of the input data. Finally, the results were written out.

There are many other patterns that appear in computer programs but this is one of the most common. In addition, the input, process, and output steps may each be quite complex, especially the process step.

In this chapter we discuss the input and output steps in detail. We describe the FORTRAN statements necessary to do basic input and output programming. With these statements, simple programs that do nothing more than input and output can be written. However, as we have seen these steps are a necessary part of more complex programs. In the chapters that follow we will discuss the various types of processing activities that can be performed in a FORTRAN program.

3-1. THE ELEMENTS OF FORTRAN INPUT/OUTPUT PROGRAMMING

To program a computer for input and output operations we need three things:

1. A way of instructing the computer to transfer data from an input device to the CPU; that is, we need an *input* instruction.
2. A way of instructing the computer to transfer data from the CPU to an output device; that is, we need an *output* instruction.
3. A way of telling the computer the arrangement or *format* of the input and output data.

The FORTRAN statements that may be used to accomplish these depend on the version of FORTRAN that is used. The main difference has to do with the third item listed. With some versions of FORTRAN the format of the input and output data must be specified in the program. That is, the program must indicate the arrangement of the fields in the input and output records. This is done with a special statement in the program. With other versions of FORTRAN, the format of the input and output data is preset outside of the program. That is, the input data must be prepared in a prescribed fashion and the output data always appears in a particular, preset form.

When the input and output formats are specified within the program, the input/output system is called *formatted* I/O. If the input/output formats are preset, then *format-free* (or *list-directed*) I/O is used. All versions of FORTRAN provide formatted I/O. Many versions also allow the use of format-free I/O.

When formatted I/O is used for the input process, two statements are required—the READ statement and the FORMAT statement. The READ statement tells the computer to read data using a specific input device (such as a card reader) and to store the data in the computer's internal storage. The FORMAT statement tells the computer the format or arrangement of the data on the input medium (such as a punched card). For example, the following statements might be used for input in a typical program:

```
READ(5,10) A,B,I,J
10 FORMAT(F10.2,F8.4,I4,I6)
```

(In writing a FORTRAN statement without a coding form, we assume that the statement begins in column 7 or beyond and that the statement number, if it exists, falls anywhere in columns 1 to 5.)

The READ statement instructs the computer to perform an input

40

or read operation. The letters A, B, I, and J are symbols that tell the computer where in internal storage the input data is to be stored. The first number in parentheses is a code that tells the computer what input device is to be used to read the input data. In this case the code 5 stands for the card reader. The second number in parentheses — 10 — is the statement number of a FORMAT statement that corresponds to this READ statement.

The FORMAT statement is a nonexecutable statement that tells the computer the arrangement of the input data on the input medium. In this example the input medium is a punched card, and the characters in parentheses following the keyword FORMAT are codes that describe the fields on the card. Notice that the FORMAT statement has a statement number — 10 — that corresponds to the second number in parentheses in the READ statement.

With format-free input the FORMAT statement is not used. Instead, the input data is arranged in a preset format known to the programmer. The READ statement is also somewhat different. Instead of two numbers in parentheses, an asterisk (*) followed by a comma is used. (Some versions of FORTRAN omit the asterisk.) For example, the following statement reads the same data as in the previous example but uses format-free input:

$$READ\ *,A,B,I,J$$

The asterisk indicates that format-free input is to be used. As before the letters A, B, I, and J indicate where the input data is to be stored in the internal storage.

When formatted output is used, two statements are required — the WRITE statement and the FORMAT statement. The WRITE statement instructs the computer to write with a specific output device (such as a printer). The data to be written is found in certain locations in the computer's internal storage. The FORMAT statement tells the computer how the data is to be arranged on the output medium (such as a printed document).

The following statements illustrate a typical output sequence:

```
    WRITE(6,15) X,K,Y
15 FORMAT(1X,F12.3,I5,F8.2)
```

The WRITE statement causes the computer to perform an output operation. The symbols X, K, and Y tell the computer what data is to be written. The first number in parentheses is a code that specifies the actual output device. In this case the code 6 stands for the printer. The second number in parentheses — 15 — is the statement number of a corresponding FORMAT statement.

The nonexecutable FORMAT statement describes the arrangement of the data on the output medium. In this example the codes in parentheses describe the arrangement of the output data on a printed document. The statement number of the FORMAT statement corresponds to the second number in parentheses in the WRITE statement.

Notice the similarity between the input sequence and the output sequence with formatted I/O. The READ and WRITE statements have very similar syntax; that is, the way in which the statements are written is almost the same. Each requires a corresponding FORMAT statement. Thus, the FORMAT statement is a dual-purpose statement. When used in conjunction with a READ statement, it describes input data format; when used with a WRITE statement, it describes the arrangement of output data. The READ or WRITE statement is linked to its corresponding FORMAT statement by the number of the FORMAT statement.

For format-free output the arrangement of the output data is preset. Hence the FORMAT statement is not needed. In addition the PRINT statement is used instead of the WRITE statement. For example, to write the same data as in the previous example but with format-free output we use the following statement:

$$\text{PRINT } *,X,K,Y$$

The word PRINT is used instead of WRITE and the asterisk indicates that the output is format-free. (The asterisk is not used in some versions of FORTRAN.) The letters X, K, and Y specify what data is to be written.

We can see from these examples that the advantage of format-free I/O is that the programmer does not have to write extra statements in the program to give the format of the input and output data. However, the disadvantage is that the programmer cannot control the arrangement of the input or output data since the format is preset. With formatted I/O the programmer has complete control over the input/output formats but extra statements are required in the program to accomplish this.

In this book we describe both format-free and formatted I/O. The reader who wishes to learn only one of the input/output systems may skip the applicable sections in this chapter and in Chapter 7. The next section in this chapter describes various background concepts necessary to understand the input/output process. Then Section 3–3 explains the format-free I/O system. Sections 3–4, 3–5, and 3–6 are devoted to formatted I/O. Finally Section 3–7 explains how to write complete programs using either system.

3-2. INTERNAL STORAGE AND FORTRAN DATA

In order to understand the effect of the FORTRAN input and output statements it is necessary to be familiar with the internal storage component of the computer. In this section we explain the basic structure of internal storage and show the relationship to FORTRAN.

Internal Storage

A computer's internal storage is a complex unit composed of a large number of electronic and magnetic parts. The various parts of the internal storage are grouped to form *storage locations*. One way of thinking of a computer's internal storage is in terms of a large number of boxes similar to post office boxes. Figure 3-1 illustrates this idea; each box represents a storage location. In this example there are twelve storage locations and in each location the computer can store one number. Once data is placed in a storage location it remains there for use by the computer. However, if new data is placed in the same storage location, then the old data is destroyed.

The computer keeps track of storage locations by giving each location a unique number called an *address*. In Fig. 3-1 the address of each storage location is shown in the small box. Post office boxes have addresses to distinguish them. To find a particular post office box, we search through the boxes until the one with the desired address is located. Similarly, the computer identifies a particular storage location by means of its address.

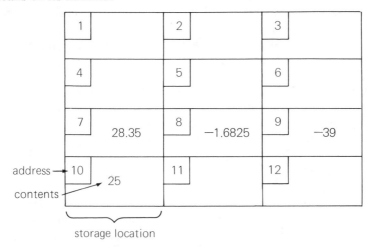

FIGURE 3-1. Internal storage.

It is important not to confuse a storage address with the contents of the storage location. A storage location contains data which can change from time to time. However, the address of each location is fixed. The computer uses the address to find the storage location. Once the storage location is found, the computer can put data in the location or retrieve data from the location. For example, in Fig. 3-1, if the computer is told to retrieve the contents of storage location 10, it gets the number 25. If it is told to put the number 35 in location 10, then the value that is in this location is destroyed and replaced by the new data.

FORTRAN Variables

In the simplified internal storage illustrated in Fig. 3-1, there are only twelve storage locations. In actual computers there are thousands, even hundreds of thousands of storage locations. For example, one common computer has about 250,000 locations in its internal storage. Other computers have up to several million storage locations.

To keep track of that many storage locations and their addresses would be quite a complex task for a programmer. Fortunately FORTRAN does not require the programmer to use addresses to identify locations in storage. Instead, symbolic names are used. For example, in the sample program from the previous chapter, the symbolic names TS1 and TOTAL identify two storage locations.

It is not necessary to give a symbolic name to every location in the computer's internal storage; it is only necessary to name those locations that are used in the program. In fact, it is not even necessary for the programmer to worry about which storage locations and addresses are being used. The programmer merely uses a symbolic name, and the computer automatically reserves a storage location for that name and keeps track of its address. Most FORTRAN programmers think in terms of data and assign symbolic names to data used in the program. Thus, the name TOTAL stands for the value that is found by adding the data referred to by the names TS1, TS2, and TS3.

A *variable* in FORTRAN is a value that is identified in a program by a symbolic name. The name that is used is called a *variable name*. Since the variable name does not specify exactly what the value is but rather specifies where it is stored, the quantity may change or vary from time to time in a program. Thus, the name TOTAL may have a particular value at one point in a program and then another value later in the program. Any time that a variable name is used (for example, for output), the current value of that variable name is retrieved by the computer. Any time that a value is assigned to a variable name (for example, through an input operation), the old value of that variable name is destroyed and the new value replaces it.

Figure 3-2 illustrates this concept with the variable names A, B, I, and J. Each name identifies a storage location in the computer's internal storage that contains a variable value. For example, the name A refers to location 7 which contains the value 28.35. Similarly, the other variable names refer to other storage locations. If the variable name A is used in the program then the computer goes to location 7 and retrieves the value 28.35. If a value is assigned to A then 28.35 is destroyed and replaced by the new value.

Variable Names

It is the programmer's responsibility to select names for all variables used in a program; however, the selections must follow certain rules. In FORTRAN a variable name may be one to six characters in length. (Some versions of FORTRAN restrict variable names to five characters. A few versions allow more than six characters in a name.) The name may contain any alphabetic or numeric characters but may not contain any special characters. However, the first character must always be an alphabetic character. For example, the following variable names are valid.

TOTAL
A
X
K
EV86D
K3
ZZZ

The following variable names are invalid for the reasons given:

2M35	(first character is not alphabetic)
M93LZTS	(contains more than six characters)
X.95Z	(contains a special character)

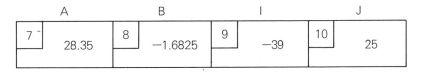

FIGURE 3-2. Variable names and internal storage.

Note that it is not just the first character that defines the variable name; it is all of the characters that make the name unique. Thus, K and K3 are two separate variable names that refer to different storage locations in the computer's internal storage.

In writing a program the programmer should attempt to select meaningful variable names. This helps the programmer, or anyone else who examines the program, remember the function of each variable name. For example, in the sample program from the previous chapter the variable name TS1 stood for the test score on test 1, TS2 identified the score on test 2, and TS3 stood for the score on the third test. Similarly the name TOTAL identified the total of the test scores and AVE stood for their average. In a business application PRICE might stand for the unit price of an item, QTY the quantity purchased, and COST the total cost of the order. In a program that analyzes the results of a sociological questionnaire, the variable names AGE, STATUS, and SEX might identify a respondent's age, marital status, and sex, respectively.

Data Types

In FORTRAN, there are two basic types of numeric data — integer and real. *Integer data*, or simply *integers*, are written without decimal points — that is, as whole numbers. For example, 25 and –38 are integers. *Real data*, or just *reals*, are written with decimal points. For example, 25.0, –6.2, and .083 are real data. Integers are sometimes called *fixed-point data*, and reals are often referred to as *floating-point data*.

The distinction between integers and reals may seem trivial but in FORTRAN it is very important. Basically the distinction is made because the data is stored in different forms in the computer's internal storage. Integers are stored similarly to the way that they are commonly written. For example, the number 25 occupies a storage location and is stored as shown in Fig. 3-3. (The actual representation of an integer is in the binary number system, but the principle is the same. Binary representation of data is discussed in Chapter 13.)

Real data is stored in a form similar to scientific notation. This is known as *floating-point notation* and involves rewriting the number as a fraction times some power of ten. For example, 28.35 is written as $.2835 \times 10^2$ and .058 is $.58 \times 10^{-1}$. In remembering a number in this form, it is necessary to remember only the fraction and the exponent.

storage location

| +000000025 | = 25 |

FIGURE 3-3.   Internal storage of an integer value.

For example, assume that we know that the fraction is 2835 and the exponent is 2. The decimal point is always just to the left of the fraction and the exponent is a power of ten. Hence we know that the number must be .2835 $\times$ 10^2 or 28.35. In floating-point notation this approach is used and only the fraction and exponent are stored. In the computer the value 28.35 is stored as shown in Fig. 3-4.

It is not important at the beginning of the study of FORTRAN to know precisely the internal representation of integers and reals. However, it is important to remember that there is a difference, and that the difference is significant. The difference is most important for variable names.

A FORTRAN variable name can refer to a storage location that contains an integer or a real. However, the computer must know what type of data is being referred to by the variable name. In addition, once the computer has been told that a particular variable name refers to integer data, that same name cannot be used for real data. Similarly, a real variable name cannot refer to integer data.

In FORTRAN the computer is told by the first letter of the variable name what type of numeric value is being referred to. If the first letter is an I, J, K, L, M, or N, then the variable name refers to an integer value. If the first letter is any other letter of the alphabet, then the name refers to a real value. For example, the following are integer variable names:

$$I$$
$$J$$
$$K3$$
$$NUM$$

The following are real variable names:

$$A$$
$$TOTAL$$
$$AVE$$
$$X$$
$$EV86D$$

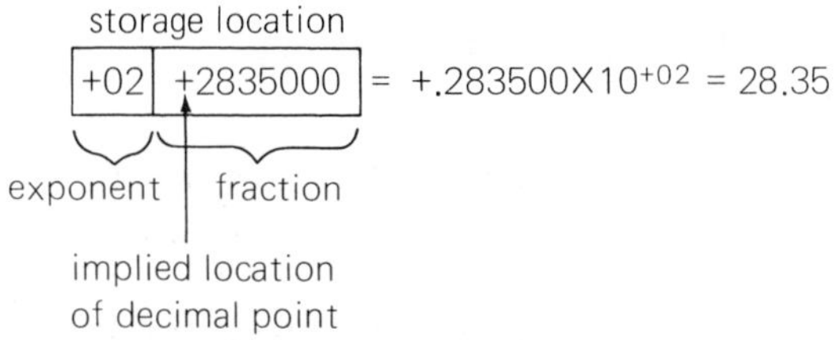

FIGURE 3-4. Internal storage representation of a real value.

Limitations on Data Values

The FORTRAN language does not set any limit on the size of numbers that can be assigned to variable names. However, computers have limited capacity and therefore there are practical maximum and minimum values that can be stored. These limits depend on the type of computer being used. We will use a common computer, the IBM System/370 to illustrate.

For integer data the maximum value on the IBM System/370 is +2,147,483,647 and the minimum value is –2,147,483,648. These seemingly arbitrary numbers result from the binary representation of integers in the computer. (See Chapter 13.) Any integer between these limits can be assigned to an integer variable name; however, if an attempt is made to store a value outside of this range then the results will be unknown.

With real data the limits are not expressed as easily. Since a real value is stored in floating-point notation, limitations must be given for the exponent and for the fraction. On the IBM System/370, the maximum exponent is approximately 75 and the minimum is about –78. The fraction can have at most approximately seven digits. These values are approximate because the internal representation is in the binary mode. (See Chapter 13.) For example, 583079000000000.00 is an acceptable real number. In floating-point notation this is interpreted as .583079 $\times$ 10^{15}. Notice that there are less than seven digits in the fraction and the exponent is between –78 and 75. However, 39025672.53 is not acceptable. In floating-point form this value is interpreted as .3902567253 $\times$ 10^8. Although the exponent is within the required range, the fraction contains more than seven digits; hence, the number cannot be stored.

It is important to know the limitations for the computer being used. Any input data that is read must be within the limits for integer or real data, as the case may be. Similarly, no attempt should be made to compute a value that violates the restrictions and thus no output can be produced that is not within the limits.

3-3. FORMAT-FREE INPUT/OUTPUT

As we saw in Section 3–1, format-free I/O uses the READ statement for input and the PRINT statement for output. In this section we describe these statements and explain their use.

The general form of the READ statement for format-free input is as follows:

READ *, *list*

where *list* is a list of variable names separated by commas.

The asterisk indicates that format-free input is to be used. (With some versions of FORTRAN the asterisk is not used but the comma following it is still required.) The computer assumes that the input data will come from a standard input device such as a card reader or terminal keyboard. We will assume that a card reader is used in the following examples.

The list of variable names, called an *I/O list*, indicates how many values are to be read and the names that are used to refer to the values in the program. The computer automatically assigns a storage location to each variable name. When the READ statement is executed, one value for each variable name in the list is read and stored in its respective location. As an example, consider the following READ statement:

```
READ *,NUM,P,AZ
```

Three values are read with this statement. The first is an integer and the other two are reals. If the three input values are 158, –17.63, and .0035 respectively, then after execution of this statement the value of NUM is 158, P is –17.63, and AZ is .0035. Notice that the variable names in the list are separated by commas but that there is no punctuation after the last variable name.

In preparing input data, the values are punched or typed one after the other, separated by commas or blanks. For example, an input card for the previous READ statement could be punched as follows:

```
123456789.......... (card columns)

158,-17.63,.0035
```

If an interactive rather than batch system is used, then the input data is typed exactly as it would be punched on a card. (Usually with an interactive system the computer prints or displays a question mark when a READ statement is encountered. Then the data is typed after the question mark and the RETURN key is pressed at the end of the line.)

Between each input value there must be a comma or a blank. Blanks can be used before or after the comma or several blanks can be left between each value without a comma. However, a blank or a comma must never be put in the middle of a value.

If the value to be read is integer, then it must not have a decimal point. A real value requires a decimal point unless the decimal point is on the right in which case it is optional. If the value is negative then a minus sign is required. For a positive value, a plus sign may be used or no sign·can be included.

It is important that the type of the variable name and the type of the data correspond. That is, if the variable name is integer then the value read must be integer and if the name is real then the input data must be real. Thus in the previous example, the first input value is integer and the next two are real, corresponding with the order of the variable names in the READ statement list.

As another example consider the following READ statement:

$$\text{READ } *,X,Y,K,L$$

Assume that an input card is punched as follows:

```
    123456789.........
  _____
 /    4.53  62  18  -37
(
```

Notice that the input data does not have to begin in column 1. In addition, blanks may be used to separate values instead of commas. After the READ statement reads this card the value of X is 4.53, Y is 62., K is 18, and L is -37. Notice that the value for Y is punched without a decimal point even though Y is a real variable name. This is because the decimal point, if punched, would be on the right and thus it is optional.

Each READ statement causes the computer to begin reading a new card. (With interactive processing, each READ statement displays a question mark and accepts a new typed line of input.) Thus the following statements cause two cards to be read:

$$\text{READ } *,X,Y$$
$$\text{READ } *,K,L$$

The first card contains the values for X and Y; the second contains data for K and L.

If there are more values on a card than there are variable names in the READ statement list, then any excess data is ignored. Thus if there are six numbers and only four variable names, then the last two numbers would not be read. If there are fewer values on a card than there are variable names then the computer continues to read from the next card. For example, if there are four variable names in the READ statement list and two values on each of two input cards, then the computer will read the data on the first card and assign it to the first two variable names. Then the data from the second card will be read and assigned to the third and fourth variable names.

For format-free output, the PRINT statement is used. The general form of this statement is as follows:

PRINT *, *list*

where *list* is a list of variable names separated by commas.

The asterisk indicates format-free output. (An asterisk is not used in some versions of FORTRAN.) A standard output device such as a printer or video display is assumed. We will use a printer for the output device in the following examples.

The I/O list gives the variable names of the values to be printed. When the PRINT statement is executed the computer writes the current value of each variable name in the list. For example, the following PRINT statement causes the computer to write two values:

```
PRINT *,X,I
```

The first value printed is real and the second value is integer. Notice that commas must be used between the variable names. If X is 4.53 and L is –37 in the computer's internal storage, then execution of this statement causes the computer to write these two values.

The way in which the output is printed depends on the computer being used. As an example, the previous PRINT statement might result in the following output:

```
123456789....................(print positions)
```
```
    4.530000                -37
```

The values are printed across the paper in the order in which the corresponding variable names appear in the PRINT statement list. Thus the first number printed is the value of X, followed by the value of L. The values are separated by one or more blanks to make the output readable. If the number is negative, a minus sign is printed; otherwise no sign appears.

An integer is always printed as it would normally be written, as in the example above. The output format for a real number depends on its size. If the value requires relatively few print positions, as in the previous example, then the number is printed as we would normally write it, but with extra zeros added if necessary so that the number always has a certain number of digits. For quantities that require many print positions, the output appears in exponential notation. (Some versions of FORTRAN print all real output in exponential notation.) In this notation the number appears in a form somewhat similar to floating-point notation. The output consists of a fraction followed by the letter E and then the exponent. For example, assume that the value of the variable named S is 583079000000000.0. If the computer executes the following PRINT statement

$$\text{PRINT *,S}$$

then the output would appear as follows:

```
123456789.........
```
```
   0.5830790E 15
```

This is interpreted as 0.5830790×10^{15}. If the value to be printed is very small, then the exponent will be negative. For example, if the value of T is .0000000000038045, then execution of the statement

$$\text{PRINT *,T}$$

results in the following output

```
123456789.........
```
```
   0.3804500E-11
```

This is interpreted as $0.3804500 \times 10^{-11}$.

It is easy to convert exponential notation to our usual way of writing numbers by shifting the decimal point. If the exponent is positive, then the decimal point should be shifted to the right the number of places given by the exponent. For a negative exponent, the decimal point should be shifted to the left. Thus in the first example above, the decimal point should be shifted 15 places to the right to get the equivalent value. In the second example, the decimal point should be shifted eleven places to the left.

Each PRINT statement causes the computer to start a new line. If there are more values to be printed than can fit on a line, then the computer automatically continues on to the next line. Thus if only eight values can be printed on a line and there are twelve variable names in the PRINT statement list, then the values of the first eight variables will be printed on the first line and the last four values will appear on the second line. The next PRINT statement will start printing on the third line.

The READ and PRINT statements perform basic format-free input and output. In Section 3-7 we will show their use in complete programs.

3-4. FORMATTED INPUT/OUTPUT

Three statements are needed for formatted I/O. The READ statement is used for an input operation. For output, the WRITE statement is used. The FORMAT statement is needed for both input and output. In this section we describe these statements and explain their use.

The general form of the READ statement for formatted input is as follows:

> READ (i,n) *list*

where i is the device code.

n is the statement number of the FORMAT statement describing the input data format.

list is a list of variable names separated by commas.

The *device code* (also called the *logical unit number* or *data set reference number*) specifies the particular device that is used for the input data. The code that is used for any specific input device depends on the computer system. In this text, the device code 5 signifies the card reader. (A different code would be used for a terminal keyboard.)

As we recall, for each READ statement there must be a corresponding FORMAT statement. The two statements are linked by the statement number of the FORMAT statement. This number must appear in parentheses, separated from the device code by a comma.

The list of variable names, called the *I/O list*, specifies how many values are to be read and the names that are used to refer to the values in the program. The computer automatically assigns a storage location to each variable name. When the READ statement is executed, one value for each variable name in the list is read and stored in its respective location. For example, the following READ statement causes four values to be read:

```
READ(5,10) AMT,B5,K,JNUM
```

The first two values are real and are stored at locations reserved for the variables named AMT and B5 respectively. The second two values are integer and are identified by K and JNUM in the program. If the four values punched on a card are 5.8, 183.52, –18, and 0, then after execution of this statement the value of AMT is 5.8, B5 is 183.52, K is –18, and JNUM is 0. Note that the variable names in the list are separated by commas but that there is no punctuation after the last variable name in the list. In this example, the device code 5 means that input is from the card reader. The statement number of the corresponding FORMAT statement is 10.

Each READ statement causes the computer to begin reading a new card (or a new type line if interactive processing is used). Thus the following statements cause the computer to read two cards:

$$\text{READ}(5,20) \ A$$
$$\text{READ}(5,30) \ X,J$$

The first card contains the value for A; the second card contains data for X and J.

For formatted output, the WRITE statement is used. The general form of this statement is as follows:

WRITE (i,n) *list*

where i is the device code.

n is the statement number of the FORMAT statement describing the output data format.

list is a list of variable names separated by commas.

The device code for the WRITE statement specifies the output device. In this text, the device code 6 is used for the printer. (A different code would be used for a terminal.) As with the READ statement, the WRITE statement must have a corresponding FORMAT statement. Again the link between the two statements is the statement number of the FORMAT statement.

The I/O list gives the variable names of the values to be printed. When the WRITE statement is executed, the computer writes the current value of each variable named in the list. For example, the following WRITE statement causes three values to be written:

$$\text{WRITE}(6,15) \ X,\text{KNT},\text{YVAL}$$

The first and last values are real. The second value is an integer. If X is 25.82, KNT is 139, and YVAL is –5.6 in the computer's internal storage, then execution of this statement causes these three values to be written by the printer (device code 6) in the arrangement specified by the FORMAT statement whose number is 15.

Each WRITE statement causes the computer to start a new output

line. Hence, the following statements cause the computer to write three
lines: .

```
WRITE(6,25) A,I
WRITE(6,35) J
WRITE(6,45) X,Y,Z
```

The first line contains the values of A and I. In the second line the
value of J is printed. The third line contains the values of X, Y, and Z.

Linked to each READ or WRITE statement must be a FORMAT
statement. This statement describes the arrangement of the input or
output data on the external medium. Internally, all data is represented
in a standard form. Section 3-2 discussed briefly the internal form of
integer and real numbers. (A more complete discussion is contained in
Chapter 13). It is not necessary for the programmer to have a detailed
understanding of the internal form of data since the computer handles
this automatically. What is required is that the programmer tell the
computer the external form of the data. In the case of input, the computer must know the arrangement of the input data so that it can
properly convert the data to its internal form. For output, the external
form of the data is required so that proper conversion from the internal
form can be accomplished. This is the function of the FORMAT
statement.

The general form of the FORMAT statement is as follows:

   n FORMAT (*format codes*)

   where *n* is a statement number.
   format codes specify the external data format.

A statement number is required for any FORMAT statement. This
same statement number must appear in the corresponding READ or
WRITE statement. The *format codes*, also called *data conversion codes*,
describe how data fields are arranged on the external medium, and what
type of conversion is to take place between the internal data representation and the external data form. There are a number of format codes
available in FORTRAN. In the following sections we consider I-format,
F-format, and X-format. In later chapters we examine other format
codes.

As an example of the use of the FORMAT statement, consider the
following statements:

```
    READ(5,40) A,J
40 FORMAT(F10.2,I5)
    WRITE(6,45) A,J
45 FORMAT(1X,F10.2,2X,I5)
```

The READ statement instructs the computer to read data for A and J using the format given in statement 40. The format codes (F10.2,I5) give the arrangement of the input data. The WRITE statement causes the computer to print the values of A and J in the format given in statement 45. The codes (1X,F10.2,2X,I5) describe the output format.

In the next two sections we describe the format codes used for input and for output respectively. Then in Section 3-7 we show the use of the READ, WRITE, and FORMAT statements in complete programs.

3-5. FORMAT CODES FOR INPUT

Format codes can be used to specify the arrangement of both input and output data. However, their function when used for input is different than when used for output. First we will examine the function of several codes for input and then consider their use for output.

I-Format Code for Input

Different format codes are used to specify the arrangement of different types of data. The I-format code is used for integer data. Only integers may be read using I-format.

The general form of the I-format code is as follows:

Iw

where w is the width of the field.

As an example of the use of I-format, consider the following READ statement and corresponding FORMAT statement:

```
     READ(5,105) K,L
105 FORMAT(I4,I5)
```

In this example, there are two integer variable names — K and L — in the READ statement list. Thus, two values are read. In the FORMAT statement there are two I-format codes — I4 and I5. These are separated by commas, and they correspond to the two input variable names respectively. Thus, the value for K is read in format I4, and L is read in format I5.

The numbers following the letter I specify the width of the field on the external medium which is a punched card in our examples.

The first field, containing the value for K, is four columns wide and begins in column 1. Immediately following this field is a five-column field that contains the value for L. If the values to be read for K and L are 25 and -36 respectively, then the input card must be punched as follows:

123456789...(card columns)

```
     ┌──────┬─────┐
    /    25 │ -36 │
   (         │     │
```

(Vertical lines are used to designate fields but do not necessarily appear on the card. Note that if an interactive rather than a batch system is used, then the input data is typed exactly as it would be punched on a card). After execution of the READ statement, the values of the input variable names are as desired.

It is important to remember the correspondence between the variable names in the READ statement, the format codes in the FORMAT statement, and the fields on the input card. Figure 3-5 summarizes the correspondence for this example.

In this example the selection of K and L as the integer variable names is arbitrary. The programmer may select any names as long as they begin with one of the letters, I, J, K, L, M, or N and follow the other rules for FORTRAN variable names. For example, NUM and M5 would work equally well. In addition, the location of the fields on the input card may be different. One part of planning a program is to determine the layout of the input data. In this example the value for K is punched in columns 1 through 4, and the value for L is punched in columns 5 through 9. However, the input data card may be arranged in another manner as long as the READ and FORMAT statements correspond to the card layout. For example, assume that the card is punched with the value for L in columns 1 through 5 and the value

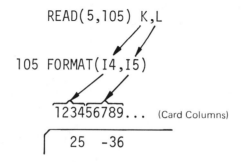

FIGURE 3-5. Correspondence between variable names, format codes, and card input fields.

for K in columns 6 through 12. Then the READ and FORMAT statements are:

READ(5,106) L,K
106 FORMAT(I5,I7)

In this case L is read in format I5, and K is read in format I7. Finally, note that it is not necessary to know the actual data values when preparing the READ and FORMAT statements. All that is needed is knowledge of the location of the fields on the input data card.

When an integer value is recorded on a punched card, it must not be punched with a decimal point. If the value is negative, it must have a minus sign in front of it. If it is positive, the plus sign is optional. No commas may appear in the value. An integer must be recorded as far to the right in its field as possible. That is, integers must be *right-justified*. If an integer is not right-justified, then any blanks that appear in the field after the value are interpreted as zeros. For example, consider a data card punched as follows:

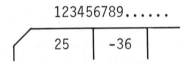

If this card is read by the previous READ statement, then the value of L is 25000 and K is –3600.

F-Format Code for Input

When an integer value is to be read, only I-format code may be used. The F-format code is used to describe the arrangement of real data (floating-point data). Only real values may be read using F-format.

The general form of the F-format code is:

  F$w.d$

  where w is the width of the field.
     d is the number of places to the right of the decimal point.

The following example illustrates the use of F-format for input:

READ(5,20) X,Y,Z
20 FORMAT(F8.2,F10.4,F4.0)

Three real values are read and assigned to the storage locations reserved for variable names X, Y, and Z. (Recall that real variable names begin with any letter other than I, J, K, L, M, or N.) The three F-format codes, separated by commas, correspond to the three variable names in the input list. The value for X is read in format F8.2, Y is read in format F10.4, and Z is read in format F4.0.

Like I-format, the field width in F-format is written immediately following the letter F. Thus, the value for X in the previous example occupies the first eight columns of the input card, the value for Y is punched in columns 9 through 18, and Z is punched in columns 19 through 22. However, since F-format is used for real data, additional information about the number of decimal positions is required. This information is coded after the field width and is separated from the field width by a decimal point. In the preceding example, the value for X has two places to the right of the decimal point, Y has four places to the right, and the value of Z has no places to the right of the decimal point. Note that even though Z has no decimal places it has a decimal point and is assigned to a real variable name.

Consider a data card punched as follows:

```
123456789...............
   ┌──────────────────────────────────
  /      36.25  │    -.2738│ 45.│
 /
```

If this card is read by the previous READ statement, then the value of X is 36.25, Y is –.2738, and Z is 45.

When a real value is recorded on a punched card it is often punched with a decimal point in the proper position. However, this is not required. If the decimal point is omitted, then the computer uses the F-format code to locate where the decimal point should be. For example, assume that the data card is punched as follows:

```
123456789...............
   ┌──────────────────────────────────
  /       3625 │    -2738│ 45│
 /
```

Then the result is the same as in the previous example. The computer examines the format codes and determines how many places should be to the right of the decimal point. For example, format code F8.2 tells the computer that there are two decimal places. The computer counts the number of places specified *from the right-most column in the field*, and reads the value as if a decimal point were punched in the indicated position. In this example the value for X is read as 36.25. It is important when using this feature of the F-format that the data be right-justified. Assume for example, that the first field is not right-justified but instead is punched as:

123456789...

3625

Then the computer interprets any trailing blanks as zeros, and, counting two decimal places from the right, the value is read as 362.50.

If a decimal point is included in the punched card data, then it need not correspond with the format code, and the value need not be right-justified. For example, consider the following punched card data:

123456789...

36.2587

The actual location of the decimal point on the data card overrides the specified location in the format code, and in this case, with format code F8.2, the value is read as 36.2587.

F-format and I-format may be used in the same FORMAT statement. For example, the following statements are valid:

```
     READ(5,10) A,B,I,J
10   FORMAT(F10.2,F8.4,I4,I6)
```

The values for A and B are read in formats F10.2 and F8.4 respectively; the values for I and J are read in formats I4 and I6. However, care should be taken not to read or write a real value using I-format, or an integer value using F-format. For example, assume that the above READ statement is accidentally coded as follows:

```
     READ(5,10) A,I,B,J
```

In this case an error occurs since the computer tries to read a value for the integer variable name I in format F8.4, and a value for the real variable name B in format I4.

X-Format Code for Input

In the examples considered so far the first input field has always begun in column 1. If additional fields are read, they begin in the next column following the previous field. Commonly the computer begins reading in column 1 and continues through successive columns until all of the required fields on the card are read. However, by using X-format it is possible to have the computer skip columns. Thus, data fields can be spaced across the punched card.

The general form of the X-format code is:

wX

where w is the width of the field to be skipped; that is, w is the number of columns to be skipped.

For example, consider the following statements:

```
        READ(5,25) AMT,KT
     25 FORMAT(F5.2,4X,I3)
```

In this example, the value for the real variable named AMT is read in format F5.2. Then the format 4X tells the computer to skip the next four columns. Finally, the value for the integer variable named KT is read in format I3. Thus, if some values, say 2.58 and –10, are to be read and assigned to AMT and KT respectively, then the data card is punched as follows:

```
        123456789......
```

```
          2.58    -10
```

As another example, consider the following READ and FORMAT statements:

```
        READ(5,26) ID,COST
     26 FORMAT(5X,I4,1X,F10.2)
```

The format 5X tells the computer to skip the first five columns. Then the value of ID is read in format I4. Next, the code 1X causes one column to be skipped. Finally, the value of the variable name COST is read in format F10.2.

Repeat Specification

If an F- or I-format code is repeated successively in a FORMAT statement, the code may be written once and immediately preceded by a number that specifies the number of times that the code should be repeated. For example, in the following FORMAT statement, FORMAT code F10.2 is repeated three times in succession:

$$55 \ \text{FORMAT}(\text{F10.2,F10.2,F10.2})$$

Using a repeat specification, the statement may be shortened to the following:

$$55 \ \text{FORMAT}(\text{3F10.2})$$

The 3 in front of the format code specifies that this code should be repeated three times.

As another example, consider the following FORMAT statement:

$$56 \ \text{FORMAT}(\text{F12.6,F12.6,I2,I2,I2})$$

The format F12.6 is repeated twice followed by three repetitions of the I2 format. Thus, the statement may be shortened to

$$56 \ \text{FORMAT}(\text{2F12.6,3I2})$$

A repeat specification can be used for both input and output formats.

3-6. FORMAT CODES FOR OUTPUT

In the last section we explained the use of I-, F-, and X-format codes for describing the arrangement of input data. In this section the use of these codes for output is discussed. However, to understand how these codes are used we must reexamine the organization of output records.

Output Records

In Chapter 1 we saw that a *record* is a group of fields. In FORTRAN the fields that are read from one input card comprise one input record. Similarly, the fields to be written as a printed line make up one output record.

When dealing with punched card input, we think in terms of the card columns in which the data are punched. A printed line is organized into character positions or *print positions* that are similar to card columns. The maximum number of print positions per output line varies with the printer, but common sizes are 120, 132, and 144 print positions. The print positions are numbered, beginning with 1 on the left and continuing to the maximum on the right. These numbers do not appear on the printout paper, but when discussing output formats it is convenient to think in terms of numbered print positions.

With punched card input, the data is read beginning in column 1. Similarly, with printed output, the printing begins in print position 1; however, the character in the first position in the *output record* (described by the FORMAT statement) is *not* printed. Printing begins in print position 1 with the character in the *second* position in the output record. The reason for this is that the first character of a printed output record is used to control the movement of the paper in the printer. The details of this are discussed in Chapter 7, but for now we need a way of skipping the first position of the output record. The simplest approach is to use the X-format code. By using 1X as the first code in the FORMAT statement, the first position in the output record is skipped and printing begins in print position 1 with the next character.

I-Format Code for Output

As an example of output record organization and the use of the I-format code, consider the following statements:

```
        WRITE(6,87) K,L
    87 FORMAT(1X,I2,I4)
```

The result of the execution of the WRITE statement is that the current values of K and L are printed. The value of K is printed in format I2, and L is printed in format I4. If this is executed when the values of K and L are 25 and –36 respectively, then the output appears as follows:

```
    123456789...              (print positions)
  ┌─────────────────────
  │   25│ -36│
  └─────────────────────
```

(Vertical lines are used to designate fields, but are not printed by the printer.)

When the FORMAT statement is used for output, the statement describes the arrangement of the characters in the output record. In this example the first position in the output record is skipped, because the first code in the FORMAT statement is 1X. The value of K is placed in the next two positions in the output record, followed by the value of L in the next four positions. Since printing begins with the *second* position in the output record, the value of K is printed in the first two print positions and the value of L is printed in print positions 3 through 6. This is summarized in Fig. 3-6.

The importance of skipping the first position in a printed output record can be seen more clearly now. Assume that the 1X code had been left out, and that the statements had been coded as follows:

```
        WRITE(6,87) K,J
     87 FORMAT(I2,I4)
```

In this case the value of K occupies the first two positions in the output record. However, the first character in a printed output record is never printed; the printing begins with the second character. Hence, if K is 25, the 2 is not printed, and the 5 is printed in the first print position. This is summarized in Fig. 3-7. Note that this applies to printed output only and does not apply to any other form of output or any form of input.

When using I-format for output, the output data is automatically printed right-justified in its fields. Since these values are integers, no decimal points are printed. If the value is positive, no sign is printed. If it is negative, a minus sign is printed immediately to the left of the value. The minus sign occupies a print position and enough room must be left for all digits in the value and any sign. If the field size is not large enough to contain the output, an error condition occurs. On many computer systems such an error field is filled with asterisks. For example, if the previous FORMAT statement is coded

```
     87 FORMAT(1X,I2,I2)
```

then with K equal to 25 and L equal to -36, the resulting output

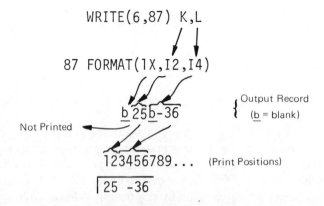

FIGURE 3-6.   Correspondence between variable names, format codes, and printed output fields.

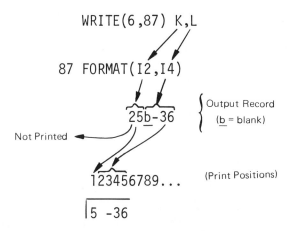

FIGURE 3-7. Result of an incorrectly coded FORMAT
statement for printed output.

appears as follows:

```
123456789...
 25|**|
```

Since −36 requires three print positions, and only two print positions
have been specified for this field in the FORMAT statement, an error
occurs. Hence the field is filled with asterisks.

The I-format code describes the external format of integer data.
Internally all integer data are represented in the same general form.
Thus, a value that is read in one format may be written in another. For
example, the value of L may be read in format I5 and written in format
I4. In addition, there may be as many format codes in a FORMAT statement as needed. The only restriction is that the total number of columns
specified for input does not exceed 80, and that the number of output
print positions does not exceed the capacity of the printer.

F-Format Code for Output

The following example illustrates the use of F-format for output:

```
WRITE(6,75) X,Z
75 FORMAT(1X,F8.2,F6.0)
```

If the WRITE statement is executed when the value of X is 36.25 and the value of Z is 45., then the output appears as follows:

```
123456789........
```
```
|      36.25|  45.|
```

The value of X is printed in format F8.2, and Z is printed in format F6.0. Note that the input format need not agree with the output format. For example, the value of Z may be read in format F4.0 and written in format F6.0. Format codes describe the external representation of the data; internally, real data is represented in a standard form which is unrelated to the external form.

Output with F-format is always right-justified in its field. A decimal point is always printed, whether or not there are places to the right of the decimal point. There should be enough field width to accommodate the value and any punctuation. The minus sign and the decimal point each require a full print position. In addition, on most computers a fraction is printed with a leading zero. Thus, if Y is –.2738 and the following WRITE statement is executed:

```
    WRITE(6,185) Y
185 FORMAT(1X,F10.4)
```

then the result is printed as follows:

```
123456789...
```
```
|    -0.2738|
```

F-format input and output differ in that when F-format is used for output the number of decimal positions specified is always the controlling factor. If the number of decimal positions specified is greater than the number in the value to be written, then trailing positions are filled with zeros. For example, consider the following statements:

```
    WRITE(6,410) X
410 FORMAT(1X,F12.4)
```

In this example, four decimal positions are specified, but the value of X (36.25) has only two decimal positions. The resulting output is:

```
123456789......
```
```
|      36.2500|
```

If the number of decimal positions specified is less than the actual number in the data value, then the value is rounded to the specified number of decimal positions before printing. For example, if Y is –0.2738 and the following statements are coded

```
      WRITE(6,65) Y
   65 FORMAT(1X,F6.3)
```

then the output appears as follows:

```
    123456789...
   ┌──────────────────────┐
   │  -0.274│
   │        │
```

Notice that –0.2738 has been rounded off to –0.274 before printing.

In some versions of FORTRAN rounding does not take place when excess decimal positions are present. Instead, excess decimal positions are dropped or *truncated*. In such a case the output from the previous WRITE statement is as follows:

```
    123456789...
   ┌──────────────────────┐
   │  -0.273│
   │        │
```

Notice in this example that the last digit in –0.2738 is dropped and the value is not rounded off.

X-Format Code for Output

As we have seen, the X-format code may be used to skip positions in an output record; in fact, X-format causes blank characters to be printed. For example, the following statements cause the values of AMT and KT to be printed with five blank characters at the beginning and three blanks between the fields:

```
      WRITE(6,26) AMT,KT
   26 FORMAT(6X,F5.2,3X,I3)
```

If AMT is 2.58 and KT is –10, then the output is printed as:

```
    123456789..........
   ┌───────────┐┌─────┐
   │      2.58││-10│
   │          ││   │
```

Notice that the first format code is 6X, even though only five blanks appear in the final output. This is because printing begins with the second character in the output record. In the past we have skipped the first position in the output record with a 1X code. Here we skip five positions with a 6X code. In other words, 6X is equivalent to 1X, 5X.

3-7. WRITING COMPLETE FORTRAN PROGRAMS

A FORTRAN program is a meaningful sequence of FORTRAN statements. The statements in the program are executed by the computer in the order in which they appear. Although only input and output statements have been considered so far, it is possible (with the addition of two simple statements) to write complete programs.

For example, consider the simple problem of reading a real value from a card and then printing the value. The following sequence of statements accomplishes this task using format-free I/O:

```
READ *,A
PRINT *,A
```

With formatted I/O the statements are as follows:

```
   READ(5,10) A
10 FORMAT(F8.2)
   WRITE(6,20) A
20 FORMAT(1X,F8.2)
```

The computer executes the statements in the sequence in which they are written. The effect is shown in Fig. 3–8. First, the READ statement causes the computer to read one number and to store it in the storage location identified by the variable name A. In the format-free case, the input format is preset. In the formatted I/O example, the format of the input is given by the FORMAT statement numbered 10. Next the PRINT or WRITE statement is executed causing the computer to print the value of A. The output format is preset in the format-free example and given by the statement number 20 in the formatted case. Notice that the variable name used in the output statement is the same as the name in the READ statement. It wouldn't make any sense to read a value for A and then print, for example, the value of B.

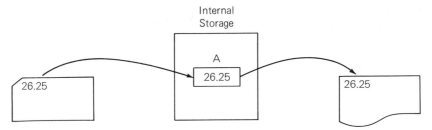

FIGURE 3-8. Effect of execution of a simple program.

Terminal Statements

This simple program has two executable statements in it. But what does the computer do after it executes the output statement? One rule in programming is that the computer must be told everything, including when to stop. For this purpose, FORTRAN supplies the STOP statement. This statement is just the keyword STOP. Its function is to cause the computer to cease processing the present program and go on to the next program.

In addition to the STOP statement, every FORTRAN program must have an END statement as the last statement in the program. While the STOP statement specifies the *logical* end of the program during execution, the END statement signals the *physical* end of the program for the FORTRAN compiler. During translation of the FORTRAN source program into machine language, the compiler processes each statement in turn until it encounters the END statement. At that point the compiler knows that there are no more source statements; compilation is terminated, and execution of the program is begun.

Illustrative Programs — Format-Free I/O

To complete the previous format-free example we add a STOP and an END statement. This results in the following complete FORTRAN program:

```
READ *,A
PRINT *,A
STOP
END
```

The computer first reads a value for A, then prints A, and finally stops execution.

The order of the statements on the program is important. The computer executes the statements in the order in which they are written. Thus, the statements must be logically arranged. For example, the following program is incorrect:

```
PRINT *,A
READ *,A
STOP
END
```

In this example, the value of A is printed before it is read which is clearly impossible.

For each input card that is to be read, a separate READ statement is usually used. In addition, each line to be printed requires a separate PRINT statement. For example, the following program reads two cards and prints two lines of output:

```
READ *,A
READ *,B
PRINT *,A
PRINT *,B
STOP
END
```

In this example, the first input card contains the value for A and the second card contains the value of B. The values of A and B are then printed on two successive lines.

A program need not read all input before printing some of the output. For example, the following program reads one card and prints a line, then reads a second card and prints another line:

```
READ *,A
PRINT *,A
READ *,B
PRINT *,B
STOP
END
```

In addition, a variable name may be reused after its value is no longer needed in the program. For example, the previous program could be coded as follows:

```
READ *,A
PRINT *,A
READ *,A
PRINT *,A
STOP
END
```

In this case, the variable A is used for both input values. The first READ statement causes the first input card to be read and a value to be assigned to A. When the second READ statement is executed, a second card is read. The previous value of A is destroyed and replaced with the new data. However, this is acceptable in this program since the previous value has already been printed.

In a more complicated situation it may be necessary to print the output in a different order than the input. The following program reads two cards and produces three lines of output:

```
READ *,I,J,K
READ *,X,Y,Z
PRINT *,I,X
PRINT *,J,Y
PRINT *,K,Z
STOP
END
```

The first input card contains three integers and the second card contains three reals. The output is printed with one integer and one real per line.

As a final example assume that the test data for two students is punched in two input cards. Each card contains one student's identification number followed by his or her score on two examinations. It is necessary to list the data for the students. Each line of output should contain the data for one student. A program to accomplish this is shown in Fig. 3-9(a). The output that results from running the program is shown in Fig. 3-9(b).

```
READ *,ID,SCR1,SCR2
PRINT *,ID,SCR1,SCR2
READ *,ID,SCR1,SCR2
PRINT *,ID,SCR1,SCR2
STOP
END
```

(a)

```
12841    98.50000       83.00000
20853    92.00000       85.50000
```

(b)

FIGURE 3-9. An illustrative program — format-free I/O:
(a) the program; (b) the output.

Illustrative Programs — Formatted I/O

With the addition of the two terminal statements STOP and END, the formatted I/O example at the beginning of this section becomes a complete FORTRAN program:

```
      READ(5,10) A
   10 FORMAT(F8.2)
      WRITE(6,20) A
   20 FORMAT(1X,F8.2)
      STOP
      END
```

A value for A is read in the format given by FORMAT statement 10. Then A is printed using the format in FORMAT statement 20. Finally the program stops executing.

The READ and WRITE statements are executable statements. The computer executes these statements in the order in which they appear in the program. Hence it would be unacceptable to code the previous program as follows:

```
      WRITE(6,20) A
   20 FORMAT(F8.2)
      READ(5,10) A
   10 FORMAT(1X,F8.2)
      STOP
      END
```

The value of A cannot be written before it is read and thus this program is logically incorrect.

FORMAT statements are nonexecutable statements. They are used during input and output operations but they are not executed by themselves. Hence FORMAT statements may appear anywhere in the program before the END statement. Many programmers place all FORMAT statements together at the beginning or end of the program. For example, in the following program we have grouped all FORMAT statements at the end of the program, after the STOP statement but before the END statement:

```
      READ(5,10) A
      WRITE(6,20) A
      STOP
   10 FORMAT(F8.2)
   20 FORMAT(1X,F8.2)
      END
```

The computer locates the appropriate FORMAT statement by the statement number given in the READ or WRITE statement. Each FORMAT statement must have a unique statement number so it can be found.

For each input card that is read, a separate READ statement is usually used. In addition, a separate WRITE statement is needed for each line to be printed. For example, the following program reads two cards and prints two lines:

```
      READ(5,10) A
      READ(5,10) B
      WRITE(6,20) A
      WRITE(6,20) B
      STOP
   10 FORMAT(F8.2)
   20 FORMAT(1X,F8.2)
      END
```

Notice that FORMAT statement 10 is used with both READ statements and that statement 20 is used with both WRITE statements. It is *not* required that each READ and WRITE statement refer to a unique FORMAT statement. If an input or output format is identical for several records, then the appropriate FORMAT statement may be referred to by several READ or WRITE statements.

The previous program could also be written as follows:

```
      READ(5,10) A
      WRITE(6,20) A
      READ(5,10) B
      WRITE(6,20) B
      STOP
   10 FORMAT(F8.2)
   20 FORMAT(1X,F8.2)
      END
```

In this example the first value is read and printed before the second value is read. Another way of writing this program is to reuse the variable name A. For example, the program can be coded as follows:

```
      READ(5,10) A
      WRITE(6,20) A
      READ(5,20) A
      WRITE(6,20) A
      STOP
```

```
10 FORMAT(F8.2)
20 FORMAT(1X,F8.2)
   END
```

In this program, the first READ causes the first input card to be read and a value to be assigned to A. The second READ statement reads the next input card. The old value of A is destroyed and replaced by a new value. This is acceptable in this program since the old value has already been printed.

Many times the output data needs to be printed in a different format than the input data. For example, the following program reads three integers from one card and three reals from a second card. Then the output is printed with one integer and one real per line.

```
   READ(5,30) I,J,K
   READ(5,40) X,Y,Z
   WRITE(6,50) I,X
   WRITE(6,50) J,Y
   WRITE(6,50) K,Z
   STOP
30 FORMAT(3I5)
40 FORMAT(3F10.2)
50 FORMAT(1X,I5,2X,F10.2)
   END
```

Notice that a repeat specification is used in FORMAT statements 30 and 40.

Figure 3-10(a) shows our final illustrative program. This program reads two input cards, each containing the identification number for a student and two examination scores. The output lists the input data; one line is printed for each student. Figure 3-10(b) shows the output that results from running this program.

3-8. PROGRAM REPETITION

The programs in the previous section illustrate the use of input and output operations. Each program follows the same basic pattern. That is, each program reads some input data, writes some output, and then stops. One problem with this pattern is that if there is a lot of data to be read or written then the program becomes very large. For example, in the sample programs in Figs. 3-9 and 3-10 there are two READ statements, one for each input card. If there is more input

```
      READ(5,100) ID,SCR1,SCR2
      WRITE(6,200) ID,SCR1,SCR2
      READ(5,100) ID,SCR1,SCR2
      WRITE(6,200) ID,SCR1,SCR2
      STOP
  100 FORMAT(I5,5X,2F5.1)
  200 FORMAT(1X,I5,5X,F5.1,5X,F5.1)
      END
```

(a)

```
  12841     98.5     83.0
  20853     92.0     85.5
```

(b)

FIGURE 3-10. An illustrative program—formatted I/O:
(a) the program; (b) the output.

data, then additional READ statements would be required. Thus if there are 10 or 100 or 1000 input cards then an equal number of READ statements is needed. Obviously the size of the program gets out of hand very quickly.

In the sample programs in Figs. 3-9 and 3-10, each input card has the same type of data in the same format. That is, even though the numbers are different, the first value is always the student's identification number and the next two values are always test scores. In addition, the format of the output is the same for each line. Thus we could use just one READ statement and one WRITE or PRINT statement if we had some way of causing the computer to use these statements more than once. In fact, as we will see, we want to be able to repeatedly execute the statements in a program until there is no more input data.

The way that we accomplish this in FORTRAN is by using a GO TO statement. The syntax of the GO TO statement is simply the words GO TO followed by a statement number. For example, GO TO 50 is a valid GO TO statement. The number must correspond with some other statement in the program. (Recall that any statement in a program can have a number, although the only statements that we have numbered so far have been FORMAT statements.) The effec: of the GO TO statement is to cause the computer to go to the statement whose number is given in the GO TO statement and to continue execution from that point. We will have more to say about the GO TO statement in Chapter 5, but for now we want to see how to use this statement to cause the computer to repeat the execution of statements in a program.

Figure 3-11 shows the use of the GO TO statement in a sample program. This program reads and writes student identification numbers and test scores. Notice that the READ statement is numbered 10. Execution of the READ statement causes values to be read for ID, SCR1, and SCR2. Then the WRITE or PRINT statement writes the output. After this the GO TO statement causes the computer to go to the statement numbered 10 and to continue execution with that statement. But since statement 10 is the READ statement the computer reads another input card. The data that is read is assigned to ID, SCR1, and SCR2, replacing the previous values that were read. Execution of the output statement causes the current values of these variables to be written on the next line. Then the GO TO statement causes the computer to repeat the program, reading another card and printing another line, and so forth.

Notice that in this program there is no STOP statement. In fact, the GO TO statement appears in the place where we would expect the STOP statement. Thus, this program appears not to have any way of terminating execution. In fact, the program will continue to execute as long as input data is supplied. The program will read an input record and write a line until there is no more input. On a batch processing system, this will usually result in an execution error. If interactive processing is used, the programmer can press a special key (usually the BREAK or ATTN key) when no more data is to be supplied. Then the program will stop execution.

The statements in this sample program are executed over and over again. In general, a group of statements that are repeatedly executed

```
10 READ *,ID,SCR1,SCR2
   PRINT *,ID,SCR1,SCR2
   GO TO 10
   END
```

(a)

```
10 READ(5,100) ID,SCR1,SCR2
   WRITE(6,200) ID,SCR1,SCR2
   GO TO 10
100 FORMAT(I5,5X,2F5.1)
200 FORMAT(1X,I5,5X,F5.1,5X,F5.1)
   END
```

(b)

FIGURE 3-11.   Illustrative programs with repetition: (a) format-free input/output; (b) formatted input/output.

is called a *loop*. The process of repeatedly executing the statements in
a loop is called *looping*. In this example, the loop consists of the READ
statement through the GO TO statement. We will have more to say
about loops and looping in Chapter 6.

3-9. PROGRAM STYLE

The most important objective of the programming process is to produce
a program that correctly solves the required problem. The process of
program testing, discussed briefly in Chapter 2, is designed to help
locate errors in a program. We will have more to say about program
testing in a later chapter.

After correctness, the most important characteristic of a program
is its understandability. By this we mean the qualities of the program
that make it understandable or readable to a human. Program understandability is important because programs are often reviewed by
people other than the original programmer. For example, the programming manager may review the program to check for completeness
and consistency with the problem definition. Other programmers may
have to read the program to make corrections for errors that are not
detected until after the program has been in use for awhile. Often
modifications are necessary in the program because of changing requirements. For example, payroll programs have to be modified
regularly because of changing tax structures. Sometimes it is decided
to enhance the program so that it does more than was originally
planned. In all of these situations, someone must look at the program
often several months or even years after it was originally coded. Even
if the original programmer is given the task, he or she may have a
difficult time remembering the program's logic unless the program
is easily understood.

Program style deals with those characteristics of a program that
make it more understandable to a human. Even though we have only
covered a few features of the FORTRAN language, it is possible to
begin incorporating good style into our programs. One rule that is
very basic is to use variable names that symbolize the data to which
they refer. For example, in the programs in Fig. 3-11 we used ID for
the student's identification number. Similarly the name SCR1 identified
the first test score and SCR2 referred to the second score.

Another good style rule is to use statement numbers that increase
in sequence. It is possible to use any valid statement number for any
statement as long as the number is not used elsewhere in the program.
However, for a large program it is often difficult to locate a particular

statement if the numbers are out of sequence. Thus statement numbers that increase through the program should be used.

If formatted I/O is used all FORMAT statements should be grouped together at the beginning or end of the program. By doing this, the main part of the program only contains executable statements. Thus these statements are easier to follow.

The style rules discussed here are illustrated in the programs shown in Fig. 3-11. As we explain other features of the FORTRAN language we will give more rules for style that help improve the understandability of any program.

PROGRAMMING PROBLEMS

In each of the following problems, the requirements are given for a computer program. A complete FORTRAN program should be prepared according to the requirements. The program should be fully debugged and tested on a computer using the test data given. The first seven problems may be solved using format-free I/O. The remaining problems require formatted I/O.

1. Write a FORTRAN program to list the data punched on a card. The input consists of three numbers. The first is real and the second and third are integers. Print the data in the same order as the input. Use the input values 98.6, 120, and 80 to test the program.

2. Input to a program consists of one card punched with four integers. Write a FORTRAN program to print the input data in a column; that is, print each value on a separate line. Use the values 47, –13, 29, and 148 to test the program.

3. Write a FORTRAN program that reads two input cards. The first card is punched with two integers and the second card is punched with two reals. Print the data on one line with the first integer followed by the first real, then the second integer followed by the second real. Test the program with the following input data: 1083, 2174, 47.49, 63.95.

4. The results of the analysis of a survey need to be printed. Input consists of three cards each punched with the following data:

    Survey number (integer)
    Number of respondents (integer)
    Percent responding (real)

Write a FORTRAN program to print the input data in three columns with the survey numbers on the first line, the number of respondents on the second line, and the percent responding on the third line. Use the following data to test the program:

Survey Number	Number Respondents	Percent Responding
146	375	46.5%
205	139	28.6%
439	643	67.3%

5. A list of student grade point averages is needed. Input consists of one card for each student giving his or her identification number (integer) followed by his or her grade point average (real). An unknown number of input records is to be processed. Write a FORTRAN program that prints one line for each input card listing the data on the card. Use the following data to test the program:

Student Number	Grade Point Average
10837	2.67
14836	3.50
15006	2.99
17113	1.85
17280	3.89
19463	2.25

6. An unknown number of input cards each contain a product number (integer), unit price (real), and quantity sold (integer). Write a FORTRAN program to list the data punched on the cards. One line should be printed for each input card. Use the following input data to test the program:

Product Number	Unit Price	Quantity Sold
147	$1.29	50
153	$4.25	29
185	$2.50	138
187	$6.95	250
228	$3.49	73

7. The first input card in a data deck contains an automobile identification number (integer). Following this card are an unknown number of cards each containing the results of a mileage test. The first number on each card is a test number (integer), the next is a test type (integer), and the last value is the miles per gallon (real). Write a FORTRAN

program that prints the identification number on the first line of output. Then list the input data with one line for each mileage test. Use the following input data for the program:

Automobile ID number: 4836

Test Number	Test Type	Miles Per Gallon
1	2	23.8
2	1	18.6
3	3	28.6
4	4	31.5
5	1	17.3
6	2	24.0
7	1	19.2
8	3	26.4

8. A FORTRAN program is needed to list the data punched in two fields of a card. The value in the first field is integer. It is punched in card columns 1 through 5. A real value with two places to the right of the decimal point is punched in columns 6 through 12.

Write a FORTRAN program that reads the data in these two fields, then prints the data in the same format. To test the program, punch 21835 in the first field of the data card and 472.80 in the second field.

9. Three values are punched in a card. The first and second values are integers punched in columns 6 and 7, and 11 and 12 respectively. The third value is real with one place to the right of the decimal point. It is punched in columns 14 through 18.

Write a FORTRAN program that reads the values and then prints them with five spaces between the output fields. To test the program let the three values be 25, 16, and 147.3.

10. Four values are punched in a card. The first two are integer. They are punched in columns 11 to 14 and 16 to 18. The next value is real with three places to the right of the decimal point. It is punched in columns 21 to 28. The last value is real with one place to the right of the decimal point. It is punched in columns 31 to 34.

Write a FORTRAN program to read all four values. Then on one line print the first integer followed by the first real, then the second integer followed by the second real. Separate all output fields by three spaces. To test your program, let the four values be 1821, 793, -45.637, and 21.4 respectively.

11. Two cards need to be read and printed on two separate lines of output. Each card has an integer and a real punched in format (4X, I3, 3X, F6.2).

Write a FORTRAN program that reads the cards and then prints the data in the same format as the input. To test the program, punch 482 and 37.35 in the first card, and 913 and 125.42 in the second card.

12. Each of three input cards contains data in the following format:

Card Columns	Field
1–3	Station number (integer)
5–10	Gallons of gasoline solid (integer)
21–24	Average price per gallon (real with one decimal position)

Write a FORTRAN program that reads the data punched in the three cards, then prints the data in three columns. The station numbers should be printed on the first line of the output record, the gallons of gasoline sold for each station should appear on the second line, and the average price per gallon for each station should be printed on the third line. Use the following data to test the program:

Station	Gallons	Price
128	20,532	79.9
389	17,835	85.3
405	23,562	77.5

13. Input data for a program is punched in the following format:

Card Columns	Field
1–5	Item number (integer)
6–10	Quantity on hand (integer)
21–25	Unit price (real, 2 decimal positions)

There is an unknown number of input cards. Write a FORTRAN program that lists the input data. One line should be printed for each card. Use the following data to test the program:

Item Number	Quantity On Hand	Unit Price
13721	47	$4.75
19821	253	$16.95
20056	89	$28.30
21306	465	$7.56
22465	0	$63.50
22851	360	$1.29
24711	28	$12.95

14. Input to a program consists of several cards giving information about a student's grades in the courses he or she took. The first card consists of the student's identification number (integer) in columns 1 through 5. Following this is an unknown number of course cards containing data in the following format:

Card Columns	Field
1–4	Course number (integer)
23–25	Units (real, one decimal position)
26–28	Grade (real, one decimal position)

Course grades are expressed as numbers in the input (for example, A is 4.0, A- is 3.7, B+ is 3.3, etc.). Write a FORTRAN program that prints the student's identification number on the first line. Then print one line for each course card listing the data on the card with five spaces between each output field. Use the following input data to test the program:

Student Number: 28601

Course Number	Units	Grade
1308	3.0	2.3
5872	2.0	4.0
1591	4.0	2.7
2811	3.0	3.3
4605	0.5	2.0

Chapter 4

ARITHMETIC PROGRAMMING

Using the statements discussed in Chapter 3, we can prepare programs that read and write data. However, after a program reads input data, it normally *processes* the data, and then writes the results. Processing includes many types of data manipulation but the most common is arithmetic processing. In this chapter we describe the FORTRAN elements necessary to do arithmetic and we discuss programming for arithmetic processing.

4-1. FORTRAN CONSTANTS

As we saw in Chapter 3, a symbolic name for a data value that occupies a storage location is called a *variable name*. The value in that storage location can change or vary and is referred to in the program by the variable name. A data value that does not change during execution of the program is called a *constant*. Like the value of a variable name, a constant occupies a storage location. However, a constant is not identified by a variable name. It appears as a number in a FORTRAN statement. For example, the following are valid constants in FORTRAN:

$$
\begin{array}{ll}
482.59 & 0 \\
25 & 5.83 \\
-18 & 0.0 \\
10 & -1.6258
\end{array}
$$

Just as there are two types of variables—integer and real—there are also two types of constants. An integer constant is any numeric value that does not have a decimal point. The following are valid integer constants:

$$1$$
$$91$$
$$-173$$
$$+24567$$

Commas are not permitted in a constant. If the constant is integer, no decimal point is allowed. A minus sign is required if the value of a constant is negative; a plus sign is optional for positive constants. The following are invalid integer constants for the reasons given:

3.2	(contains a decimal point)
27.	(contains a decimal point)
5,468	(contains a comma)

A real constant is any numeric value that has a decimal point. For example, the following are valid real constants:

$$0.0$$
$$+58.3$$
$$.00392$$
$$145.$$
$$-2538.63$$

Commas are not acceptable. A minus sign is required for negative values, but a plus sign is optional for positive values. A leading zero for a value with a fractional part is also optional. Thus, 0.05 and .05 are equivalent. Trailing zeros for a value with no fractional part are also optional. For example, 58., 58.0, and 58.00 are equivalent. However, a decimal point is required. Thus, 58. is real and 58 is integer.

In Section 3–2 we discussed limitations on the size of numbers that can be used for input data. These limitations also apply to constants and depend on the computer being used. Thus, an integer constant must be within a certain range which, on the IBM System/370, is from +2,147,483,647 to –2,147,483,648. Any integer between these values, including zero, is an acceptable integer constant. A real constant is stored in floating-point notation and thus has limitations on its fraction and its exponent. On the IBM System/370 a real constant must have no more than seven digits in its fraction, and its exponent must be between –78 and +75. Any positive or negative real constant within these limits, including zero, is valid.

4-2. ARITHMETIC EXPRESSIONS

An arithmetic expression is an instruction to the computer to perform arithmetic. Arithmetic expressions are formed from constants, variable names, and arithmetic operators.

Arithmetic operators are symbols which indicate what form of arithmetic is to be performed. The symbols used in FORTRAN and their meanings are as follows:

+   addition
−   subtraction
*   multiplication
/   division
**   exponentiation

To form a simple arithmetic expression using these symbols we write an unsigned constant or variable name on each side of the operator. For example, the following are valid arithmetic expressions in FORTRAN:

```
A+B
X-Y
2*K
TOTAL/3.0
X**2
```

Each of these expressions tells the computer to perform the indicated operation using the values of the variables and constants. For example, A+B means add the value of A and the value of B. If A is 8.3 and B is 5.2, then the value of A+B is 13.5. With subtraction, the value on the right of the subtraction operator is subtracted from the value on the left. Thus X−Y means subtract the value of Y from the value of X. Notice that multiplication is indicated by the asterisk symbol. Hence, 2*K means multiply the value of K by the constant 2. With division, the value on the left of the division operator is divided by the value on the right. TOTAL/3.0 means divide the value of TOTAL by 3.0. Exponentiation means raise the value on the left of the operator to the power of the value on the right. Hence X**2 means raise the value of X to the second power (that is, square the value of X).

The addition and subtraction symbols may be used alone in front of a single constant or variable name to form an arithmetic expression. In fact, a variable name or constant by itself is considered to be an arithmetic expression. Hence, each of the following are arithmetic expressions:

```
3
J
+7.5
+P
-.0063
-A
```

In the last example, if the value of A is –6.2, then the value of the arithmetic expression is –(–6.2) or 6.2.

To form more complex arithmetic expressions, several arithmetic operators are used. For example, the following are valid arithmetic expressions:

```
EL/F3+2.0
8-I*J
A*X**2+B*X-C
3.14159*R**2
-B+B/2.0/A
```

With complex arithmetic expressions, the order in which the operations are performed is very important. The order is always as follows:

1. All exponentiation is performed.
2. All multiplication and division is performed left-to-right.
3. All addition and subtraction is performed left-to-right.

For example, consider the following expression:

```
3.7-A*2.5/C+D**2+E
```

This expression is evaluated in the following order:

1. D is raised to the second power.
2. A is multiplied by 2.5 and the result divided by C.
3. The answer from Step 2 is subtracted from 3.7; the result is added to the result of Step 1; and finally E is added to get the final value of the expression.

In algebraic notation, the expression appears as follows:

$$3.7 - \frac{A \times 2.5}{C} + D^2 + E$$

To change the order of evaluation, arithmetic expressions may be enclosed in parentheses and combined with other expressions. When this is done, expressions in parentheses are evaluated before operations outside of the parentheses are performed. For example, consider the following modification of the previous expression:

$$3.7-A*2.5/(C+D**2)+E$$

The expression C+D**2 is enclosed in parentheses and is evaluated before any other operations are performed. Thus, the computer first raises D to the second power and adds the result to C. Next A is multiplied by 2.5, and the result is divided by the value of C+D**2. Finally, the other addition and subtraction is performed. The result in algebraic notation is as follows:

$$3.7 - \frac{A \times 2.5}{C + D^2} + E$$

Arithmetic expressions in parentheses may be imbedded in other parenthetic expressions. When this is done, the computer evaluates the expression in the innermost parentheses before continuing with the expression in the next level of parentheses. For example, consider the following:

$$3.7-A*(2.5/(C+D**2)+E)$$

First the computer evaluates C+D**2. The result is then divided into 2.5 and the value of E is added. The final multiplication by A and subtraction from 3.7 are then performed. In algebraic notation, this expression is as follows:

$$3.7 - A \times \left[\frac{2.5}{C + D^2} + E \right]$$

Notice that when using parentheses, as in these examples, each left parenthesis must have a matching right parenthesis.

A common mistake when writing an arithmetic expression is to forget that certain operations are done before others. For example, assume that the programmer must write an arithmetic expression in FORTRAN for the following algebraic expression:

$$\frac{A + B}{C + D}$$

In coding the expression, the programmer may hastily write the following:

$$A+B/C+D$$

This is incorrect since division is done ahead of addition and thus this arithmetic expression is interpreted as follows:

$$A + \frac{B}{C} + D$$

To force the additions to be done before the division the programmer must use parentheses. Hence the correct arithmetic expression is as follows:

$$(A+B)/(C+D)$$

It is important to remember that when there are a series of multiplications and divisions, then the order of evaluations is left to right. Thus, in the expression A/B*C the division is performed first and the result is multiplied by C. Hence, in algebraic notation the expression is

$$\frac{A}{B} \times C$$

If we wish to write the algebraic expression

$$\frac{A}{B \times C}$$

in FORTRAN, then we must use parentheses to force the multiplication to be done ahead of the division. Hence the equivalent FORTRAN expression for this example is A/(B*C).

The left-to-right evaluation also applies to addition and subtraction. For example, in the expression J-K+L the subtraction is done first followed by the addition. If J is 3, K is 2, and L is 1 then the value of this expression is 2. Had we interpreted the expression incorrectly and assumed that the addition is done first, then we get zero as the result. But because of the left-to-right order of evaluation this is incorrect. To change the order we would have to use parentheses and write the expression as J-(K+L).

With a series of exponentiations, the order of evaluation is right to left, the opposite of the order for the other operators. Hence the expression X**Y**Z is interpreted as X**(Y**Z). If we want to have the computer evaluate the expression left to right then we must use parentheses and write the expression as (X∗∗Y)∗∗Z.

Unlike algebra, leaving out an arithmetic operator does not mean multiplication. For example, 3K is invalid and must be written 3∗K. Similarly, parentheses may not be used to imply multiplication. For example, (A+B)(C+D) is invalid and must be written as (A+B)∗(C+D).

Two arithmetic operators may not appear adjacent to each other. For example, A/−B is invalid. However, −B by itself is an arithmetic expression and therefore may be enclosed in parentheses to give meaning to the expression. This example may be written correctly as A/(−B). The same does not hold true for the invalid expression A∗/B; there is no way of making this expression meaningful.

A final consideration in arithmetic expressions is the *mode* of the expression. The mode of an arithmetic expression is determined by the types of constants and variable names in the expression. An expression is said to be in the *integer mode* if all constants and variable names are integer. The following are integer mode arithmetic expressions:

```
I+2
K3*(6-L)
MON**2+18/J
```

A *real mode* expression contains all real constants and variable names except that the exponents may be integer constants, variable names, or arithmetic expressions in parentheses. The following are real mode expressions:

```
A+7.8*B**1.5
Y**Y-5.38
2.73/AMT**2
VALUE**(I+2)
```

Note that exponents in real mode expressions may be real or integer.

An expression that contains any other combination of integer and real constants and variable names is called *mixed mode*. The following are mixed mode expressions:

```
A-2*B+3.5
C+I**2.5
4-A/B
```

Mixed mode expressions are not valid in some versions of FORTRAN. On some computers they may be evaluated. However, their evaluation follows complex rules, so their use should be avoided.

4-3. THE ARITHMETIC ASSIGNMENT STATEMENT

An arithmetic expression by itself is not a FORTRAN statement. Rather, arithmetic expressions are parts of statements which are then used in programs. The most common statement in which an arithmetic expression appears is the arithmetic assignment statement. This statement causes the computer to evaluate an arithmetic expression and then to assign the result to a variable name.

The general form of an arithmetic assignment statement is as follows:

variable name = arithmetic expression

On the left of the equals sign is a single integer or real variable name. On the right is any valid arithmetic expression. For example, the following are valid arithmetic assignment statements:

```
TOTAL=TS1+TS2+TS3
AVE=TOTAL/3.0
Y=A*X**2+B*X+C
A=3.14159*(D/2.0)**2
```

In each of these, the computer uses the current values of the variable names to evaluate the arithmetic expression. Then the result is stored at the storage location identified by the variable name on the left. For example, in the statement

```
TOTAL=TS1+TS2+TS3
```

if the value of TS1 is 78.0, TS2 is 92.0, and TS3 is 83.0, then after execution of this statement the value of TOTAL is 253.0. This replaces the previous value for TOTAL and is the value that is retrieved at any subsequent use of the variable named TOTAL.

It is important to remember that the equal sign does not mean equality in FORTRAN; it means *assignment*. That is, the equal sign tells the computer that the value of the expression on the right is to be *assigned* to the left-hand variable name. This is why there must be one variable name to the left of the equal sign. For example, the statement

```
A+B=X+Y
```

is invalid because it implies assignment of the value of the expression

X+Y to the expression A+B. Since the left-hand expression is not a single storage location, such assignment is meaningless and therefore not allowed. There must always be a single variable name on the left.

A further consequence of this concept of assignment is that some algebraically invalid equations become valid statements in FORTRAN. For example, the following statement is valid and often useful:

$$K=K+1$$

The meaning of this statement is that 1 is added to the current value of K and the result returned to the storage area reserved for K. (See Fig. 4-1.) Thus, the value of K is increased by 1. Similarly, the following statement causes the current value of A to be replaced by a value that is five times as large:

$$A=5.0*A$$

On the right of the equal sign may be an integer mode or a real mode expression. The usual situation is that the arithmetic expression is the same mode as the variable name on the left. This eliminates any problem with conversion from one mode to another. However, mixed mode arithmetic assignment statements are acceptable in most versions of FORTRAN. (Some computers do not accept mixed mode arithmetic assignment statements; Section 4-4 discusses ways of overcoming this.) The effect of a mixed mode statement is that the expression on the right is evaluated in the mode in which it is written. Then the result is converted to the mode of the variable name on the left. If the expression is integer, and the left-hand variable name is real, the conversion involves changing the integer form of a numeric value into its real form. However, if the expression is real, and the left-hand variable name is integer, then the conversion is more complex. Since the internal representation of an integer does not allow for a fractional part, any digits

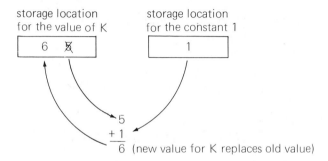

FIGURE 4-1.   Evaluation of the statement K = K + 1.

to the right of the decimal point must be dropped. That is, the value is truncated. For example, consider the following statement:

$$K=A+B$$

If the value of A is 5.0 and B is 7.8, then the value of A+B is 12.8. Since this must be assigned to an integer variable name, the fractional part is dropped and K becomes 12. Note that although the left-hand variable name and the arithmetic expression in an arithmetic assignment statement may have different modes, the expression on the right should not be mixed mode. (See Section 4-2.)

The test score averaging program in Chapter 2 illustrates a complete program that involves arithmetic processing. As another example, assume that it is necessary to compute the gross pay, withholding tax, and net pay for an employee. Input to the program consists of the employee's identification number (ID) and his or her hours work (HOURS). The gross pay (GROSS) is to be computed at the rate of $4.50 per hour; the withholding tax (TAX) is 18% of the gross pay; the net pay (PAY) is the gross pay less the withholding tax. Output should list the employee's identification number, gross pay, withholding tax, and net pay.

The program in Fig. 4-2 satisfies these requirements. First the input data is read. (We will use formatted input/output in all examples in this and subsequent chapters but the programs can be written with format-free input/output.) Next the gross pay, withholding tax, and net pay are computed. Notice that the order of the three assignment statements is important. The gross pay must be computed first since it is needed in the calculation of the withholding tax. In addition, the tax must be computed before the net pay can be found. After all calculations are completed, the output is printed.

Notice that this program stops after reading one input card, processing the data on the card, and printing the output. Usually more than

```
    READ(5,100) ID,HOURS
    GROSS=4.50*HOURS
    TAX=.18*GROSS
    PAY=GROSS-TAX
    WRITE(6,200) ID,GROSS,TAX,PAY
    STOP
100 FORMAT(I5,F5.1)
200 FORMAT(1X,I5,3X,F6.2,3X,F5.2,3X,F6.2)
    END
```

FIGURE 4-2. A payroll calculation program.

```
 10  READ(5,100) ID,HOURS
     GROSS=4.50*HOURS
     TAX=.18*GROSS
     PAY=GROSS-TAX
     WRITE(6,200) ID,GROSS,TAX,PAY
     GO TO 10
100  FORMAT(I5,F5.1)
200  FORMAT(1X,I5,3X,F6.2,3X,F5.2,3X,F6.2)
     END
```

FIGURE 4-3. A payroll calculation program with a loop.

one set of input needs to be processed by a program. As we saw in Section 3-8 we can repeat the process by incorporating a loop in the program. This is done by replacing the STOP statement with a GO TO statement that branches to the READ statement.

The program in Fig. 4-3 incorporates this modification. The loop consists of the READ statement through the GO TO statement. The first time the loop is executed the first input card is read and the data is assigned to ID and HOURS. This data is processed and one line is printed. Then the computer executes the GO TO statement, returning to the READ statement. This causes the computer to read the second input card. The data from this card is assigned to ID and HOURS, replacing the old values of these variables. Hence, the second time through the loop the calculations use the data from the second input card; the second line printed gives the results for these calculations. Then the computer goes to the READ statement again, reads the third card, and proceeds as before. The program continues to loop until no more input data is available.

As a final example, assume that it is necessary to calculate the area of the floor of a room so that new carpeting can be ordered. The input to the program consists of the room's length (XLEN) and width (WIDTH) in feet. The output should be the number of square feet (NSF) of carpeting to order. The problem is complicated by the fact that we can only order a whole number of square feet and the amount ordered must be greater than or equal to the actual area. Thus, if the dimensions are 10.3 feet by 14.5 feet, then the area (10.3 × 14.5) is 149.35 square feet. Hence we must order 150 square feet of carpet.

The program in Fig. 4-4 is a solution to this problem. After reading the input data the number of square feet is computed by multiplying XLEN by WIDTH. The result of the multiplication is a real number (149.35 in our example) but it is assigned to an integer variable name (NSF). Hence, the fraction is truncated when the assignment takes place. (Thus NSF will be 149 in our case.) To make sure that an

```
      READ(5,110) XLEN,WIDTH
      NSF=XLEN*WIDTH
      NSF=NSF+1
      WRITE(6,220) NSF
      STOP
  110 FORMAT(2F4.1)
  220 FORMAT(1X,I5)
      END
```

FIGURE 4-4.   A program to calculate floor area.

adequate amount of carpeting is ordered, we add one to NSF before printing the result. (Thus, the output will be 150 square feet for the data that we are using.)[†]

As we can see from these examples, the arithmetic assignment statement is the basic statement that is used in FORTRAN for arithmetic processing. The statement assigns the value of an arithmetic expression to a variable name. This is one use of arithmetic expressions. Other uses will be discussed in later chapters.

4-4. FORTRAN-SUPPLIED FUNCTIONS

There are many common processing activities that are regularly required in FORTRAN programs. For example, converting a value from integer to real and finding the square root of a quantity are common processing tasks. In order to relieve the programmer of repeatedly preparing the instructions necessary to perform these tasks, FORTRAN supplies special programs called functions. A *function* is a separate program that performs a special task. Each function has a name and is written in the program by coding the name of the function followed by an arithmetic expression in parentheses. The resulting reference to the function is used as part of an arithmetic expression.

An example of a function is SQRT. This function finds the square root of a nonnegative, real value. For example, the following statement calculates the square root of the value of B and assigns the result to C:

$$C=SQRT(B)$$

It is important to remember that the SQRT function operates only on nonnegative, real values. For example, the expression SQRT(K) is in-

---

[†]This program gives one extra square foot if the actual area is a whole number. An interesting exercise is to try to figure out a way of overcoming this.

valid because K is an integer variable name. However, a complex arithmetic expression may be used if the expression is real and its value is non-negative. Thus SQRT (X+3.5*Y) is valid; the square root of the value of the expression is found.

Functions may be used in simple or complex arithmetic expressions. For example, the following statement shows a valid use of the square root function:

$$ROOT=(-B+SQRT(B**2-4.0*A*C))/(2.0*A)$$

To overcome the problems of mixed mode in arithmetic expressions and arithmetic assignment statements, FORTRAN supplies two functions called FLOAT and IFIX. The general form of the FLOAT function is:

FLOAT (*integer mode arithmetic expression*)

The effect of this function is to change the value of the expression to real. For example, assume that it is necessary to add the value of M+N to the value of A and assign the result to B. The statement B=A+M+N is incorrect because the right-hand-side expression is mixed mode. However, using the FLOAT function the statement can be correctly coded as follows:

B=A+FLOAT(M+N)

The effect of this function reference is to evaluate the expression M+N, and then to convert the result to a real value. The real value is then added to the value of A and the result assigned to B.

The following are other examples of valid uses of the FLOAT function:

```
A=FLOAT(K-5)*6.25
Y=-2.83*FLOAT(3*L)+FLOAT(M)
X=SQRT(FLOAT(-K))
Z=FLOAT(J)
```

In any of these statements the contents of the storage locations reserved for integer variable names are not changed by the function. For example, in the last statement above the value of J is converted to real only for the purpose of assigning it to the variable named Z. At the storage location reserved for the value of J, the original integer value is retained.

The general form of the IFIX function is:

IFIX (*real mode arithmetic expression*)

The effect of this function is to change the value of the expression to integer. For example, consider the following statement.

K=IFIX(2.5*A)+7

In evaluating this statement, the real value of 2.5*A is calculated. The result is then converted to an integer by the IFIX function. Finally, the constant 7 is added to the integer value and the result assigned to K.

In converting a real value to an integer, any fractional part of the real is dropped. That is, the value is truncated. For example, consider the following statement:

M=IFIX(X)

If the value of X is 25.83, then after execution of this statement, M is 25. If X is negative, then the fraction is dropped but the sign is retained. Thus if X is -4.6, then M will be -4 after execution of this statement. Note that X retains its original value; conversion from one mode to another does not change the contents of the storage location reserved for the variable name.

If it is necessary to round off rather than truncate a positive real value when converting to an integer, a technique called *half-adjusting* can be used. With this technique, one half (.5) is added to the value before using the IFIX function. Thus, with half-adjusting, the previous statement is written as follows:

M=IFIX(X+.5)

For example, if X is 25.5 or greater but less than 26.0, then X + .5 is 26.0 or greater. Then truncation results in the integer 26 which is assigned to M. However, if X is less than 25.5 but greater than or equal to 25.0, then X+.5 is less than 26.0 and truncation yields 25. Hence, the value of X is correctly rounded with this technique. Note that if X is negative then -.5 must be added to correctly half-adjust.

The IFIX function can be used in a variety of ways in a FORTRAN program. The following statements show valid examples of the use of the IFIX function:

```
I=82*IFIX(W)
N=IFIX(7.3-B*28.97)+K
L=-3*J*IFIX(3.0-FLOAT(I))
```

```
      READ(5,120) NSF
      RNSF=FLOAT(NSF)
      SIDE=SQRT(RNSF)
      ISIDE=IFIX(SIDE)
      WRITE(6,220) ISIDE
      STOP
  120 FORMAT(I5)
  220 FORMAT(1X,I5)
      END
```

FIGURE 4-5.   A program to calculate floor dimensions.

As an example of the use of the SQRT, FLOAT, and IFIX functions, assume that the input to a program is an integer which gives the number of square feet (NSF) of carpeting purchased to cover a floor. The program must compute and print the integer length of the side (ISIDE) of the largest square floor that can be covered by this amount of carpet. The program in Fig. 4-5 accomplishes this. After reading the value of NSF, the program converts the square footage to real (RNSF) so it can be used with the SQRT function. The square root of RNSF gives the length of the side of a square floor that can be covered by the carpet. Converting this to integer (ISIDE) gives the final result. Notice that since only ISIDE is printed the three assignment statements can be reduced to one statement as follows:

```
      ISIDE=IFIX(SQRT(FLOAT(NSF)))
```

In addition to SQRT, FLOAT, and IFIX, there are many other FORTRAN-supplied functions. Appendix B contains a list of the functions available in FORTRAN.

4-5. INTEGER AND REAL ARITHMETIC

There are significant differences between calculations involving integers and reals. Without going into detail, this section discusses some of the important considerations in real and integer arithmetic.

Consider the integer expression J/K. If J is 9 and K is 5, the result of evaluating this expression is 1.8. But since the result must be integer, the fractional part is lost. Thus, the actual answer is 1. Note that the result is not rounded; it is truncated. This rule, together with the rules for the order of execution of operations in an arithmetic expression, yields some peculiar results:

$$1/2=0$$
$$1/2+2/3=0+0=0$$
$$2/5*5=0*5=0$$
$$2/3*3/2=0*3/2=0/2=0$$

All of these are correct, according to the FORTRAN rules for integer arithmetic.

The truncation characteristic of integer division can be both a hindrance and an aid. For example, the program in Fig. 4-6 uses this characteristic to calculate the number of dozen in a given number of eggs (NEGG). The first arithmetic assignment statement calculates the number of dozen (NDOZ), truncating any fractional part. The second arithmetic assignment statement calculates the number remaining (NREM) after the calculated number of dozen are removed. If the input value is 226 eggs, then the output is 18 dozen with 10 remaining.

Another problem that sometimes occurs with integer arithmetic is *overflow*. This occurs when the result of an arithmetic operation is greater than the maximum value that the computer can store. For example, if J is 5000 and K is 1000000, then J*K is 5000000000. For most systems, this is greater than the maximum integer value that the computer can store; hence, an overflow condition occurs. If the result of an arithmetic calculation is less than the minimum acceptable value, the condition is called *underflow*. Overflow and underflow can occur in real arithmetic when the exponent of the result of a calculation is outside of the acceptable exponent range. When overflow or underflow occurs, the result of the calculation is not correct. Thus, care should be taken to avoid such situations.

Both integer and real arithmetic can be used in the same program; for certain types of operations, however, one is preferred to the other. For problems involving whole numbers, integer arithmetic is preferred. Integers are most often used for counting, keeping tallies, and similar operations. If an exponent is a whole number, an integer should always

```
        READ(5,130) NEGG
        NDOZ=NEGG/12
        NREM=NEGG-NDOZ*12
        WRITE(6,230) NDOZ,NREM
        STOP
    130 FORMAT(I3)
    230 FORMAT(1X,I2,3X,I2)
        END
```

FIGURE 4-6. The egg program.

be used. In addition, operations involving whole numbers are usually faster using integer arithmetic than using real arithmetic.

Obviously, integers cannot be used when a fractional part is necessary. Reals are used whenever the result may contain an important fraction. Much larger values can be stored as reals than as integers, but for whole numbers the values are usually not as accurate as their integer equivalent. This is because of the difference in the way reals and integers are stored in the computer's internal storage. In Chapter 13 we will have more to say about the internal representation of integers and reals.

PROGRAMMING PROBLEMS

For each of the following problems, use either format-free or formatted input/output. If formatted I/O is used, you will have to design your own input and output formats.

1. The annual depreciation of an asset by the straight-line method is calculated by the following formula:

$$\text{Depreciation} = \frac{\text{Cost} - \text{Salvage value}}{\text{Service life}}$$

Write a FORTRAN program that reads the cost, salvage value, and service life. Then calculate the depreciation and write the result. Test the program using $13,525.00 for the cost, $1,500.00 for the salvage value, and 7 years for the service life.

2. Fahrenheit temperature is converted to Celsius temperature by the following formula:

$$C = \frac{5}{9} \times (F - 32)$$

In this formula F is the temperature in degrees Fahrenheit, and C is the temperature in degrees Celsius. Write a FORTRAN program to read the temperature in Fahrenheit, calculate the equivalent temperature in Celsius using the above formula, and write the result. To test the program use the following Fahrenheit temperatures as input data:

```
    78.4
   -50
    98.6
     0
    32
   212
```

3. In economic theory, supply and demand curves can sometimes be represented by the following equations:

$$\text{Supply: } P = A \times Q + B$$
$$\text{Demand: } P = C \times Q + D$$

In these equations, P represents the price and Q the quantity. The values of A, B, C, and D determine the actual curves.

These equations can be solved for P and Q, giving the equilibrium price and quantity for any commodity. The formulas are as follows:

$$P = \frac{C \times B - A \times D}{C - A}$$

$$Q = \frac{D - B}{A - C}$$

Write a FORTRAN program to calculate the equilibrium price and quantity for a product. Input to the program should be the values of A, B, C, and D. Output should be the price and quantity at equilibrium. Test the program with the following data:

$$A = \ \ .19$$
$$B = 1.20$$
$$C = -.42$$
$$D = 8.50$$

4. The system of linear equations

$$ax + by = c$$
$$dx + ey = f$$

has the following solution:

$$x = \frac{ce - bf}{ae - bd}$$

$$y = \frac{af - cd}{ae - bd}$$

Write a FORTRAN program to solve the system and to print the values of x and y. Input consists of the values of a, b, c, d, e, and f. Use the following data to test the program:

a	b	c	d	e	f
1.0	2.0	3.0	4.0	5.0	6.0
5.2	8.9	13.2	-6.3	7.2	2.1
-83.82	42.61	-59.55	14.73	5.32	-39.99
.035	-.327	1.621	.243	.006	.592

5. Several calculations are important in analyzing the current position of a company. The formulas for the calculations are as follows:

$$\text{Working capital} = \text{Current assets} - \text{Current liabilities}$$

$$\text{Current ratio} = \frac{\text{Current assets}}{\text{Current liabilities}}$$

$$\text{Acid-test ratio} = \frac{\text{Cash} + \text{Accounts receivable}}{\text{Current liabilities}}$$

Assume that the cash, accounts receivable, current assets, and current liabilities are available for input. Write a FORTRAN program to read these data, perform the above calculations, and print the results. Use the following data to test the program:

Cash: 10,620
Accounts receivable: 5,850
Current assets: 22,770
Current liabilities: 14,680

6. The final score for a particular test is equal to the number of questions answered correctly minus one fourth of the number answered incorrectly. Assume that test data available for input includes the student's identification number, number correct on the test, and number incorrect, all of which are integers. Write a program to calculate the final score from this data and to print the results along with the input data. Note that the number correct and incorrect are integers and should be printed as integers but must be converted to reals before doing the calculations.

Use the following input data to test the program:

Student Number	Number Correct	Number Incorrect
1	90	10
2	75	20
3	84	0
4	57	35
5	10	50
6	95	5

7. The interest and maturity value of a promissory note can be calculated as follows:

$$\text{Interest} = \frac{\text{Principal} \times \text{Rate} \times \text{Time}}{360}$$

Maturity value = Principal + Interest

Write a FORTRAN program that accepts as input the loan number, principal, rate (percent), and time (days), performs the above calculations, and prints the loan number, rate, time, interest, and maturity value. Note that the rate is expressed in percent for input purposes but must be converted to decimal form for the calculation (e.g., 5% = .05). This conversion should be done within the program; the input and output of the rate should be in percent. Use the program to find the interest and maturity value of loan number 1875 which is a $450 note with a rate of 6% for 60 days.

8. The payroll in a particular business is calculated as follows:
   (a) Gross pay is the hours worked times the pay rate.
   (b) Withholding tax is found by subtracting thirteen times the number of exemptions from the gross pay and multiplying the result by the tax rate.
   (c) Social security tax is 6.05% of the gross pay.
   (d) Net pay is the gross pay less all taxes.

Write a FORTRAN program that accepts as input an employee's identification number, hours worked, pay rate, tax rate, and number of exemptions. Then calculate the employee's gross pay, withholding and social security taxes, and net pay. Print these results along with the employee's identification number.

Use the following input data to test the program:

Employee Number	Hours Worked	Pay Rate	Tax Rate	Number of Exemptions
1001	40	4.50	20%	3
1002	36	3.75	17.5%	4
1003	47	6.50	24%	0
1004	25	5.25	22.5%	2

9. Grade point average is calculated by multiplying the units for each course that a student takes by the numeric grade that he or she receives in the course (A = 4.0, B = 3.0, C = 2.0, D = 1.0, F = 0.0), totaling for all courses, and dividing by the total number of units. For example, assume that a student received a C (2.0) in a four-unit course and a B

(3.0) in a two-unit course. Then his or her GPA is calculated as follows:

$$\frac{4 \times 2.0 + 2 \times 3.0}{4 + 2} = 2.33$$

Write a FORTRAN program to calculate one student's GPA, given the units and grade in each of five courses that he or she took. Input for the program is the student's identification number and the units (integer) and numeric grade (real) for each of the five courses. Output from the program should list the student's number, total units (integer), and grade point average (real).

Test the program with data for student number 18357, who got an A in a two-unit course, a C in a three-unit course, a D in a one-unit course, a C in a four-unit course, and a B in a three-unit course.

10. A projectile is fired with an initial velocity v, at an angle θ, and it reaches a maximum height h, in time t, given by the following equation:

$$h = \frac{1}{2} \frac{v^2 \sin^2 \theta}{32}$$

$$t = \frac{v \sin \theta}{32}$$

The sine of an angle is found using the function SIN; the angle must be in radians. (One radian equals 57.2958 degrees.)

Write a FORTRAN program that reads the values of v and θ (in degrees) and computes h and t. Print the values of v, θ (in degrees), h, and t. Use the following input data to test the program:

Velocity	Angle
247.38	45
100.00	72.5
360.00	0
282.61	90
75.32	25.6

11. Write a FORTRAN program that converts seconds into hours, minutes, and seconds remaining. Input should be the amount of time in seconds. Output should be the number of seconds and its equivalent in hours, minutes, and seconds remaining. For example, 4372 seconds is equivalent to one hour, twelve minutes, and 52 seconds. Test the program using 28,635 seconds.

12. There are 3.281 feet in a meter and 0.3937 inches in a centimeter. Write a program that reads a distance in feet and inches and computes and prints the equivalent distance in meters and centimeters. Give the answer in whole meters and centimeters rounded to the nearest centimeter. Test the program with the distance six feet, nine inches.

13. The percent correct for each part of a three-part test needs to be calculated. The number of questions in each part varies but is always less than 100. Write a FORTRAN program to do the necessary calculations. Input consists of one record containing the number of questions on each of the three parts. Following this is one input record for each student giving the student's number followed by his or her scores on each of the three parts. The program should calculate the percent correct for each part and the percent correct on all three parts combined. Output should give the number of questions on each part and the total number of questions for all three parts. Then for each student the output shoud list the number correct, the percent correct on each part, and the total percent correct.

To test the program assume that Part I contains 50 questions, Part II contains 90 questions, and Part III contains 40 questions. The students' results are as follows:

Student Number	Part I Correct	Part II Correct	Part III Correct
18372	37	83	28
19204	25	30	30
20013	45	87	36
21563	0	53	40

14. The economic order quantity represents the most economic quantity of inventory that should be ordered for each item in stock. The formula for calculating the economic order quantity is:

$$Q = \sqrt{\frac{2 \times R \times S}{H}}$$

In this formula Q is the quantity ordered, R is the demand rate, S is the set-up or ordering cost, and H is the inventory holding cost. If C represents unit cost, then the average cost per unit of inventory held is given by the following formula:

$$A = C + \frac{S}{Q} + \frac{H \times Q}{2 \times R}$$

Write a FORTRAN program to calculate the economic order quantity and the average cost per unit when this quantity is ordered. Read the values for *R, S, H,* and *C.* Print the values for the economic order quantity and the average cost per unit. Be sure to print the economic order quantity as a whole number, correctly rounded.

Finally, calculate the average cost per unit when the quantity ordered is 30% more than the economic order quantity. Print that quantity and the average cost. Do the same for an order quantity that is 30% less than the economic order quantity.

Use the following data to test the program:

R = 1025
S = $75
H = $60
C = $235

Chapter 5

PROGRAMMING FOR DECISIONS

If a program contains a sequence of input/output and arithmetic assignment statements, then these statements are executed in the order in which they are written. We saw this in the examples in the previous two chapters. Sometimes we wish to alter this normal sequential execution. For example, we may want the computer to select between several sequences of statements based upon some condition or to repeat a group of statements until a particular condition occurs. These activities involve controlling the order of execution within a program. The statements that are used in FORTRAN to accomplish this are called *control statements*.

In this chapter we begin the discussion of program control and control statements by examining programming for decision making. Decision making involves selecting between alternative sequences of statements based upon some condition that occurs during the execution of the program. For example, assume that we need to write a program that calculates the tuition for a college student based on the number of units that the student is taking. If the student is taking fewer than a certain number of units, then the tuition is calculated one way, otherwise a different calculation is used. Thus the computer must select between two calculations based on a particular condition.

In this chapter we describe the FORTRAN control statements necessary for decision making and discuss related program logic. In the next chapter we discuss other aspects of program control.

5-1. THE UNCONDITIONAL GO TO STATEMENT

In Section 3-8 we mentioned the GO TO statement and demonstrated its use in program loops. In fact this form of the GO TO statement is called the *unconditional* GO TO statement. (We will see another type of GO TO statement in a later section.) The general form of the unconditional GO TO statement is as follows:

GO TO n

> where n is the statement number of an executable statement in the program.

For example, the following is a valid GO TO statement:

GO TO 50

The GO TO statement is a control statement. It causes the computer to interrupt the normal sequential execution of the program and to continue execution at the statement whose number is given in the GO TO statement. This process of breaking execution of the program at a point and continuing elsewhere is called *branching* or *transfer of control*. For example, the following statement causes the computer to branch to statement 105.

GO TO 105

Upon execution of this statement the computer does not continue with the next statement in sequence. Instead it goes to the statement numbered 105 and continues execution from that point.

Note that the statement number used in a GO TO statement must be that of an *executable* statement. The only nonexecutable statement that we have considered so far is the FORMAT statement. Even though it has a number, it is not valid to branch to a FORMAT statement.

It is possible to branch from a point in a program either in the direction of the beginning of the program (that is, "up" the program) or towards the end of the program ("down" the program). In previous examples we have always branched "up" the program so as to create a loop. In this chapter we will see many examples in which it is necessary to branch "down" the program.

5-2. THE LOGICAL IF STATEMENT

The most commonly used statement in FORTRAN for decision making is the logical IF statement. This statement is available in most versions of FORTRAN. For those versions of FORTRAN that do not allow the use of the logical IF statement, the arithmetic IF statement is provided. In this section we describe the logical IF statement and demonstrate its use in FORTRAN. The arithmetic IF statement is explained in a later section of this chapter.

The general form of the logical IF statement is as follows:

IF (*logical expression*) *executable statement*

A logical expression is an expression that is either true or false. A common type of logical expression is called a *relational expression*, which we describe below. (Other types of logical expressions are discussed in Chapter 9.) The logical expression is enclosed in parentheses following the keyword IF. Following this is any executable statement except another logical IF statement or a DO statement (discussed in Chapter 6). For example, the following is a valid logical IF statement:

$$IF(A.GT.B) \ C=A-B$$

In this example A.GT.B is a logical expression (in this case, a relational expression) and C = A – B is an arithmetic assignment statement within the logical IF statement.

Execution of a logical IF statement causes the computer to evaluate the logical expression and determine whether it is true or false. If the expression is true, then the statement in the IF statement is executed next. If the logical expression is false, then this statement is skipped, and execution continues with the next statement in sequence. In the previous example the expression A.GT.B causes the computer to determine whether or not the value of A is greater than the value of B. If this condition is true then the computer executes the statement C = A – B. If A is not greater than B, then the computer bypasses the statement and goes on to the next statement in sequence.

Any executable statement may be used in the logical IF statement (with the exceptions given above). For example, the following are valid logical IF statements:

```
IF(X.LT.Y) READ(5,10) A,B,C
IF(K.EQ.7) WRITE(6,20) K
IF(U.LE.12.0) GO TO 35
```

In each of these examples, the computer either executes the statement in the IF statement or skips it depending on whether or not the logical expression is true. If the condition is true, then after the statement in the IF statement is executed, the computer goes on to the next statement in sequence unless a GO TO statement or other branching statement has been executed.

Relational Expressions

The most common type of logical expression is the relational expression. This expression compares the values of two arithmetic expressions. Values may be compared to determine whether one is greater than or less than the other, whether they are equal or not equal, or whether combinations of these conditions are true. The relational expression has a *truth value* of true or false, depending on whether the indicated comparison is correct or not correct.

The way in which the values of the arithmetic expressions are compared is given by a *relational operator*. The following are the relational operators used in FORTRAN and their meanings:

Relational Operator	Meaning
.LT.	Less than
.LE.	Less than or equal to
.GT.	Greater than
.GE.	Greater than or equal to
.EQ.	Equal to
.NE.	Not equal to

Notice that each relational operator begins and ends with a period.

The simplest form of a relational expression is a constant or a variable name followed by a relational operator and then another constant or variable name. For example, the following are valid relational expressions:

```
J.LT.K
6..LE.C
Q.GT.5.6
K.GE.-5
A.EQ.B
7.NE.J
```

To evaluate each of these, the values of the variables and constants are compared according to the relational operator. For example, if J is 6 and K is 5, then the first expression is *false*. Similarly, if both J and K are equal to 6 then the expression is *false*. However, if J is 6 and K is 7, then the expression is *true*.

Mixed mode may or may not be allowed in relational expressions, depending on the version of FORTRAN. For example, the expression A.L.T.K. may not be valid because it attempts to compare a real value with an integer. Even if mixed mode relational expressions are acceptable, they should not be used since their evaluation is complex. This problem can always be overcome by using the FLOAT or IFIX functions. Thus the following expression is valid in all versions of FORTRAN:

$$A.LT.FLOAT(K)$$

When comparing a real constant without decimal positions, the situation is particularly error prone. For example, 6.LE.C is mixed mode since the period belongs with the less than operator and not with the digit six. This can be overcome in this example by adding a decimal point. The resulting expression is as follows:

$$6..LE.C$$

Relational operators may be used to compare the values of complex arithmetic expressions. For example, the following relational expressions are valid:

```
Q.GT.P-5.6
K+8.GE.-5-L
X+Y/(4.56-Z).EQ.(Z-FLOAT(M))
IFIX(A)-(I+1).NE.(K-5)
```

Notice that parentheses may be used to enclose part or all of either arithmetic expression in a relational expression.

In evaluating a relational expression containing arithmetic expressions, current values of the variable names are used to evaluate each arithmetic expression. The resulting values of the arithmetic expressions are then compared according to the relational operator to determine the truth value of the relational expression. If the condition specified by the relational operator is correct, then the relational expression is *true*. If the condition is not correct, the relational expression is *false*. For example, consider the following relational expression:

$$N-3.GE.5$$

If N has a value of 10, then N-3 has a value of 7. Since 7 is greater than 5, the relational expression is true. However, if N has a value of 4, then N–3 is 1. Since 1 is not greater than or equal to 5, the expression is false. If N is 8, then N–3 is 5 and the relational expression is true.

A relational expression may not be written with just one arithmetic expression. For example, the following expression is invalid because it lacks an arithmetic expression on the left of the relational operator:

$$.GT.P-5.6$$

If we had wanted to compare the value of Q with the value of P–5.6, then the correct expression would be

$$Q.GT.P-5.6$$

In addition, the relational operator must always begin and end with a period. The following expression is invalid because the period on the right of the relational operator is missing:

$$K+8.GE \ -5-L$$

This is correctly coded as follows:

$$K+8.GE.-5-L$$

An Illustrative Program

To illustrate the use of the logical IF statement and relational expressions in a program, assume that we need to write a program that calculates the tuition for a college student. The input data is the student's identification number and number of units. The tuition is $350 if the student is taking twelve or less units. However, if the student is taking more than twelve units, the tuition is $350 plus $20 per unit for all units over twelve. The program must print the student's identification number and tuition for any valid input.

The program to accomplish this requires decision making. First the input data must be read. Then the computer must examine the number of units to determine the tuition. This decision-making step can be stated as follows: If the number of units is less than or equal to twelve, then the tuition is $350; otherwise the tuition is $350 plus $20 per unit for all units over twelve. In other words, the computer must select between two ways of calculating the tuition based on a comparison between the number of units in which the student is enrolled and twelve. After the tuition is calculated, the output can be written.

The program in Fig. 5-1 solves this problem. The READ statement reads the student's number (ID) and number of units (UNITS). Then the IF statement compares the number of units with 12.0. If UNITS is greater than 12.0, then the GO TO statement in the IF statement is executed and the computer branches to statement 20. The tuition (TUIT) is calculated at $350 plus $20 per unit for all units over twelve. Then the output is written. If UNITS is less than or equal to 12.0, then the GO TO statement is not executed. The computer goes on to the next statement in sequence and the tuition is set equal to $350. The purpose of the GO TO statement following this assignment statement is to branch around statement 20 to the WRITE statement so that the output can be printed.

It is important to understand why the statement GO TO 30 is necessary in this program. Recall that the statements in a program are executed in sequence unless the sequence is broken with a branch instruction. If this GO TO statement is omitted and the number of units is less than or equal to twelve, then the result would be incorrect. In this case the computer would set TUIT equal to $350.00. Then, since the GO TO statement would be missing, the next statement in sequence would be statement 20. Hence the tuition would be calculated again, this time incorrectly. This second value for the tuition would replace the first and would be the value printed. This situation is avoided by including the GO TO statement to branch around statement 20.

This program has a loop in it so that it will be repeated until no more input is supplied. If there is only one set of input data, so that a loop is not needed, then the statement GO TO 10 can be replaced with a STOP statement.

```
 10 READ(5,100) ID,UNITS
    IF(UNITS.GT.12.0) GO TO 20
    TUIT=350.00
    GO TO 30
 20 TUIT=350.00+20.00*(UNITS-12.0)
 30 WRITE(6,200) ID,TUIT
    GO TO 10
100 FORMAT(I4,F4.1)
200 FORMAT(1X,I4,3X,F7.2)
    END
```

FIGURE 5-1. The tuition calculation program.

5-3. PROGRAM LOGIC FOR DECISION MAKING

The pattern of program logic in the example at the end of the last section is used in many decision problems. The pattern is represented by the diagram in Fig. 5-2. Usually what we wish to do is to test a logical condition. If the condition is true, then one group of statements is executed; if the condition is false, then another set of statements is performed. After doing either group of statements then we want the computer to continue with the next statement in sequence.

We can express this pattern of logic in the form shown in Fig. 5-3. We call the statements to be executed if the condition is true the *true part* of the decision and the statements to be executed if the condition is false the *false part*. Figure 5-3 shows that if the condition is true, then the true part is executed, else (or otherwise) the false part is executed.

While the form in Fig. 5-3 expresses very clearly the logic that we wish to use in decision making, it is not the pattern used by the logical IF statement. (In the next section we will discuss the block IF statement which is available in some versions of FORTRAN and which does follow this pattern.) With the logical IF statement, only one statement can be executed or bypassed depending on the truth or falsity of a logical expression. Hence, if we wish to accomplish the same thing as in the pattern shown in Fig. 5-3, then we must branch to the true part. The false part must follow the IF statement and end with a GO TO statement which branches around the true part. This pattern is shown in Fig. 5-4.

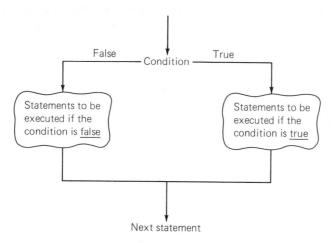

FIGURE 5-2. Decision-making logic.

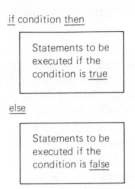

if condition then

> Statements to be
> executed if the
> condition is true

else

> Statements to be
> executed if the
> condition is false

FIGURE 5-3. A basic decision-making pattern.

The tuition calculation program illustrated this approach. The decision-making step in this program is as follows:

```
    IF(UNITS.GT.12.0) GO TO 20
    TUIT=350.00
    GO TO 30
 20 TUIT=350.00+20.00*(UNITS-12.0)
 30 (next statement)
```

If the condition that the number of units is greater than twelve is true, then the computer branches to the second tuition calculation. If the condition is false, then the computer goes on (we say that it "falls through") to the next statement in sequence. The statement GO TO 30 is necessary to branch around the true part.

Sometimes the decision logic is easier to think about if we use the complementary condition in the IF statement. The complement

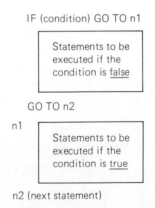

IF (condition) GO TO n1

> Statements to be
> executed if the
> condition is false

GO TO n2

n1

> Statements to be
> executed if the
> condition is true

n2 (next statement)

FIGURE 5-4. The basic decision-making pattern using a
logical IF statement.

of a condition is the condition that is true if the original condition is false, and vice versa. For example, the complement of "less than" is "greater than or equal to." Similarly, the complement of "equal to" is "not equal to." As an example of the use of a complementary condition in a program, assume that if A is greater than B then we wish to print the value of A otherwise we want to print B. We could write this section of the program as follows:

```
        IF(A.GT.B) GO TO 10
        WRITE(6,200) B
        GO TO 20
     10 WRITE(6,200) A
     20 (next statement)
```

Alternatively we could use the complement of the "greater than" condition which is the "less than or equal to" condition. Then the true and false parts can be exchanged and the program segment written as follows:

```
        IF(A.LE.B) GO TO 10
        WRITE(6,200) A
        GO TO 20
     10 WRITE(6,200) B
     20 (next statement)
```

Whether or not the programmer wishes to do this depends on what he or she finds easier to understand. If we use the complementary condition in the tuition calculation then the decision-making step is as follows:

```
        IF(UNITS.LE.12.0) GO TO 20
        TUIT=350.00+20.00*(UNITS-12.0)
        GO TO 30
     20 TUIT=350.00
     30 (next statement)
```

In the examples so far, there is only one statement to be executed if the condition is true and one if the condition is false. In fact, there may be any number of statements in the true and false parts. For example, assume that we wish to calculate employee pay. The gross pay is $4.50 per hour for the first forty hours worked and $6.75 per hour for all time over forty hours. In addition, the withholding tax is 18% of the gross pay if 40 or fewer hours are worked and 20% of the pay if more than 40 hours are recorded. The net pay is the gross pay less the withholding tax.

```
10 READ(5,100) ID,HOURS
   IF(HOURS.GT.40.0) GO TO 20
   GROSS=4.50*HOURS
   TAX=.18*GROSS
   GO TO 30
20 GROSS=180.00+6.75*(HOURS-40.0)
   TAX=.20*GROSS
30 PAY=GROSS-TAX
   WRITE(6,200) ID,GROSS,TAX,PAY
   GO TO 10
100 FORMAT(I5,F5.1)
200 FORMAT(1X,I5,3X,F6.2,3X,F5.2,3X,F6.2)
   END
```

FIGURE 5-5. A payroll program.

The program in Fig. 5-5 satisfies these requirements. The program first reads the input data. Then the hours worked is compared with forty. If the hours are less than or equal to forty then the payroll calculations following the IF statement are performed and the computer branches to statement 30. However, if the hours are greater than forty, then the computer branches to statement 20 and performs the payroll calculations beginning there. After the gross pay and withholding tax are computed by one of the two methods, then the net pay is computed and the output is printed.

Program Style

To make the decision logic easier to understand in the program, many programmers indent the true and false parts. For example, the decision part of the previous payroll program could be coded as follows:

```
   IF(HOURS.GT.40.0) GO TO 20
      GROSS=4.50*HOURS
      TAX=.18*GROSS
   GO TO 30
20    GROSS=180.00+6.75*(HOURS-40.0)
      TAX=.20*GROSS
30 NET=GROSS-TAX
```

The statements indented between the IF statement and the GO TO 30 statement are the false part of the decision. The indented statements after GO TO 30 are the true part. Whether or not a style such as this is used depends on whether the programmer feels it helps him or her understand the program logic.

One-sided Decisions

The decision-making pattern that we have described requires the computer to select between two alternative sequences of statements based on a logical condition. Sometimes it is only necessary to either select or bypass a set of statements based on a condition. This "one-sided" decision logic can be represented by the diagram in Fig. 5-6. If only one statement needs to be executed or bypassed then that statement may be included in the logical IF statement. For example, the statement

$$IF(A.GT.B) \ C=A-B$$

either executes the statement C=A−B or bypasses it based on whether or not A is greater than B.

If multiple statements need to be executed or bypassed, then the problem is more complex. Figure 5-7 shows a way of representing the desired pattern. If the condition is true, then the true part is executed, otherwise the computer bypasses this part and goes on to the next statement in sequence. To implement this pattern using the logical IF statement we must use the complementary condition in the IF

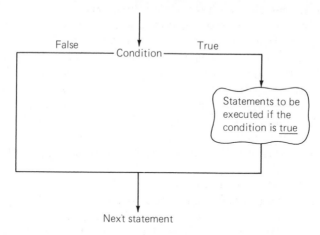

FIGURE 5-6. One-sided decision-making logic.

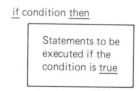

FIGURE 5-7. A one-sided decision-making pattern.

statement and branch around the true part if this condition is true. The technique is shown in Fig. 5-8.

To illustrate the use of this technique assume that if A is greater than B then we must not only calculate C=A-B but also print C. Then the necessary statements are as follows:

```
      IF(A.LE.B) GO TO 10
      C=A-B
      WRITE(6,200) C
   10 (next statement)
```

The complement of the "greater than" condition is "less than or equal to." If this condition is true, then we branch around the next two statements. Otherwise, these statements are executed.

Nested Decisions

Within the true or false parts of a decision-making structure there may be any number or type of statements. In fact, there may be other IF statements. When an IF statement is included within a set of statements that is executed depending on the condition in another IF statement, then we say that we have *nested decisions.*

As an example of nested decisions assume that the tuition charged a college student is not only based on the number of units but also on whether or not the student is a resident of the state. If the number of units are less than or equal to twelve and the student is a state resident, then the tuition is \$350. However, if the student is not a resident (and the units are less than or equal to twelve) then the tuition is \$800. If the number of units is greater than 12, and the student is a resident then the tuition is \$350 plus \$20 for all units over twelve. For a nonresident with more than twelve units, the tuition is \$800 plus \$45 for each excess unit.

This problem involves first deciding if the number of units is or is not greater than twelve and then in each case determining if the student is or is not a state resident. Assume that the input data is the student's identification number (ID), the number of units (UNITS),

IF(complement of condition) GO TO n

```
┌─────────────────────────────┐
│ Statements to be            │
│ executed if the             │
│ condition is true           │
│ (i.e. if complement is false).│
└─────────────────────────────┘
```

n (next statement)

FIGURE 5-8.   The one-sided decision-making pattern using a logical IF statement.

and an in-state code (INST) which is 1 if the student is a state resident and 0 otherwise. A program to accomplish this is shown in Fig. 5-9. After reading the input data, the program compares UNITS with 12.0. If UNITS is less than or equal to 12.0, then the computer falls through to the second IF statement. This statement checks INST to determine whether or not the student is a state resident. If UNITS is greater than 12.0, then the computer branches to statement 20 which again checks INST. The actual tuition depends on both the number of units and the in-state code.

Within a nested decision there may be other nested decisions. In fact, there may be as many nested decisions as the programmer wants. Usually, though, nesting more than one or two decisions makes the program harder to understand.

Selection

A special type of nested decision involves selecting from among several cases. For example, assume that the tuition charge is based on the following schedule:

Units	Tuition
0.1 to 6.0	$200
6.1 to 12.0	$200 + $25/unit over 6
12.1 to 18.0	$350 + $20/unit over 12
18.1 and up	$470 + $15/unit over 18

```
 10 READ(5,100) ID,UNITS,INST
    IF(UNITS.GT.12.0) GO TO 20
    IF(INST.EQ.0) GO TO 15
    TUIT=350.00
    GO TO 30
 15 TUIT=800.00
    GO TO 30
 20 IF(INST.EQ.0) GO TO 25
    TUIT=350.00+20.00*(UNITS-12.0)
    GO TO 30
 25 TUIT=800.00+45.00*(UNITS-12.0)
 30 WRITE(6,200) ID,TUIT
    GO TO 10
100 FORMAT(I4,F4.1,I1)
200 FORMAT(1X,I4,3X,F7.2)
    END
```

FIGURE 5-9. Tuition calculation with nested decisions.

```
 10 READ(5,100) ID,UNITS
    IF(UNITS.GT.6.0) GO TO 20
    TUIT=200.00
    GO TO 50
 20 IF(UNITS.GT.12.0) GO TO 30
    TUIT=200.00+25.00*(UNITS-6.0)
    GO TO 50
 30 IF(UNITS.GT.18.0) GO TO 40
    TUIT=350.00+20.00*(UNITS-12.0)
    GO TO 50
 40 TUIT=470.00+15.00*(UNITS-18.0)
 50 WRITE(6,200) ID,TUIT
    GO TO 10
100 FORMAT(I4,F4.1)
200 FORMAT(1X,I4,3X,F7.2)
    END
```

FIGURE 5-10. Tuition calculation with selection.

There are four cases, depending on the number of units that the student is taking. We wish to write the program to select the appropriate case and do the required calculations.

The selection process can be done using nested decisions by first determining if the number of units is less than or equal to six. If it is, then we select the first case and the tuition is $200. However, if the number of units is greater than six then we must check to see if the number is less than or equal to twelve. If it is, then we have the second case and the tuition can be calculated appropriately. However, if the number of units is greater than twelve then we compare the number with eighteen. If it is less than or equal to eighteen, then we select the third case, otherwise we have the fourth case.

Figure 5-10 shows the tuition calculating program using this selection logic. The program selects the appropriate case by comparing UNITS with 6.0, 12.0, and 18.0. After the tuition is calculated the output is printed. The three GO TO 50 statements are required to branch around the other cases to the WRITE statement when the first, second, or third case is selected.

For certain very specialized types of case selection, FORTRAN provides the computed GO TO statement. We will discuss this statement in Section 5-5.

5-4. THE BLOCK IF STATEMENTS

Some versions of FORTRAN provide special decision-making statements. These are called the block IF statements. There are four statements in all that are used in combinations of two or more to form different types of decision-making structures. In this section we explain these statements and demonstrate their use in decision making.

To form the basic decision-making pattern shown in Fig. 5–3 we use the IF-THEN statement, the ELSE statement and the END IF statement. The general form is as follows:

IF (*logical expression*) THEN
    .
    .
    .
  statements
    .
    .
    .
ELSE
    .
    .
    .
  statements
    .
    .
    .
END IF

When the computer executes this sequence of statements it first determines if the logical expression is true or false. If the expression is true, then the computer executes the statements between the IF-THEN statement and the ELSE statement (the true part). If the condition is false, then the statements between the ELSE statement and the END IF statement (the false part) are executed. After doing either the true part or the false part the computer continues with the next statement following the END IF statement (unless a branch statement has been executed).

As an example, consider the simple tuition calculation program in Fig. 5-1. Using block IF statements, the decision-making step can be written as follows:

```
IF (UNITS.LE.12.0) THEN
  TUIT=350.00
ELSE
  TUIT=350.00+20.00*(UNITS-12.0)
END IF
```

If the number of units is less than or equal to 12.0, then TUIT is set equal to $350. Otherwise, the value of TUIT is computed by the second assignment statement. Notice that GO TO statements are not needed with these statements. The computer automatically goes to the true or false part and then to the statement following END IF. Also, it is unnecessary to use the complementary condition in the IF statement. These features make the block IF statements especially easy to use.

In this example we have indented the true and false parts. This is a common program style used with the block IF statements. It helps the programmer see the structure of the decision logic.

There may be any number of statements between the IF-THEN statement and the ELSE statement, and between the ELSE statement and the END IF statement. The computer will execute all statements in the true or false part depending on the logical expression. However, the END IF statement is essential. If it is left out, the computer will not know the extent of the false part.

The one-sided decision-making pattern shown in Fig. 5-7 is coded using the IF-THEN and END IF statements. The general form is as follows:

IF (*logical expression*) THEN
.
.
.
statements
.
.
.

END IF

If the logical expression is true, then the statements between the IF-THEN statement and the END IF statement are executed. Otherwise, these statements are skipped. For example, consider the following sequence of statements:

```
IF (A.GT.B) THEN
   C=A-B
   WRITE(6,200) C
END IF
```

If A is greater then B, then the computer will execute the assignment and WRITE statements and then go on to the next statement following END IF. Otherwise, it will skip these statements and go directly to the next statement after the END IF statement.

Block IF statements may be used for nested decision. The only restriction is that each IF-THEN statement must have a corresponding END IF statement. For example, consider the tuition calculation in the program in Fig. 5-9. The nested decisions could be written as follows using block IF statements:

```
IF (UNITS.LE.12.0) THEN
  IF (INST.EQ.1) THEN
    TUIT=350.00
  ELSE
    TUIT=800.00
  END IF
ELSE
  IF (INST.EQ.1) THEN
    TUIT=350.00+20.00*(UNITS-12.0)
  ELSE
    TUIT=800.00+45.00*(UNITS-12.0)
  END IF
END IF
```

The first END IF statement corresponds with the second IF statement. The second END IF statement corresponds with the third IF statement. The last END IF statement is paired with the first IF statement. All of these are required for the nested decision to function properly. Other valid patterns of nested decisions are shown in Fig. 5-11. Brackets show the pairing of IF-THEN and END IF statements in this diagram.

Selecting from among several cases can be done using nested decisions or using the ELSE-IF-THEN statement. The general form of this statement is as follows:

ELSE IF (*logical expression*) THEN

Between an IF-THEN statement and its END IF may be any number of ELSE-IF-THEN statements. If an ELSE statement is used then it must appear after the last ELSE-IF-THEN statement. As an example of the use of this statement, consider the tuition calculation shown in Fig. 5-10. The selection of the appropriate calculation can be written as follows:

```
IF (UNITS.LE.6.0) THEN
  TUIT=200.00
ELSE IF (UNITS.LE.12.0) THEN
  TUIT=200.00+25.00*(UNITS-6.0)
ELSE IF (UNITS.LE.18.0) THEN
  TUIT=350.00+20.00*(UNITS-12.0)
ELSE
  TUIT=470.00+15.00*(UNITS-18.0)
END IF
```

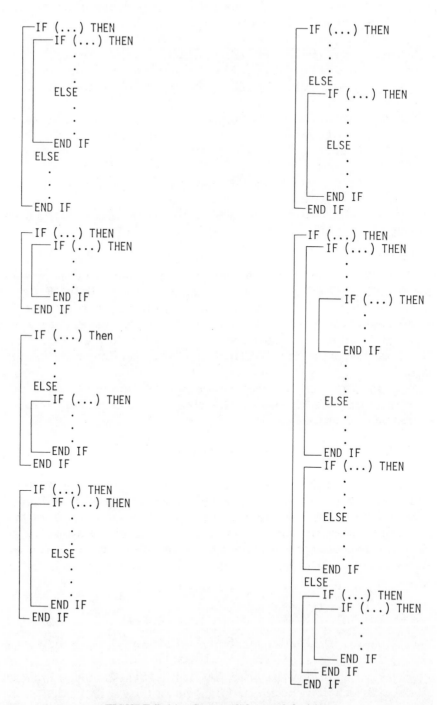

FIGURE 5-11. Some valid nested decisions.

If the first condition is true, then TUIT is assigned the value of 200.00 and the computer continues with the next statement following the END IF statement. If the first condition is false, then the computer checks the condition in the first ELSE-IF-THEN statement. If this condition is true, then the tuition is calculated by the second assignment statement, otherwise the condition in the second ELSE-IF-THEN statement is checked. If none of the conditions is true then the assignment statement following the ELSE statement is executed. Notice that there are no matching END IF statements for the ELSE-IF-THEN statement. The END IF statement is only used with the IF-THEN statement.

The block IF statements discussed in this section can make programming for decisions considerably easier than using the logical IF statement. While not currently available on all versions of FORTRAN, their availability is expected to increase in the future.

5-5. THE COMPUTED GO TO STATEMENT

The computed GO TO statement is used to branch to one of a group of statements based on the value of an integer variable name. The general form of the computed GO TO statement is as follows:

GO TO $(n1, n2, \ldots, nm), i$

where $n1, n2, \ldots, nm$ are statement numbers.
i is an integer variable name.

The effect of this is a branch to the statement holding the numbered position that is indicated by the value of the integer variable name. That is, if the value of i is 1, the computer branches to the statement numbered $n1$. If the value of i is 2, the branch is made to the statement numbered $n2$. If the value of i is k, the computer branches to the statement numbered nk.

As an example of the computed GO TO statement, consider the following:

```
GO TO (25,30,12), K
```

This statement causes the computer to branch to statement 25 if K has a value of 1. If K is 2, the branch is to the statement numbered 30, which is in second position in the list. If K is 3, the computer branches to the statement numbered 12 which holds the third position in the list.

As another example, consider the following statement:

GO TO (15,16,16,13,15,17,17), N

If N has a value of 1 or 5, the computer branches to the statement numbered 15. If N is 2 or 3, the branch is to the statement numbered 16. If N is 4, the branch is to the statement numbered 13. Finally, if N has a value of 6 or 7, the branch is made to the statement numbered 17. Notice that the variable name used in a computed GO TO statement must always be integer and that a comma is required after the list of statement numbers.

The value of the integer variable name in the computed GO TO statement should normally be between one and the number of statement numbers in the list. For example, if there are six statement numbers then the variable name should have an integer value between one and six. If the value is less than one or greater than six then the result depends on which version of FORTRAN is being used. With some versions of FORTRAN this results in an execution error. However, with other versions of FORTRAN, there is no error; instead the computer continues with the next statement in sequence.

Some versions of FORTRAN allow the use of an integer arithmetic expression in the computed GO TO statement. When this is done the value of the expression is computed and the computed GO TO statement is evaluated as before. In addition the comma after the list of statement numbers is optional in some versions of FORTRAN.

The computed GO TO statement is usually used to select one of a number of cases based on the value of an integer variable name. For example, in the tuition calculation problem, assume that a variable named KODE indicates the amount of the scholarship that a student is to receive. If the value of KODE is 1, then the scholarship is $100. If KODE is 2 or 3 then the scholarship is $150. A value of 4 indicates a $300 scholarship while if KODE equals 5, then the scholarship is $400. In the program, the following sequence of statements can be used to select the appropriate scholarship:

```
        GO TO (10,20,20,30,40), KODE
    10  SCLSP=100.00
        GO TO 50
    20  SCLSP=150.00
        GO TO 50
    30  SCLSP=300.00
        GO TO 50
    40  SCLSP=400.00
    50  (next statement)
```

```
 10 READ(5,100) ID,HOURS,ISHIFT
    GO TO (20,30,40), ISHIFT
 20 GROSS=4.50*HOURS
    GO TO 50
 30 GROSS=6.75*HOURS
    GO TO 50
 40 GROSS=9.00*HOURS
 50 WRITE(6,200) ID,GROSS
    GO TO 10
100 FORMAT(I5,F4.1,I1)
200 FORMAT(1X,I5,3X,F6.2)
    END
```

FIGURE 5-12.   A payroll program.

The computed GO TO statement branches to statements 10, 20, 30, or 40 based on the value of KODE. Then the variable named SCLSP is assigned the appropriate scholarship amount. Notice that after each assignment statement (except the last where it is not necessary) the statement GO TO 50 causes the computer to bypass other cases and go on to the next part of the program.

   As another example of the use of the computed GO TO statement, assume that the employee's pay rate is based on the shift that the employee works. The input contains a code that indicates the shift. If the code is 1, then the employee works the day shift at the rate of $4.50 per hour. A shift code equal to 2 indicates that the employee works the evening shift at $6.75 per hour. A night shift employee has a code equal to 3 and earns $9.00 per hour. Figure 5-12 shows the program that computes the employee's gross pay based on this schedule. Input consists of the employee's identification number (ID), hours worked (HOURS), and shift code (ISHIFT). The computed GO TO statement selects the appropriate calculation based on the value of ISHIFT. Then the output is written.

5-6.   THE ARITHMETIC IF STATEMENT

Some versions of FORTRAN do not allow the use of the logical IF statement. Instead, the arithmetic IF statement is provided. While the same effect can be accomplished using either statement, it is generally easier and less error prone to use the logical IF statement. In this section we describe the arithmetic IF statement and show how programs written with logical IF statements can be translated into ones using arithmetic IFs. If logical IF statements are available with the version of FORTRAN being used, then this section need not be read. If only arithmetic IF statements are available, then the reader should develop skill in translating from logical to arithmetic IFs.

The general form of the arithmetic IF statement is:

IF(*arithmetic expression*) *n1,n2,n3*

where *n1*, *n2*, and *n3* are statement numbers of executable statements in the program.

The effect of this statement is to cause the computer to branch to the statement numbered *n1*, *n2*, or *n3*, depending on the value of the arithmetic expression. If the value of the arithmetic expression is *less than zero*, then the computer branches to the statement numbered *n1*. If the expression has a value *equal to zero*, then the computer branches to the statement numbered *n2*. If the value of the expression is *greater than zero*, then control transfers to the statement numbered *n3*.

As an example of the arithmetic IF statement, consider the following:

$$IF(B+C*(3.5-X))\ \ 12,72,38$$

The arithmetic expression B+C*(3.5-X) is evaluated by substituting the current values of the variables named B, C, and X. The value of this arithmetic expression is then compared with zero. If the value is less than zero, control transfers to the statement numbered 12. If the value of the expression equals zero, then the computer branches to the statement whose number is 72. If the arithmetic expression has a value greater than zero, then the computer branches to the statement numbered 38.

Sometimes branching is based on the value of only one variable name. For example, assume that it is necessary to branch to the statement numbered 1 if the value of A is less than zero and to branch to the statement numbered 2 if A's value is equal to or greater than zero. The following IF statement accomplishes this:

$$IF(A)\ \ 1,2,2$$

The arithmetic IF statement compares the value of the arithmetic expression with zero. Sometimes it may be necessary to branch on the basis of a comparison of the value of a variable name and a constant. For example, assume that it is necessary to branch to the statement numbered 50 if the value of KOUNT is less than or equal to 25. If

KOUNT is greater than 25, then control should transfer to the statement numbered 60. To solve this problem we note that if the value of the expression KOUNT-25 is less than or equal to zero, then the value of KOUNT must be less than or equal to 25. Similarly, if KOUNT-25 is greater than zero, then KOUNT must be greater than 25. Thus, the problem can be solved with the following IF statement:

```
IF(KOUNT-25) 50,50,60
```

As an illustration of the use of the arithmetic IF statement in a program, consider the problem of calculating the tuition for a college student discussed earlier. The tuition is $350 if the number of units is less than or equal to twelve; otherwise, the tuition is $350 plus $20 for each unit over twelve. The following program solves the problem using an arithmetic IF statement:

```
 10 READ(5,100) ID,UNITS
    IF(UNITS-12.0) 15,15,20
 15 TUIT=350.00
    GO TO 30
 20 TUIT=350.00+20.00*(UNITS-12.0)
 30 WRITE(6,200) ID,TUIT
    GO TO 10
100 FORMAT(I4,F4.1)
200 FORMAT(1X,I4,3X,F7.2)
    END
```

After the input data is read, the IF statement compares the number of units (UNITS) with 12.0. If UNITS is less than or equal to 12.0, then the computer branches to statement 15 and the tuition is set equal to 350.00. If UNITS is greater than 12.0, then the computer branches to statement 20 and the tuition is calculated. The GO TO statement between statements 15 and 20 causes the computer to branch around statement 20 to the WRITE statement if the tuition is calculated by statement 15.

Notice that whenever an arithmetic IF or a GO TO statement is used, the next statement in sequence should have a number. If the statement following an IF or GO TO statement is not numbered, then there is no way that the statement can be identified later and executed. For example, consider the following sequence of statements:

```
  IF(A) 1,2,2
  X=Y+Z
1 B=X
  GO TO 3
```

```
    X=Y-Z
  2 B=-X
  3 (next statement)
```

In this example, the IF statement causes the computer to branch either to statement 1 or to statement 2. Thus, the statement immediately following the IF statement is not executed. Since it does not have a statement number there is no way that another statement can branch to it. Therefore, the statement X=Y+Z following the IF statement can never be executed. Similarly, the statement immediately following the GO TO statement in this example can never be executed.

We can see from the tuition calculating program that it is easy to translate a program using a logical IF statement into one using an arithmetic IF statement. In the version of the program in Fig. 5-1 we used the following logical IF statement:

$$IF(UNITS.GT.12.0) \ GO \ TO \ 20$$

To convert this to an arithmetic IF statement we change the logical expression UNITS.GT.12.0 into the arithmetic expression UNITS-12.0. Then we number the next statement in sequence with some number not used elsewhere in the program, such as 15. Finally, since the greater than relational operator is used, we wish to branch to statement 15 if UNITS-12.0 is less than or equal to zero, and to statement 20 if UNITS-12.0 is greater than zero. Hence the complete arithmetic IF statement is as follows:

$$IF(UNITS-12.0) \ 15,15,20$$

Except for adding the statement number 15, the rest of the program remains unchanged.

If either arithmetic expression compared in a relational expression is more than a single variable name or constant, then, in general, the expression should be enclosed in parentheses when converting to an arithmetic IF statement. For example, consider the following logical IF statement:

$$IF(3.5*A.GE.X+Y) \ GO \ TO \ 80$$

If we number the next statement in sequence 75, then the corresponding arithmetic IF statement is:

$$IF((3.5*A)-(X+Y)) \ 75,80,80$$

In this example the parentheses around 3.5*A are not essential but are included for consistency. However, the parentheses around X+Y are required to get the same effect as in the previous logical IF statement. In general it is easiest to parenthesize both expressions whether or not it is required, so that there is no possibility of an error.

Figure 5-13 summarizes the conversion of logical IF statements to arithmetic IF statements. In each case we have assumed that a GO TO statement is included in the logical IF statement. If some other statement is used then the conversion is somewhat different. For example, consider the following logical IF statement:

$$IF(A.GT.B) \ C=A-B$$

To convert this to an arithmetic IF statement we make C=A-B the next statement in sequence and supply it with a number not used elsewhere in the program, such as 25. We also supply the statement following it with a number, such as 30. Then the corresponding sequence using an arithmetic IF statement is as follows:

```
      IF(A-B) 30,30,25
   25 C=A-B
   30 (next statement)
```

A similar technique may be used for the other relational operators.

We have demonstrated in this section how to convert logical IF statements to equivalent arithmetic IFs. If the version of FORTRAN being used has both types of IF statements available, then generally it is easier to use the logical type. However, if only the arithmetic IF statement is available, then the program can be written using logical IF statements and then converted to one using arithmetic IFs by following the procedures in this section.

Logical IF Statement	Arithmetic IF Statement*
IF(exp1.GT.exp2) GO TO n1	IF((exp1)-(exp2)) n2,n2,n1
IF(exp1.GE.exp2) GO TO n1	IF((exp1)-(exp2)) n2,n1,n1
IF(exp1.LT.exp2) GO TO n1	IF((exp1)-(exp2)) n1,n2,n2
IF(exp1.LE.exp2) GO TO n1	IF((exp1)-(exp2)) n1,n1,n2
IF(exp1.EQ.exp2) GO TO n1	IF((exp1)-(exp2)) n2,n1,n2
IF(exp1.NE.exp2) GO TO n1	IF((exp1)-(exp2)) n1,n2,n1

*n2 is the number of the next statement in sequence

FIGURE 5-13. Conversion of logical IF statements with the GO TO statement to arithmetic IF statements.

PROGRAMMING PROBLEMS

1. Commission paid to a salesperson is often based on the amount sold by the person. Assume that the commission is 7½% if a person's sales total less than $10,000 and 9% if sales total $10,000 or more. Then the commission is calculated by multiplying the person's sales by the appropriate commission percentage.

   Write a FORTRAN program that reads the salesperson's identification number and total sales, calculates the commission, and prints the result along with the identification number. Test the program with data for salesperson number 18735 with sales of $11,250, data for salesperson number 27630 whose sales total $6500, and data for salesperson 31084 whose sales were $10,000.

2. The telephone company charge for long-distance calls is based not only on distance but on the length of time of a call. Assume that between two cities the rate is $1.10 for the first three minutes or fraction thereof, and $.40 for each additional minute. Data for a number of customers who made calls between these two cities consist of the customer's number and length of call.

   Write a FORTRAN program to read the customer number and length of call, calculate the charge, and print the customer number, length of call, and the charge. Use the following data to test the program:

Customer Number	Length of Call
9606	8
9735	3
2802	2
7921	5
1509	4
5371	1

3. Write a FORTRAN program to find the absolute value of a number. The absolute value of x is x if x is nonnegative and $-x$ if x is negative. Input should be the number; output should give the original number and its absolute value. Do *not* use the FORTRAN-supplied absolute value function. Use the following input data to test the program:

        25.0
       -25.0
         0.0
       -84.6
       132.5

132

4. A real estate office employs several salespeople. At the end of each month the total value of all property sold by each salesperson is used to calculate the person's commission. If total sales exceed $200,000, the commission is 3½% of the sales. If the sales are greater than $100,000 but not more than $200,000, the commission is 3% of sales. Otherwise, the commission is 2½% of the sales.

Write a FORTRAN program that reads the salesperson's number and total sales, performs the necessary commission calculation, and prints the result along with the salesperson's number and total sales.

Use the following data to test the program:

Salesperson's Number	Total Sales
1085	$252,350
1720	$42,500
2531	$95,000
3007	$155,500
3219	$73,250
4806	$282,950
6111	$110,000
7932	$118,000

5. An electric company charges its customers 5 cents per kilowatt-hour for electricity used up to the first 100 kilowatt-hours, 4 cents per hour for each of the next 200 kilowatt-hours (up to 300 kilowatt-hours), and 3 cents per hour for all electricity used over 300 kilowatt-hours. Write a FORTRAN program to calculate the total charge for each customer. Input to the program consists of the customer's number and kilowatt-hours used. Output from the program should list the customer number, the kilowatt-hours used, and the total charge. Use the following data to test the program:

Customer Number	Kilowatt-hours Used
1065	640
2837	85
3832	220
6721	300
8475	100

6. Write a FORTRAN program that finds the maximum of three numbers. Input consists of the three numbers; output should be the largest of the three. Do *not* use the FORTRAN-supplied maximum function. Use the following sets of input data to test the program:

```
    10,25,16
    17,38,41
   100,52,77
    -3,-8,-1
     0,45,-6
   -37,0,-42
    39,39,39
    14,14,8
```

7. Write a FORTRAN program to determine whether a student is a freshman, sophomore, junior, or senior based on the number of units that the student has completed. Input to the program consists of the student's number and the number of units completed.

A student's classification is based on his or her units completed according to the following schedule:

Units Completed	Classification	Code
Less than 30 units	freshman	1
30 units or more but less than 60 units	sophomore	2
60 units or more but less than 90 units	junior	3
90 units or more	senior	4

The output from the program should give the student's number, units completed, and the classification code (1, 2, 3, or 4). Use the following data to test the program:

Student Number	Units Completed
2352	38.0
3639	15.5
4007	29.5
4560	67.0
4915	103.5
8473	89.0

8. Write a FORTRAN program to evaluate the following function:

$$f(x) = \begin{cases} -x \text{ if } x < 0 \\ 1 \text{ if } x = 0 \\ 0 \text{ if } x > 0 \text{ and } x \leqslant 10 \\ 2x \text{ if } x > 10 \end{cases}$$

Input is the value of x; print the values of x and $f(x)$. Use the following data to test the program:

       38.60
        9.00
       10.00
        0.00
      -45.60
        0.01
       -0.01
       10.53

9. The basic charge for computer time is based on the number of hours of time used during a month. The schedule is as follows:

Hours Used	Basic Charge
0.00 to 5.00	$200
5.01 to 15.00	$200 plus $35 per hour for all time over 5 hours
15.01 and up	$550 plus $30 per hour for all time over 15 hours

In addition there is a surcharge added to the basic charge based on the priority used. The priority is indicated by a code. The surcharge is as follows:

Priority Code	Surcharge
0	0
1	$50
2	$150

Write a FORTRAN program that reads a customer's account number, number of hours used, and priority code. Then calculate the total charge. Print the account number and charge. Use the following data to test the program:

Account Number	Hours Used	Priority Code
11825	3.52	0
14063	17.06	1
17185	7.93	1
19111	12.00	2
20045	5.00	1
21352	5.84	0
22841	27.94	2
23051	1.55	2
29118	15.02	0

10. The results of a psychological experiment need to be analyzed. Each card in an input deck is punched with information about how an individual subject in the experiment did in a series of tests. Each of the subjects took from one to four tests. The number of tests taken, the test scores, and the subject's identification code are punched on a card. Write a FORTRAN program to calculate the average test score for each subject. Use a computed GO TO statement to branch to the appropriate averaging routine based on the number of tests completed. The output should list each subject's identification code, the number of tests completed, the score on each test, and the average score.

Use the following data to test the program:

Identification Code	Number of Tests Taken	Test Scores
408	3	17, 16, 21
519	1	24
523	2	14, 18
584	4	22, 16, 17, 14
601	1	12
677	3	25, 23, 24
701	4	17, 18, 21, 15
713	2	13, 12

11. Write a FORTRAN program that computes the coordinates of the point of intersection of two straight lines. Assume that the lines are given by the following equations:

$$y = sx + a$$
$$y = tx + b$$

where s and t are the slopes, and a and b are the intercepts. In addition, determine the number of the quadrant (1, 2, 3, or 4) of the point of intersection. (If the point of intersection falls on an axis, use the lower quadrant number of the quadrants separated by the axis.)

The program should read the values of s, a, t, and b, do the necessary computations, and print the coordinates of the point of intersection and the quadrant number. Use the following data to test the program:

s	a	t	b
18.0	6.0	30.0	6.0
2.0	8.0	-3.0	-2.0
1.0	8.0	-2.0	-22.0
3.0	-7.0	1.0	-1.0
-0.5	-3.0	2.0	-8.0

12. Input to a payroll program consists of the employee's number, year-to-date pay, base pay rate, shift code, and hours worked. Write a program to read these data, compute the employee's gross pay, withholding tax, social security tax, and net pay, and print these results along with the employee's number.

The gross pay is found by multiplying the hours worked by the pay rate where the pay rate is the product of the base pay rate and the shift factor. The shift factor comes from the following table:

Shift Code	Shift Factor
0	1.00
1	1.25
2	1.50

The withholding tax is the product of the gross pay and the tax rate. The tax rate is found from the following table:

Gross Pay	Tax Rate
Less than $100.00	0
$100.00 to $149.99	8%
$150.00 to $199.00	12%
$200.00 to $299.00	15%
$300.00 or more	17.5%

The social security tax (F.I.C.A. tax) depends on the gross pay and the year-to-date pay. If the year-to-date pay is greater than $17,300, then there is no social security tax. If the year-to-date pay plus the gross pay is less than or equal to $17,300, then the social security tax is 6.05% of the gross pay. If the year-to-date pay is less than $17,300, but the sum of the year-to-date and gross pay is greater than $17,300, then the tax is 6.05% of the difference between $17,300 and the year-to-date pay.

The net pay is computed by subtracting the withholding tax and social security tax from the gross pay.

Use the following input data to test the program:

Employee Number	Year-to-date Pay	Base Pay Rate	Shift Code	Hours Worked
1001	10,312.00	4.50	1	34.5
1002	3,888.75	3.25	0	25.0
1003	12,365.50	4.00	0	30.0
1004	15,284.25	5.25	2	38.5
1005	17,138.50	6.25	0	40.0
1006	18,465.00	8.95	2	48.0
1007	12,061.25	5.00	1	35.0
1008	17,225.00	6.00	1	40.0

Chapter 6

PROGRAMMING FOR REPETITION

As we have seen, a group of statements that is repeatedly executed is called a loop. In Chapter 3 we introduced the use of a loop to repeat the steps of a program so that more than one set of input data can be processed. We call such a loop an *input loop* since there is an input operation within the loop. Sometimes a loop does not contain an input operation but rather just processes data. We call this type of loop a *processing loop.* We will see a number of examples of processing loops in this chapter.

Whenever there is a loop in a program one important question is how to *control* the loop. By this we mean, how do we get the computer to *stop* looping? For example, consider the tuition calculation program shown in Fig. 6-1. (This is the same program as shown in Fig. 5-1.) The loop consists of statement 10 through the GO TO 10 statement. Notice that there is not a STOP statement in this program. The program will continue to loop as long as input data is supplied. When there is no more input data the computer will stop the program and go on to another program. (This is usually considered an execution error.)

The type of loop in this program is called an *uncontrolled loop* because there is no mechanism within the program to stop the repetition. As another example of an uncontrolled loop consider the following statements:

```
5 K=1
  GO TO 5
```

If these statements were in a program then the computer would continue to loop until stopped by the computer operator. Again there is

```
 10 READ(5,100) ID,UNITS
    IF(UNITS.GT.12.0) GO TO 20
    TUIT=350.00
    GO TO 30
 20 TUIT=350.00+20.00*(UNITS-12.0)
 30 WRITE(6,200) ID,TUIT
    GO TO 10
100 FORMAT(I4,F4.1)
200 FORMAT(1X,I4,3X,F7.2)
    END
```

FIGURE 6-1. The tuition calculation program.

nothing within this group of statements that causes the computer to stop after a period of time. Hence this is an uncontrolled loop.

In this chapter we discuss programming techniques for controlling loops. We also describe special FORTRAN statements that are used specifically for loop control.

6-1. CONTROLLING LOOPS

As we have seen, the GO TO statement may be used to create a loop by branching from the end of a group of statements to the beginning. To control such a loop we normally use an IF statement to branch out of the loop when some condition occurs. The techniques discussed in this section illustrate this approach to loop control for input loops and processing loops.

Input Loops

The program in Fig. 6-1 contains an uncontrolled input loop. Each time the loop is executed a new set of input data is read. A common technique for controlling such a loop is to use a special set of input data at the end of the regular data. If the input data is punched in cards, then this special end-of-data card is called a *trailer card* (or a *sentinel card*). Each time that a set of input data is read, the program checks to see if this special data has been read. If not, then the program continues with the normal execution of the statements in the loop. When the end-of-data input has been read, the program branches out of the loop.

Usually the end-of-data input contains a value in one of its fields that is not found in the same field in any other set of input data. We call such a value a *trailer value*. (This is also called a *sentinel*.) For example, in the tuition calculation program in Fig. 6-1 the input consists of the student's identification number and number of units. The identification number is a four-digit integer field. If we select a value for this field that is not found in any other set of input, then we can test for this value each time that the loop is executed. This value is the trailer value.

We will assume that the trailer value for the tuition data is 9999 in the identification number field. Then Fig. 6-2 shows the program with this form of loop control. First the program reads the identification number (ID) and number of units. Then it checks the value of ID. If ID is *not* equal to 9999, the program continues with the next statement in sequence. If the value of ID equals 9999, then the program branches out of the loop to the STOP statement. Notice that the end-of-data test comes immediately after the READ statement. We must check for the end of the input at this time since we do not want to process the trailer data.

In this program we could have written the second statement as follows:

```
IF(ID.EQ.9999) STOP
```

Then statement 40, the STOP statement, would not be needed. While this approach is appropriate for this problem, there are situations where we must branch out of the loop when the trailer value has been read. This is the case where there is additional processing that must be done after all data has been read. We will see an example of this later in this chapter.

```
 10 READ(5,100) ID,UNITS
    IF(ID.EQ.9999) GO TO 40
    IF(UNITS.GT.12.0) GO TO 20
    TUIT=350.00
    GO TO 30
 20 TUIT=350.00+20.00*(UNITS-12.0)
 30 WRITE(6,200) ID,TUIT
    GO TO 10
 40 STOP
100 FORMAT(I4,F4.1)
200 FORMAT(1X,I4,3X,F7.2)
    END
```

FIGURE 6-2. The tuition calculation program with input loop control.

Processing Loops

A processing loop is a loop that is controlled by some condition on the data that is processed in the loop, not by an input value. Usually within the loop, computations take place that affect the value of some variable. Each time the loop is executed, the variable is used in a logical test to determine whether or not to terminate the loop. If the loop is properly designed then eventually the condition will become true and the program will branch out of the loop.

For example, consider the problem of determining the amount of time that it will take for a bank deposit to double at a given interest rate. Assume that $1000 is put into a bank at 5% interest compounded annually. This means that at the end of the first year, the interest will be 5% of $1000 or $50 which is added to the original deposit to give a balance of $1050. At the end of the second year, the interest will be 5% of $1050 or $52.50. The balance will then be $1102.50. Thus the interest is added to the balance at the end of each year and used in the next year's interest calculation. Our problem is to write a program that prints a table of yearly interest and balance until the deposit has doubled to $2000.

Figure 6-3(a) shows a program that accomplishes this. Notice that there is not an input statement in the program; this program does not require any input data. The variable named BAL is equal to the bank balance; initially BAL is $1000.00. IYEAR is an integer variable which counts the number of years. For the first year's calculation IYEAR is one. The loop consists of statement 10 through the GO TO 10 statement. The IF statement, numbered 10, terminates the loop when BAL is greater than or equal to $2000.00. Within the loop, the current year's interest (XINT) is calculated by multiplying BAL by .05. XINT is then added to BAL to give the new balance. (Recall from Chapter 4 that the statement BAL=BAL+XINT adds XINT to the old value of BAL and assigns the result to BAL.) Then the output is printed and IYEAR is increased by 1 for the next year. The GO TO statement branches back to the beginning of the loop (which is *not* the first statement in the program). The processing is repeated as long as BAL is less than $2000.00. The output from the program is the table shown in Fig. 6-3(b). The first column is the year, the second column is the interest for the year, and the last column is the year-end balance.

Counting Loops

A special type of processing loop control that is often used involves counting the number of times that a loop is executed and branching out of the loop when the count reaches some desired number. This ap-

```
        BAL=1000.00
        IYEAR=1
    10  IF(BAL.GE.2000.00) GO TO 20
        XINT=.05*BAL
        BAL=BAL+XINT
        WRITE(6,200) IYEAR,XINT,BAL
        IYEAR=IYEAR+1
        GO TO 10
    20  STOP
   200  FORMAT(1X,I3,3X,F6.2,3X,F8.2)
        END
```

(a)

1	50.00	1050.00
2	52.50	1102.50
3	55.13	1157.63
4	57.88	1215.51
5	60.78	1276.29
6	63.81	1340.10
7	67.01	1407.11
8	70.36	1477.47
9	73.87	1551.34
10	77.57	1628.91
11	81.45	1710.36
12	85.52	1795.88
13	89.79	1885.67
14	94.28	1979.95
15	99.00	2078.95

(b)

FIGURE 6-3. The interest calculation program: (a) the
program; (b) the output.

proach uses a variable name as a *counter* or *index*. Before entering the
loop, the counter is *initialized* to some beginning value. Each time that
the loop is executed the value of the counter is *modified*, usually by
increasing or *incrementing* its value by 1. Also each time that the loop
is executed the counter is tested and the loop repeated as long as the
value of the counter does not exceed some final value.

For example, the following statements show the general form of a
loop that is to be executed 100 times:

```
    K=1                                    (initialize counter)
10 (first statement in loop)
    .
    .
    .
```

```
(statements in loop)
  .
  .
  .
K=K+1                              (modify counter)
IF(K.LE.100) GO TO 10             (test counter)
(next statement)
```

In this example, the counter is the variable named K. Initially K is assigned the value 1. Then the statements in the loop are executed. At the end of the loop, the value of K is increased by 1 and then tested to see if it exceeds 100. If K is less than or equal to 100, the loop is repeated. If K is greater than 100, the computer leaves the loop.

Notice here that the IF statement branches to the beginning of the loop if the counter is less than *or equal to* the maximum number of times that the loop is to be executed. This is necessary to insure that the loop is executed exactly 100 times. If the IF statement were coded so that the computer branched out of the loop when the counter equaled 100, then the loop would be executed only 99 times.

We can use this technique in the interest calculation program. Assume that we only wish to print a table of interest and balance for ten years. The variable named IYEAR may be used to count the number of years and, at the same time, the number of times that the loop is executed. The program is shown in Fig. 6-4. IYEAR is initialized to one. Each time through the loop, IYEAR is incremented by 1. The loop is repeated as long as IYEAR is less than or equal to ten.

Notice in these examples that the variable name use for the counter is integer. It is usually best to select integer variable names for this purpose because integer arithmetic is faster and more accurate for counting purposes.

As another example of this form of loop control consider the problem of finding the total and average of fifty test scores. Assume that the test scores are punched one per card on fifty cards with no trailer card. The program must read the data, calculate the total and average, and print the results.

One way to write the program would be to use fifty variable names, one for each test score. However, such a program would be tedious to code. A better approach is to read and process the data within a loop. Although the loop in this case contains a READ statement, we cannot use an end-of-data check to terminate it since there is not a trailer value. However, since we know that there are exactly fifty input cards, we can control the loop by counting the number of times that the loop is executed.

The program is shown in Fig. 6-5. The variable named TOTAL is used to accumulate the total of the test scores. Each time through the loop the READ statement reads a test score (SCORE). Then the

```
        BAL=1000.00
        IYEAR=1
     10 XINT=.05*BAL
        BAL=BAL+XINT
        WRITE(6,200) IYEAR,XINT,BAL
        IYEAR=IYEAR+1
        IF(IYEAR.LE.10) GO TO 10
        STOP
    200 FORMAT(1X,I3,3X,F6.2,3X,F8.2)
        END
```

FIGURE 6-4. The interest calculation program with a counting loop.

value of SCORE is added to TOTAL and the result is assigned to TOTAL. Notice that TOTAL must be initially set equal to zero outside of the loop so that with the first execution of the loop the first test score is added to zero. Each successive time through the loop TOTAL is increased by the value of another test score until all fifty scores have been read and added.

The loop in this program is controlled by using the variable named KOUNT as a counter. Initially KOUNT is set equal to one. Each time through the loop KOUNT is increased by one and tested to see if it is less than or equal to fifty. When KOUNT exceeds fifty, the program falls through to the statement after the IF statement and calculates the average by dividing TOTAL by fifty. Then the output is printed and the program terminates.

This program processes exactly fifty test scores. A variation on the program is to read the number of test scores to be processed from an input card that comes ahead of the other data. Such a card is often called a *header card*. The header card contains a count of the number

```
        TOTAL=0.0
        KOUNT=1
     10 READ(5,110) SCORE
        TOTAL=TOTAL+SCORE
        KOUNT=KOUNT+1
        IF(KOUNT.LE.50) GO TO 10
        AVE=TOTAL/50.0
        WRITE(6,200) TOTAL,AVE
        STOP
    110 FORMAT(F3.0)
    200 FORMAT(1X,F5.0,3X,F5.1)
        END
```

FIGURE 6-5. A program to total and average fifty test scores.

```
      READ(5,100) NUM
      TOTAL=0.0
      KOUNT=1
   10 READ(5,110) SCORE
      TOTAL=TOTAL+SCORE
      KOUNT=KOUNT+1
      IF(KOUNT.LE.NUM) GO TO 10
      AVE=TOTAL/FLOAT(NUM)
      WRITE(6,200) TOTAL,AVE
      STOP
  100 FORMAT(I3)
  110 FORMAT(F3.0)
  200 FORMAT(1X,F5.0,3X,F5.1)
      END
```

FIGURE 6-6. A program to total and average a given
number of test scores.

of cards that follow. Hence the program is not limited to processing
exactly fifty values.

The program with this modification is shown in Fig. 6-6. The
first READ statement reads the number of test scores from the header
card and assigns the value to the variable named NUM. The rest of the
program up to the IF statement is the same as before. In the IF state-
met, the counter is compared with NUM and the loop is repeated as
long as KOUNT is less than or equal to the number of test scores. The
average is computed by dividing TOTAL by the real equivalent of
NUM.

In these examples the testing step is at the end of the loop. However, this is not essential. We could put the testing step in the middle
or the beginning of the loop depending on the requirements of the
problem. For example, the following statements execute a loop 100
times but with the counter test at the beginning of the loop:

```
    K=1                          (initialize counter)
 10 IF(K.GT.100) GO TO 20       (test counter)
    .
    .
    .
   (statements in loop)
    .
    .
    .
    K=K+1                        (modify counter)
    GO TO 10                     (repeat)
 20 (next statement)
```

Note that we branch out of the loop when the value of the counter is *greater than* 100.

We can also vary the way in which counting is done. The initial value of the counter does not have to be one. It can be any value depending on the problem. In addition, we need not count by ones. We can modify the counter by adding or subtracting any reasonable value. The test condition is determined by the initial value of the counter, how it is modified each time through the loop, and the number of times we wish to execute the loop.

To illustrate these variations, the following sequence counts from 0 to 20 by 2's:

```
      L=0
   20 (first statement in loop)
       .
       .
       .
      L=L+2
      IF(L.LE.20) GO TO 20
      (next statement)
```

Another alternative is to count backwards as in the following example that counts from 10 to 1:

```
      M=10
   30 (first statement in loop)
       .
       .
       .
      M=M-1
      IF(M.GE.1) GO TO 30
      (next statement)
```

Notice in this example that each time through the loop we decrease or *decrement* the counter by one. We can also modify the counter by a fractional amount. For example, the following statement counts from 0 to 1 in increments of .05:

```
      X=0.0
   40 (first statement in loop)
       .
       .
       .
      X=X+.05
```

```
IF(X.LE.1.0) GO TO 40
(next statement)
```

Notice that we must use a real variable name in this example.

Patterns of Loop Control

The discussion and examples in this section illustrate several different patterns of loop control. In all patterns the loop is repeated until some condition occurs that signals the end of the loop. However, the patterns vary in the placement of the end-of-loop test. Figure 6–7 summarizes the differences graphically.

Figure 6–7(a) shows the basic loop pattern with the termination test in the middle of the loop. In Fig. 6–7(b), the test is at the beginning of the loop. This pattern is called a *pre-test* loop. When the test is the last statement in the loop, as in Figure 6–7(c), the pattern is

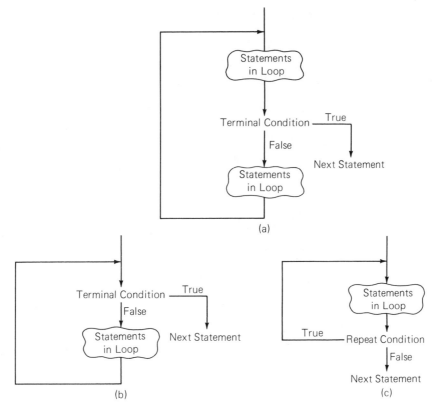

FIGURE 6-7. Patterns of loop control: (a) basic loop pattern; (b) pre-test pattern; (c) post-test pattern.

called a *post-test* loop. All loops in programs fall into one of these patterns. The implementation of these patterns in FORTRAN using IF and GO TO statements is shown in Fig. 6–8.

```
n1 (first statement in loop)
    .
    .
    .
   IF(terminal condition) GO TO n2
    .
    .
    .
   GO TO n1
n2 (next statement)
```

(a)

```
n1 IF(terminal condition) GO TO n2
    .
    .
    .
   (statements in loop)
    .
    .
    .
   GO TO n1
n2 (next statement)
```

(b)

```
n1 (first statement in loop)
    .
    .
    .
   (statements in loop)
    .
    .
    .
   IF(repeat condition) GO TO n1
   (next statement)
```

(c)

FIGURE 6–8.   Loop control patterns using IF and GO TO statements: (a) basic loop pattern; (b) pre-test pattern; (c) post-test pattern.

Program Style

To make the loop structure easier to understand in the program, many programmers indent the statements within a loop. For example, the loop part of the interest calculation program in Fig. 6-3 might be coded as follows:

```
10 IF(BAL.GE.2000.00) GO TO 20
      XINT=.05*BAL
      BAL=BAL+XINT
      WRITE(6,200) IYEAR,XINT,BAL
      IYEAR=IYEAR+1
   GO TO 10
```

The statements indented between the IF statement and the GO TO 10 statement form the main part of the loop. Whether or not a style such as this is used depends on whether the programmer feels it helps him or her understand the program logic.

Nested Loops

Within a loop there may be other loops. Such a combination of loops is referred to as *nested loops*. Any of the loop patterns in Fig. 6-7 may be nested within any other. The effect is that an inner loop is completely executed for each time that an outer loop is performed.

For example, assume that we wish to determine the amount of time that it will take for a bank deposit to double at interest rates varying from 3% to 7% in 1% increments. One approach is to run the program in Fig. 6-3 five times, each time using a different interest rate in the interest calculation. However, a better approach is to put another loop in the program that repeats the interest calculation five times, each with a different rate. The resulting program is shown in Fig. 6-9.

In this program the statement BAL=1000.00 through the GO TO 10 statement are the same as in the previous program with the exception that a variable name (RATE) is used for the interest rate in the interest calculation. The value of RATE is controlled by a loop that surrounds this group of statements. Initially RATE is set equal to .03. Each succeeding time through the loop, RATE is increased by .01. This loop is terminated when RATE becomes greater than .07.

Notice in this program that the inner loop (statement 10 through the GO TO 10 statement) is completely contained in the outer loop (statement 5 through the GO TO 5 statement). (Brackets are used in the diagram to show the nested loops.) Each time that the outer loop is repeated the inner loop will be completely executed. Since the outer

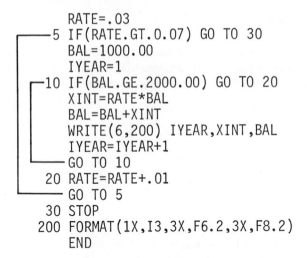

```
     RATE=.03
   5 IF(RATE.GT.0.07) GO TO 30
     BAL=1000.00
     IYEAR=1
  10 IF(BAL.GE.2000.00) GO TO 20
     XINT=RATE*BAL
     BAL=BAL+XINT
     WRITE(6,200) IYEAR,XINT,BAL
     IYEAR=IYEAR+1
     GO TO 10
  20 RATE=RATE+.01
     GO TO 5
  30 STOP
 200 FORMAT(1X,I3,3X,F6.2,3X,F8.2)
     END
```

FIGURE 6-9. The interest calculation program with nested loops.

loop is done five times, the inner loop will be completely performed five times. Hence the program will produce five tables, each similar to that shown in Fig. 6-3(b), but with a different interest rate used in the calculation of each table.

6-2. WHILE LOOPS

Some versions of FORTRAN provide special statements for general loop control. These are the WHILE and END WHILE statements.[†] Together these statements are used to form a *WHILE loop*.

The general form of a WHILE loop is as follows:

WHILE (*logical expression*) DO

.

.

.

statements

.·

.

.

END WHILE

[†] The statements described in this section are available in the WATFIV-S version of FORTRAN and some other versions.

The first statement, a WHILE statement, includes a logical expression in parentheses. Following this is a sequence of statements that is to be repeatedly executed. At the end of the loop must be an END WHILE statement. For example, the following is a valid WHILE loop:

```
WHILE (I.LE.10) DO
   WRITE(6,200) I
   I=I+1
END WHILE
```

The effect of the WHILE loop is to repeatedly execute the statements in the loop as long as the logical expression in parentheses is true. In the above example the WRITE and assignment statements will be repeatedly executed as long as I is less than or equal to 10. As soon as the logical expression becomes false, the computer branches out of the loop and continues with the next statement following the END WHILE statement.

A WHILE loop is actually a pre-test loop. The pattern is shown graphically in Fig. 6-10. When a WHILE statement is encountered, the computer first evaluates the logical expression. If the expression is false, then it branches to the next statement following the END WHILE statement. If the expression is true, then the computer executes the statements in the loop up to the END WHILE statement. The logical expression is again evaluated and, if true, then the loop is repeated. This continues until the logical expression becomes false and control transfers to the statement after the END WHILE statement. Notice that because the expression is evaluated at the beginning of the loop it is possible that the loop will not be executed at all. If the logical expression is false when the WHILE statement is first encountered, the loop will be bypassed completely.

With a WHILE loop we do not need an IF statement or GO TO statements for loop control. The testing and looping functions are built into the WHILE and END WHILE statements. However, we can

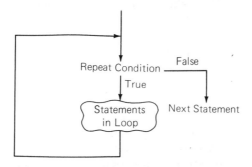

FIGURE 6-10. The WHILE loop pattern.

create the same effect using an IF statement and GO TO statements in a pre-test pattern. To do this we must use the complement of the condition in the WHILE statement. Thus the following sequence of statements is equivalent to the WHILE loop at the beginning of this section:

```
10 IF(I.GT.10) GO TO 20
     WRITE(6,200) I
     I=I+1
   GO TO 10
20 (next statement)
```

In a WHILE loop there may be any number of statements between the WHILE and END WHILE statements. The computer will repeatedly execute all statements while the logical expression is true. However, the END WHILE statement is essential. If it is left out, the computer will not know where the end of the loop is located.

Notice in our example that we have indented the statements in the loop. Although this is not required, it is a common programming style that makes it easier to see the loop structure in a program.

We can use a WHILE loop for control of any of the types of loop discussed in the previous section. Sometimes, though, the structure of the program must be modified slightly. For example, to control an input loop with a trailer value, we must have two READ statements. One READ statement is outside of the WHILE loop and reads the first set of input data. The other READ statement is in the WHILE loop (usually the last statement) and reads each successive set of input data. The logical expression in the WHILE statement checks for the absence of the trailer value. Figure 6-11 shows the pattern in the tuition calculation program (Fig. 6-2). (Notice that we have used the block IF statements in this program. Usually if a version of FORTRAN provides WHILE loops it also allows block IF statements.)

In this program, the first READ statement reads the first set of input data. The WHILE statement tests the value of ID to see if it is *not* equal to 9999, the trailer value. When the loop is executed, the tuition is calculated and the output is written. Then the READ statement at the end of the loop reads the next set of input data. The logical expression is checked again and if true the loop is repeated. Finally, after the last set of input data has been read and processed, the trailer card is read with a value of 9999 in the ID field. Since the logical expression is no longer true, execution continues with the next statement after the END WHILE statement.

The interest calculation program in Fig. 6-3 can easily be written with a WHILE loop. Since this program uses a pre-test loop we can replace the IF statement with a WHILE statement using the com-

```
      READ(5,100) ID,UNITS
      WHILE (ID.NE.9999) DO
        IF (UNITS.LE.12.0) THEN
          TUIT=350.00
        ELSE
          TUIT=350.00+20.00*(UNITS-12.0)
        END IF
        WRITE(6,200) ID,TUIT
        READ(5,100) ID,UNITS
      END WHILE
      STOP
  100 FORMAT(I4,F4.1)
  200 FORMAT(1X,I4,3X,F7.2)
      END
```

FIGURE 6-11. The tuition calculation program with a
              WHILE loop.

plementary condition and replace the GO TO 10 statement with an
END WHILE statement. The modified program is shown in Fig. 6-12.

The program to total and average fifty test scores in Fig. 6-5
used a post-test counting loop. We can rewrite this program fairly
easily with a WHILE loop. The result is shown in Fig. 6-13. The counter
must be initialized outside of the loop. Within the loop, the counter
is incremented. The WHILE statement causes the loop to be repeated
as long as the counter is less than or equal to 50.

WHILE loops may be nested. The only restriction is that each
WHILE statement must have a corresponding END WHILE statement.
For example, the interest calculation program in Fig. 6-9 uses nested
loops. This program may be rewritten with WHILE loops as shown in
Fig. 6-14. Notice that each WHILE statement has a matching END

```
      BAL=1000.00
      IYEAR=1
      WHILE (BAL.LT.2000.00) DO
        XINT=.05*BAL
        BAL=BAL+XINT
        WRITE(6,200) IYEAR,XINT,BAL
        IYEAR=IYEAR+1
      END WHILE
      STOP
  200 FORMAT(1X,I3,3X,F6.2,3X,F8.2)
      END
```

FIGURE 6-12. The interest calculation program with a
              WHILE loop.

```
      TOTAL=0.0
      KOUNT=1
      WHILE (KOUNT.LE.50) DO
         READ(5,110) SCORE
         TOTAL=TOTAL+SCORE
         KOUNT=KOUNT+1
      END WHILE
      AVE=TOTAL/50.0
      WRITE(6,200) TOTAL,AVE
      STOP
  110 FORMAT(F3.0)
  200 FORMAT(1X,F5.0,3X,F5.1)
      END
```

FIGURE 6-13. A program to total and average fifty test
scores with a WHILE loop.

WHILE statement. (Brackets are used in the diagram to better show the nested loop structure.) The effect of execution is that the inner WHILE loop will be completely executed for each repetition of the outer WHILE loop.

One important thing to notice in all of these examples of the use of WHILE loops is the lack of GO TO statements and the infrequent need for statement numbers. If block IF statements and WHILE loops are available in the version of FORTRAN being used, it is completely unnecessary to use GO TO statements and the only statements that need to be numbered are FORMAT statements. In general, this greatly reduces the complexity of programs. A program written with few

```
      RATE=.03
    ┌ WHILE (RATE.LE.0.07) DO
    │    BAL=1000.00
    │    IYEAR=1
    │  ┌ WHILE (BAL.LT.2000.00) DO
    │  │    XINT=RATE*BAL
    │  │    BAL=BAL+XINT
    │  │    WRITE(6,200) IYEAR,XINT,BAL
    │  │    IYEAR=IYEAR+1
    │  └ END WHILE
    │     RATE=RATE+.01
    └ END WHILE
      STOP
  200 FORMAT(1X,I3,3X,F6.2,3X,F8.2)
      END
```

FIGURE 6-14. A program with nested WHILE loops.

or no GO TO statements is generally easier to understand, debug, and modify than an equivalent program written with many GO TO statements.

6-3. DO LOOPS

Counting loops play an important role in programming. In Section 6-1 we saw several examples of the use of counting loops. Later chapters will show more examples. Because of the importance of this type of loop, FORTRAN provides a special statement, the DO statement, for control of counting loops. A loop that is controlled by a DO statement is called a *DO loop*. In this section we describe the DO statement and discuss programming with DO loops.

The basic steps for controlling a counting loop involve initializing a counter, modifying the counter after the statements in the loop have been executed, and testing the counter to determine whether or not the loop should be repeated. The program to total and average fifty test scores in Fig. 6-5 illustrated these steps. The following is the main loop in this program:

```
      KOUNT=1
   10 READ(5,110) SCORE
      TOTAL=TOTAL+SCORE
      KOUNT=KOUNT+1
      IF(KOUNT.LE.50) GO TO 10
```

Using a DO loop to control this loop we can rewrite this sequence of statements as follows:

```
      DO 20 KOUNT=1,50,1
         READ(5,110) SCORE
         TOTAL=TOTAL+SCORE
   20 CONTINUE
```

The first statement in this example is a DO statement. Whenever a DO statement is used, the statements that initialize, modify, and test the counter are not needed. Instead, the DO statement combines these functions. Here the effect of the DO statement is to cause the computer to repeatedly execute the statements following the DO statement up to and including the statement numbered 20. The first time that the loop is executed, KOUNT is assigned the value 1. Each succeeding pass through the loop, the value of KOUNT is increased by 1 until it exceeds 50. Then control transfers out of the loop to the next statement following the statement numbered 20. Statement 20 in this example is a CONTINUE statement which is a special statement that is often used as the last statement in a DO loop.

The DO Statement

The general form of the basic DO statement is as follows:

DO n $i=m1,m2,m3$

where n is the statement number of an executable statement that follows the DO statement.
i is an integer variable name.
$m1$, $m2$, and $m3$ are unsigned integer constants or variable names.

The effect of this statement is to cause the computer to repeatedly execute the statements following the DO statement up to and including the statement numbered n. The first time that the statements are executed, i is assigned the value of $m1$. Each succeeding time the value of i is incremented by $m3$. When the value of i becomes greater than $m2$, the computer branches to the next statement following the statement numbered n.

The *range* of a DO loop is the group of statements that is to be repeatedly executed. The range begins with the first statement that follows the DO statement and ends with the statement numbered n. This last statement in the range is called the *terminal statement* or *range limit*.

The integer variable name i is called the *DO-variable* or *control variable*. The DO-variable is incremented for each execution of the range. The value of the integer constant or variable name $m1$ is called the *initial value* or *initial parameter*. It is the value assigned to the DO-variable for the first execution of the range. The initial value must be 1 or greater.

The value of $m2$ is called the *test value* or *terminal parameter*. At the end of the execution of the range, after the DO-variable has been incremented, the value of the DO-variable is compared with the test value. If it is greater than the test value, control transfers to the next statement following the terminal statement. The test value must be 1 or greater.

The *increment* or *incrementation parameter* is the value of $m3$. It is the amount by which the value of the DO-variable is increased after each execution of the range. It must be 1 or greater. The increment may be omitted from the DO statement, in which case it is assumed to be 1.

The following DO statement, from the previous example, illustrates these concepts:

DO 20 KOUNT=1,50,1

The terminal statement of the loop described by this statement is the statement numbered 20. The DO-variable for the loop is the integer variable named KOUNT. The initial value of the DO-variable is 1, the test value is 50, and the increment is 1. Since the increment is 1 it may be omitted and the statement may be coded as follows:

DO 20 KOUNT=1,50

As another example, consider

DO 200 I=10,20,3

In this example, the terminal statement is the statement numbered 200, the DO-variable is the integer variable named I, the initial value is 10, the test value is 20, and the increment is 3.

Variable names may be used for any or all of the parameters. For example, the following DO statement uses variable names for the initial value and the test value:

DO 300 K=KN,KT,5

Note that the value of all parameters, whether variable names or constants, must be positive integers.

In a program that uses a DO loop the initialization, incrementation, and testing of the DO-variable are not coded directly. These operations are specified by the DO statement alone. However, the programmer must be aware of the order in which these operations are performed. Fig. 6-15 shows the pattern of execution that a DO loop usually follows. First, the DO-variable is initialized. Then the statements in the range are executed. After execution of the range, the DO-variable is incremented and tested. If the value of the DO-variable is less than or equal to the test value, the loop is repeated. Otherwise, execution of the program continues with the next statement following the terminal statement.

Notice that with this pattern the incrementation and testing of the DO-variable occur *after* the range is executed. Such a DO loop is always executed at least once. For example, consider the following:

DO 400 J=I,M

If I has a value of 50 and M is 40 at the time that the DO loop is exe-

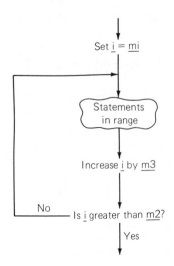

FIGURE 6-15.   Execution of a DO loop.

cuted, then the initial value of the DO-variable is greater than the test value. However, since the test is not made until after execution of the range, the loop is performed once before continuing with the statement that follows the terminal statement.

The number of times that a loop·is executed depends on the parameters. For example, the loop defined by the following statement is performed 50 times:

```
DO 20 KOUNT=1,50,1
```

As another example, consider the following DO statement:

```
DO 200 I=10,20,3
```

The loop described here is executed four times. The first time that the range is executed, the DO-variable has the value of 10. Then the DO-variable is incremented by 3 and is assigned the value 13 for the second execution of the range. For the third execution of the range, the DO-variable has the value of 16, and for the fourth time the value of the index is 19. After execution of the range for the fourth time, the DO-variable is incremented by 3 to 22. Then the test of the DO-variable determines that its value is greater than the test value (20), and the computer branches to the next statement following the terminal statement.

The CONTINUE Statement

The terminal statement in a DO loop may be an executable state-ment with certain exceptions such as a GO TO statement, STOP statement, or DO statement. However, usually programmers use a CONTINUE statement as the last statement in a DO loop. The CON-TINUE statement is simply the word CONTINUE. If used anywhere in the program except as the terminal statement of a DO loop, the CONTINUE statement has no effect on the program. That is, the computer just passes through the CONTINUE statement to the next statement in sequence. However, if a CONTINUE statement is the terminal statement of a DO loop then it has the *effect* of incrementing and testing the DO-variable.

The following DO loop illustrates the use of the CONTINUE statement:

```
      DO 20 KOUNT=1,50
         READ(5,110) SCORE
         TOTAL=TOTAL+SCORE
   20 CONTINUE
```

The CONTINUE statement is numbered 20 and hence is the terminal statement of the DO loop. Each time the loop is executed, the CON-TINUE statement has the effect of causing the value of KOUNT to be incremented and tested to determine whether or not to repeat the loop.

Notice in this example that we have indented the statements between the DO statement and the CONTINUE statement. This is a common program style that helps set off the statements in the loop so that the program is easier to understand.

Although a CONTINUE statement is not required for a DO loop, most programmers use it. The reason for this is that by using the CONTINUE statement, the DO loop is clearly set off in the program. In addition, there are certain times when it is necessary to have a special statement such as a CONTINUE statement at the end of the loop. We will see an example of this in the next subsection.

Illustrative Programs

A program to total and average fifty test scores illustrates the use of a DO loop. The complete program is shown in Fig. 6–16. After initializing TOTAL to zero, the program accumulates the total of the fifty test scores by reading each score and adding it to the total. After

```
          TOTAL=0.0
          DO 20 KOUNT=1,50
            READ(5,110) SCORE
            TOTAL=TOTAL+SCORE
       20 CONTINUE
          AVE=TOTAL/50.0
          WRITE(6,200) TOTAL,AVE
          STOP
      110 FORMAT(F3.0)
      200 FORMAT(1X,F5.0,3X,F5.1)
          END
```

FIGURE 6-16. A program to total and average fifty test
scores with a DO loop.

the DO loop is executed, the average is calculated and the results are printed.

A modification of this program is to read the number of test scores to be averaged from a header card. Then the value from the header card becomes the test value for the loop. The program in Fig. 6-17 illustrates this technique. Notice that the value of NUM is read with the first READ statement. Then NUM is used as the test value in the DO statement.

In Fig. 6-4 we showed a program that prints a table giving the interest and balance on an original deposit of $1000 at 5% interest compounded annually. The program required a counting loop and thus can be written with a DO loop. The equivalent program with a DO loop is shown in Fig. 6-18. Notice that the value of IYEAR is

```
          READ(5,100) NUM
          TOTAL=0.0
          DO 20 KOUNT=1,NUM
            READ(5,110) SCORE
            TOTAL=TOTAL+SCORE
       20 CONTINUE
          AVE=TOTAL/FLOAT(NUM)
          WRITE(6,200) TOTAL,AVE
          STOP
      100 FORMAT(I3)
      110 FORMAT(F3.0)
      200 FORMAT(1X,F5.0,3X,F5.1)
          END
```

FIGURE 6-17. A program to total and average a given
number of test scores with a DO loop.

```
        BAL=1000.00
        DO 20 IYEAR=1,10
          XINT=.05*BAL
          BAL=BAL+XINT
          WRITE(6,200) IYEAR,XINT,BAL
    20 CONTINUE
        STOP
   200 FORMAT(1X,I3,3X,F6.2,3X,F8.2)
        END
```

FIGURE 6-18. The interest calculation program with a
DO loop.

controlled with the DO statement. In addition, the value of this variable
is printed each time through the loop.

This example illustrates the use of the DO-variable within the range
of the DO loop. Any time the DO-variable is used in the loop its value
depends on the initial value, the increment, and the number of times
that the range has been executed. Figure 6-19 shows another program
that uses the DO-variable within the DO loop. This program finds the
total of the even integers from 2 to 20. In this example, the DO-
variable is used in the arithmetic assignment statement that calculates
the sum. Initially, zero is assigned to the variable named ISUM. With the
first execution of the range, the initial value of the DO-variable (2) is
added to ISUM and the result replaces the original value of ISUM. Thus,
after the first execution of the loop, ISUM has a value of 0+2 or 2. With
each succeeding execution of the range, the current value of the DO-
variable is added to ISUM. After the second execution of the range,
ISUM has a value of 0+2+4 or 6; after the third execution of the range,
ISUM is 0+2+4+6 or 12. This continues until after 10 executions of the
range the value of ISUM is 0+2+4+6+8+10+12+14+16+18+20, or 110.
Then the DO-variable is incremented to a value greater than the test
value and the loop is terminated.

```
        ISUM=0
        DO 50 I=2,20,2
          ISUM=ISUM+I
    50 CONTINUE
        WRITE(6,200) ISUM
        STOP
   200 FORMAT(1X,I4)
        END
```

FIGURE 6-19. A program to find the sum of the even
integers from two to twenty.

Within thè range of a DO loop, the DO-variable, initial value, test value, and increment cannot be used in such a way that their values are changed. For example, the following loop is invalid:

DO 75 J=1,10
.
.
.
J=5
.
.
.
75 CONTINUE

In this loop the DO-variable (J) is assigned a value through the DO statement but the value is illegally modified by the statement J=5. Similarly, the values of the DO-variable or the parameters cannot be modified by execution of a READ statement.

Sometimes within a DO loop it is necessary to bypass some of the statements in a loop under certain conditions and go directly to the incrementation and testing of the DO-variable. For example, assume as before that there are fifty test scores punched on cards. However, this time we wish to total and average only those scores that are 60 or greater (that is, passing scores). The program must read a test score from a card and determine if it is greater than or equal to 60. If it is, then the score must be added to the total. If not, then the program must bypass the totaling step. In addition, a count of the number of scores greater than or equal to 60 must be kept for the averaging step.

Figure 6–20 shows a program that accomplishes this. Before entering the loop the program initializes TOTAL to zero. In addition, a variable named NPASS is initially set equal to zero. This variable is used to count the number of passing test scores (that is, the number that are 60 or greater) and is used in the average calculation. In the DO loop, the READ statement reads a test score. The program must then check the score to see if it is greater than or equal to 60. If it is, then the score must be added to TOTAL and NPASS must be increased by one. To do this the IF statement in the loop causes the computer to bypass the assignment statements if SCORE is less than 60. Notice that the IF statement branches to the *end* of the DO loop (that is, to the CONTINUE statement). A common mistake in this type of problem is to branch to the DO statement. If this were done, then the computer would reset the DO-variable to its initial value and restart the loop. Any time the computer branches to a DO statement it initializes the DO-variable and starts processing the loop. If this were done in this example, the program would not process the loop in the required way.

```
      TOTAL=0.0
      NPASS=0
      DO 20 KOUNT=1,50
        READ(5,110) SCORE
        IF(SCORE.LT.60.0) GO TO 20
        TOTAL=TOTAL+SCORE
        NPASS=NPASS+1
   20 CONTINUE
      AVE=TOTAL/FLOAT(NPASS)
      WRITE(6,200) TOTAL,AVE
      STOP
  110 FORMAT(F3.0)
  200 FORMAT(1X,F5.0,3X,F5.1)
      END
```

FIGURE 6-20. A program to total and average passing
test scores.

This example shows an important use of the CONTINUE statement. In situations where the last part of a DO loop must be bypassed and loop processing continued in the normal way, it is necessary to branch to the end of the loop. While we could use any insignificant statement as the last statement in the DO loop in circumstances such as this, the CONTINUE statement serves the purpose well. If a CONTINUE statement is used as the terminal statement for every loop then we are less likely to make the mistake of branching to the DO statement.

Branching Into and Out of a DO Loop

It is permissible to branch out of a DO loop at any time. For example, assume that we wish to find the total and average of an unknown number of test scores. Each score is punched in a card. The last card in the data deck is a trailer card with zero punched in the test score field. If we assume that there are less than 100 input cards, then a DO loop that is executed 100 times may be used to read the data and total the scores. However, after each card is read, a test for the trailer card must be made. When the trailer card is detected, the program must branch out of the DO loop.

The program to accomplish this is shown in Fig. 6-21.[†] Notice that after the program branches out of the loop, the number of test scores is calculated by subtracting one from the DO-variable. The DO-variable equals the last value assigned to it in the DO loop. For each

---

[†] Although this program is valid in FORTRAN, we will see in Chapter 8 that it violates certain principles of good program structure.

```
      TOTAL=0.0
      DO 20 KOUNT=1,100
         READ(5,110) SCORE
         IF(SCORE.EQ.0.0) GO TO 30
         TOTAL=TOTAL+SCORE
   20 CONTINUE
   30 NUM=KOUNT-1
      AVE=TOTAL/FLOAT(NUM)
      WRITE(6,200) TOTAL,AVE
      STOP
  110 FORMAT(F3.0)
  200 FORMAT(1X,F5.0,3X,F5.1)
      END
```

FIGURE 6-21.   A program to total and average an unknown
number of test scores.

card that is read, the variable is incremented by one. Thus, the DO-variable counts the number of input cards. However, the trailer card does not contain a test score and must not be included in the count. To correct for this, the value of the DO-variable is reduced by one after the program branches out of the loop. The number of test scores is then used to calculate the average score.

Although it is permissible to branch out of a DO loop, most versions of FORTRAN do not allow the program to branch into the range of a DO loop. Some versions of FORTRAN do allow this under very restrictive conditions. However, the conditions are complex and generally the situation should be avoided. This does not mean, though, that branching to the DO statement itself is restricted. The program can branch to a DO statement from outside of the DO loop at any time and thus begin the loop processing.

Nested DO Loops

Within the range of a DO loop may be another DO loop. Such a combination of loops is referred to as *nested DO loops*. As an example of the use of nested DO loops consider the problem of finding the total and average of five groups of fifty test scores each. One approach would be to execute the program in Fig. 6-16 five separate times. Each time, a different set of input data would be processed by the program. A better approach is to put another loop in the program to repeat the totaling and averaging statements five times. The resulting program is shown in Fig. 6-22. With this program all data can be processed at one time.

In this program, the first DO statement initializes the DO-variable KLASS to 1. Then the variable named TOTAL is assigned the value

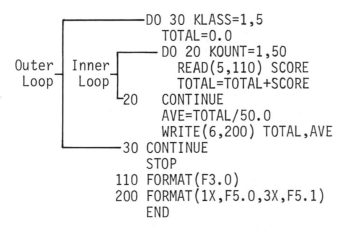

```
                            DO 30 KLASS=1,5
                            TOTAL=0.0
                             DO 20 KOUNT=1,50
 Outer   Inner                  READ(5,110) SCORE
 Loop    Loop                   TOTAL=TOTAL+SCORE
                        20    CONTINUE
                            AVE=TOTAL/50.0
                            WRITE(6,200) TOTAL,AVE
                        30 CONTINUE
                           STOP
                       110 FORMAT(F3.0)
                       200 FORMAT(1X,F5.0,3X,F5.1)
                           END
```

FIGURE 6-22. A program with nested DO loops.

zero. The second DO statement initializes the DO-variable KOUNT
to 1. Next the range of the inner DO loop is executed. When the
terminal statement of the inner DO loop is encountered, KOUNT is
incremented and tested. The inner loop is repeated until its DO-variable
exceeds the test value. At that point, the computer executes the statements following the terminal statement of the inner DO loop. In this
case, the average is computed and the output is printed. Then the
terminal statement of the outer loop is encountered, and the DO-
variable KLASS is incremented and tested.

With the second execution of the outer DO loop, the value of the
variable named TOTAL is reset to zero. Then the inner DO statement
is encountered. This causes KOUNT to be set to 1. Then the inner loop
is executed 50 times. Next the average is calculated and the WRITE
statement is executed. Then the outer loop DO-variable is incremented
and tested. This continues for a total of five times. Each time that the
outer loop is executed, the statements in the inner loops are performed
50 times.

We can see from the example how nested DO loops are executed.
The basic rule is that each time that an outer loop is performed, the
inner loop is completely executed. In the previous example, the statements in the inner loop are executed a total of 250 times.

As another example, consider the following outline of nested DO
loops:

```
                     DO 300 L=11,20
                       DO 200 M=1,5
                         DO 100 N=2,6,2
                           .
                           .
                           .
```

```
100     CONTINUE
200    CONTINUE
300 CONTINUE
```

In this example, the inner-most loop is executed three times for each execution of the intermediate loop. The intermediate loop is executed five times for each execution of the outermost loop. Since the outermost loop is executed 10 times, the intermediate loop is executed a total of 50 times (10 × 5), and the innermost loop is performed 150 times (10 × 5 × 3).

Notice that the DO-variables of the loops in a nest are different variable names. A unique name must be used for the DO-variable of each loop in a nest of DO loops.

When using nested DO loops the range of an inner loop must be completely contained within the range of the next outer loop. Hence the following pattern of DO loops is invalid:

```
DO 70 I=1,20
DO 80 J=1,5
        .
        .
        .
70 CONTINUE
80 CONTINUE
```

This pattern is unacceptable because, if executed, the terminal statement of the outer loop is encountered while performing the inner loop.

Nested DO loops may have the same terminal statement. For example, the following pattern of nested loops is valid:

```
DO 90 M=3,18,4
DO 90 N=1,7
        .
        .
        .
90 CONTINUE
```

This has the same effect as if each loop had a separate terminal statement. Figure 6-23 summarizes several valid and invalid patterns for nested DO loops.

Variations on the DO Statement

The DO statement described above is the most commonly available form of this statement. However, some versions of FORTRAN allow

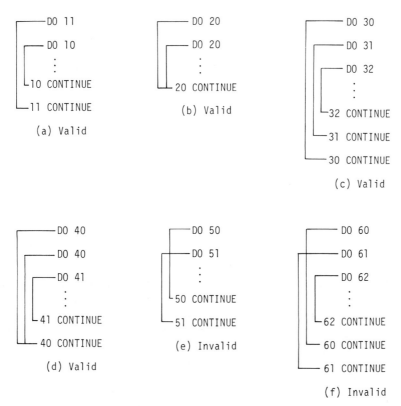

FIGURE 6-23. Valid and invalid patterns for nested DO
              loops.

variations in the DO statement. In some cases it is acceptable to have
nonpositive values for the initial value, final value, and increment.
The only restriction is that the increment must not be zero. For example, the following DO statement is valid in some versions of FORTRAN:

$$DO\ 300\ I=-10,0,1$$

The first time the DO loop for this statement is executed, the value of
I is -10. Then one is added to I, making it -9 for the second execution
of the loop. The value of I is incremented by 1 for each successive
time through the loop. The last time the loop is executed, I is zero.

   If the increment is negative, then the DO loop, in effect, counts
backwards. For example, the following DO statement causes the value
of J to be decreased by one each time the loop is executed:

$$DO\ 310\ J=10,1,-1$$

When the increment is negative, the loop terminates when the value of the DO-variable is *less than* the test value. In this example, the value of J is one during the last execution of the loop. Then –1 is added to J, decreasing its value to 0. Since J is now less than 1, the test value, the loop is not repeated again.

Some versions of FORTRAN allow a real variable name for the DO-variable and real values for the parameters. For example, the following DO statement is valid in some versions of FORTRAN:

```
DO 320 X=.05,1.00,.01
```

The DO-variable in this example is X, a real variable name. The initial value is .05, the test value is 1.00, and the increment is .01. Thus X varies from .05 to 1.00 in increments of .01. If the parameters are not the same type as the DO-variable, then they are automatically converted to the appropriate type using the FLOAT or IFIX function.

As we have seen, the parameters may be constants or variable names. However, sometimes arithmetic expressions are allowed. The expressions may be integer or real. In evaluating the DO statement, the value of any expression is evaluated at the time the statement is encountered. The resulting value is then used for loop control. For example, the following DO statement is valid in some versions of FORTRAN:

```
DO 330 Y=A,A+B,2.0*C
```

If A is 5.0, B is 20.0, and C is 3.0 when this statement is executed, then the initial value of Y is 5.0, the test value is 25.0 and the increment is 6.0.

The order in which the loop control processing is done is sometimes different than that described previously. Usually, the testing step occurs at the end of the loop, after incrementing the DO-variable. This post-test pattern results in a DO loop that is always executed at least once, no matter what the initial and final values are. In some versions of FORTRAN the testing is done at the beginning of the loop, before the loop is even executed once (that is, a pre-test loop). This means that if the magnitude of the initial value is greater than the final value before the first execution of the loop, the loop will not be executed at all. The incrementation is still done at the end of the loop and, except for this one case, loop processing is identical whether the DO loop is the pre-test or the post-test type.

The variations of the DO statement described here apply to few versions of FORTRAN. However, if available they can affect the way a program is written. The programmer should determine if any of these variations apply to the version of FORTRAN being used.

PROGRAMMING PROBLEMS

1. Complete the program for problem 2 or problem 5 in Chapter 5 with the modification that the program terminates when the customer number is 9999.

2. Complete the program for problem 4 in Chapter 5 with the modification that the total commission for all salespeople is accumulated and printed at the end of the regular output. Add a trailer card with zero in the salesperson number field to control the input loop.

3. Write a FORTRAN program to create a table for converting Fahrenheit temperature to Celsius. (See problem 2 in Chapter 4 for the appropriate conversion formula.) The table should list the Fahrenheit temperatures from 32 to 212 degrees in two-degree increments and the equivalent of each temperature in Celsius.

4. A classic exercise in computer programming is sometimes called the "Manhattan Problem." It is based on the historical fact that in 1627 the Dutch purchased Manhattan Island from the Indians for the equivalent of $24. Currently the assessed value of Manhattan is over eight billion dollars. Did the Dutch make a good investment, or would it have been better to have deposited the original $24 in a bank at a fixed interest rate and left it for all these years?

Assume that the original $24 used to purchase Manhattan Island was deposited in a bank that paid 3% interest compounded annually. Write a FORTRAN program to determine the account total at the end of 1981 (355 years later). Do not use an interest formula to calculate the amount at the end of the time period; instead, accumulate the total one year at a time.

5. A company agrees to pay one of its employees in grains of rice instead of money. The employee receives one grain on the first day, two grains the second day, four grains the third day, eight grains the fourth day, and so forth. In other words, each succeeding day the employee receives twice as many grains as he or she did the day before. The employee works for the company for 15 days.

Write a FORTRAN program to determine the number of grains of rice that the employee receives on each day that he or she works. Also, accumulate the total of the rice earnings. There is no input for this program. Output should consist of 15 lines each with the day number, the number of grains received on that day, and the accumulated number of grains received to date.

6. Assume that a pair of rabbits can produce a new pair in one month's time. Each new pair becomes fertile at one month of age and begins the cycle of reproducing a new pair every month. If rabbits never die, how many pairs of rabbits are produced from a single pair in N months' time?

If N ranges from 1 to some maximum value, then the solution to this problem creates a sequence of numbers known as the Fibonacci sequence after the Italian mathematician who first posed the problem. For $N = 1$, the value in the sequence is 1. (That is, at the end of the first month, one new pair of rabbits is produced.) For $N = 2$, the value is also 1. For any N greater than 2, the value in the sequence is the sum of the two previous values. Thus, the sequence is as follows:

Number of Months	Number of Pairs of Rabbits
1	1
2	1
3	2
4	3
5	5
6	8
7	13
.	.
.	.
.	.

Let N range from 1 to 24. Write a FORTRAN program to compute and print a table of the number of rabbits produced from the original pair at the end of month N. There is no input for this program.

7. Each student in a class of 15 took two examinations. A program is needed to calculate the total and the average test score for each student, the total and average for the entire class on each test, and the total and average of all 30 test scores. Input to the program is one card for each student with his or her identification number and score on each of the two tests. Output should list the input data and all required totals and averages. Use the following data to test the program:

Identification Number	Score on First Test	Score on Second Test
101	88	73
102	100	92
103	45	78
104	63	69
105	84	87
106	92	88
107	91	100
108	61	75
109	78	73
110	99	94
111	74	82
112	83	69
113	100	100
114	52	69
115	85	85

Notice that the data does not include a trailer card. The program should use a DO loop to process exactly 15 input cards.

8. Complete the program for problem 12 in Chapter 5 with the modification that the total gross pay, withholding tax, social security tax, and net pay is accumulated and printed at the end of the regular output. Add a trailer card with 9999 in the employee number field to control the input loop.

9. Write a FORTRAN program that produces a table of Fahrenheit and equivalent Celsius temperature. The equation is given in problem 2 of Chapter 4. The program should be designed to begin the table at any initial Fahrenheit temperature, end at any final temperature, and increment between the initial and final temperatures by any given value. Input for the program is the initial Fahrenheit temperature, the final temperature, and the increment. Use the following sets of input data to test the program:

Initial	Final	Increment
32	212	10
70	71	.1
40	30	−1
−10	0	2
0	0	0

The program should terminate if the increment is 0.

10. In problem 10 of Chapter 4 are the equations for the height h, and time of travel t, for a projectile fired in the air at an initial velocity, v, and angle of inclination, θ. Let θ range from 0 to 90 degrees by 5-degree increments. Write a FORTRAN program that produces a table listing the value of θ and the corresponding values of h and t. Use an initial velocity of 247.38 to test the program.

11. The value of e^x can be found from the following infinite series:

$$e^x = 1 + x + \frac{x^2}{2!} + \frac{x^3}{3!} + \frac{x^4}{4!} + \ldots$$

$$= 1 + \sum_{i=1}^{\infty} \frac{x^i}{i!}$$

Notice that the nth term (where the 1st term is 1) is the previous term times $\frac{x}{n-1}$.

An approximation to the value of e^x can be computed by carrying out this summation to a finite number of terms. Write a FORTRAN program to approximate e^x using 6 terms in the summation. Print out the approximate value of e^x. Also compute and print the value of e^x using the EXP function. Test the program with the following values of x:

    1
    0
    −1
    2.7183
    5
    −5

12. A tabulation of exam scores is needed for the students in a class. The scores vary from 0 to 100. Write a FORTRAN program to determine the number of scores in ranges 90 to 100, 80 to 89, 70 to 79, 60 to 69, and 0 to 59. Also determine the percent of the total number of test scores that fall in each range. Print all results.

Input to the program is one card for each exam score. The last card in the deck contains 999 in the exam score field. Use the following exam scores to test the program:

85	100	80	76	42	65	89
91	90	37	72	83	88	69
94	85	48	66	92	45	100
73	87	70	60	80	72	59
61	78	61	91	75	78	74
82	76	75	85	91	79	75

13. A problem in timber management is to determine how much of an area to leave uncut so that the harvested area is reforested in a certain period of time. It is assumed that reforestation takes place at a known rate per year, depending on climate and soil conditions. The reforestation rate expresses this growth as a function of the amount of timber standing. For example, if 100 acres are left standing and the reforestation rate is .05, then at the end of the first year there are 100 + .05 × 100 or 105 acres forested. At the end of the second year the number of acres forested is 105 + .05 × 105, or 110.25 acres.

Assume that the total area to be forested, the uncut area, and the reforestation rate are known. Write a FORTRAN program to determine the percent of the total area that is forested after 20 years. Output should list the input data plus the number of acres forested and the percentage of the total that this represents. Use the following data to test the program:

Area Number	Total Area	Uncut Area	Reforestation Rate
045	10,000	100	.05
083	1,000	50	.08
153	20,000	500	.10
192	14,000	3,000	.02
234	6,000	1,000	.01
416	18,000	1,500	.05
999 (trailer card)			

14. The rate of inflation is the annual percent increase in the cost of goods and services. For example, assume that an item costs $10.00 today and the rate of inflation is 10%. Then the cost of the item in one year is 10.00 + .10 × 10.00 or $11.00. In two years the item will cost 11.00 + .10 × 11.00 or $12.10.

Write a FORTRAN program to find the cost of a $12.00 item in fifteen years if the rate of inflation is 2%, 3%, 4%, and so forth up to 10%. That is, the program should give the cost after fifteen years at each inflation rate. (*Hint:* Use nested DO loops.)

Also determine the overall increase in the cost of the item. For example, if a $10.00 item costs $18.00 after 15 years, then the increase is 80%; if it costs $24.00, the increase is 140%. Compute the overall increase for the $12.00 item after fifteen years at each inflation rate.

There is no input for this program. Output should list the final results after fifteen years for each inflation rate.

Chapter 7

PROGRAMMING FOR NONNUMERIC INPUT AND OUTPUT

In Chapter 3 we discussed input and output of numeric data. It is also possible to read and write *nonnumeric* data, that is, letters and words. In this chapter we describe format-free and formatted I/O for this type of data. We also discuss several advanced input and output features.

7-1. NONNUMERIC OUTPUT

Most programs not only print the results of processing but also print words and phrases that describe the output. This is so that a person reading the output will know what the data represents. Sometimes a word or phrase is printed followed by the results of a computation. At other times, headings are printed above columns of output. There are many variations that are used to make the output more readable. In this section we describe the FORTRAN elements necessary to print nonnumeric data.

Format-free Nonnumeric Output

If format-free I/O is available, then nonnumeric output can be produced by enclosing the words to be printed in apostrophes. The combination of words and apostrophes is called a *character constant*. The character constant is then included in the I/O list of the PRINT

174

statement. When the PRINT statement is executed, the character constant is printed without the apostrophes. The values of any variable names in the I/O list are also printed.

For example, consider the following PRINT statement:

```
PRINT *,'THE SOLUTION IS',X
```

The character constant in this statement is 'THE SOLUTION IS'. Note that the comma separating the constant and the variable name X is required. Execution of this statement causes the phrase in the character constant to be printed followed by the value of X. If X is 125.25, then the output will appear as follows:

```
123456789..................

THE SOLUTION IS    125.2500
```

Notice that the apostrophes are not printed; only the characters between the apostrophes appear in the output.

There may be as many character constants in a PRINT statement as are needed. For example, the following statement includes two character constants:

```
PRINT *,' AMOUNT = ',AMT,'COUNT = ',KT
```

If AMT is 2.58 and KT is –10, then the output from execution of this statement is as follows:

```
123456789....................................

  AMOUNT =     2.580000    COUNT =              -10
```

A character constant by itself can be printed without printing the value of a variable name. The following statement illustrates this:

```
PRINT *,'STATISTICAL DATA'
```

The effect of execution of this statement is that the only output that will be printed is the character constant. This is often used to print headings to describe the output that follows.

Any printable characters may appear in a character constant. Letters, digits, and special characters including blanks are all permitted.

However, if an apostrophe is to be printed then two consecutive apostrophes must be used in the character constant. For example, to print the word JOHN'S we must use the character constant 'JOHN''S'. The two consecutive apostrophes indicate that one apostrophe is to appear in that position in the actual output.

Figure 7-1 shows a program with nonnumeric output. This program lists student identification numbers and test scores (see Figure 3-11(a)). At the top of the output is printed a heading that describes the columns of data that are printed. Notice that the PRINT statement for the headings is outside of the loop. If this statement were inside the loop, then the headings would be printed each time a value is read. The extra spaces in the character constant in the PRINT statement are necessary to align the headings above the appropriate columns. The actual spacing will depend on how the output is printed on the computer being used.

Formatted Nonnumeric Output

With formatted I/O, the H-format code is used to print nonnumeric data. The general form of the H-format code is as follows:

   *w*H*literal*

where w is the width of the field to be printed.
   literal is the w characters that are to be printed.

```
    PRINT *,'          ID     1ST TEST          2ND TEST'
 10 READ *,ID,SCR1,SCR2
    PRINT *,ID SCR1,SCR2
    GO TO 10
    END
```

(a)

```
      ID    1ST TEST      2ND TEST
   12841    98.50000      83.00000
   20853    92.00000      85.50000
   23841    75.00000      63.00000
   28006    81.50000      87.00000
```

(b)

FIGURE 7-1. A program with format-free nonnumeric output.

The following statements illustrate the use of the H-format code:

```
     WRITE(6,35) X
  35 FORMAT(1X,15HTHE SOLUTION IS,2X,F6.2)
```

The H-format specifies that a field containing 15 characters is to be printed. The characters that are to be printed follow the letter H. This is called a *literal* and includes any blanks that are specified. If the value of X is 125.25 in the computer's internal storage, then the output is printed as follows:

```
       123456789................
      ┌─────────────────┬────────┐
      │ THE SOLUTION IS │ 125.25 │
      └─────────────────┴────────┘
```

It is important to remember that the number that appears in front of the H must be an *exact* count of the number of characters (including any blanks) in the literal following the H. This is a common source of errors.

The following example illustrates the use of two H-format codes in one FORMAT statement:

```
     WRITE(6,36) AMT,KT
  36 FORMAT(1X,10H AMOUNT = ,F5.2,2X,8HCOUNT = ,I3)
```

The output for this example appears as follows:

```
       123456789......................
      ┌──────────┬──────┬─────────┬─────┐
      │ AMOUNT = │ 2.58 │ COUNT = │ -10 │
      └──────────┴──────┴─────────┴─────┘
```

Note that in a WRITE statement a list of variable names is not required. Thus, it is possible to print headings and captions without printing the value of a variable name. For example, the following sequence of statements causes the specified heading to be printed:

```
      WRITE(6,101)
  101 FORMAT(1X,16HSTATISTICAL DATA)
```

A common mistake when using H-format is to try to print more characters than there are print positions on a line. If several long literals are used in one FORMAT statement, this can easily happen. This usually results in an execution error when the program is run.

Another common error occurs when continuing a FORMAT statement from one line to the next in a program. Whenever a statement is so long that it cannot fit between columns 7 and 72, the statement must be continued onto the next line. However, it is not necessary to fill out the line to column 72 before continuing; most statements can be broken at *almost* any point and continued onto the next line. However, with a FORMAT statement a problem occurs when breaking the statement in the middle of a literal. In this case it is essential that the statement be carried out to exactly column 72 and continued beginning in column 7. Otherwise the character count in the H-format code will not coincide with the number of characters in the literal. For example, assume that a programmer wrote the FORMAT statement shown in Fig. 7-2(a). In this example column 72 is two spaces beyond the word TOTAL. These spaces would be counted as part of the literal. Since the character count is twelve, the computer would assume that the literal ends with the letter I on the next line. A compilation error would result because the letter S is not part of the literal. To correct this example, the I should be in column 72 and the S on the next line in column 7, as shown in Fig. 7-2(b). A better approach is to only break the FORMAT statement after a comma separating format codes, as shown in Fig. 7-2(c). Then this type of error cannot occur.

Many versions of FORTRAN allow the use of apostrophes to set off literals in addition to H-format. For example, often we can write the following:

```
       WRITE(6,35) X
    35 FORMAT(1X,'THE SOLUTION IS',2X,F6.2)
```

The effect is the same as if H-format were used; that is, the literal is printed (but without the apostrophes). When an apostrophe is to be printed as part of the output then two consecutive apostrophes must be used in the literal. Thus to print the word JOHN'S we must use 'JOHN''S' in the FORMAT statement. The advantage of using apostrophes instead of H-format is that it is unnecessary to count the number of characters in the literal. Hence, the programmer is relieved of one of the common sources of errors in FORMAT statements.

Figure 7-3 shows a program with formatted nonnumeric output. The program lists student identification numbers and test scores (see Fig. 3-11(b)). At the top of the output is printed a heading that describes the columns of data that follow. Notice that the WRITE statement for the heading must be outside the loop since otherwise the heading would be printed each time a value is read.

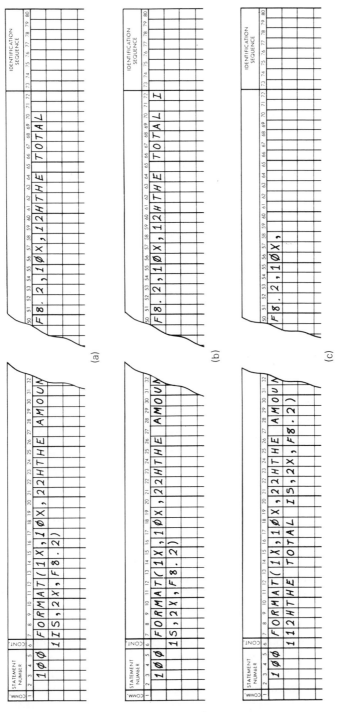

FIGURE 7-2. Continuing a FORMAT statement.

179

```
      WRITE(6,150)
   10 READ(5,100) ID,SCR1,SCR2
      WRITE(6,200) ID,SCR1,SCR2
      GO TO 10
  100 FORMAT(I5,5X,2F5.1)
  150 FORMAT(1X,4H ID,5X,8H1ST TEST,2X,8H2ND TEST)
  200 FORMAT(1X,I5,5X,F5.1,5X,F5.1)
      END
```

(a)

```
      ID      1ST TEST  2ND TEST
    12841       98.5      83.0
    20853       92.0      85.5
    23841       75.0      63.0
    28006       81.5      87.0
```

(b)

FIGURE 7-3. A program with formatted nonnumeric
output: (a) the program; (b) the output.

7-2. CARRIAGE CONTROL

As we have seen, each time that a READ statement is executed, a new
input record is read. For punched card input, this means that the next
card in sequence is read. With terminal input, each READ statement
causes a new typed line to be accepted. No additional programming is
needed to control which record is read; the computer always reads the
next record in sequence.

In a similar fashion, each time a WRITE or a PRINT statement is
executed, a new output record is written; that is, a new line is printed.
In the examples we have seen so far, the new line appears immediately
after the previous line. In other words, the printed output is single
spaced. Many times, though, this automatic single spacing is not acceptable. For example, we may wish to double space the output, or
skip part of a page so that the output begins at the top of a new page.
To do this we need an additional programming feature. This feature
is referred to as *carriage control* and is only used with formatted I/O.

Computer output is not usually printed on individual sheets of
paper but rather on continuous perforated paper forms. Figure 7–4
illustrates continuous form output and the printer mechanism for
controlling it. Most printed output consists of individual sheets of
paper connected together along perforated top and bottom edges.

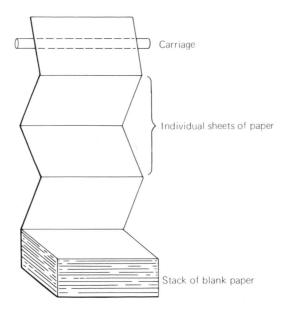

FIGURE 7-4. Continuous form output.

This creates a continuous form that moves through the printer. The movement of the forms is controlled by a *carriage* similar to a typewriter carriage. As the carriage rotates, the forms move, exposing blank paper to the printing mechanism. The carriage can move one line at a time or it can skip to the top of the next page.

In most versions of FORTRAN special characters are used to control carriage movement. The carriage control character occupies the first position in the output record. Recall from Chapter 3 that the character in this position is never printed. It is merely examined by the computer and interpreted as an instruction of how to move the carriage before printing the line described in the rest of the FORMAT statement.

The standard carriage control characters in FORTRAN are as follows:

Blank — advance one line before printing (single space)
    0 — advance two lines before printing (double space)
    1 — advance to the first line of the next page before printing
    + — no advance before printing

There are several approaches to using carriage control characters. The simplest is to place as the first code in the FORMAT statement a 1Hx, where the appropriate carriage control character is substituted for x. The number 1 in front of the H tells the computer that there is one character in the literal that follows the H. Since this is the first character in the output record, it controls the carriage.

For example, if double spacing is desired, the correct coding for one of the previous examples is as follows:

```
35 FORMAT(1H0,15HTHE SOLUTION IS,2X,F6.2)
```

The first character of the output record is defined by the one-character literal that follows the H in the first format code. Here the character is a zero, so the carriage advances two lines before printing.

If single spacing is required, the correct coding is as follows:

```
35 FORMAT(1H ,15HTHE SOLUTION IS,2X,F6.2)
```

Since the one-character literal that follows the H in the first format code is a blank (a valid character in FORTRAN) the carriage advances one line before printing. If one wishes the computer to skip to the top of the next page before printing, the correct coding is:

```
35 FORMAT(1H1,15HTHE SOLUTION IS,2X,F6.2)
```

Note that the first character (the carriage control character) is not printed; that is, the 0 or 1 in these examples does not appear in the output.

An alternate approach is to put the carriage control character in the first position in the main literal. For example, double spacing may be accomplished equally well with the following statement:

```
35 FORMAT(16H0THE SOLUTION IS,2X,F6.2)
```

In this example, the literal is sixteen characters in length with zero as the first character. Since this is the first character in the output record, it is considered the carriage control character.

In the earlier examples of output formats we have used 1X as the first code in the FORMAT statement. This places a blank in the first position in the output record. This is equivalent to using $1Hb$ ($b =$ blank) as the first format code.

Carriage control can be executed without any actual printing. For example, the following statements cause the computer to skip to the top of the next page with no printed output:

```
        WRITE(3,75)
75 FORMAT(1H1)
```

One reason that this may be done is to position the paper at the top of a new page before printing any output data.

If apostrophes can be used to set off literals, then the carriage control character can be enclosed in apostrophes. Thus the first example above can be written as follows:

```
35 FORMAT('0','THE SOLUTION IS',2X,F6.2)
```

Since 0 is the first character in the output record in this example, it serves as the carriage control character and is not printed. Alternatively, we could include the 0 in the main literal and write the statement as follows:

```
35 FORMAT('0THE SOLUTION IS',2X,F6.2)
```

Any of the carriage control characters can be used in this manner.

We can modify the program in Fig. 7-3(a) to include carriage control. If we wish to start the output at the top of a new page, then statement 150 should be written as follows:

```
150 FORMAT(1H1,4H  ID,5X,8H1ST TEST,2X,8H2ND TEST)
```

When the WRITE statement for this FORMAT statement is executed, the 1H1 at the beginning causes the digit 1 to be put in the first position of the output record. Hence, the printer skips to the top of the next page before printing the record.

7-3. CHARACTER INPUT AND OUTPUT

Nonnumeric data is often referred to as *character* data or as *alphanumeric* data since it can consist of both alphabetic and numeric characters. In many programs it is necessary to read and write character data. For example, the input to a payroll program may include the employee's name. This information must be read by the program so that it can be printed along with the results of the payroll calculations. In this section we discuss input and output of character data.

There are several approaches to character I/O depending on the version of FORTRAN being used. In all versions of FORTRAN character data is read and assigned to a variable name just as with numeric data. With some versions of FORTRAN numeric variable names (either real or integer) are used to refer to character data. In other versions, special character variable names are used. In addition, some versions of FORTRAN allow format-free I/O of character data while others only permit formatted I/O of this type of data. In this section we first discuss character variable names. Then we describe format-free I/O of character data which uses character variables. Finally we discuss two types of formatted character I/O, first using character variables then with numeric variables. Only those subsections that apply to the version of FORTRAN being used need to be read.

Character Variables

A character variable name is a name that refers to character data. The name is formed just like a numeric variable name. However, to indicate that the variable name refers to character data instead of integer or real numeric data, the name must be included in a CHARACTER statement. In its simplest form this statement is the keyword CHARACTER followed by a list of variable names separated by commas. For example, the following statement identifies the names A, B, I, and J as character variable names:

```
CHARACTER A,B,I,J
```

In the program, these names would refer to character data and cannot be used for numeric data.

The CHARACTER statement is a type of nonexecutable statement known as a *specification statement*. In general, specification statements describe characteristics of the data to be processed by a program. In this case the CHARACTER statement specifies that certain variable names will refer to character data and not numeric data. Since this information is needed prior to the execution of any statement using a character variable name, all CHARACTER statements must appear at the beginning of the program.

Each character variable has a *length* associated with it. The length is the maximum number of characters that can be assigned to the variable. For example, if a character variable has a length of ten, then any group of ten or fewer characters can be assigned to the variable. The length of each character variable is indicated by the CHARACTER statement. If the statement is written as described above, then the length of each variable is one. Thus in the previous example the character variable names A, B, I, and J can each refer to only one character.

To indicate lengths longer than one, two approaches are possible. The first is to follow the keyword CHARACTER with an asterisk and then a length. The length then applies to each variable name in the list. For example, the following CHARACTER statement specifies three character variables each of length twelve:

CHARACTER*12 X,Y,Z

Another approach is to include a separate length specification for each variable. This is done by following each variable name in the list with an asterisk and then its length. The following statement illustrates this approach:

CHARACTER NAME*18,DATE*6

This statement specifies two character variables. The first, NAME, is of length eighteen and the second, DATE, is of length six. These two approaches can be used in the same statement. Any variable name without its own length specification has the length given after the keyword CHARACTER. For example, in the following statement P has a length of eight, Q and R have lengths of ten, and S has a length of two:

CHARACTER*10 P*8,Q,R,S*2

Character variables are used with format-free I/O of character data. Some versions of FORTRAN also use character variables with formatted character I/O. In addition, in some versions of FORTRAN character variables are used for manipulation of character data as discussed in Chapter 9.

Format-free Character I/O

If format-free I/O is available, then character data can be read and written using the READ and PRINT statements. Any character variable name must first be specified in a CHARACTER statement. Values for character variable names can be read from punch cards or from a terminal using the READ statement. The values can then be printed using a PRINT statement. For example, the following simple program reads a four-character value, assigns it to the variable named N, and then prints the value of N:

```
CHARACTER*4 N
READ *,N
PRINT *,N
STOP
END
```

Character input data must be enclosed in apostrophes. As we saw in Section 7-1, this is called a character constant. For example, if the value to be read for N in the previous program is JOHN then it must be punched on a card as 'JOHN'. In this example the value is the same length (four) as the character variable. If the input value has fewer characters than the length of the character variable, then the value is assigned to the left-most part of the variable and blanks are added on the right to fill out the entire length. Thus, in the previous example, if the input data is 'ED', then the value of N after execution of the READ statement will be ED*bb* (*b* = blank). If the input value is longer than the length of the character variable, then the left part of the input data is assigned to the variable. For example, if the input is 'SALLY', then the value of N after execution of the READ statement in the previous program will be SALL.

With character data output, the value that is printed is whatever the variable is equal to. In the previous example, if N is equal to JOHN, then this is the value printed. Notice that surrounding apostrophes are *not* printed. If extra blanks have been added because the input data is shorter than the length of the character variable, then these blanks appear in the output.

Any printable characters can appear in a character constant. If an apostrophe is to be included within the input data, then it must be represented by two successive apostrophes. For example, if the value to be read by the previous program is ED'S, then the input data must be 'ED''S'. The value of N will be ED'S after execution of the READ statement. Notice that the apostrophe counts as one of the characters and thus the length is four in this example. When the value of N is printed it will appear as ED'S with a single apostrophe.

More than one character value can be read or written with one statement. In addition, character and numeric data can be read and written with the same statement. For example, the following program reads and writes two character values and one numeric value:

```
CHARACTER NAME*18,DATE*14
READ *,NAME,DATE,GPA
PRINT *,NAME,DATE,GPA
STOP
END
```

Input data for this program must be separated by commas or blank. For example, the following would be acceptable input for this program:

```
123456789.......................

 'JOHN SMITH','AUG 5,1956',3.45
```

The output will appear as follows:

```
123456789..................................

JOHN SMITH          AUG 5,1956        3.450000
```

Formatted Character I/O with Character Variables

With formatted character I/O using character variables, character variable names refer to the input and output data. Any character variable name must first be specified in a CHARACTER statement. Then the *A-format* code is used in the FORMAT statement to describe the input or output format. (The A signifies alphanumeric data.) The general form of the A-format code for this type of character I/O is as follows:

> A   or   A*w*

where *w* is the field width.

The code may be used for both input and output.

When the A-format code is used without a width specification, then the field width is given by the length of the character variable. For example, consider the following program:

```
        CHARACTER*4 N
        READ(5,100) N
        WRITE(6,200) N
        STOP
100     FORMAT(A)
200     FORMAT(1X,A)
        END
```

This program reads a character value for N in A-format and then prints the value of N. Since the format code does not specify a width, the field width is assumed to be the length of the character variable named N. In this case the length is four. Hence the first four columns of the input card are read and assigned to N. Assume that the input data is punched as follows:

```
123456789...

JOHN
```

Then the value of N after execution of the READ statement is JOHN. The WRITE statement prints this value in the first four print positions. (The 1X code is used to skip the first character in the output record.) Hence the output from this program is as follows:

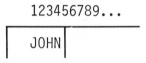

If a field width is given in the A-format code, then this indicates the width of the input or output field. When the width is the same as the length of the character variable, then the code functions the same as if it did not have a field width. If the field width is less than the character variable's length, then only the number of characters indicated by the width are read or written. For input, the data is read and assigned to the left-most part of the character variable with blanks added on the right to fill out the variable. For example, consider the following statements:

```
      CHARACTER*4 N
      READ(5,101) N
  101 FORMAT(A2)
```

In this example N has length four but its value is read in format A2. Assume that the input data is punched as follows:

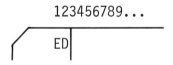

The READ statement will read the first two columns of the input card, assign the data to N, and fill out the value of N with blanks. Hence N will be EDbb (b = blank) after execution of the READ statement. On output, only the left-most characters of the variable are printed up to the width given in the A-format code. Thus, if N is equal to JOHN and we write it in format A2, then the letters JO will be printed.

If the field width is greater than the length of the character variable then, for input, the entire field will be read. However, the value assigned to the variable will be taken from the right-most part of the field. For example, consider the following statements:

```
      CHARACTER*4 N
      READ(5,103) N
  104 FORMAT(A10)
```

In this example N is of length four but the field is ten columns in length. Assume that the input data is punched as follows:

123456789....

```
  /    JOHN SMITH|
 (                |
```

All ten characters will be read from the card but only the right-most four will be assigned to N. Hence, after execution of the READ statement, N will have a value of MITH. On output, if the field width is greater than the length of the character variable, then the data is printed right justified. For example, assume that the following statements appear after the READ statement above:

WRITE(6,103) N
103 FORMAT(1X,A8)

Then the output will be as follows:

123456789...

```
  |          |
  |     MITH |
```

Formatted Character I/O with Numeric Variables

With formatted character I/O using numeric variables, either real or integer variable names may refer to the input and output data. The A-format code describes the input or output format. The general form of the A-format code for this type of character I/O is as follows:

Aw

where w is the field width.

The code may be used for both input and output.

The following statements illustrate the use of A-format for input:

READ(5,115) D1,D2,D3
115 FORMAT(2A4,A2)

The effect of execution of this READ statement is to cause three fields to be read (A4 is used two times and A2 once). The data from the fields are assigned to the variables named D1, D2, and D3. The first two fields (2A4) are each four columns wide; the third field (A2) occupies two columns. Assume that the input card read by this READ statement is punched as follows:

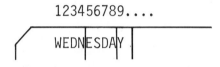

After execution, the variable named D1 has the value WEDN, D2 has the value ESDA, and D3 is Yb, where b stands for a blank.

When A-format is used for output the current values of the variable names in the WRITE statement list are printed. For example, consider the following statements:

```
WRITE(6,116) D1,D2,D3
116 FORMAT(1X,2A4,A2)
```

If this WRITE statement is executed after the previous READ statement, then the output will be as follows:

Note that a 1X code is used at the beginning of the FORMAT statement to skip the first character in this output record.

One problem with A-format that is of no concern when using other format codes is the maximum allowable field width. The maximum field width depends on the type of computer being used and whether the variable name that identifies the field is integer or real. Since a maximum field width of four characters is common, it is used here for illustrative purposes.

If the field width is greater than the limit, only the maximum number of characters is read or written. For input, the data is taken from the right-most part of the field. For example, if the format code is A10, the first six characters are skipped and the last four are read. With output, the data is right-justified in the field. Thus, if the format code A8 is used, four print positions are skipped and the data is printed in the remaining four positions.

When the field width is less than the maximum, only the number of characters specified is read or written. For example, the READ and FORMAT statements from the beginning of this section could be coded as follows:

```
    READ(5,114) D1,D2,D3,D4,D5,D6,D7,D8,D9,D10
114 FORMAT(10A1)
```

However, unless there is a special reason for using this approach, it should be avoided since excessive internal storage is used for the data.

One of the main uses of A-format is to manipulate character data. For example, data can be read in one format, then rearranged when it is written. To illustrate, assume that a person's last name is punched in the first 12 columns of an input card and his or her initials are punched in columns 13 and 14. We wish to print the name with the initials first, punctuated and separated by blanks. The following sequence of statements accomplishes this:

```
    READ(5,125) S1,S2,S3,I1,I2
125 FORMAT(3A4,2A1)
    WRITE(6,126) I1,I2,S1,S2,S3
126 FORMAT(1X,A1,1H.,1X,A1,1H.,1X,3A4)
```

Assume that the input card is punched with the following data:

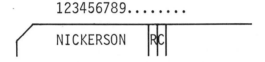

After execution of the statements in the example, the output appears as

```
    123456789...........
   ┌─────────────────────────
   │  R. C. NICKERSON
```

An Illustrative Program with Formatted I/O

Figure 7-5 shows a complete program with character I/O and other features discussed in this chapter. Input to the program consists of one card for each student giving his or her identification number in columns 1 through 4, name in columns 5 through 20, and scores on three tests in three successive four-column fields. Output consists of a main heading, headings for the columns of output, and one line for each input record giving the input data and the total and average of the test scores. The program stops when there is no more input data. Figure 7-5(a) shows the program using a character variable for the character I/O. In

```
      CHARACTER*16 NAME
      WRITE(6,200)
      WRITE(6,210)
   10 READ(5,100) ID,NAME,TS1,TS2,TS3
      TOTAL=TS1+TS2+TS3
      AVE=TOTAL/3.0
      WRITE(6,220) ID,NAME,TS1,TS2,TS3,TOTAL,AVE
      GO TO 10
   20 STOP
  100 FORMAT(I4,A16,3F4.0)
  200 FORMAT(1H1,26X,19HTEST SCORE ANALYSIS)
  210 FORMAT(1H0,6HNUMBER,5X,12HSTUDENT NAME,5X,6HTEST 1,3X,
     1            6HTEST 2,3X,6HTEST 3,3X,5HTOTAL,3X,7HAVERAGE)
  220 FORMAT(1H ,1X,I4,4X,A16,4X,F4.0,5X,F4.0,5X,F4.0,4X,F5.0,4X,F5.1)
      END
```

(a)

```
      WRITE(6,200)
      WRITE(6,210)
   10 READ(5,100) ID,N1,N2,N3,N4,TS1,TS2,TS3
      TOTAL=TS1+TS2+TS3
      AVE=TOTAL/3.0
      WRITE(6,220) ID,N1,N2,N3,N4,TS1,TS2,TS3,TOTAL,AVE
      GO TO 10
   20 STOP
  100 FORMAT(I4,4A4,3F4.0)
  200 FORMAT(1H1,26X,19HTEST SCORE ANALYSIS)
  210 FORMAT(1H0,6HNUMBER,5X,12HSTUDENT NAME,5X,6HTEST 1,3X,
     1            6HTEST 2,3X,6HTEST 3,3X,5HTOTAL,3X,7HAVERAGE)
  220 FORMAT(1H ,1X,I4,4X,4A4,4X,F4.0,5X,F4.0,5X,F4.0,4X,F5.0,4X,F5.1)
      END
```

(b)

TEST SCORE ANALYSIS

NUMBER	STUDENT NAME	TEST 1	TEST 2	TEST 3	TOTAL	AVERAGE
1841	JOHNSON ROBERT	78.	92.	83.	253.	84.3
1906	SMITH MARY	100.	95.	97.	292.	97.3
2133	ANDERSON RICHARD	65.	72.	57.	194.	64.7
2784	WILSON ALEX	73.	69.	78.	220.	73.3
2895	BOYD DEAN	42.	56.	47.	145.	48.3
3047	EMERY ELIZABETH	91.	100.	92.	283.	94.3
3260	COLE JAMES	75.	78.	73.	226.	75.3
3335	GUINN DOROTHY	86.	82.	74.	242.	80.7
3819	JONES ED	71.	85.	78.	234.	78.0

(c)

FIGURE 7-5. An illustrative program: (a) the program using a character variable for character I/O; (b) the program using numeric variables for character I/O; (c) the output.

Fig. 7-5(b) the same program appears using numeric variables for the character data.

The first WRITE statement in the program prints the main heading after skipping to the top of the next page. The next WRITE statement prints the column headings after double spacing. The READ statement reads the input data including the student's name. A-format is used in statement 100 for the character data. After calculating the total and average, the results are printed along with the input data. The student's name is printed using A-format in statement 220. This output line is single spaced from the previous line. The program then branches to the READ statement to get the next input record. Notice that the headings are printed outside of the loop so that they are only printed once. Figure 7-5(c) shows how the output appears.

7-4. ADDITIONAL FORMAT-FREE I/O FEATURES

There are several additional features that are available with format-free I/O. In this section we describe these features.

With format-free input any valid constant is acceptable as an input value. The only restriction is that the constant's type must be the same as the type of the variable name in the I/O list. Thus we can read integer, real, or character data from an input card. In addition, a *null value* can be specified on a data card. This is done by punching two successive commas. In effect, this indicates that no value is to be read for the corresponding variable name in the I/O list. As a result, the value of the variable name is unchanged. For example, assume that the following READ statement appears in a program:

```
READ *,A,I,J,B
```

If we wish to read the values 12.5, 63, and 85.4 for A, I, and B respectively but not change the value of J, then we would punch the input data as follows:

```
123456789.......

       12.5,63,,85.4
```

The two commas in the place where a value for J should appear indicate that the no value is to be read for J. Hence, after execution of this statement the value of J is whatever it was before the statement was executed.

If the values to be read for several successive variables in an I/O list are the same, then the constant can be punched once with a *duplication factor*. The factor indicates how many times the constant is to be repeated. For example, assume that we have the following READ statement in a program:

$$\text{READ *,A,B,C,D,E}$$

We wish to read the value zero for each of the five variable names in the I/O list. One way to do this is to punch the input data with five zeros separated by commas or blanks. However, since the same value is to be read for each of the five variables, we can use a duplication factor of five on the data card. This factor is followed by an asterisk and then the constant to be duplicated which is 0.0 in this example. Thus the input card can be punched as follows:

```
123456789...
        5*0.0
```

The effect is as if 0.0 were punched on the card five times. We can use a duplication factor with any type of constant (integer, real, or character). In addition, we can duplicate a null value by not punching any value after the asterisk. We can have unduplicated constants along with ones with duplication factors on the same card. Thus, the following input card is acceptable:

```
123456789.....................
     3.5,4*,'JOHN',3*'MARY',2*1
```

The first value read is 3.5. Then four null values appear. Next the character constant 'JOHN' is read followed by 'MARY' which is repeated three times. Finally, two 1's are read.

Sometimes we wish to stop reading before reaching the end of the I/O list. For example, assume that we have the following statement in a program:

$$\text{READ *,I,J,K,X,Y,Z}$$

We wish to read values for I, J, and K, but not for X, Y, and Z. In effect, we want to supply null values for X, Y, and Z. One way to do this is to punch the card with extra commas for the null values as follows:

```
123456789...
/
  5,6,7,,,,
|
```

An easier approach is to use a slash (/) after the last constant on the data card. That is, the card can be punched as follows:

```
123456789...
/
  5,6,7/
|
```

This has the effect of stopping execution of the READ statement after the last constant has been read and assigned to its corresponding variable name.

With format-free output, any valid variable name can be used in the I/O list. Thus we can print the value of an integer, real, or character variable. We can also put any acceptable constant in the list. We have seen this already with character constants but we can also print the value of an integer or real constant. For example, the following PRINT statement is valid:

$$\text{PRINT } *,1,I,T,98.6$$

In addition to the values of the variables I and T, the constants 1 and 98.6 are printed. We can also use expressions in the list. For example, the following PRINT statement is valid:

$$\text{PRINT } *,I+J,7.5-3.2*A$$

The effect is that any expression is first evaluated and then the resulting value is printed.

7-5. ADDITIONAL FORMATTED I/O FEATURES

Several additional features for formatted I/O are often used. These are described in this section.

End-of-File Specifier

The end-of-file specifier is used to indicate what is to be done when there is no more input data. In most of the examples in Chapters

2 through 5 we have included a loop that repeats the main part of the program so that more than one set of input can be processed. However, whenever one of these programs is run, an execution error will occur when the input file is out of data. The end-of-file specifier is used to overcome this error.

The general form of the end-of-file specifier is as follows:

END = *statement number*

The specifier is included in the parenthesized part of the READ statement after the FORMAT statement number. For example, the following READ statement shows the use of an end-of-file specifier:

READ(5,100,END=50) A,B,C

The effect of the specifier is that if, when the READ statement is executed, no more input data is available (that is, the end of the input file has been reached), then the program branches to the statement whose number appears in the end-of-file specifier. Thus in this example, if there is no more input data, then the program branches to statement 50.

We can use an end-of-file specifier in many of the programs in the previous chapters. For example, the following program appears in Fig. 3–11(b):

```
10  READ(5,100) ID,SCR1,SCR2
    WRITE(6,200) ID,SCR1,SCR2
    GO TO 10
100 FORMAT(...)
200 FORMAT(...)
    END
```

This program will stop with an execution error when it runs out of data. However, if we add an end-of-file specifier that branches to a STOP statement, then the program will terminate in a normal fashion. The following is the modified program:

```
10  READ(5,100,END=20) ID,SCR1,SCR2
    WRITE(6,200) ID,SCR1,SCR2
    GO TO 10
20  STOP
100 FORMAT(...)
200 FORMAT(...)
    END
```

When the end of the input file is reached, this program branches to statement 20 and stops execution.

Group Repetition

In Section 3-5 we discussed the use of the repeat specification to indicate that a format code should be repeated. When a group of format codes is to be repeated, the group may be enclosed in parentheses and a repeat specification placed in front of the group. For example, consider the following FORMAT statement:

$$57 \ \text{FORMAT}(F8.3,I4,F8.3,I4,F12.2)$$

In this statement, the group F8.3,I4 is repeated twice. This may be shortened to the following:

$$57 \ \text{FORMAT}(2(F8.3,I4),F12.2)$$

Notice that the F12.2 is not part of the group and therefore does not appear within the parentheses of the group.

Group repetition may also be used to repeat literal data for output. For example, the following causes 80 asterisks to be printed at the top of the page:

$$\text{WRITE}(6,58)$$
$$58 \ \text{FORMAT}(1H1,80(1H*))$$

In some versions of FORTRAN only one level of group repetition is allowed. In other versions, a repeated group may be included within another group. This is called *nested group repetition*. For example, the following FORMAT statement has nested group repetition:

$$59 \ \text{FORMAT}(2(F8.1,3(I2,I3),F8.2))$$

The innermost group (I2, I3) is repeated three times for each repetition of the outer group. Thus, this statement is equivalent to the following:

$$59 \ \text{FORMAT}(F8.1,I2,I3,I2,I3,I2,I3,F8.2,F8.1,I2,I3,I2,I3,I2,I3,F8.2)$$

New Record Specification

So far, a comma has been used in the FORMAT statement to separate format codes. However, it is also possible to use a slash (/) or several slashes between format codes. Whenever a slash is encountered in a list of format codes, the computer begins a new record; that is, it begins reading a new card or line from a terminal, or writing a new print line. For example, the following statements cause four values to be read, each from a separate card:

```
    READ(5,60) A,B,C,D
 60 FORMAT(F10.2/F10.2/F10.2/F10.2)
```

In this example the computer reads the value of A from the first 10 columns of the first input card. Then the slash in the FORMAT statement tells the computer to begin a new record. Thus, the value of B is read from the first 10 columns of the second card. Then the next slash starts a new record, and so on until all of the data has been read.

For output, the first character of a record is the carriage control character and is not printed. Thus, the first character in a record that follows a slash must be a carriage control character. For example, the following statements cause two lines to be printed with double spacing between the lines:

```
    WRITE(6,61) I,J,K,L
 61 FORMAT(1H1,2I5/1H0,2I5)
```

The values for I and J are on the first line; the values for K and L are printed on the second line. The 1H0 following the slash is required to control the carriage before printing the second line.

Multiple slashes may also be used to skip several cards or lines. If *n* slashes appear at the beginning or end of the FORMAT statement, then *n* input records are skipped or *n* blank records are inserted between output records. If *n* slashes appear elsewhere in the statement, then one less than *n* records are skipped or blank records inserted. For example, the following statements cause four cards to be skipped, then two values read from the next card, then two cards skipped, and one value read from the succeeding card:

```
    READ(5,62) AMT,KNT,DUE
 62 FORMAT(////F6.2,I3///F10.2)
```

Underloading An I/O List

For each variable name in an input or output list, there must be a corresponding format code in the FORMAT statement. It is possible to have more format codes than there are variable names however. This is called underloading an I/O list. When this happens, the computer reads or writes only the number of values specified in the I/O list. That is, the controlling factor is the number of variable names in the I/O list. Additional format codes in the FORMAT statement are not used (except for any H-format that might be specified immediately following the last numeric code).

There is an advantage in underloading an I/O list in that a single FORMAT statement can be used by several READ or WRITE statements with differing numbers of variable names in their lists. As an illustration, consider the following statements:

```
      READ(5,15) J,B
   15 FORMAT(I5,5X,F10.4)
      READ(5,16) K
   16 FORMAT(I5)
```

Since the fields that contain the values of J and K are in identical positions on two separate cards, both READ statements can refer to the same FORMAT statement:

```
      READ(5,15) J,B
      READ(5,15) K
   15 FORMAT(I5,5X,F10.4)
```

The first READ statement uses all of the format codes. The second READ statement has an underloaded input list and uses only the first format code.

Overloading An I/O List

The opposite of underloading is overloading an I/O list. In this case there are more variable names in the I/O list than there are format codes. As always, the controlling factor is the number of variable names in the I/O list. When there is no group repetition the rule that applies is that if there are more variable names after the available format codes are used, then control returns to the beginning of the FORMAT statement, a new record is begun, and the same format codes are used again. For example, consider the following sequence of statements:

```
      WRITE(6,70) A,B,C,D,E
   70 FORMAT(1H0,F6.2,F8.3,F4.1)
```

In executing the WRITE statement, the value of A is written in format F6.2 after double spacing, B is written in format F8.3, and C is written in format F4.1. At this point, no more format codes are available, so the computer returns control to the beginning of the format codes and starts a new record. Since a new record is begun, the first character in the record is considered carriage control. Thus the 1H0 code causes double spacing. Then D is printed in format F6.2 and E is printed in format F8.3. At this point, the execution of the WRITE statement terminates. An alternate way of accomplishing the same thing is with a slash in the FORMAT statement. The following statement yields the same result as before:

```
70 FORMAT(1H0,F6.2,F8.3,F4.1/1H0,F6.2,F8.3)
```

The advantage of the overloading technique is most apparent with large volumes of data. For example, consider the following:

```
   READ(5,71) X1,X2,X3,X4,X5,X6,X7
71 FORMAT(F12.3)
```

This FORMAT statement, coupled with the READ statement, causes seven cards to be read. The first card contains the value of X1 in format F12.3. Then, since there are no more format codes, a new card that contains the value of X2 in format F12.3 is read. This continues until all variable names in the input list are satisfied.

If there is group repetition in the FORMAT statement, control returns to the beginning of the last major group when an I/O list is overloaded. For example, consider the following statements:

```
   READ(1,72) A1,A2,A3,A4,A5,B1,B2,B3,B4
72 FORMAT(F8.2,2(F4.2,F10.4))
```

In this example, the values of the first five variable names are read from one card. Since there are more variable names in the input list, control returns to the beginning of the group repetition specification and the values for the next four variable names are read from a new card. In effect, this FORMAT statement is equivalent to

```
72 FORMAT(F8.2,F4.2,F10.4,F4.2,F10.4/F4.2,F10.4,F4.2,F10.4)
```

PROGRAMMING PROBLEMS

The following problems are exercises in the topics of this chapter. In addition, many of the problems in previous chapters can be completed with headings or other descriptive output, carriage control, and character input and output.

1. The results of a questionnaire survey need to be printed in sentence

form. The data consists of the sample identification number, the number of questionnaires processed, and the average age of the respondents. The output should appear as follows:

```
RESULTS FROM SAMPLE XXXXX.
WITH XXX QUESTIONNAIRES PROCESSED,
THE AVERAGE AGE OF THE RESPONDENTS IS XX.X YEARS.
```

(X's represent the location of output fields.) Input data is punched in two cards. The first card contains the sample number and the number of questionnaires. The second card contains the average age.

Write a FORTRAN program to prepare the specified output from the input. Test the program using 10083 for the sample number, 253 for the number of questionnaires, and 37.3 for the average age.

2. A summary of a student's grades is needed. The information is punched in two cards. The first card contains a one-digit value representing the semester followed by a two-digit value representing the year. The second card contains the student's identification number followed by five pairs of fields where each pair represents a course number and the grade received in the course. The course numbers are four digits in length. The grades are each punched in a three-column field with one decimal position. (For example, 4.0 is an A, 3.7 is an A-, 3.3 is a B+, etc.) A sample of how the output should appear is shown:

SUMMARY OF GRADES FOR STUDENT NUMBER 4837
Semester 1   Year 1980

Course	Grade
1308	4.0
5872	2.3
1591	3.0
2811	2.7
4605	3.3

Write a FORTRAN program to prepare this summary of grades from the specified input. Use the data shown in the sample output above to test the program.

3. A tabulation of a statistical survey of voter preference by age groups is needed. A sample of how the output should appear follows:

AGE GROUP	18–20	21–30	31–45	46–60	OVER 60
CANDIDATE X	64.7%	59.1%	41.8%	18.2%	10.1%
CANDIDATE Y	21.5%	27.3%	43.0%	67.5%	65.3%
CANDIDATE Z	2.3%	4.2%	10.6%	10.3%	18.7%
UNDECIDED	11.5%	9.4%	4.6%	4.0%	5.9%

Write a FORTRAN program to prepare the voter preference tabulation from input data consisting of one card for each age group giving the percentages for the four choices. In other words, there are five input cards, each punched with four fields. Test the program with the data shown in the sample output.

4. A graphic representation of a student's class schedule is:

TIME	8-9	9-10	10-11	11-12	12-1	1-2	2-2	3-4
MONDAY	1	0	0	1	0	1	1	1
TUESDAY	0	1	1	1	0	0	0	0
WEDNESDAY	1	0	0	1	0	1	1	1
THURSDAY	0	1	1	1	0	0	0	0
FRIDAY	1	0	0	1	0	0	0	0

The digit 1 indicates hours when the student is in class; the digit 0 indicates hours when he or she is out of class.

Write a FORTRAN program that produces this graphic output. Input to the program is one card for each day with the student's study schedule for that day punched as a series of ones and zeros. Use the data shown in the preceding graph to test the program.

5. Write a program that reads and prints a list of names. Each name is punched in the first eighteen columns of a card. Supply six to eight names as test data for the program.

6. Write a program that reads a person's first name, middle initial, and last name. Print the name with the last name first, followed by a comma, and then the first name and the middle initial. Supply several names as test data for the program.

7. Write a program that reads a name of up to six characters. Then print the name on a diagonal. For example, the name ROBERT should print as follows:

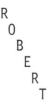

Supply several names to test the program.

8. A palindrome is a word, phrase, or number that reads the same forward or backward. For example, "Mom" is a palindrome. Write a program that reads a group of ten characters and prints the characters both forwards and backwards to check if it is palindromic. Use the following data to test the program:

    RADAR
    TOOT TOOT
    1881
    ABLE WAS I
    DAD
    PALINDROME
    33-22-33

Chapter 8

PROGRAM DEVELOPMENT

In previous chapters we have discussed different aspects of the process of developing computer programs. Many of the ideas about program development were presented without explanation while illustrating some feature of FORTRAN. In this chapter we bring together these ideas and discuss program development in detail.

8-1. PROGRAM STRUCTURE

A central aspect of program development is the concept of program structure. The *structure* of a program is the way in which the instructions in the program are organized. When a programmer develops a FORTRAN program he or she builds a structure of FORTRAN statements. If the structure is well built, then the program is correct, easy to understand, and easily modified. On the other hand, a poorly structured program may have errors that are difficult to detect, or it may be hard to read or troublesome to change.

There are three basic structures of statements in a program: sequence structures, decision structures, and loop structures. They are illustrated in Figure 8-1. In a *sequence structure*, the statements are executed in the order in which they are written, one after the other. For example, a series of assignment statements that performs some calculation is a sequence structure. A *decision structure* (also called *selection* or *alternation*) is used to decide which of two other structures is to be executed next based on some logical condition. In FORTRAN, the IF statement, coupled with the necessary GO TO statements, may be used to create a decision structure. If the condition in the IF statement is true, then one group of statements is executed; otherwise

204

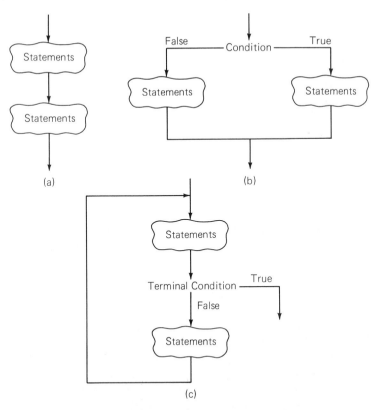

FIGURE 8-1. Basic program structures: (a) sequence
structures; (b) decision structure; (c)
loop structure.

another set of statements is performed. (The block IF statements, if
available, also create a decision structure.) In a *loop structure* (also
called *repetition* or *iteration*), a group of statements is executed repeatedly until some condition indicates that the loop should be terminated. In FORTRAN we use a GO TO statement at the end of a set of
statements to branch to the beginning and thus create a loop. The loop
is controlled by checking a condition in an IF statement each time the
loop is executed. (The WHILE statement, when available, also creates
a loop structure. In addition, the DO statement forms a special type of
loop structure.)

Figure 8-1 summarizes the three basic structures. Figure 8-1(a)
shows a sequence structure in which one group of statements is performed after another. In Fig. 8-1(b), a decision structure is shown in
which one of two alternative groups of statements is executed based on
some condition. We can also create a one-sided decision by not executing any statements when the condition is false (see Fig. 5-6). The loop
structure in Fig. 8-1(c) is such that a group of statements is executed,

then a terminal condition is checked, and then another group of statements is executed before repeating the pattern. If no statements are performed in the loop before the terminal condition is checked, then we have a pre-test pattern (see Fig. 6–7(b)). Similarly, if the structure is such that there are not any statements executed after the condition is checked, then the pattern is that of a post-test loop (see Fig. 6–7(c)).

One characteristic that is common to all of these structures is that there is only one way of entering each structure and only one way of leaving. That is, it is not possible to branch into the middle of any of the structures or to branch out of any structure in more than one place. We say that each structure has one *entry point* and one *exit point*. We will see that this is an important characteristic of these structures.

Within a structure, we can embed any other structure that we need. This is the idea of nesting that we have discussed in relation to decisions and loops. In fact, we can nest any structure within any other. For example, within a loop we may have a sequence of statements, decision structures, and other loops. Within a decision structure we can have sequences, loops, and other decisions. In terms of the diagrams in Fig. 8–1, this means that we can substitute any structure for any block of statements within any structure.

We can use this idea of nesting to build a program as shown in Fig. 8–2. We might start with a single block and substitute a loop for it. Then we replace the statements at the beginning of the loop with a decision and the statements at the end with a sequence. Finally, we nest a loop in the decision. We can continue in this manner to build arbitrarily complex programs. Notice, however, that because each structure has one entry point and one exit point, the final program has only one entry point (that is, one point where execution of the program starts) and one exit point (that is, one point where the program stops execution).

There are other program structures that can appear in a program. For example, a computed GO TO statement can be used to create a special type of selection known as a *case structure*. However, we can accomplish the same thing as the computed GO TO statement by using nested IF statements. In fact, *any* other structure can be created out of the three basic structures. This fact was proven by two computer scientists. They showed that any program that has a single entry point and a single exit point can be written using just the three basic structures.[†] Thus, if we know how to create these structures in a programming language, then we don't need any other structures.

[†]C. Böhm and G. Jacopini, "Flow Diagrams, Turing Machines and Languages with Only Two Formation Rules," *Communications of the ACM*, 9, 5 (May 1966), 366–71. In proving their result, Böhm and Jacopini used a different loop structure from the one shown in Fig. 8–1(c). However, it can be shown that the general loop structure in the text can be constructed from the Böhm and Jacopini structures.

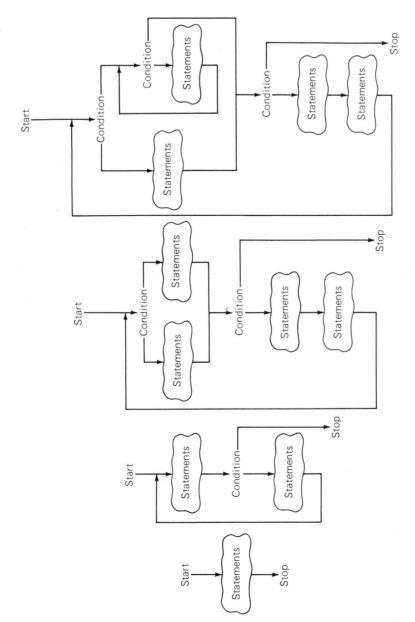

FIGURE 8-2. Nesting program structures.

8-2. PROGRAM UNDERSTANDABILITY

In Section 3-9 we discussed the importance of producing an understandable program. A program must be easily understood because people, including the original programmer, must understand the program in order to correct, modify, and enhance it.

Program structure can contribute greatly to program understandability. The problem with trying to understand the logic of a complex program is that there are really two versions of the program. One is the *static* version that is represented by the listing of the program on paper. The other version is the *dynamic* form of the program that can only be understood by following the logic of the program as it is being executed. When a programmer reads a source listing he or she is reading the static form of the program. As with the lines in a book, each statement is normally read in sequence from the top of the page down. The dynamic version may be different from the static version because the statements are not executed in the order in which they are written. For example, when a GO TO statement is encountered in a program, the next statement in the dynamic version of the program (that is, the statement to which the program branches) is not the same as the next statement in the static version (which is the next statement in sequence). To understand the dynamic version, the programmer may have to jump all over the source listing instead of reading the program sequentially.

One of the basic principles of producing understandable programs is to make the dynamic version of the program as close as possible to the static form. The ideal situation is to have the program execute from top to bottom just as it is read. However, if branching is required this is not possible. The next best situation is to have the program execute from top to bottom through a sequence of basic program structures. That is, the program first executes the statements in one structure (for example, a loop), then executes the statements in the next structure (such as a decision), and so on to the end of the program. Of course, other structures may be nested in these structures, as we saw in the last section. But this top-to-bottom execution using only the three basic program structures brings the dynamic version of the program as close as possible to the static form. In addition, we know that we can solve any problem using just these three structures.

The structure of a program can be greatly complicated by the uncontrolled use of GO TO statements. The problem with GO TO statements is that we don't always know where we came from. Although this may sound funny, it makes a lot of sense. For example, assume that we are trying to understand the conditions under which a particular statement is executed. If it is possible to branch to that statement from a number of different points in the program, then we don't know how we got to the statement without going back to all of the GO TO statements that branched to it. The logic may become even more complex if there are multiple ways to get to each of these GO TO statements. (There is a famous letter entitled "GO TO Statement Considered Harmful" which discusses this point of view.[†])

The ultimate situation would be to eliminate all GO TO statements from the program. In FORTRAN this can be done if the block IF and WHILE statements are available. Since the former is used for decision making and the latter for loop control, we have a sufficient set of control structures. We can write any program we want using these. There need not be any GO TO statements in such a program and the only statement numbers required would be those for FORMAT statements. Figure 6-11 showed an example of such a program. (Although it is not necessary, we may also want to use a DO statement for loop control. Then a statement number is needed for the CONTINUE statement at the end of the loop.)

If the block IF and WHILE statements are not available, then the equivalent structures must be created using IF statements and GO TO statements. The various patterns were shown in Figs. 5-4, 5-8, and 6-8. In Fig. 8-3 the patterns that are equivalent to the block IF statements and WHILE loops are given. Although these structures require the use of GO TO statements, the logic of the program is kept as simple as possible if we only use GO TO statements in the particular way that is shown.

To summarize, the basic approach to producing understandable programs is to design the program so that it executes from top to bottom and only uses sequences, decisions, and loops.

8-3. PROGRAM STYLE

Program style refers to those characteristics of a program that make it easier to read and hence easier to understand. In previous chapters we have mentioned a number of style rules. The following are some of the rules that have been discussed plus a few that have not been previously mentioned:

1. Use meaningful variable names. This helps the programmer remember what each name refers to.

[†] Dijkstra, Edsger W., "GO TO Statement Considered Harmful," *Communications of the ACM*, 11, 3 (March 1968), 147-148. The letter begins with the statement, "For a number of years I have been familiar with the observation that the quality of programmers is a decreasing function of the density of *go to* statements in the programs they produce."

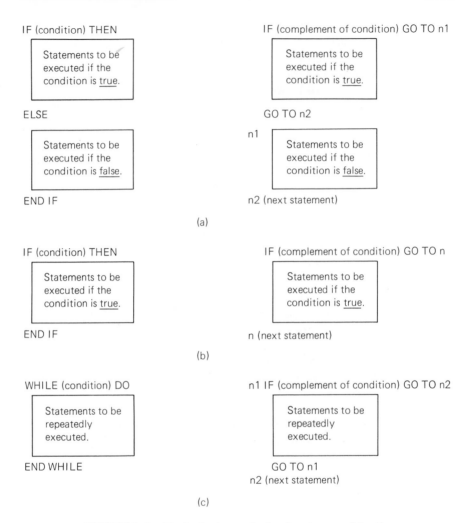

FIGURE 8-3. Equivalent control structures: (a) the
IF-THEN-ELSE structure; (b) the IF-
THEN structure; (c) the WHILE loop.

2. Use statement numbers that increase in sequence through the
   program. This helps the programmer locate statements in a
   large program.
3. Assign statement numbers in some logical pattern. For example,
   the statements in the first section of the program may be assigned numbers between 100 and 199, the statements in the
   second section may be assigned numbers between 200 and 299,
   and so forth for other sections of the program.
4. Put all FORMAT statements at the end of the program and

number them accordingly (for example, with numbers between 900 and 999).

5. Use parentheses in expressions to show the order of evaluation even if they are not needed.

6. Don't use the arithmetic IF statement if possible.

7. Always terminate a DO loop with a CONTINUE statement.

Program style can also help display the structure of the program. If block IF statements are used, then the true and false parts should be indented several columns. This helps the programmer see the structure more quickly. Similarly with WHILE loops, the statements in the loop should be indented. Indentation should also be used with DO loops.

When IF and GO TO statements must be used for decision and loop structures, then indentation may help show the structure or it may make the logic more confusing. This depends to a large extent on the individual programmer. Some programmers advocate using a CONTINUE statement as the target of each GO TO statement. Although we have only used CONTINUE statements at the end of DO loops so far, it is possible to put a CONTINUE statement at any point in a program. If we branch to a CONTINUE statement or reach one in the normal sequential execution of the program, then the computer just goes on to the next statement in sequence (unless, of course, the CONTINUE statement is the last statement in a DO loop). Using this style and indentation, we would write the program in Fig. 6-11 as shown in Fig. 8-4. Whether or not this style is used depends on the individual preference of the programmer.

Another way of improving the readability of a program is to use comments to explain the function of different parts of the program. In Chapter 2 we mentioned that a comment can be placed anywhere in the program by coding a C in column 1. We have purposefully avoided using comments in our illustrative programs so as to concentrate on the logic of the program. However, as programs become more complex, comments can help explain the program.

The basic principle in using comments is that each comment should explain some characteristic of the program that is not immediately obvious. Usually there should be a comment before each important loop or decision in the program indicating the function of the code that follows. For example, in the program in Fig. 8-4 we might insert the following comment before statement 10:

```
C     REPEAT INPUT LOOP UNTIL TRAILER CARD IS READ
```

While the information in this comment can be gleaned from the pro-

```
      READ(5,100) ID,UNITS
 10 CONTINUE
      IF(ID.EQ.9999) GO TO 40
        IF(UNITS.GT.12.0) GO TO 20
          TUIT=350.00
          GO TO 30
 20     CONTINUE
          TUIT=350.00+20.00*(UNITS-12.0)
 30     CONTINUE
        WRITE(6,200) ID,TUIT
        READ(5,100) ID,UNITS
        GO TO 10
 40 CONTINUE
      STOP
100 FORMAT(I4,F4.1)
200 FORMAT(1X,I4,3X,F7.2)
      END
```

FIGURE 8-4. A program with branching to CONTINUE statements.

gram, the comment makes the process of understanding the program easier. As another example we may put the following comment before the second IF statement in Fig. 8-4:

```
C          CALCULATE TUITION
```

This comment describes the function of the decision structure that follows.

A common mistake in using comments is to simply parrot the code that follows. For example, consider the following sequence that might be used in the program in Fig. 8-4:

```
C          SET TUITION EQUAL TO $350.00
           TUIT=350.00
```

The comment is unnecessary since it simply repeats the statement that follows. Another example of this unnecessary use of comments is the following:

```
C          INCREASE I BY 1
           I=I+1
```

Again, the comment merely echoes the next statement.

Another common problem with the use of comments is that a

comment may say one thing while the program does something else. This may be because the programmer wrote the comment incorrectly or wrote a correct comment but incorrect code, or perhaps because the code was modified sometime after the original program was written. When comments are used, it is essential that they correctly describe the program. Otherwise the programmer may read the comment and think the program does one thing while, in fact, it does something else. (Because of this, some programmers advocate deleting all comments while debugging a program.)

One test that is sometimes applied to determine if the comments in a program are sufficient is to just read the comments and not the code. If the basic logic of the program—but not the detail—can be understood from the comments, then the comments are sufficient. The problem with this test is that it sometimes results in too many comments or comments containing too much detail. By remembering that comments should help explain difficult parts of the program but not simply repeat the code, the best level of commenting can be achieved.

Besides describing how a program works, comments can be used to document important information about the program. This information includes such things as who wrote the program, when it was written, what the purpose of the program is, and what the variable names in the program mean. Usually such information is put into a block of comments at the beginning of the program. For example, the following comments might be used at the beginning of the program in Fig. 8-4:

```
C
C
C       TITLE: TUITION CALCULATION PROGRAM
C
C       PROGRAMMER: ROBERT C. NICKERSON
C       DATE: NOVEMBER 3, 1980
C
C       PURPOSE: THIS PROGRAM COMPUTES TUITION FOR A COLLEGE STUDENT
C                BASED ON THE NUMBER OF UNITS THAT THE STUDENT IS TAKING.
C
C       VARIABLE NAMES:
C           ID    = STUDENT IDENTIFICATION NUMBER (INPUT/OUTPUT)
C           UNITS = NUMBER OF UNITS (INPUT)
C           TUIT  = TUITION (OUTPUT)
C
```

Notice in this example that blank comment lines (that is, lines with just a C in column 1) are used to separate groups of comments. This helps make the comments more readable. Blank comment lines may also be used to separate groups of statements in the program and thus improve the readability of the code.

In this section we have given a number of rules to improve the readability of a program. There are many other rules of program style that are advocated. As the programmer becomes more experienced, he or she should investigate alternative approaches to program style. Then the programmer should select the style with which he or she is most comfortable and that at the same time makes the program readable and the logic understandable.[†]

8-4. PROGRAM REFINEMENT

Developing the logic of a complex program can be a difficult task. A technique that is often advocated is to develop the program through a sequence of refinement steps. The idea is to start with a general statement of the solution and to gradually refine this statement. Each refinement should bring the program closer to the final version. The last step in the process produces the coded program. This technique is often called *stepwise program refinement*.

To illustrate this technique we consider the problem of rearranging three real values into ascending (or increasing) numerical order. This process is called sorting. (In a later chapter we will see how to sort large amounts of data.) We assume that the three real numbers are input data. The numbers may be in any order initially. In the program we will refer to the numbers by the variable names V1, V2, and V3. The program must read values for V1, V2, and V3. Then it must rearrange the values so that V1 equals the smallest value, V2 is the middle value, and V3 equals the largest value. Finally the sorted values must be printed.

As a first step in developing the program we write the following:

```
        READ(5,100) V1,V2,V3
        Sort V1, V2, and V3 into ascending order.
        WRITE(6,200) V1,V2,V3
        STOP
100     FORMAT(3F4.0)
200     FORMAT(1X,3F4.0)
        END
```

This program is complete except for the second line, which is written in English, not FORTRAN. If we can refine this line to a set of FOR-

---

[†] A good place to start is with the book by Brian W. Kernighan and P. J. Plauger entitled *The Elements of Program Style* published by McGraw-Hill Book Company.

TRAN statements that accomplishes the sorting process, then the program will be complete.

One way to sort the three numbers is to move the largest value to V3 and then move the next largest value to V2. If this is done without destroying any of the values, then V1 will be equal to the smallest value. Hence the numbers will be sorted. For example, assume that initially the data is as follows:

        V1 = 7.0
        V2 = 9.0
        V3 = 5.0

Moving the largest value, 9.0, to V3 results in the data being rearranged into the following order:

        V1 = 7.0
        V2 = 5.0
        V3 = 9.0

Then moving the next largest value, 7.0, to V2 results in the following:

        V1 = 5.0
        V2 = 7.0
        V3 = 9.0

Thus, the smallest value, 5.0, is automatically moved to V1. Incorporating this refinement into our program we get the following:

```
READ(5,100) V1,V2,V3
Move largest value to V3.
Move next largest value to V2.
WRITE(6,200) V1,V2,V3
```

(We will leave out the other statements until the final version of the program.)

To move the largest value to V3, we first move the larger of V1 and V2 to V2, and then move the larger of V2 and V3 to V3. After doing this we move the next larger to V2 by moving the larger of V1 and V2 to V2. Hence the program can be refined again to the following:

```
READ(5,100) V1,V2,V3
Move larger of V1 and V2 to V2.
Move larger of V2 and V3 to V3.
Move larger of V1 and V2 to V2.
WRITE(6,200) V1,V2,V3
```

To move the larger of V1 and V2 to V2, we compare V1 and V2. Then if V1 is larger than V2, we switch the values of V1 and V2. In effect, we are asking if V1 and V2 are in proper sequence with respect to one another. If they are not, then we switch their values. We do similar comparisons and switching for V2 and V3 and again for V1 and V2. Incorporating this refinement into the program we get the following:

```
   READ(5,100) V1,V2,V3
   IF(V1.LE.V2) GO TO 10
      Switch V1 and V2.
10 IF(V2.LE.V3) GO TO 20
      Switch V2 and V3.
20 IF(V1.LE.V2) GO TO 30
      Switch V1 and V2.
30 WRITE(6,200) V1,V2,V3
```

The only thing that remains to complete the program is to include the necessary statements to switch the values of the variables. Figure 8-5 shows how the switching is done for V1 and V2. First V1 is assigned to a temporary variable, TEMP. Then V2 is assigned to V1. Finally, the value of TEMP is assigned to V2. Thus the following three statements are needed to switch the values of V1 and V2:

```
TEMP=V1
V1=V2
V2=TEMP
```

Writing similar sets of statements for the other switching steps and

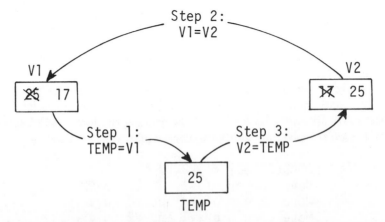

FIGURE 8-5. Switching the value of two variables.

```
      READ(5,100) V1,V2,V3
      IF(V1.LE.V2) GO TO 10
      TEMP=V1
      V1=V2
      V2=TEMP
   10 IF(V2.LE.V3) GO TO 20
      TEMP=V2
      V2=V3
      V3=TEMP
   20 IF(V1.LE.V2) GO TO 30
      TEMP=V1
      V1=V2
      V2=TEMP
   30 WRITE(6,200) V1,V2,V3
      STOP
  100 FORMAT(3F4.0)
  200 FORMAT(1X,3F4.0)
      END
```

FIGURE 8-6. The sorting program.

including these in the program, we get the final versions of the sorting program shown in Fig. 8-6.

To illustrate how the program works consider the following worst possible case:

    V1 = 9.0
    V2 = 7.0
    V3 = 5.0

The data is completely out of order. After the first switch the values will be as follows:

    V1 = 7.0
    V2 = 9.0
    V3 = 5.0

That is, the larger of V1 and V2 is moved to V2. After the next switch the values will be in the following order:

    V1 = 7.0
    V2 = 5.0
    V3 = 9.0

The larger of V2 and V3 is moved to V3. The effect of both switches is that the largest of all three is moved to V3. The final switch results in the following:

V1 = 5.0
V2 = 7.0
V3 = 9.0

The larger of V1 and V2 is moved to V2. In effect, the next largest of all three is moved to V2 and at the same time, the smallest value ends up in V1. Hence, the data is sorted.

This example illustrates how the techniques of stepwise refinement can be applied to a problem solution. The technique allows the programmer to concentrate on small parts of the program in successively more detail. The programmer does not try to figure out the whole solution at one time but rather thinks about the solution in pieces. This usually makes program development easier.

8-5. THE PROGRAMMING PROCESS

At the end of Chapter 2 we discussed briefly the process of preparing a computer program. We mentioned five activities that make up the programming process. These activities are:

1. Understanding and defining the problem.
2. Designing the program.
3. Coding the program.
4. Showing that the program is correct.
5. Documenting the program.

In this section we discuss each of these activities in detail.

The five activities in the programming process are not necessarily performed in sequence. In fact, several activities usually take place at the same time. For example, later we will see that documenting begins when we are trying to define and understand the problem. In addition, we can begin to show correctness of the program during the designing activity. The activities are listed not in the order in which they are *started* but rather in the order in which they are *finished*. For example, we cannot finish designing the program until we have finished understanding and defining the problem. However, we may have started the designing activity before the first activity is finished. Similarly, final coding cannot be completed until program design is done, showing that the program is correct cannot be finished until coding is completed, and documentation cannot be finalized until all other activities have been completed.

Problem Definition

The first activity in the programming process is to understand and carefully define the problem to be solved. The most difficult step often is recognizing that a problem exists for which a programmed solution is appropriate. However, it is usually not the programmer's responsibility to recognize the need for a program to solve a problem. Most often the programmer receives a general statement of the problem, either verbally or in writing, and begins the programming process from that point.

At first the programmer should try to understand the problem as a whole. What is required by the problem? Usually this involves determining what output is to be produced. What data is available? Answering this question often involves determining what input data is to be processed. The programmer tries to get a general understanding of the problem as a whole without going into details about the input, the output, and the calculations.

After the programmer has a general understanding of the problem he or she should refine the problem definition to include specific information about input and output layouts, calculations, and logical operations. The refinement of the problem definition should continue until the programmer obtains sufficient detail to begin designing a solution. As a minimum the problem definition must give the following:

1. What output is to be produced and its layout.
2. What input data is available and its layout.
3. What computations are to be performed.
4. What logical conditions affect processing.

Sometimes the programmer may have difficulty understanding a given problem. When this happens it often helps to try to isolate parts of the problem and work with each part separately. Another approach is to think of a simpler but similar problem and try to understand it first. The programmer may get some insight from the simpler problem that helps explain the more complex problem.

Some problems cannot be solved with a computer. In mathematics there are a number of problems that we know do not have solutions. In addition, some problems may be too large for a computer or take too long to solve. Problems that cannot be solved do not often arise. However, we still must be careful in defining a problem to be sure that it is reasonable to attempt a programmed solution.

As an example of the programming process we are going to consider a variation of the test score averaging problem discussed in previous chapters. The problem is to calculate a weighted average of three test scores. We assume that the best test score counts 50%, the next best score is weighted 35%, and the worst test score only counts 15%. In addition to calculating the weighted average, the program must print the corresponding letter grade based on a straight percentage scale (that is, 90% to 100% is an A, 80% to 89% is a B, 70% to 79% is a C, 60% to 69% is a D, and 59% or less is an F).

Already we begin to have an understanding of the problem. A program is needed that produces a report giving the weighted average and letter grade for each student in a class. The input to the program must be three test scores. In addition, there must be some way of identifying the student to whom the scores belong (such as a student identification number). The program must determine which is the best test score, which score is worst, and which test score falls in between. Then the program must apply the appropriate percentages to arrive at the average. In addition, the program must determine which grade category the average falls into so that the appropriate letter grade can be printed.

We can refine the problem definition at this point to specify input and output formats. We may even assign variable names to the input and output data. An acceptable input format is as follows:

Card Columns	Field	Variable Name	Type
1–4	Identification number	ID	Integer
5–8	First test score	TS1	Real
9–12	Second test score	TS2	Real
13–16	Third test score	TS3	Real

For real values we need to be concerned with the number of decimal positions. In this example we will assume that each test score has no places to the right of the decimal point.

For the output format, we must be concerned with the print positions in which the data is printed. A useful tool is to use a piece of graph paper or a special form called a *print chart* to sketch the output. Figure 8–7 shows the output format for this program on a print chart. The numbers across the top give the print positions. Headings are written on the chart exactly as they are to be printed. Variable information, such as the student's identification number, average score, and letter grade are indicated by Xs in the print position in which they are to be printed. By sketching the output format first on a chart such as this it is much easier to code the necessary FORMAT statements.

A question that has not been considered is how the input loop is to be controlled. As we have seen, there are a number of techniques for

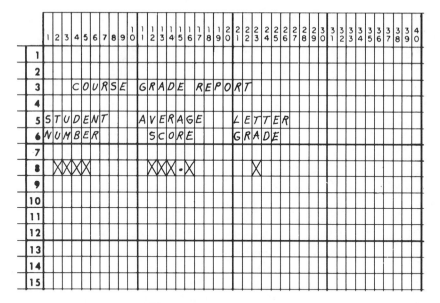

FIGURE 8-7. A print chart.

loop control. We will assume in this example that the last data card contains 9999 in the student number field and use this to control the loop.

Program Design

After the problem has been carefully defined, we can begin to design an appropriate program. The objective during the program designing activity is to devise a plan for a program that solves the problem. This does not mean that the program is coded at this stage. Before coding can begin a solution procedure must be developed. The procedure should, of course, be correct.

In general, a procedure for solving a problem is called an algorithm. An *algorithm* is a set of instructions that, if carried out, results in the solution of a problem. An algorithm may be represented in many forms. For example, an algorithm may be written in English or using mathematical notation. A recipe to bake a cake is an algorithm in a form that is understandable to a cook. A computer programming language is used to represent an algorithm so that it can be carried out by a computer.

During the program design activity an algorithm is developed to solve the problem. This is usually the most difficult task in the programming process and there are many strategies that help. One thing that is important is that the programmer have a repertoire of algorithms upon which he or she can draw. Then when a problem or a part of a problem requires a particular algorithm in the programmer's repertoire, he or she can quickly supply the appropriate procedure.

When a necessary algorithm is not known, then the programmer must devise one of his or her own. The use of stepwise program refinement, discussed in the last section, can help in designing an algorithm. In addition to producing the necessary algorithm, this procedure leads naturally to the use of basic control structures in nested patterns as discussed in Section 8-1. If the programmer sticks with the basic control structures during the refinement process, then the final program will have a single entry point and a single exit point, and will flow from top to bottom through a sequence of loops and decisions. Thus, this program refinement strategy not only helps in devising an algorithm but it also leads to the most understandable program.

When developing an algorithm it is important that the structure of the data be kept in mind. Although we have only worked with simple data structures so far, we can already see that an algorithm cannot be developed without knowing how the data is going to be organized. For example, the programmer must know the organization of the input and output files before developing an algorithm to do the necessary processing. In later chapters we will discuss more complex data structures and it will be seen that the algorithm depends on the structure of the data. Thus the development of an algorithm is *not* independent of the development of the data structure.

Many times alternative algorithms are developed. Then the question of which algorithm to select becomes important. The objective is to select the best algorithm that correctly solves the problem. However, which algorithm is "best" depends on trade-offs among such factors as speed of execution, storage utilization, and algorithm understandability.

Sometimes it is difficult to devise an algorithm for a problem. When this happens it often helps to think of a related problem and try to develop an algorithm for it. Another approach is to simplify the problem by discarding some of the conditions and then try to develop an algorithm for the simpler version. Sometimes it is necessary to go back to the problem definition and see if anything has been left out. Any of these approaches may help the programmer develop an algorithm for the problem.

There are various tools that are available to help in developing an algorithm. One tool that is sometimes used is a flowchart. A *flowchart* is a graphical representation of the logic in an algorithm. Many programmers find it helpful to draw a flowchart of the algorithm so they can see the logic pictorially. Then the program can be coded from the flowchart. In Appendix E we discuss program flowcharting in detail.

When a program is especially large it often helps to divide the program into sections or *modules*. Each module performs some function related to the overall processing of the program. The advantage of this modular programming is that each module can be worked on separately. The programmer can develop an algorithm for each module without worrying about the logic of the other modules. In addition, each module can be coded and tested before going on to the next module. Thus errors are isolated and easier to locate with modular programming.

When programming in a modular fashion each module can be thought of as a subalgorithm. The logic of a module can be developed through stepwise refinement. Using only the three basic control structures results in a module with only one entry point and one exit point. The exit point for one module then leads to the entry point of the next module. Thus the complete program is a sequence of modules. (A related idea is the use of subroutines to modularize a program. FORTRAN subroutines are discussed in Chapter 12.)

To illustrate many of the ideas in this subsection we continue with the development of the grade report program. We might start by writing the overall algorithm as follows:

Write the headings.
Repeat the following until there is no more input data:
    Read an input record.
    Calculate the average score.
    Determine the grade category based on the average and write
        an appropriate output record for each category.

At this point we could begin to code some of the instructions in the program. However, before we do this and get bogged down in details we should continue to refine some of the steps that are not immediately obvious.

The step to calculate the average score needs further refinement. We recall that the average score is found by taking 50% of the best test score, 35% of the next best, and 15% of the worst score. Hence we must first determine the best score, the next best score, and the worst score. Thus we could refine this step as follows:

Find the best score.
Find the next best score.
Find the worst score.
Compute the weighted average.

However, we can easily do the first three steps above by simply sorting the test scores into ascending order. Then the algorithm can be expressed as follows:

Sort the test scores into ascending order.
Compute the weighted average.

Since we already know a sorting algorithm for three numbers we can use this algorithm in the first step. Thus the refinement of the average calculation is complete (except for the final coding).

We should also refine the step that determines the grade category and writes the output. Since there are five grade categories we can think of this as a selection process and refine it as follows:

Select the appropriate grade category:

90–100: Write output record with "A".
80–89: Write output record with "B".
70–79: Write output record with "C".
60–69: Write output record with "D".
 0–59: Write output record with "F".

Although this doesn't look like one of the three basic structures, we know that we can code it as nested decisions.

The only other step that needs some refinement is the input loop control. We wish to repeat the loop until there is no more input data. To refine this further we need to know more about the structure of the input file. During the problem definition stage we decided that the last input record will contain 9999 in the student number field. Hence we can control the input by testing for this trailer value after each record is read.

Incorporating all of the refinements discussed here we get the algorithm shown in Fig. 8-8. We can now begin the final program refinement, that of writing the code for the program.

Program Coding

The objective during the program coding activity is to implement the algorithm in a specific programming language. In effect, this is the last step in the program refinement. Each part of the algorithm must be translated into a group of statements. The final code will be correct if the algorithm is correct and the translation is done correctly.

Sometimes during the coding activity an error is discovered in the algorithm's logic. When this happens, the programmer must go back and redesign the program. It may even be necessary to return to the prob-

```
Write the headings.
Repeat the following loop:
    Read an input record.
    If the trailer value is read, stop the program.
    Sort the test scores into ascending order.
    Compute the weighted average.
    Select the appropriate grade category:
        90-100: Write output record with "A".
        80- 89: Write output record with "B".
        70- 79: Write output record with "C".
        60- 69: Write output record with "D".
         0- 59: Write output record with "F".
```

FIGURE 8-8. Grade report algorithm.

lem definition and work forward again if a serious error or misunderstanding is discovered.

During program coding, style rules, as discussed in Section 8-3, should be followed. This helps make the program more readable and the structure more understandable. Comments should be included as the program is coded. When the coding activity is complete, the program should be in its final form (except for the correction of possible errors).

The coding for the grade report program is shown in Fig. 8-9. Each step in the algorithm is translated into one or more FORTRAN statements. For example, the sorting step results in twelve statements while the average calculation requires only one statement. Notice that the comments in the body of the program follow closely the algorithm given in Fig. 8-8. This is a common approach for commenting a program. Notice also the use of introductory comments in the program.

The program is built from the basic program structures discussed in Section 8-1. The main logic is a sequence consisting of a step to write the headings and an input loop that is terminated when a trailer value is read. The loop contains a sequence of decisions for sorting, a calculation step for the average, and a nested decision for the output. Style rules have been followed to make the program more readable and understandable.

There are alternative ways of accomplishing different steps in this program, depending on the language features that are available. For example, if block IF statements and WHILE loops can be used, then the program can be written with these and the final code may be more understandable. Another example is the way in which the letter grade is printed. Using some language features discussed in Chapter 9, these steps can be simplified. The programmer should be familiar with as much of the programming language as possible and use those features that make the program easiest to code and as understandable as possible.

```
C
C      TITLE: GRADE REPORT PROGRAM
C
C      PROGRAMMER: ROBERT C. NICKERSON
C      DATE: NOVEMBER 10, 1980
C
C      PURPOSE: THIS PROGRAM COMPUTES A WEIGHTED AVERAGE OF THREE
C               TEST SCORES AND ASSIGNS APPROPRIATE LETTER GRADES.
C
C      VARIABLE NAMES:
C           ID    = STUDENT IDENTIFICATION NUMBER (INPUT/OUTPUT)
C           TS1   = TEST SCORE ON FIRST TEST (INPUT)
C           TS2   = TEST SCORE ON SECOND TEST (INPUT)
C           TS3   = TEST SCORE ON THIRD TEST (INPUT)
C           AVE   = WEIGHTED AVERAGE SCORE (OUTPUT)
C           TEMP  = TEMPORARY VARIABLE (INTERNAL)
C
C
C      WRITE HEADINGS
C
       WRITE(6,900)
C
C      BEGIN INPUT LOOP
C
  100  READ(5,800) ID,TS1,TS2,TS3
       IF(ID.EQ.9999) GO TO 500
C
C      SORT TEST SCORES INTO ASCENDING ORDER
C
       IF(TS1.LE.TS2) GO TO 210
       TEMP=TS1
       TS1=TS2
       TS2=TEMP
  210  IF(TS2.LE.TS3) GO TO 220
       TEMP=TS2
       TS2=TS3
       TS3=TEMP
  220  IF(TS1.LE.TS2) GO TO 230
       TEMP=TS1
       TS1=TS2
       TS2=TEMP
C
C      CALCULATE WEIGHTED AVERAGE
C
  230  AVE=.15*TS1+.35*TS2+.50*TS3
```

FIGURE 8-9. Grade report program (Part 1).

```
C
C      SELECT GRADE CATEGORY AND WRITE OUTPUT
C
       IF(AVE.LT.90.0) GO TO 310
C      GRADE IS "A"
       WRITE(6,910) ID,AVE
       GO TO 400
   310 IF(AVE.LT.80.0) GO TO 320
C      GRADE IS "B"
       WRITE(6,920) ID,AVE
       GO TO 400
   320 IF(AVE.LT.70.0) GO TO 330
C      GRADE IS "C"
       WRITE(6,930) ID,AVE
       GO TO 400
   330 IF(AVE.LT.60.0) GO TO 340
C      GRADE IS "D"
       WRITE(6,940) ID,AVE
       GO TO 400
C      GRADE IS "F"
   340 WRITE(6,950) ID,AVE
C
C      REPEAT INPUT LOOP
C
   400 GO TO 100
C
   500 STOP
C
C      INPUT FORMAT
C
   800 FORMAT(I4,3F4.0)
C
C      OUTPUT FORMATS
C
   900 FORMAT(1H1,3X,19HCOURSE GRADE REPORT/
      1        1H0,7HSTUDENT,3X,7HAVERAGE,3X,6HLETTER/
      2        1H ,6HNUMBER,5X,5HSCORE,4X,5HGRADE/)
   910 FORMAT(1H ,1X,I4,6X,F5.1,6X,1HA)
   920 FORMAT(1H ,1X,I4,6X,F5.1,6X,1HB)
   930 FORMAT(1H ,1X,I4,6X,F5.1,6X,1HC)
   940 FORMAT(1H ,1X,I4,6X,F5.1,6X,1HD)
   950 FORMAT(1H ,1X,I4,6X,F5.1,6X,1HF)
C
       END
```

FIGURE 8-9. Grade report program (Part 2).

Program Correctness

In Chapter 2 we discussed the three types of errors that can occur in a program. These are compilation errors, execution errors, and logic errors. Compilation errors are detected by the compiler during the compilation of the program. An error message is printed for each compilation error. To correct such errors the programmer must interpret the error message and make appropriate changes in the source program. Usually compilation errors result from the misuse of the programming language. Since these errors are detected by the computer they are usually easy to correct.

Execution errors occur during the execution of the program. The program must not have any serious compilation errors in order to be executed. Therefore, any execution error is the result of some condition that can be detected only during execution. Some examples of execution errors are dividing by zero, attempting to read when there is no more input data, and calculating a number that is too large for a variable. When such an error is detected the computer normally stops execution of the program and prints an error message explaining the cause of the error. It is the programmer's responsibility to interpret the error message and to make the necessary correction.

If the program compiles and executes without errors it still may not be correct. Errors may exist in the logic of the program. These are the most difficult errors to detect. The usual approach is to make up test data and determine by hand what output is expected from the data. Then the program is run with the test data and the actual output is compared with the expected output. If the outputs do not agree then there is an error which must be located and corrected.

A program testing procedure such as this only shows the *presence* of errors, not their *absence*. To show that a program is correct we must show that under all circumstances the program produces the correct result. To do this by using test data would require running the program with all possible combinations of data and comparing the output with the expected output calculated by hand. In addition to being an enormous task this would be senseless, since then we would have all possible outputs calculated by hand and there would be no need for a program (except, perhaps, to check our hand calculations). Thus we need some other way of showing that the program is logically correct.

It is sometimes possible to prove that a program is correct in a mathematical sense. However, this approach is usually too complex and tedious for the average programmer. However, we can informally "prove" a program's correctness through the stepwise program refinement process. Recall that in this approach we start with a general statement of the problem and then refine this statement by determining what things must be done to accomplish it. At each step in the development we refine the statements of the previous step until we reach the coded program. To show that a program is correct we need to show that each refinement accomplishes the task specified at the previous step.

As an example, consider the sorting program developed in Section 8-4. The problem is to sort three numbers into ascending sequence. The first step in the refinement includes the following statement:

>Sort V1, V2, and V3 into ascending order.

We assume that this is a correct definition of the problem and begin to refine it. The refinement results in the following:

>Move largest value to V3.
>Move next largest value to V2.

We can say that the program is correct at this point because we know that to sort the values we need only do the two things listed above. We then refine each of these two things separately and show that each refinement is a correct way of accomplishing the task that is being described. Thus we can refine the first statement above to the following:

>Move larger of V1 and V2 to V2.
>Move larger of V2 and V3 to V3.

Then the program is correct at this level of refinement. We continue in this manner, showing that each successive step is a correct refinement of the previous step. Finally, we code the program, and, if there are no coding errors, then the coded program is logically correct.

This method of showing program correctness through stepwise refinement is a very important part of programming. Most programmers do this even though they may not think they are "proving" that the program is correct. However, if this is done carefully and explicitly then the chance of serious logic errors in the program is greatly reduced. Thus the development of the program is the most important step in the programming process.

Even if a program is developed in the manner described here, logic errors may occur. Often small things are forgotten or a logical step in the development is passed over too quickly. Therefore, a thorough testing of the program should be performed to try to bring out any hidden errors. The programmer should be merciless in his or her testing of the program. Some organizations have a different programmer do the testing so that the original programmer is not tempted to pass over possible weaknesses just to get the job done. The objective of program testing is to force errors to reveal themselves.

If the program is written in a modular fashion then each module can be tested separately. Sometimes testing can begin on an incomplete program by inserting "dummy" modules for incomplete parts of the program. After the modules are tested separately the interaction between the modules can be tested. Pairs of modules can be tested, then three modules at a time, and so forth until finally the entire program is tested as a whole.

The first tests of the program should be simple to make sure that the program works in the simplest cases. Obvious errors such as mis-spelling of headings or alignment of columns can be corrected at this point. Then more complex tests can be performed.

At a minimum every statement in the program should be executed at least once using test data and the results compared with the expected output. However, this strategy will not catch all obvious errors. For example, consider the following sequence of statements from the payroll program in Fig. 5-5:

```
      IF(HOURS.GT.40.0) GO TO 20
      GROSS=4.50*HOURS
      TAX=.18*GROSS
      GO TO 30
   20 GROSS=180.00+6.75*(HOURS-40.0)
      TAX=.20*GROSS
   30 (next statement)
```

To test this section of code we might supply two sets of test data, one with the hours equal to 35.0 and the other with the hours equal to 45.0. These data would cause every statement in this sequence to be executed at least once. However, the sequence may still be in error. For example, assume that the IF statement had been incorrectly coded as follows:

```
      IF(HOURS.GE.40.0) GO TO 20
```

Then testing with only the two sets of input would not detect this error. We must also test the case where the hours is equal to 40.0.

We now have three sets of test data for this program. However, even with these data, errors may still be present. For example, the following erroneous IF statement would not be detected with these test data:

```
      IF(HOURS.GT.41.0) GO TO 20
```

What we need is a test case that is just greater than 40.0, such as 40.1. Then this error would be detected.

We can see from this example the beginning of a general strategy for generating test data for this type of program. For this program the input value for the hours field can range from zero to some practical limit such as eighty. We can divide this range into two subranges based on the calculations that are to be performed. If the hours are between zero and forty, then one set of calculations should be performed. However, if the hours are greater than forty but less than or equal to the upper limit, then another set of calculations are to be done. Then the testing strategy is as follows: For each subrange, test the program with the maximum and minimum values in the subrange and with some representative value within the subrange. Applying this strategy to the payroll program we would test the program with the hours field equal to 0.0, 35.0, 40.0, 40.1, 45.0, and 80.0. If the program works for each of these cases then we are reasonably assured that it will work for other cases.

To generate test data for the grade report program is much more complex. The best approach is to analyze the different parts of the program separately and to design appropriate test data for each part. We can apply the previous strategy to the grade selection algorithm in the program. We note that the grade is based on the average test score. The actual grade depends on which of the following ranges the average falls into:

     90–100
     80–89
     70–79
     60–69
      0–59

We must select input data for the three test scores that will generate values for the average that are equal to the maximum and minimum value in each range and values in between each set of limits. This results in fifteen test cases in all.

The sorting algorithm is more complex. We notice that the algorithm does not depend on whether any of the test scores are equal. Hence, for testing purposes we can assume that each score is different. Then there are six possible cases to test, based on the relative values of TS1, TS2, and TS3. These cases are as follows:

Smallest		Largest
TS1	TS2	TS3
TS1	TS3	TS2
TS2	TS1	TS3
TS2	TS3	TS1
TS3	TS1	TS2
TS3	TS2	TS1

We must supply input test data for each of these cases. We can combine these six cases with the fifteen needed for the grade selection algorithm. One additional case with 9999 in the ID field, is needed to test the termination condition on the input loop.

A complete set of input data that satisfies these requirements is given in Fig. 8-10. Tests number 2, 3, 5, 6, 8, and 9 correspond with the six cases listed above for the sorting algorithm. For each set of data, the expected output is also shown. The test data should be shuffled so that the tests are not done in any particular order (except for the trailer value test). Then the program should be run with the data and the actual output compared with what is expected. Any discrepancy indicates an error.

The tests listed here will not detect all errors. For example, errors in input data, such as negative test scores or scores greater than 100, will not be detected by the program. In general, we should make up special tests for the worst possible cases. Errors often occur at the beginning or end of processing. Hence special tests should be made with the first and last input record. Tests should be made to see what happens when there is too much or too little data. The program should be run without any input data to see what happens. Every possible worst case that can be thought of should be tested.

When an error is detected it is necessary to locate the cause of the error in the program and to correct it. Testing each module or section separately helps isolate errors. Since many errors are the result of

Test Number	Input Test Data				Expected Output	
	ID	TS1	TS2	TS3	Average	Grade
1	1001	100	100	100	100.0	A
2	1002	83	93	100	95.0	A
3	1003	70	96	90	90.0	A
4	1004	90	90	89	89.9	B
5	1005	83	73	90	85.0	B
6	1006	86	60	80	80.0	B
7	1007	79	80	80	79.9	C
8	1008	73	80	63	75.0	C
9	1009	76	70	50	70.0	C
10	1010	70	69	70	69.9	D
11	1011	80	50	50	65.0	D
12	1012	45	75	45	60.0	D
13	1013	75	55	21	59.9	F
14	1014	40	40	70	55.0	F
15	1015	0	0	0	0.0	F
16	9999	0	0	0	—	—

FIGURE 8-10.   Test data and expected output for the grade report program.

incorrect input data, a good practice during debugging is to print all input data immediately after reading it. This is called *echo printing* and it allows the programmer to check that the desired input data has been read. Another technique is to print the values of variables that are not printed in an output record. This lets the programmer check the results of various intermediate calculations. A common technique is to *trace* the execution of the program. The idea is to show the actual order of execution of various parts of the program. This can be done by inserting WRITE or PRINT statements at different points in the program. The statements should print simple phrases that identify where in the program each statement is located. This allows the programmer to compare the actual sequence of execution with what was expected.

The techniques discussed here can help detect and locate errors in a program. However, if a program has been developed by following a logical, systematic approach then errors should be at a minimum. It is the programmer's responsibility to take whatever steps are necessary to guarantee that his or her program is correct. A program is correct when there are no logic errors as well as no compilation and execution errors.

Program Documentation

Documentation of a program serves the purpose of providing information so that others can understand how to use the program and how the program works. Documentation of how to use the program is provided mainly for people wishing to use the program to solve a particular problem. This is often called *user documentation*. It includes instructions for running the program on the computer including what input to use and what to expect for the output. (When this type of documentation is oriented toward computer operators it is commonly called *operator documentation*.) Documentation on how the program works is provided for other programmers in case errors must be corrected or modifications in the program need to be made. This is usually called *program documentation*. In this section we are concerned with this type of documentation.

Documenting the program begins during the problem definition activity. Any written specifications of the program prepared at this stage are part of the documentation. For example, input and output layouts are part of the problem definition and should be included in the final program documentation. During program planning, flow-charts may be prepared. These, too, should be included in the final documentation. Listings of the test data used and sample outputs also should be part of the program documentation.

This type of documentation is external to the source program.

Much of the documentation can be included within the program itself. This is the primary purpose of comments in the program. As we have seen, comments can be used to describe the general features of the program and the detailed logic of the algorithm. A well-commented program is an important part of the documentation. The grade report program in Fig. 8-9 illustrates such a program.

A complete documentation package for a program might contain the following:

1. A program summary or abstract that provides a brief statement of the overall function of the program.
2. A program narrative that describes the detailed logic of the program.
3. Program flowcharts, if prepared.
4. Input record layouts.
5. Output report layouts.
6. A list of the test data used.
7. Sample output using the test data.
8. The source program listing including all comments.

The complete set of documents should be bound together with a title page and a table of contents. There should be one binder for each program and the entire library of program documentation should be under the control of one or more documentation librarians. If a program is changed it is important that the documentation be updated. No programmer should ever consider his or her job done until the final documentation is prepared or appropriately modified.

8-6. CONCLUSION

Computer programming is a process that includes several activities. One of the common misconceptions is that programming only involves the activity of writing the program. However, as we have seen, this activity, which is usually called coding, is only one part of the whole programming process. When we use the word "programming" we mean the whole set of activities associated with preparing a computer program. This includes the five activities discussed in Section 8-5.

The approach to programming that is emphasized in this chapter is commonly called *structured programming*. There is a lot of disagreement about what is meant by structured programming; a single definition does not exist. However, most people agree that structured programming involves a systematic process that results in programs that are well structured, that are easily understood, maintained, and modified, and that can be shown to be correct.

In this chapter we emphasize developing programs through stepwise refinement. This approach helps us show the correctness of the program. Using the three basic control structures leads to programs that are well structured and are easy to understand and to change. The style rules discussed in the chapter also aid in producing readable programs.

Structured programming is really just good programming. By following the guidelines set down in this chapter the programmer can produce good, correct programs.

PROGRAMMING PROBLEMS

1. In the economic measurement of consumer behavior the price elasticity of demand for a product is given by the following formula:

$$- \frac{(Q_2 - Q_1)/Q_1}{(P_2 - P_1)/P_1}$$

In this formula, Q stands for quality sold and P for price.

If the elasticity is less than 1, the demand is said to be *inelastic*. If the elasticity equals 1, the demand is said to be *unit elastic*. If elasticity is greater than 1, the demand is *elastic*.

Write a FORTRAN program to calculate the elasticity of demand for a particular product. Input is the product number and the relevant prices and quantities. Output from the program should be the product number, the elasticity of demand, and a statement of whether the demand is elastic, inelastic, or unit elastic.

Use the following data to test the program:

Product Number	P_1	Q_1	P_2	Q_2
103	25.00	100	17.50	135
108	20.00	200	10.00	300
112	125.00	35	95.00	37
115	32.50	512	27.00	713
128	44.00	80	33.00	100
132	15.75	72	10.25	63
999	(trailer card)			

Note that the data includes a trailer card that should be used to terminate processing.

2. A classic problem in computer programming is the "automatic change-maker" problem. The problem involves determining the breakdown of a customer's change into various denominations.

Write a FORTRAN program that solves the automatic change-maker problem. The program should accept as input the customer's name, the amount of a customer's bill, and the cash payment. Then print the name, the amount of the bill, the payment, and the change, if any. If there is no change, an appropriate message should be printed. Similarly, if the payment is less than the bill, a message should be printed.

For each transaction in which there is change, show the number and kind of each denomination in the change. The total number of bills and coins should be kept to a minimum. Assume that only pennies ($.01), nickels ($.05), dimes ($.10), quarters ($.25), and one dollar bills are available for change.

Use the following data to test the program:

Customer's Name	Customer's Bill	Payment
JOHN	$ 3.59	$ 5.00
MARY	8.00	8.00
SUSAN	14.95	14.00
ED	21.03	25.00
ALFRED	9.95	50.00
LISA	.29	1.00
	.00	(trailer card)

3. A theater sells tickets for $3.00 and averages 100 tickets sold for each performance. At this rate the theater's cost per patron is $1.20. The theater manager has estimated that for each 10¢ reduction in ticket price the number of tickets sold will increase by 20 and the theater's cost per patron will increase by 4¢.

Write a FORTRAN program to calculate and print a table listing the ticket price, the number of tickets sold, the gross revenue (ticket price multiplied by the number of tickets sold), the theater's total cost (cost per patron times number of tickets sold), and the net profit (revenue minus theatre's total cost) for each ticket price ranging from $3.00 to $2.00.

As the ticket price decreases from $3.00 to $2.00, the profit will steadily increase to a maximum and then start to decrease. Use this fact to print the phrase MAXIMUM PROFIT on the line in the table that corresponds to the greatest profit.

4. Write a FORTRAN program that finds the day of the week for any date in the twentieth century. Input to the program is the month, day, and year of any date between 1900 and 1999. The month should be numeric and the year should be two digits. For example, January 21, 1946, should be entered as 01 21 46. Output should give the day of the week for the given date (e.g., MONDAY).

The procedure to find the day of the week is as follows. Add the year, one fourth of the year (truncated), the day of the month, and the code for the month from the following table:

Month	Code
June	0
Sept., Dec.	1
April, July	2
Jan., Oct.	3
May	4
Aug.	5
Feb., March, Nov.	6

If the year is a leap year (that is, if it is evenly divisible by four) then the code is one less for January and February.

From the sum subtract two and divide the result by seven. The remainder from the division is the day of the week with 0 denoting Saturday, 1 Sunday, 2 Monday, and so forth.

For example, the day of the week for January 21, 1946, is found as follows:

Year	46
$\frac{1}{4}$ of year	11
Day of month	21
Code	3
Subtotal	81
Subtract	2
Total	79

Dividing 79 by 7 gives 11 with a remainder of 2. Hence, January 21, 1946, was a Monday.

Test the program with the following dates:

    October 25, 1978
    March 7, 1944
    December 6, 1973
    April 18, 1906
    January 1, 1984
    February 29, 1952

Use a trailer value to terminate the program.

5. Write a FORTRAN program that will print student grade reports. Input to the program consists of a varying number of course grade cards for each student. Each card contains the student's identification number, course identification number, course units, and numeric course

grade (equal to 4, 3, 2, 1, or 0). The input data is arranged in ascending numerical sequence by the students' identification numbers.

The program must calculate the grade point average (GPA) for each student. This is done by multiplying the number of units for each course by the grade, totaling for all courses, and dividing by the total number of units taken.

The output from the program should list for each student the student's identification number, the number of units and grade for each course that the student took, and the student's GPA. In addition, if the GPA is 3.5 or greater, then the message HONOR LIST should be printed. If the GPA is less than 1.5, then the message PROBATION should be printed.

Design appropriate input data that thoroughly tests the program. Note that the number of courses taken by a student varies.

6. Given the slopes, s and t, and intercepts, a and b, of two lines, i.e., the lines whose equations are

$$y = sx + a$$
$$y = tx + b$$

compute the coordinates of the point of intersection of the lines. Then print the name of the quadrant (FIRST, SECOND, THIRD, FOURTH) in which the point lies. If the point of intersection falls on an axis, print the name of the axis (X-AXIS or Y-AXIS). If the point of intersection is the origin, print the word ORIGIN. Include a provision in the program to check if the lines are parallel (i.e., $s = t$, $a \neq b$) or if the equations are for the same line (i.e., $s = t$, $a = b$) and print an appropriate phrase if either case holds.

Input to the program is the data identification number (integer) and the values of s, a, t, and b (each real with two places to the right of the decimal point). Use the following data to test the program:

ID	s	a	t	b
101	2.00	8.00	−3.00	−2.00
102	4.38	4.25	−7.11	−18.92
103	.50	3.50	− .75	16.00
104	.50	0.00	− .50	0.00
105	.38	−15.79	.38	−28.35
106	.50	5.00	− .50	5.00
107	.50	5.00	− .50	−5.00
108	−5.63	28.91	6.21	14.35
109	4.87	.08	4.87	.08
110	−.50	−5.00	.50	−5.00
111	.50	−5.00	−.50	5.00
112	−.03	−16.92	1.72	24.38
113	−1.00	−4.00	−2.00	6.00

At the end of the input data place a trailer value of 999 in the ID field and use this to stop processing.

7. Write a program to calculate the accumulated amount of a bank deposit at any interest rate for any period of time. Input to the program is the depositor's number and name, the amount of his deposit, the interest rate the deposit earns, and the number of years that he leaves the deposit. The basic problem assumes that interest is compounded annually. This means that the interest earned one year is added to the deposit and multiplied by the annual interest rate to get next year's interest. For example, if the initial deposit is $1000, the interest rate is 5%, and the deposit is left for 3 years, then the first year's interest is $1000 × .05 = $50. At the end of the first year, the accumulated amount of the deposit is $1000 + $50 = $1050. Interest for the second year is $1050 × .05 = $52.50. The accumulated amount of the deposit at the end of the second year is $1050 + $52.50 = $1102.50. The third year's interest is $1102.50 × .05 = $55.12. Thus, the accumulated amount of the deposit at the end of 3 years is $1102.50 + $55.12 = $1157.62.

The following are the requirements for this program:

(a) Read and print the input data. List each set of data, beginning at the top of a new page. Output should include appropriate titles to identify each item. Character I/O must be used to read and print the depositor's name.

(b) For each set of input data, print, below appropriate headings, the year and the accumulated amount of the deposit at the end of the year. Assume that the deposit is made at the beginning of year 1. Then the accumulated amount of the deposit at the end of year 1 is the amount of the deposit plus the interest for that year. Continue the process for the other years, making sure that the interest is compounded annually.

(c) In part (b), we assumed that interest was compounded only once a year. It is possible to compound interest more frequently by incorporating a "compounding factor" into the program. This factor represents the number of times per year that interest is to be compounded. For example, a compounding factor of 4 means that interest is compounded four times per year (i.e. every 3 months). A compounding factor of 1 means that interest is compounded once per year (i.e., annually). When interest is compounded more than once a year, the interest rate used in the calculation is the annual interest rate divided by the compounding factor. For example, if the annual interest rate is 5% and the compounding factor is 4, then the interest rate used to calculate interest every 3 months is .05/4 = .0125. Interest is calculated at this rate four times a year. Each time the interest is calculated, it is added to the deposit to get a new accumulated deposit that is used for the next interest calculation. Calculate the accumulated amount of the deposit at the end of each year for each set of input data, assuming compounding factors of 2, 4, 8, and 12. Note that these compounding factors are not input data but must be generated in the program. (Hint: It may be useful to use a computed GO TO statement and nested DO loops.) For each compounding factor print the factor and the *final* accumulated amount of the deposit with appropriate titles. Thus, in addition to the output already described, there will be four additional lines of output for each set of data.

Use the following data to test the program:

Depositor's Number	Depositor's Name	Amount of Deposit	Interest Rate	Time (years)
10851	SMITH JOHN J	$1000.00	5%	3
13751	ABERCROMBY ARNOLD	1000.00	4½%	3
18645	ZANDER STEVEN P	1000.00	5¼%	3
19541	PALMER JOSEPH Q	50.00	3¾%	25
24712	HARWELL HOWARD H	3500.00	6¾%	10
24839	WASHINGTON JOHN J	3500.00	7%	10
26213	CATO MARTIN P	3500.00	7¼%	10
28721	JOHNSON PETER	3500.00	7%	5
00000	(trailer card)			

8. In a geographic area the population in each of three socio-economic groups is increasing at a known percent per year. Current total population of the area and distribution (percent) of the population among the three groups is also known. Several things can be determined from this information, including the expected population in each group after a certain amount of time and the total population of the area.

Assume that the following information for each geographic area is punched in cards: the area code number, the area description, the current total population of the area, the percent of the current population that comprises each of the three socio-economic groups, and the annual growth percentage rate of each group. Write a FORTRAN program to process these data according to the following specifications:

(a) Read and print the input data with appropriate headings. Note that character I/O must be used to read and print the area description.

(b) For each group calculate the current population and the expected population after 10 years. For example, if the current population of an area is 5000 and a group comprises 20% of that population, then the current population of the group is

1000. If the growth rate is 5%, then after one year the population of the group is $1000 + .05 \times 1000$ or 1050. After two years, the population is $1050 + .05 \times 1050$ or 1103. This continues for 10 years. Also calculate the total population of the area after 10 years and the percent of the total that each socio-economic group comprises. Print all results with appropriate headings.

(c) In part (b) we assumed that the growth rate for each group would remain constant. It may be that these growth rates are decreasing by some percent each year. Repeat the calculations for part (b), assuming the growth rate decreases by .1% per year until the growth rate reaches 2.1% or less, at which time it levels off. For example, if the growth rate this year is 2.7%, then next year it will be 2.6%. The following year it will be 2.5%. This continues until the growth rate reaches 2.1% at which time it levels off at 2.1% for the remainder of the 10-year period. If the growth rate is currently 2.1% or less, then the rate remains unchanged for the entire 10-year period. Do this three more times using .2%, .25%, and .35% to decrease the growth rate. (Hint: It may be useful to use a computed GO TO statement and nested DO loops.)

Use the data in the following table to test the program:

Code	Description	Current Total Population	Distribution of Current Population			Annual Growth Rate		
			Group A	Group B	Group C	Group A	Group B	Group C
1083	INNER CITY AREA 1	14,283	35%	59%	6%	4.1%	5.2%	4.9%
1215	INNER CITY AREA 2	21,863	37%	42%	21%	5.8%	5.1%	5.9%
1371	INNER CITY AREA 3	8,460	73%	0%	27%	2.4%	0.0%	3.1%
1462	SUBURBAN AREA 1	5,381	55%	41%	4%	3.7%	4.2%	4.2%
1931	SUBURBAN AREA 2	12,845	90%	9%	1%	1.9%	2.2%	2.8%
9999	(trailer card)							

Chapter 9

DATA TYPES

There are many different types of data that can be processed by a computer. In previous chapters we have concentrated on two types of numeric data — integer and real. However, there are other numeric data types. In addition, computers can process nonnumeric data including logical data and character data. In this chapter we discuss different data types available in FORTRAN. We also describe a statement that can be used to initialize the values of variables.

9-1. NUMERIC DATA

One of the basic rules of FORTRAN is that a variable name must indicate the type of data that it refers to. For integer and real data this may be accomplished by assigning the first character in the variable name the task of identifying the data type. Thus, we have seen that any variable name that begins with one of the letters I, J, K, L, M, or N identifies integer data. If the variable name begins with any other letter of the alphabet it refers to real data. This approach is called *implicit typing* of variable names because the data type is implied or suggested by the name itself. Another approach is to use a *type statement* to state explicitly what data type is being identified by the variable name. When such *explicit typing* of variable names is used, the indicated type overrides the implied type. In this section we will examine a number of type statements that accomplish this. Some versions of FORTRAN do not include some of these statements.

The INTEGER and REAL Type Statements

The basic statements that are used for explicit typing of variable names are the INTEGER and REAL type statements. They are coded with the key word INTEGER or REAL to indicate the data type. Then the key word is followed by a list of variable names separated by commas. For example, the following statement identifies B, C, and VALUE as integer variable names:

```
INTEGER B,C,VALUE
```

Similarly, the following statement declares that the names ITEM and K refer to real data:

```
REAL ITEM,K
```

In both examples, the implicit type of the variable name, identified by the first letter of the name, is overriden by the type specified in the statement. Thus, even though ITEM and K are normally integer variable names, they are considered real names for the purpose of the program in which the REAL statement is included.

Although the type statements are normally used to override the implicit type of a variable name, they may include names of the same type as indicated by the statement. Thus, the following examples are valid type statements:

```
REAL AMT,M,L,C
INTEGER VOL,POP,I,J
```

Although AMT and C in the first statement are implicitly real variable names they may be included in the REAL type statement. Similarly, in the INTEGER type statement, variable names I and J, implicitly typed as integer, are included. This approach is often used so that the programmer can keep a complete list of all integer and real variable names used in the program.

The REAL and INTEGER statements are types of nonexecutable statements called *specification statements*. Specification statements provide information about the data to be processed by a program. In this case, the INTEGER and REAL statements specify that certain variable names will refer to integer and real data. Such information is needed by the compiler before the rest of the program is compiled. Hence, all INTEGER and REAL statements, and, in fact, all specification statements must appear at the beginning of the program, before the first executable statement.

The DOUBLE PRECISION Type Statement

Limits on the size of real data were discussed in Chapter 3. There it was pointed out that the fraction and exponent of a real numeric value are limited by the type of computer that is being used. For example, on the IBM System/370, the fraction may have a maximum of about seven digits and the exponent may range from about –78 to approximately 75. The number of digits in the fraction of a real value is sometimes referred to as the *precision* of the value. While it is not usually possible to extend the range of the exponent of real values, it is possible to increase the precision.

Basic real values are sometimes referred to as *single precision* data. Variable names that identify such values are also called single precision. Real values of greater size are called *double precision*. The maximum number of digits in the fraction of a double precision value depends on the type of computer. For the IBM System/370, the fraction of a double precision value has between eight and sixteen digits. (This range is approximate because the internal representation is in the binary mode. See Chapter 13.) For example, the value 28430621.92 is double precision because it contains ten digits in its fraction while the value 5837.25, which has six digits, is single precision.

Real variable names, either typed implicitly or specified in a REAL statement, refer to single precision data. In order to use a variable name to identify double precision data, the name must be specified in a DOUBLE PRECISION statement. The general form of such a statement consists of the key words DOUBLE PRECISION followed by a list of variable names separated by commas. For example, the following statement identifies the names RATE, D, L, and NUM as double precision variable names:

```
DOUBLE PRECISION RATE,D,L,NUM
```

Notice that the implicit type of a variable name appearing in a double precision statement is overridden. Thus, the first two variable names in this example are normally single precision while the last two names usually identify integer data. However, because these names are specified in a DOUBLE PRECISION type statement, they refer only to double precision data.

Like the REAL and INTEGER type statements, the DOUBLE PRECISION type statement is a specification statement. As such, it must appear at the beginning of the program before the first executable statement.

Double precision constants and input and output of double precision data are discussed in Appendix D.

9-2. THE DATA STATEMENT

Often it is necessary to assign initial values to variable names. For example, assume that it is necessary to assign the value 0 to the variable name I, and the value 2.0 to the variable names A, B, and C. This can be accomplished by a series of arithmetic assignment statements such as the following:

```
I=0
A=2.0
B=2.0
C=2.0
```

Another approach is to use the DATA statement. For example, the following statement initializes the variable names I, A, B, and C to the desired values:

DATA I/0/,A/2.0/,B/2.0/,C/2.0/

In this statement each variable name is listed followed by its initial value enclosed in slashes with commas separating the variable names. While the end result of this statement is the same as the arithmetic assignment statements above, the way in which the variable names are initialized is different. The arithmetic assignment statements cause variable names to be initialized when the program is executed. The assignment statements require instructions in the object program and time during execution to initialize the data. The DATA statement is more efficient because no object program instructions are needed and the initialization is completed before execution of the program is begun.

The general form of the DATA statement is as follows:

DATA *list/data/,list/data/,...,list/data/*

where *list* is a list of variable names separated by commas.
data is a list of constants separated by commas and enclosed in slashes.

The previous example shows one form of the DATA statement. Another way that this statement may be coded is to list several variable names together, followed by the corresponding initial values enclosed in slashes. For example, the following statement initializes the variable names I, A, B, and C to the desired values:

DATA I,A,B,C/0,2.0,2.0,2.0/

Whenever the DATA statement is used in this form, each variable name is assigned the corresponding value in the list of data. Thus, I is assigned the value 0, A is assigned the value 2.0, and so forth.

When several variable names are to be initialized to the same value, the value may be preceded by a repeat count instead of repeatedly listing it. The repeat count is an integer constant and an asterisk. For example, the entry 3*2.0 in a DATA statement means repeat the value 2.0 three times. Thus, the previous example may be shortened to the following:

$$\text{DATA I,A,B,C/0,3*2.0/}$$

When using the DATA statement in any of these forms, it is important that the number of variable names corresponds to the number of constants. For example, consider the following DATA statement that initializes three groups of variable names:

$$\text{DATA X,Y,Z/2*7.5,0.0/,K,L/3*5/,E,F,G/4.5,3.7/}$$

The first group contains three variable names as does the list of constants when the repeat count is taken into consideration. The second group contains two variable names but the list of constants indicates three values. This results in an error. Similarly, the last group is erroneous because there are three variable names but only two constants.

Any type of data may be initialized with the DATA statement. However, the data type of the constant and the type of the variable name must correspond. Thus, an integer variable name must correspond to an integer constant and a real variable name must have a corresponding real constant.

In most versions of FORTRAN, DATA statements may be placed anywhere in the program after the specification statements and before the END statement. However, the usual practice is to place all DATA statements immediately after the specification statements and before the first executable statement. Some versions of FORTRAN require that DATA statements be placed in this position in the program.

The DATA statement is available in most, but not all, versions of FORTRAN.

9-3. LOGICAL DATA

As we saw in Chapter 5, decisions in a program are based on the truth or falsity of an expression. *True* and *false* are logical data values. A logical data type is one that refers to data that can only have one of these values, that is, that can only have a value of true or false. In this section we discuss the logical data type in FORTRAN. Not all features discussed in this section are available in all versions of FORTRAN.

Logical Expressions

There are several types of expressions in FORTRAN. In Chapter 4 we discussed arithmetic expressions. An arithmetic expression is formed from numeric constants and variables, and arithmetic operators. The evaluation of an arithmetic expression results in a numeric value.

Relational expressions were discussed in Chapter 5. A relational expression is formed by combining arithmetic expressions with relational operators. A relational expression has a *truth value*, that is, it is either true or false.

Relational expressions are used in *logical expressions*. In fact, a relational expression by itself is one form of a logical expression. The more complex logical expressions are formed by combining several relational expressions with logical operators. The resulting expression is then evaluated to determine its truth value.

The logical operators used in FORTRAN and their meanings are as follows:

Logical Operator	Meaning
.AND.	Are both expressions true?
.OR.	Is one or the other expression or both true?
.NOT.	Is the expression not true?

Notice that each logical operator begins and ends with a period.

The following logical expression uses the .AND. logical operator:

$$A.GT.B.AND.C.LT.5.1$$

An alternative way of coding such expressions is to enclose the relational expressions in parentheses. The result is the same and sometimes easier to understand:

$$(A.GT.B).AND.(C.LT.5.1)$$

In evaluating a logical expression with an .AND. operator, the truth values of the relational expressions are determined first. In the previous expression it is determined whether the value of A is greater than the value of B and whether the value of C is less than 5.1. Then the logical operator .AND. determines whether both relational expressions are true. If they are, then the logical expression is true. If one or the other of the relational expressions or both are false, then the logical expression is false.

The .OR. logical operator works differently than the .AND. operator. The following logical expression illustrates its use:

$$(5.EQ.K).OR.(X.NE.Y)$$

Again, the truth values of the relational expressions are evaluated first. Then the logical operator .OR. determines whether one or the other relational expression or both are true. If such a condition exists, the logical expression is true. Only if both relational expressions are false is the logical expression false.

The .AND. and .OR. operators each require that two relational expressions be evaluated. The logical operator .NOT. is used with only one relational expression. For example, the following logical expression uses the .NOT. operator:

$$.NOT.(D+E.GE.8.69)$$

In evaluating this logical expression, the value of the relational expression must first be determined. Then the .NOT. operator determines whether the relational expression is not true—in other words, false. If the relational expression is false, then the logical expression is true. On the other hand, if the relational expression is true, then the logical expression is false.

Logical operations can be summarized most easily with *truth tables*. Such tables show all possible combinations of truth values for relational expressions and the resulting truth values of the logical expressions. Figure 9-1 shows the truth tables for the .AND., .OR., and .NOT. logical operators. In this figure, A and B represent relational expressions with the values true or false.

Simple logical expressions of the type given so far may be combined to form complex logical expressions. The following examples are valid logical expressions:

$$(K.GT.7).AND..NOT.(A.LT.5.)$$
$$(C.EQ.X).OR.(M.LE.N).OR..NOT.(A-5.5.GT.Z)$$
$$3.7.NE.W.AND.4.2.NE.X.OR.3.7.NE.Z$$

Notice that the only times that two logical operators may appear one after the other are in the following cases:

```
A  B   A.AND.B        A  B   A.OR.B

T  T      T           T  T      T

T  F      F           T  F      T

F  T      F           F  T      T

F  F      F           F  F      F

               A    .NOT.A

               T       F

               F       T
```

FIGURE 9-1. Truth tables for the logical operators.

.AND..NOT.

.OR..NOT.

Any other combination of two logical operators is invalid. Three operators in sequence should never be coded.

In evaluating a logical expression the operations are performed in this order:

1. Arithmetic expressions are evaluated to determine their numeric values.
2. Relational expressions are evaluated to determine their truth values.
3. Logical operators are evaluated in the following order:

.NOT.
.AND.
.OR.

For example, consider the following logical expression:

A-5.5.LT.B.OR..NOT.6.3+C.GT.D.AND.12.5.EQ.E

First, the arithmetic expressions A-5.5 and 6.3+C are evaluated. Then the truth values of the relational expressions are determined. There are three relational expressions in this example:

A-5.5.LT.B

6.3+C.GT.D

12.5.EQ.E

Next, the truth value of

$$.NOT.6.3+C.GT.D$$

is determined. Then the .AND. logical operator is evaluated in this expression:

$$.NOT.6.3+C.GT.D.AND.12.5.EQ.E$$

Finally, the .OR. operator is evaluated, yielding the truth value of the logical expression. These steps are summarized in Fig. 9-2.

Parentheses may be used to modify the order in which operations are performed in a logical expression. Any logical expression that is contained in parentheses is evaluated before operations outside of the parentheses are performed. To illustrate, the following expression is a modification of the previous example:

$$A-5.5.LT.B.OR..NOT.(6.3+C.GT.D.AND.12.5.EQ.E)$$

In this example, the truth value of the parenthetic expression is determined first. This includes the evaluation of the relational expressions within the parentheses and the .AND. operation. Then the operations outside of the parentheses are performed in the appropriate order. Figure 9-3 shows the evaluation steps for this example.

Extra parentheses are often used to clarify the meaning of a logical expression even though the order of evaluation of the expressions is not changed. For example, the following logical expression is evaluated in the same way as the previous example:

$$((A-5.5).LT.B).OR..NOT(((6.3+C).GT.D).AND.(12.5.EQ.E))$$

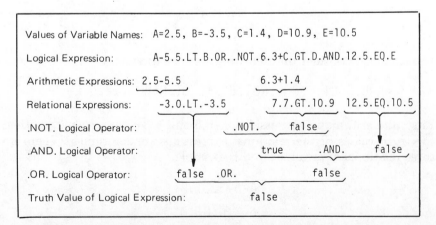

FIGURE 9-2. Evaluation of a logical expression.

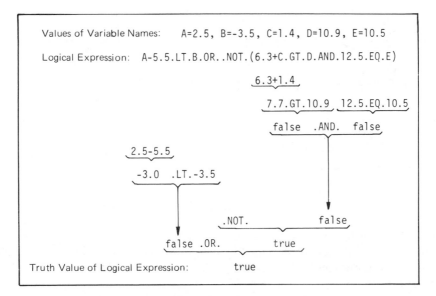

FIGURE 9-3. Evaluation of a logical expression with parentheses.

The primary use of logical expressions is in logical IF statements. We discussed this statement in Section 5-2 but only illustrated its use with relational expressions. In fact, any logical expression may be used in a logical IF statement. For example, the following are valid logical IF statements:

```
IF((K.LE.5).OR.(M.LE.5)) WRITE(6,85) X,Y
IF(.NOT.((A.GT.B).AND.(A.GT.C))) GO TO 150
IF((K1.EQ.1).OR.(K1.EQ.2).AND..NOT.(K2.EQ.1)) STOP
```

In each of these, the truth value of the logical expression is first evaluated. Then if the expression is true, the statement in the IF statement is executed next. If the logical expression is false, then this statement is skipped, and the program continues execution with the next statement in sequence.

As an example of the use of logical expressions in a program consider a variation on the tuition calculation program discussed in Section 5-2 (see Fig. 5-1). As before, we assume that the tuition is based on the number of units that the student is taking. However, there is a reduction in the tuition of $250.00 for a scholarship if the student's identification number is between 7000 and 7999. The program for this problem is shown in Fig. 9-4. Notice how the .AND. logical operator is used to test the identification number to see if it falls in the appropriate range.

Logical expressions are used in other statements besides the IF

```
 10 READ(5,100) ID,UNITS
    IF(UNITS.GT.12.0) GO TO 20
    TUIT=350.00
    GO TO 30
 20 TUIT=350.00+20.00*(UNITS-12.0)
 30 IF((ID.GE.7000).AND.(ID.LE.7999)) TUIT=TUIT-250.00
    WRITE(6,200) ID,TUIT
    GO TO 10
100 FORMAT(I4,F4.1)
200 FORMAT(1X,I4,3X,F7.2)
    END
```

FIGURE 9-4.   A tuition calculation program.

statement. For example, logical expressions are used in the WHILE statement, if it is available. Logical expressions are also used with several other logical programming features discussed in the following subsections.

Logical Constants and Variable Names

Integer and real constants and variable names are used to identify numeric data. Logical constants and variable names refer to logical data. A *logical constant* is a fixed truth value that is used in a statement. In FORTRAN, logical constants are coded .TRUE. and .FALSE.. Notice that *each constant begins and ends with a period.*

A *logical variable name* actually identifies a *storage location* that contains a truth value. In other words, the value of a logical variable name may be either true or false. A name may identify logical data only if it is specified as a logical variable name in a LOGICAL statement. The general form of this statement is the keyword LOGICAL followed by a list of variable names. For example, the following statement identifies the names LA, P, and W2 as logical variable names:

LOGICAL LA,P,W2

Note that *a variable name that has been specified as logical cannot be used to refer to integer or real data.*

The LOGICAL statement is a type of specification statement and must appear at the beginning of the program. The LOGICAL statement indicates that storage locations reserved for certain variable names contain logical data.

Logical constants and variable names may be used in logical expressions. For example, assume that the variable names LA, LB, and

LC have been specified in a LOGICAL statement. Then the following are valid logical expressions:

```
.TRUE.
LA
LB.OR.LC
(X*B).GT.-W.AND.LA
LC.AND..NOT.(LA.OR.(X.EQ.5))
```

Logical variable names may be initialized with the DATA statement by using logical constants. For example, assume that LB, LC, and LD are logical variable names. Then the following statement initializes LB to the value true and LC and LD to false values:

```
DATA LB,LC,LD/.TRUE.,2*.FALSE./
```

The Logical Assignment Statement

An arithmetic assignment statement assigns the numeric value of an arithmetic expression to a numeric variable name. A *logical assignment statement* assigns the truth value of a logical expression to a logical variable name. The general form of a logical assignment statement is as follows:

logical variable name = logical expression

On the left of the equal sign must be one logical variable name. On the right is one valid logical expression. The following are examples of logical assignment statements (assume LA, LB, and LC are logical variable names):

```
LC=.FALSE.
LB=LA
LA=LC.AND..NOT.LB
LC=X.LT.Y
LB=((S*5.2).GE.7.3).OR.LB
LA=.NOT.LB
```

When using a logical assignment statement the expression on the right of the equal sign must be a logical expression or the statement is invalid. For example, if LA is a logical variable name, then the following statement is invalid because an arithmetic expression is on the right:

```
LA=X*Y-3.5
```

Similarly, the variable name left of the equal sign in a logical assignment statement must be of logical type. The following example is invalid because it attempts to assign a logical value to a numeric variable name (X):

$$X=(K.EQ.5).OR.LB$$

One common use of logical assignment statements is to save the result of a logical expression so that the expression need be evaluated only once. For example, assume that the expression

$$(N.EQ.1).OR.(N.EQ.2)$$

is used in several logical IF statements. We can reduce the coding required for the program by assigning the value of this expression to a logical variable name, then testing the variable name by means of IF statements. The following statements illustrate this approach:

```
LOGICAL SAVE
  .
  .
  .
SAVE=(N.EQ.1).OR.(N.EQ.2)
  .
  .
  .
IF(SAVE) GO TO 10
  .
  .
  .
IF(SAVE) WRITE(6,30)
  .
  .
  .
IF(SAVE) GO TO 25
```

A similar use of the logical assignment statement is to set a flag in a program. A *flag* (also called a *signal* or a *switch*) is used to identify whether or not some condition has occurred during the processing of the program. For example, a flag may be used to signal that the end of the input file has been reached.

When a flag is needed a logical variable name is used. The flag is usually assigned an initial value of FALSE, indicating that the condition to be flagged has not occurred. Then at the appropriate points in the program, the condition can be checked and, if true, the flag is assigned a value of TRUE. At any time during the processing the flag can be tested to see whether or not the condition is true.

To illustrate this approach, assume that we need to flag the end of file condition in a program. Then the following statements might appear at appropriate points in the program:

```
LOGICAL EOF
EOF=.FALSE.
    .
    .
    .
READ(6,100) ID,...
IF(ID.EQ.9999) EOF=.TRUE.
    .
    .
    .
IF(EOF) WRITE(6,220) TOTAL
    .
    .
    .
IF(EOF) GO TO 40
```

In this sequence, EOF is the flag. Initially EOF is false. Each time an input record is read, we check for a trailer value and set EOF to TRUE when the end of the input file is reached. Then we test EOF in a logical IF statement at various other points in the program.

Input and Output of Logical Data

Input and output fields of logical data are specified by the L-format code. With this code, logical data may be read from punched cards and assigned to logical variable names. Similarly, the values of logical variable names may be printed in a format specified by the L-format code.

The general form of the L-format code is as follows:

Lw

where w is the width of the input or output field.

For input, the L-format code specifies a field of w characters that must contain a T (True) or F (False) as the first nonblank character. The field may consist of blanks, followed by a T or F, followed by a series of other characters. Blanks preceding T or F and the characters following are optional; however, the first character in the field that is not a blank *must* be a T or F. This indicates the truth value of the field.

Assume that A, B, and C have been declared as logical variable names. The following statements cause values to be read from a punched card and assigned to these names:

```
READ(5,10) A,B,C
10 FORMAT(L2,L3,L5)
```

The first input field is two columns wide; the second field occupies three columns; the third field is five columns wide. The truth values of the fields are assigned to the logical variable names A, B, and C respectively. Data may be punched in the field in a variety of forms; the following is one possibility:

```
123456789....
```

| T | F | FALSE |

In this case, the value assigned to A is true; B and C are given values of false. The same values result if the data is punched as follows:

```
123456789....
```

| T | FXX | FT |

Notice that it is the *first nonblank* character that indicates the truth value; other characters in the field have no effect on the value of the field. The first character that is not a blank must be a T or F, otherwise an error occurs. Thus, the following punched card data results in an error when the third field is read:

```
123456789....
```

| TR | FAI | NOT T |

For output, only the character T or F is printed, right-justified in the field. For example, consider the following statements:

```
WRITE(6,20) A,B,C
20 FORMAT(1X,3L4)
```

In this case, the truth values of A, B, and C are each printed in a four-position field. The first three positions in each field are blank. The last position contains a T or F, depending on the values of the logical variable names. If the value of A is true, and B and C are false, then the output appears as follows:

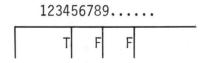

An Illustrative Program

To illustrate the logical programming features described in this section, consider the problem of analyzing the results of a true-false questionnaire. Input data consists of the respondent's identification code and the answers to four questions. Each answer is a T or F punched in a one-column field. A program is needed to print the identification code and answers to the second two questions for all respondents who answered TRUE to the first two questions. In addition, a count of the number of respondents who answered TRUE to the first two or the second two questions is needed.

Figure 9–5 shows the program for this problem. Notice the use of L-format code for input and output of logical data. The input data is read from four one-column fields. Logical output data is printed in two fields of three columns each. A logical assignment statement is used to determine if the responses to the first two questions are both

```
      LOGICAL Q1,Q2,Q3,Q4,RES
      KOUNT=0
   10 READ(5,100) ID,Q1,Q2,Q3,Q4
      IF(ID.EQ.9999) GO TO 30
      RES=Q1.AND.Q2
      IF(RES) WRITE(6,200) ID,Q3,Q4
      IF(RES.OR.(Q3.AND.Q4)) KOUNT=KOUNT+1
      GO TO 10
   20 WRITE(6,210) KOUNT
   30 STOP
  100 FORMAT(I4,4L1)
  200 FORMAT(1X,I4,2L3)
  210 FORMAT(1X,I3)
      END
```

FIGURE 9–5.   A program to analyze a true-false questionnaire.

true. The result is assigned to the logical variable named RES. This name is then used in two logical IF statements to test for this true condition.

9-4. CHARACTER DATA

In Chapter 7 we introduced the use of character data in input and output operations. Among other things, character constants and variable names were described. In this section we discuss the manipulation of character data in a program. The features explained in this section are not available in all versions of FORTRAN. Some versions of FORTRAN that do not permit the use of character data as described here, do allow a limited form of character manipulation using Hollerith constants. These are discussed in the last subsection below.

Character Constants and Variable Names

Character constants and variable names are the basic data elements used for character data manipulation. In this subsection we review these briefly.

A *character string*, or simply a *string*, consists of a group of characters. Any symbol that can be stored in the computer can be in a character string. For example, all of the following are character strings:

```
ABC
X37Z$
NEW YORK
1881
```

Notice that a blank space is a character and can be part of a character string. In fact, one or more blanks without any other characters form a character string.

A *character constant* is a character string enclosed in apostrophes. For example, the following are each valid character constants:

```
'ABC'
'X37Z$'
'NEW YORK'
'1881'
' '
```

Notice that a number enclosed in apostrophes is a character constant, not a numeric constant. The last example above is a character constant consisting of a single blank space. The *length* of a character constant is the number of characters in the character string in the constant. Thus the lengths of the character constants listed above are 3, 5, 8, 4, and 1 respectively.

A *character variable name* is a name that can refer to a character string. As discussed in Section 7-3, all character variable names must be specified in a CHARACTER statement. For example, the following statement declares CA, S, and NY as character variable names:

$$\text{CHARACTER*10 CA,S,NY*8}$$

The *length* of a character variable is the maximum number of characters to which the variable name can refer. The length is specified in the CHARACTER statement. In the above example, CA and S are of length ten and NY has a length of eight.

Input and output of character data is accomplished either using format-free I/O or with formatted I/O and the A-format code. These were discussed in Section 7-3.

The Character Assignment Statement

A character string can be assigned to a character variable name with an assignment statement. For example, assume that CA and CB have been specified as character variable names in a CHARACTER statement. Then the following assignment statements are valid:

$$\text{CA='CALIF'}$$
$$\text{CB=CA}$$

The variable name on the left of the equal sign in a character assignment statement must be of character type. On the right of the equal sign may be a character constant or character variable name (or other character elements discussed below).

If the length of the character constant or variable on the right of the equal sign is the same as the length of the character variable on the left, then the assignment takes place as we would expect. That is, the character string identified by the character constant or variable name on the right is assigned to the variable name on the left. If the length of the element on the right is *less* than the length of the variable on the left, then the character string is assigned to the left part of the variable and blanks are added on the right to fill out the variable. That is, the string to be assigned is left-justified and *padded* with blanks on the right. For example, if CA has a length of ten, then after execution of the first assignment statement above, CA will be equal to CALIF*bbbbb* (*b* = blank). When the length of the right-hand element is *greater* than the length of the variable, then the effect is that the extra characters on the right are truncated before the assignment takes place. Thus, if CB in the above example has a length of three, then after execution of the second assignment statement, CB will have a value of CAL.

Character variable names can be initialized by reading input data for the variable names, by using character assignment statements, or by initializing the names in a DATA statement. When a DATA statement is used, then the variable name must previously be specified in a CHAR-ACTER statement. Character constants are then used for the initial values. For example, consider the following DATA statement:

```
DATA CA,NY/'CALIF','NEW YORK'/,X,Y,Z/3*' '/
```

In this example, CA is initialized to CALIF, NY is initialized to NEW YORK, and X, Y, and Z are each initialized to one blank space. Note that if the length of the character variable is not the same as the length of the character constant, then padding or truncation occurs as with the character assignment statement.

Substrings

A *substring* is a group of one or more adjacent characters in a character string. For example, consider the string NEW YORK. The following are substrings of this string:

```
NEW
OR
YORK
EW YO
W
NEW YORK
```

Notice that any single character in a string is a substring, and that the entire string is a substring of itself. In addition, any group of characters that are adjacent to one another in the string forms a substring. However, if a group of characters from the string are not adjacent to each other, then they do not form a substring. Thus, NOR is *not* a substring of NEW YORK even though the characters come from the string.

In FORTRAN a substring is identified by a *substring name*. A substring name is formed from a character variable name followed by the position of the substring enclosed in parentheses. For example, the following are valid substring names:

$$CA(1:3)$$
$$NY(5:8)$$
$$NY(2:6)$$

The characters in a string are assumed to be numbered from left to right beginning with one for the first character. In a substring name the first number in parentheses gives the position of the first character in the substring and the second number specifies the position of the last character in the substring. Thus, in the first example above we are naming the substring consisting of the first character in the CA string through the third character in this string. If CA equals CALIF then CA(1:3) is CAL. In the second example, we are referring to the fifth through eighth characters in the NY string. If NY equals NEW YORK, then NY(5:8) is YORK. (Notice that the blank counts as one of the characters in the string.) The final example identifies the substring consisting of characters 2 through 6 of the NY string. For our data, NY(2:6) would be EW YO.

If we wish to identify a substring at the beginning of a string, then we can leave out the first term in parentheses. Thus, the first example above could be coded CA(:3). Similarly, when the end of a string is desired, the last term can be left out. The second example above can be coded as NY(5:) because we want the last part of the string beginning with the fifth character. A single character substring is indicated by a substring name with the same beginning and ending positions. Thus, CA(3:3) refers to the third character in the CA string. Other examples of substring names are shown in Fig. 9-6.

Variable names may be used to identify beginning and ending positions in a substring name. For example, the substring name S(I:J) is valid and refers to the Ith through Jth characters of S. Other examples are as follows:

$$T(4:K)$$
$$U(L:8)$$
$$V(:M)$$
$$W(N:)$$
$$X(I:I)$$

In the last example above, the Ith character is identified by the name. As we will see, this is often a useful substring name.

Any integer arithmetic expression can be used in a substring name. For example, the name S(J-2:3*I+1) is valid. Expressions are first evaluated and then the values are used to identify the substring. In general the values in a substring name must be between one and the length of the string, and the first value (the starting position) must be less than or equal to the second value (the ending position).

```
CHARACTER*10 ST
ST='WASHINGTON'
```

Substring Name	Substring
ST(3:7)	SHING
ST(1:4) ⎫ ST(:4) ⎬	WASH
ST(8:10) ⎫ ST(8:) ⎬	TON
ST(6:6)	N

FIGURE 9-6. Substrings.

Substring names can be used anyplace in a program that a character variable name can appear. Thus, we can use substring names in READ and WRITE statements, character assignment statements, and DATA statements. For example, the following are all valid uses of substring names:

```
READ(5,100) S(5:10),T(4:I)
WRITE(6,200) CA,NY(5:)
U(4:6)='AND'
T(2:2)=S(4:4)
DATA V(5:6)/'OK'/
```

Sometimes it is useful to be able to locate a substring in a string. This can be done with the INDEX function. This function searches through a string for a substring. If the substring is found the function gives the position of the first character in the substring. If the substring is not found, then the function returns a value of zero. For example, consider the following statement:

```
LOC=INDEX(S,'END')
```

The INDEX function will search through the string S for the substring END. If END is found, it will return the position of the first character of the substring and, in this case, the value will be assigned to the numeric variable named LOC. For example, if S is the string THE END

IS NEAR, then INDEX will return the number 5 since END begins in the fifth position. If the substring appears more than once in the string, then only the first occurrence is found. If the substring cannot be found, then INDEX indicates a value of zero.

In using the INDEX function, the first entry in parentheses identifies the string to be searched and the second entry is the substring to be located. Either entry may be a character constant, character variable name, or substring name.

Sometimes when manipulating character data we need to know the length of a string or substring. We can get this information from various sources in the program. However, it is often easiest to determine the length of a string with the LEN function. For example, the following statement assigns the length of the string identified by the name S to the variable named LS:

$$LS=LEN(S)$$

If S is of length eight, then LS will be equal to eight after execution of this statement. The entry in parentheses may be a character variable name, character constant, or a substring name. For example, we can use LEN(S(5:)) to determine the length of the substring beginning with the fifth character through the end of the character string named S.

Concatenation of Character Strings

Concatenation is the operation of putting together two strings to form one string. For example, concatenating the strings ABC and XYZ produces the string ABCXYZ. To concatenate two strings in FORTRAN we use the *concatenation operator*. This operator consists of two slashes (//). For example, to concatenate ABC and XYZ we can write

```
'ABC'//'XYZ'
```

On each side of the operator may be a character constant, character variable name, or substring name. For example, each of the following is a valid use of the concatenation operator (assuming S, T, U, and V are character variable names):

```
S//T
U//'1234'
'MY '//V
U(4:7)//S(:3)
V(4:)//T
```

In each of these cases a new string is formed consisting of the string identified by the constant, variable name, or substring name on the left of the operator followed by the string identified on the right. Thus if S equals the string ABC and T equals the string XYZ, then S//T is ABCXYZ and T//S is XYZABC.

When we use a concatenation operator we form a type of character expression. In general, a *character expression* is a character constant, character variable name, substring name, or any of these in conjunction with the concatenation operator. In addition, we can have multiple concatenations in a character expression. For example, the following is a valid character expression:

$$U//'ABC'//T(6:12)//S$$

The strings identified in the expression are concatenated from left to right.

A character expression by itself is not a FORTRAN statement. Rather it is used as part of a statement. For example, we may assign the value of a character expression to a character variable name with a character assignment statement. Thus, the following is a valid FOR-TRAN statement:

$$S=T//U//V$$

The strings identified in the character expression are concatenated and the resulting string is assigned to S.

As an example of the use of concatenation consider the problem of rearranging the order of a person's name. Assume that LSTNAM, FSTNAM, and MI are character variable names that identify a person's last name, first name, and middle initial, respectively. The problem is to create a string consisting of the person's first name followed by a space, then the person's middle initial followed by a period and a space, and then the person's last name. The following statement accomplishes this:

$$NAME=FSTNAM//' '//MI//'. '//LSTNAM$$

Notice that we must put the period and spaces in the proper place in the expression so that the final result is the way we want it. Other examples of concatenation are shown in Fig. 9–7.

String Comparison

One of the important things that we must be able to do in order to manipulate character data is to compare strings to determine if they are equal or unequal. This is accomplished in FORTRAN in the same

```
                    CHARACTER*10 ST
                    ST='WASHINGTON'
```

Operation	Result
ST//' STATE'	WASHINGTON STATE
'GEORGE '//ST	GEORGE WASHINGTON
ST(:4)//ST(5:7)//ST(8:)	WASHINGTON
ST(:3)//' '//ST(5:5)//ST(8:8)//'?'	WAS IT?
ST(10:10)//ST(9:9)//ST(8:8)	NOT

FIGURE 9-7. Concatenation.

way that we compare numeric values. We use relational expressions consisting of character expressions and relational operators. For example, the following are valid relational expressions (we assume all variable names are of character type):

```
        NAME.EQ.'JOHN'
      RES(3:5).NE.'YES'
            S.LT.T
        U//V.LE.T(:10)
      'WXYZ'.GT.V
          V.GE.U//'AA'
```

If the relational operator used is .EQ. or .NE. then the comparison is made to determine if the strings contain identical characters in identical positions. If they do, then the strings are equal. However, if they are not identical then they are not equal. For example, in the first expression above if the value of NAME is JOHN, then the expression is true, but if the name is JEAN, then the expression is false.

If the relational operator is .LT., .LE., .GT., or .GE. then the evaluation of the relational expression is based on an ordering of the characters. This ordering is called the *collating sequence*. If we just consider the letters of the alphabet, then the collating sequence is the same as the alphabetical order. That is, one string is less than another if it appears before the other in an alphabetized list. Thus, the string JEAN is less than JOHN which is less than MARY. Hence, the expression NAME.LT.'JOHN' is true if NAME is JEAN but false if it is MARY.

The way the computer makes this evaluation is by comparing the strings character-for-character, left-to-right. As soon as two corresponding characters are found not equal to each other, then the computer determines which string is the greater on the basis of which of the unequal characters is further in the alphabet. Thus, in comparing JEAN and JOHN, the computer examines the first character of each and determines that they are equal. It then compares the second character of each and determines that they are not equal. Then, since the letter O is farther in the alphabet than E, the computer would indicate that JOHN is greater than JEAN.

If a blank is included in a string, then the blank is considered to be less than any other character. Thus, JOHN*bb* (*b* = blank) is less than JOHNNY. When the strings being compared are of unequal length, the shorter string is extended with blanks until the strings are of equal length. Then the comparison is made. Thus in comparing JON with JOHN, the former would be extended to JON*b* and then the comparison would take place. In this case, JON*b* would be greater than JOHN because the third character of JON*b* is greater than the third character of JOHN.

A string of digits is evaluated in the same way as a string of letters with 0 less than 1, 1 less than 2 and so forth up to 9. Thus 123 is less than 456, as we would expect. But because a blank is less than any other character, *b*9 is less than 8*b*.

If we compare character strings consisting of both letters and digits or containing special characters, then the result depends on the computer being used. This is because different computers use different collating sequences for these characters. Thus, in general, we can't say whether X37Z is greater or less than XM7Z. The answer will depend on whether the digit 3 is greater than or less than the letter M in the collating sequence of the computer being used. Other examples of string comparison are shown in Fig. 9–8.

The primary use of relational expressions that compare strings is in IF statements. For example, the following are all valid uses of string comparisons:

```
IF(ST.LT.'CALIF') WRITE(6,250) ST
IF(INP.EQ.'END') STOP
IF((T(3:7).GT.U).AND.(T(3:7).LE.V)) GO TO 30
```

We will see other examples of the use of string comparison in the next subsection.

An Illustrative Program

To illustrate some of the character manipulation features discussed here we consider a text analysis program. Input to the program is a line

Relational Expression	Truth Value
'ED JONES'.LT.'ED SMITH'	true
'EDWARD JONES'.LT.'ED SMITH'	false
'1234'.GT.'4567'	false
'1234'.GT.' 4567'	true
'LISA '.EQ.'LISA'	true
'LISA '.EQ.' LISA'	false
' '.NE.' '	false
'X37Z'.NE.'3AY7'	true

FIGURE 9-8. String comparison.

of text (that is, a sentence) of up to eighty characters in length that ends with a period. The program must count the number of blank spaces in the line and print this count along with the original text.

Figure 9-9 shows a program that accomplishes this and the output for a representative set of input data. The program first specifies that LINE is a character variable name of length eighty. Then a line of text is read and assigned to LINE. If the first five characters of the line consist of the word STOP followed by a period, then the program terminates. That is, STOP with a period serves as a trailer value. If the trailer value has not been read, then the line is printed and a counter (KOUNT) is set equal to 0. The program then enters a loop that is executed once for each character in the line. Each time through the loop, the next character in the line is examined to determine if it is a period or a blank. This is done by using the substring name LINE(I:I) where I is a variable that is initially one and is incremented by one each time the loop is executed. Thus, when I is one, LINE(I:I) identifies the first character in the string; when I is two, LINE(I:I) refers to the second character, and so forth for the other values of I. If LINE(I:I) is a period, then the computer branches out of the loop. If LINE(I:I) is not a period but is a blank, then the counter (KOUNT) is incremented. This is repeated for each I until a period is found or until the end of the line is reached (that is, until I equals 80). After branching out of the loop, the program checks to see if the loop was terminated by finding a

```
    CHARACTER*80 LINE
 10 READ(5,100) LINE
    IF(LINE(1:5).EQ.'STOP.') GO TO 60
    WRITE(6,200) LINE
    KOUNT=0
    I=1
 20 IF((LINE(I:I).EQ.'.').OR.(I.EQ.80)) GO TO 30
    IF(LINE(I:I).EQ.' ') KOUNT=KOUNT+1
    I=I+1
    GO TO 20
 30 IF(LINE(I:I).EQ.'.') GO TO 40
    WRITE(6,210)
    GO TO 50
 40 WRITE(6,220) KOUNT
 50 GO TO 10
 60 STOP
100 FORMAT(A80)
200 FORMAT('0',A80)
210 FORMAT(' NO PERIOD AT END OF LINE')
220 FORMAT(' THERE ARE ',I2,' BLANKS IN THIS LINE')
    END
```

(a)

```
    NOW IS THE TIME.
    THERE ARE  3 BLANKS IN THIS LINE

    FOUR SCORE AND SEVEN YEARS AGO.
    THERE ARE  5 BLANKS IN THIS LINE

    THE QUICK BROWN FOX
    NO PERIOD AT END OF LINE

    HELP.
    THERE ARE  0 BLANKS IN THIS LINE
```

(b)

FIGURE 9-9. A text analysis program: (a) the program;
(b) the output.

period at the end of the line. If this is the case, then the count of the number of blanks in the line is written; otherwise an error message is printed indicating that there is not a period at the end of the line. The output shows how the program works for several sets of input data.

This program illustrates one use of the character manipulation features in FORTRAN. There are many other interesting and practical applications of character data processing. Some of these are discussed in the programming problems at the end of the chapter.

Character Manipulation
with Hollerith Constants

Some versions of FORTRAN do not allow the use of character constants and variable names as discussed in the previous subsections. Instead Hollerith constants are used to assign nonnumeric data to numeric variable names in a DATA statement. A *Hollerith constant* is coded like an H-format code in a FORMAT statement. That is, a literal is preceded by the letter H and a count of the number of characters in the literal. For example, the following are valid Hollerith constants:

```
4HJOHN
1HA
2HB3
```

The maximum length of a Hollerith constant depends on the type of computer being used. We will assume that the maximum length is four characters.

A Hollerith constant can be used in a DATA statement to assign a non-numeric value to a numeric variable name. For example, the following DATA statement assigns the value JOHN to the variable named NAME and the values A and B3 to the names K1 and K2, respectively:

```
DATA NAME,K1,K2/4HJOHN,1HA,2HB3/
```

After a variable name has been assigned a nonnumeric value in a DATA statement the name can be used in other statements to refer to the data. For example, the following statements cause the value of NAME to be printed:

```
WRITE(6,20) NAME
20 FORMAT(1X,A4)
```

Notice that A-format must be used for the output since the value is nonnumeric. Similarly, we can assign the nonnumeric value of one variable name to another name by an assignment statement. Thus, the following statement is valid:

K3=K2

We can also compare the nonnumeric values of variable names in an IF statement. For example, assume that we wish to test an alphanumeric input field called NAME1 to determine if it is equal to JOHN. Then the following statement accomplishes this:

IF(NAME1.EQ.NAME) GO TO 25

Notice that the variable name NAME is used in the IF statement since this refers to the Hollerith constant with a value of JOHN.

In the examples of assignment and IF statements above the variable names used are all of the same type, in this case integer. Whenever non-numeric data is assigned or compared, the names must be the same type; otherwise, the results may not be as we expect. In general, it is best to use integer variable names since then there is minimum likelihood for error.

Hollerith constants are available in some versions of FORTRAN. However, their use can be complex and error prone. If character data as discussed earlier is available, then it should be used for character manipulation.

PROGRAMMING PROBLEMS

1. In one business the commission paid to each salesperson is based on the product line sold and the total amount of the sales. Assume that the product line is indicated by a code that can be either 5, 8, or 17. If the code is 5 or 8, the commission rate is 7½% for the first $5000 of sales and 8½% for sales over $5000. However, if the product-line code is 17, then the commission rate is 9½% for the first $3500 of sales and 12% for sales over $3500.

Write a FORTRAN program to determine the commission for each salesperson. Input is the salesperson's number, product-line code, and total sales. Output should be the salesperson's number, total sales, and commission with appropriate headings.

Use the following data to test the program:

Salesperson's Number	Product-line Code	Total Sales
101	17	$2250
103	5	$4000
117	8	$7350
125	5	$6500
138	17	$6375
192	8	$8125
203	8	$3250
218	5	$5000
235	5	$5250
264	17	$4150
291	17	$ 750
999 (trailer card)		

2. A student is placed on the Dean's list of a college if his or her grade point average (GPA) is above a certain level. The minimum GPA necessary to make the Dean's list depends on the student's year in college. A freshman must have a 3.70 GPA or higher to make the Dean's list. For a sophomore the minimum GPA is 3.50. Juniors and seniors require a 3.30 GPA or better to make the Dean's list.

Write a FORTRAN program to print data for all students who are on the Dean's list. Input for this program is one card for each student indicating the student's identification number, year in school (1= freshman, 2=sophomore, 3=junior, 4=senior), and his or her grade point average. Output should consist of the student's number and GPA for Dean's list students only. Supply appropriate headings for the output data.

Use the following data to test the program:

Student Number	Year	GPA
1012	2	3.61
1385	1	2.63
1472	3	3.95
1981	2	3.30
2061	4	2.91
2111	4	3.30
2385	1	3.85
2500	1	3.75
2911	2	3.50
3047	3	3.28
3568	3	3.00
3910	4	3.35
9999 (trailer card)		

3. The annual bonus paid to each employee of an organization is based on the number of years of service and the age of the employee. If the employee has 5 to 9 years of service and is between 25 and 34, the annual bonus is $20. If he or she is 35 or older, with 5 to 9 years of service, the bonus is $40. If the years of service are between 10 and 19, and the age is less than 40 years, the bonus is $40. If the employee is 40 or older, with 10 to 19 years of service, the bonus is $50. If he or she has had 20 or more years of service, no matter what age, then the bonus is $60. For other employees, there is no annual bonus.

Write a FORTRAN program to determine the annual bonus for each eligible employee in the organization. Input for the program is one card for each employee with his or her identification number, age, and number of years of service. Output should include the employee's number and bonus only for those employees who receive a bonus. Supply appropriate headings for the output.

Use the following data to test the program:

Employee's Number	Age	Years of Service
1001	38	12
1121	52	28
1305	42	16
1457	29	8
1689	29	3
1810	37	9
1925	42	20
2008	33	10
2025	24	5
2133	54	23
2485	49	19
2561	24	6
2610	33	5
9999	(trailer card)	

4. A market research survey gave a number of customers a choice of two brands for each of five products and asked the customers to indicate their preference. If a customer preferred the first brand over the second, his or her response was recorded as T in a punched card. If the second brand was preferred, the response was punched as F. After the survey was completed, each punched card contained a customer code and one column for each product punched with T or F.

A FORTRAN program is needed to analyze the results of this survey. The program should determine which customers preferred the first brand for the first or second product, and print — for these customers only — the customer's code and preferences for the last three products. In addition, a count of the number of customers who preferred the first brand for any of the five products should be kept and printed at the end. Supply appropriate headings for all output.

Use the following data to test the program:

Customer's Code	Brand Preferences
11	FTFTF
12	FFFFF
13	TTFTT
14	TFFFF
15	FFFFF
16	FFTTT
17	TFTFF
18	FFFFF
19	TTFTF
20	FFTFF
00	(trailer card)

5. In a political survey a number of people were given six statements about a political candidate's involvement in illicit campaign practices. Each person was asked to indicate whether he or she felt each statement was true or false. The responses for each person were punched in a card.

A FORTRAN program is needed to analyze these data. The program should determine the answers to the following questions:

(1) What percent of the people in the survey felt that the first two statements were true and the remainder false?
(2) What percent felt that all six statements were true?
(3) What percent felt that all six were false?

Output should give the answers to these questions with appropriate descriptive headings.

Use the following data to test the program:

Survey Responses	
TFTFFF	TTFTFF
TTFFFF	TTFFFF
TTTTTT	TTFFFF
FFTTFF	FFFFFF
FFFFFF	TFFFFF
TTFTFT	TTTTTT
FTFTFF	TTFFFF
FFFFFF	FTFFFF
TTFFFF	FFFFFF

The last card in the data deck is a trailer card with a 9 punched in column 80.

6. An employee satisfaction survey asked every employee of an organization to indicate whether each of four working conditions was true or false. The results of the survey were punched in cards, with one card punched for each employee.

Write a FORTRAN program to determine how many employees answered True to all four conditions, how many answered True to any three conditions, how many responded True to any two conditions, how many felt only one condition was true. Print the totals with appropriate headings.

Use the following data to test the program:

	Employee Responses	
TTFF	FTFF	FFFF
TFTT	FFFT	TFFF
TFFF	TTTT	FFFT
FTTT	TTFT	FTFF
FFFF	FTTF	TTTT
TTTF	FTFT	FTFF
TTFF	TTTT	FFFF

The last card in the data deck is punched with a 9 in column 5.

7. Figure 9-1 shows the truth tables for the basic logical expressions. Sometimes it is necessary to develop a truth table for more complex logical expressions. For example, here is a truth table for the expression A.OR.B.AND.C:

A	*B*	*C*	*A.OR.B.AND.C*
T	T	T	T
T	T	F	T
T	F	T	T
T	F	F	T
F	T	T	T
F	T	F	F
F	F	T	F
F	F	F	F

Write a FORTRAN program to print a truth table for the expression

A.AND..NOT.B.OR.B.AND.C

(Hint: This problem can be most easily solved by using nested DO loops and the .NOT. logical operator to reverse the value of a logical variable name.)

There is no input for this program. Output for the program should list the truth table with appropriate headings.

8. A five-question true-false test needs to be graded. The correct answers are punched in the first five columns of a card. On each succeeding card is punched a student's number and his answers to the five questions. Write a FORTRAN program to determine the number of correct answers for each student. The printed output for this program should give the correct answers at the top of the page. Below this, list each student's number, his or her answers, and the number of correct answers. Supply appropriate descriptive headings for all output data.

Use the following data to test the program:

Correct answers: FTTFT

Student's Number	Student's Answers
101	FTFFT
102	TTTFF
103	TFFTF
104	FTTFT
105	TFTFT
106	FTTTT
107	FTFTF
108	TFFTF
109	FTTFT
999 (trailer card)	

9. Write a FORTRAN program to compute the average length of the words in a line of text. Assume that the line only contains alphabetic characters and blanks. Use the following lines to test the program:

        NOW IS THE TIME FOR ALL GOOD MEN
        THE QUICK BROWN FOX JUMPED OVER THE LAZY DOG
        FOUR SCORE AND SEVEN YEARS AGO
        PETER PIPER PICKED A PECK

10. Write a FORTRAN program to count the number of times that the word THE occurs in a line of text. Assume that the line only contains alphabetic characters and blanks. Use the following lines to test the program:

        THE MAN WONDERED WHETHER THE THEATER WAS
        THERE

THEN THE MAN THOUGHT THAT IT WAS HERE
BUT IT WAS NOT THERE
THE THE THE TITHE THE THE THE

11. Write a FORTRAN program that reads a person's name with the last name first followed by a comma and then the first name. The length of the last name and the first name can vary but the input field containing the complete name is eighteen characters long. After reading the data the program should rearrange and print the name with the first name first, a space, and then the last name. Use the following input data to test the program:

WASHINGTON, GEORGE
ADAMS, JOHN
JEFFERSON, THOMAS
MADISON, JAMES
MONROE, JAMES

12. A palindrome is a word, phrase, or number that reads the same forward or backward. For example, RADAR is a palindrome. Write a FORTRAN program that reads a character string containing at most twenty-five characters and determines if it is a palindrome. Print the character string and a statement as to whether or not it is a palindrome. Test the program with the following data:

RATS STAR
MOM
PALINDROME
A
11/5/11
ABLE WAS I ERE I SAW ELBA
ABABAB
1991

13. Write a FORTRAN program that right-justifies a line of text (i.e., aligns the right margin). Input to the program should be a line of no more than forty characters including blanks. Assume that the line only contains alphabetic characters and blanks. Output from the program should be the same line with the first word beginning in position one and the last word ending in position 40 (i.e., left- and right-justified). This may involve inserting extra blanks between words so that the line is properly aligned.

Make up several lines of input to test the program. There should be one test line that is exactly 40 characters in length. All other test lines should be less than 40 characters in length. There should be at least one line that is less than 30 characters in length.

14. The Roman numeral system uses the following seven symbols: M (value 1000), D (value 500), C (value 100), L (value 50), X (value 10), V (value 5), and I (value 1). The Arabic value of each symbol is shown in parentheses. The value of a Roman numeral expressed as an Arabic numeral is found by adding the Arabic value of each Roman symbol. However, if a C, X, or I is to the left of a symbol with a greater value, then the Arabic value of C, X, or I is subtracted. For example, Roman MCDLXXVI is 1476 in the Arabic system.

Write a FORTRAN program to convert Roman numerals to Arabic numerals. The program should read a string of up to 14 Roman symbols, determine the equivalent in the Arabic system, and print the Roman numeral and its Arabic equivalent. Input data should be punched with the Roman numeral in the first 14 columns of a card. By examining each character in the Roman numeral and its relation to other characters, the Arabic equivalent of the Roman numeral can be determined.

Use the following data to test the program:

```
CMXCIX
MDCCLXVI
DCCCXXXIV
MMDCCCLXXXVIII
MCMLXXIV
MCDXLII
CCIII
MMDXXII
(trailer card — all blank)
```

Chapter 10

ARRAYS

Many times it is necessary to store and process a large amount of data in a program. For example, we may need to process a list of fifty numbers, all of which must be available in the program at the same time. Using the techniques that we have discussed so far it would be necessary to use a separate variable name for each number in the list. Hence, fifty variable names would be needed.

Another approach to this type of problem is to identify the entire list of data by a single name. Then each value in the list can be referred to by indicating the position of the value in the list. In this chapter we examine this approach and its use in FORTRAN.

10-1. ARRAYS AND ARRAY ELEMENTS

An *array* is a group of data values that is identified in a program by a single name. An array may be thought of as a list or table of data. An array may contain data of any type—integer, real, double precision, logical, or character. However, all data values in any one array must be of the same type. Thus, a group of integer values may be contained in one array, but another array is necessary for a list of real numbers.

A name that identifies an array is called an *array name*. An array name must follow the rules for variable names and must be the same type as the data in the array. For example, the names X and AMT may be used to identify arrays containing real data; the names M5 and K may be used for arrays of integer data. Figure 10-1(a) shows a list of ten real values. These are identified by the array name A.

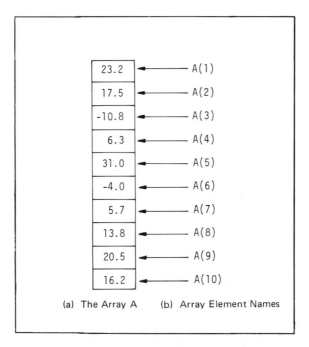

FIGURE 10-1. Arrays and array elements.

Each value in an array is called an *array element.* Thus, in the array in Fig. 10-1(a), the number 23.2 is an array element. Similarly, 17.5, –10.8, and so forth are each elements of the array A. There are ten elements in this array.

In a program we think of the elements of an array as being numbered. The first element in an array is always numbered 1, the second is numbered 2, and so forth throughout the array. The array in Fig. 10-1(a) has 10 elements; thus, the last element is numbered 10. In a program, an array element is identified by coding the name of the array followed immediately by the number of the element in parentheses. For example, the first array element shown in Fig. 10-1(a) is identified as A(1); the fifth element is A(5); the last is A(10). A data name of this sort is called an *array element name* (or sometimes a *subscripted variable name*). The number in parentheses following the array name is called a *subscript.* An array element name such as A(5) is read "A sub five." The complete list of array element names for the array in Fig. 10-1(a) is shown in Fig. 10-1(b).

It is important not to confuse an array element with its subscript. A subscript specifies which value in an array is being identified. The actual value is the array element. Thus, A(5) identifies the fifth value in the array A. The corresponding array element from Fig. 10-1(a) is 31.0.

The data in an array is referred to collectively by an array name. However, an array name may not be used by itself in a FORTRAN program except in a few specialized situations. An array name must normally be followed by a subscript to identify which element of the array is being identified. An array element name may be used like any other variable name. Thus, array element names may be used in READ and WRITE statements and in arithmetic expressions. For example, assume that X and Y identify arrays of 20 elements each. Then the following statements are valid examples of the use of array element names:

```
READ(5,10) X(1),Y(1)
W=X(5)+X(6)+X(7)
WRITE(6,20) X(5),X(6),X(7),W
Y(3)=X(2)*Y(1)/3.5
IF(X(15).GE.Y(10)) GO TO 30
```

The DIMENSION Statement

Before the FORTRAN compiler can translate a source program into machine language it must have information about any arrays that are used in the program. The compiler must know what symbolic names are array names and the number of elements in each array. Among other things, this information is used to reserve storage locations for all of the arrays.

The necessary information about arrays is provided by the DIMENSION statement. The general form of this statement is as follows:

DIMENSION $a1(k1),a2(k2),\ldots,an(kn)$

where $a1,a2,\ldots,an$ are array names.
$\qquad k1,k2,\ldots,kn$ are integer constants indicating the number of elements in the respective arrays.

For example, the following DIMENSION statement describes three arrays.

```
DIMENSION A(10),AMT(25),K(15)
```

The name of the first array is A; it has 10 elements. The second array is AMT and it has 25 elements. The third array has 15 elements and is named K. Note that if a name is specified in a DIMENSION statement, it may not be used as a simple variable name in the program. Thus, in this example the names A, AMT, and K may refer only to arrays.

As many arrays as needed may be specified for a program. All array specifications may be included in one DIMENSION statement, or several statements may be used. The following examples illustrate other DIMENSION statements:

```
DIMENSION X(20),Y(20)
DIMENSION M5(200),DAT(117),P(38),N(150)
DIMENSION SCORE(50)
```

The DIMENSION statement is one type of specification statement. Specification statements provide information to the FORTRAN compiler about the arrangement of data in internal storage. Since such information is needed before the compiler can translate the remainder of the program into machine language, all specification statements must appear at the beginning of the program. Therefore, any DIMENSION statements should be coded before the first executable statement in the program.

Explicit Typing of Arrays

When an array is dimensioned in a DIMENSION statement, it is typed implicitly. That is, the type of data in the array is indicated by the first letter in the array name. Thus, with the statement

```
DIMENSION A(10),K(15)
```

the array A will contain real data and the array K will contain integer values.

It is also possible to type arrays explicitly using INTEGER, REAL, or other type statements. This can be done by dimensioning the array in a DIMENSION statement and then giving its type in a type statement. However, a simpler approach is to include the dimension of the array in the type statement. For example, consider the following statements:

```
INTEGER A(10),X(20)
REAL K(15)
```

The first statement indicates that A and X are arrays of integer data with 10 and 20 elements, respectively. The second statement specifies that K is a 15-element array of real data. Since the dimensions of these arrays are specified in type statement, they must not appear in a DIMENSION statement.

If an array is to contain double precision data, then a DOUBLE PRECISION statement is used to specify the dimension of the array.

For example, the following statement describes a double precision array named W with 50 elements:

DOUBLE PRECISION W(50)

Arrays may also contain logical data and character data. In later sections we will show examples of the use of these types of data in arrays.

Subscripts

A subscript indicates which element of an array is being referred to. The subscript must have an integer value between one and the total number of elements in the array as specified by the DIMENSION statement. As we have seen, a subscript may be an integer constant. A subscript may also be an integer variable name. For example, A(I) is a valid array element name. This is read "A sub I." The element of array A that is being identified by this name depends on the value of I. For example, if the value of I is 3, then the third element of the array A is identified by the name A(I).

The use of a variable name as a subscript is a powerful technique in FORTRAN programming. For example, assume that 10 real values are punched in cards. A program is needed to store the 10 values in an array, accumulate the total of the values, print the array data, and then print the total. The program in Fig. 10-2 shows how this can be done. The program is complete except for the input and output of the array. (Input and output of array data is discussed in the next section.)

In this program the total of the array elements is accumulated by successively adding each element to the variable named TOTAL and storing the result as the value of TOTAL. This is accomplished in a DO

```
          DIMENSION A(10)
          (Read data for array)
          TOTAL=0.0
          DO 100 J=1,10
            TOTAL=TOTAL+A(J)
      100 CONTINUE
          (Print array data)
          WRITE(6,310) TOTAL
          STOP
      310 FORMAT(1H0,F10.2)
          END
```

FIGURE 10-2. An array processing program.

loop by using the DO-variable as the subscript for the array element name. Initially, the value of TOTAL is set to zero. With the first execution of the loop, the value of the DO-variable J is one, and the value of A(1) is added to TOTAL. The second execution of the loop causes the value of A(2) to be added to TOTAL. This continues for the remaining executions of the loop. Upon completion of the DO loop, the value of the variable named TOTAL is

```
0.0+A(1)+A(2)+A(3)+A(4)+A(5)+A(6)+A(7)+A(8)+A(9)+A(10)
```

In addition to integer constants and variable names, subscripts may be simple integer arithmetic expressions. The general forms of the allowable subscript expressions are as follows:

$v+k$
$v-k$
$c*v$
$c*v+k$
$c*v-k$
where v is an integer variable name.
c and k are unsigned integer constants.

(Some versions of FORTRAN allow a subscript to be any integer expression.)
For example, the following array element names use subscripts of these forms:

```
A(I+2)
A(L-3)
A(8*I)
A(3*M+7)
A(2*J-1)
```

The value of a subscript expression such as one of the above is determined by the current value of the variable name. For example, if the value of J is 5, then the last name above refers to the ninth element of array A.

Whether the subscript is a constant, a variable name, or an arithmetic expression, the value of the subscript may not be zero, negative, or greater than the number of elements in the array. In addition, the subscript must always have an integer value whether or not the data in the array is integer or real.

To illustrate common subscript errors, assume that the real array A has 10 elements and that the integer array K has 15 elements. Then the following array element names are invalid for the reasons given:

A(0)	(value of subscript may not be zero)
K(J) where J=-3	(value of subscript may not be negative)
A(15)	(value of subscript may not be greater than the number of elements in the array)
K(5.6)	(subscript may not be real)
A(X)	(subscript may not be real)
A(2+I)	(variable name must precede constant when addition or subtraction is indicated)
K(-3*M)	(constant must be unsigned when multiplication is indicated)
A(L-3.0)	(constant may not be real)
A(K(3))	(subscript may not contain an array element name)
K(3*L) where L=7	(value of subscript may not be greater than the number of elements in the array)

Dimension Bounds

In most versions of FORTRAN an array element name must have a subscript with a value between one and the number of elements given in the DIMENSION statement. That is, the *lower dimension bound* is one and the *upper dimension bound* is the number specified in the DIMENSION statement. However, in some versions of FORTRAN it is possible to specify a lower dimension bound that is not one. In fact, in such versions of FORTRAN the lower and upper dimension bounds can be any integer values—positive, negative, or zero—as long as the lower dimension bound is less than or equal to the upper bound.

The lower and upper dimension bounds for an array are indicated in the DIMENSION statement. The general syntax for a dimension declaration is as follows:

> *a(d1:d2)*
> where *a* is an array name.
>   *d1* is the lower dimension bound.
>   *d2* is the upper dimension bound.

For example, consider the following DIMENSION statement:

```
DIMENSION A(5:10),K(0:7),X(-10:-1)
```

This statement specifies three arrays. The first, A, has a lower dimension bound of 5 and an upper bound of 10. Hence it has six elements. The array K has eight elements with a lower dimension bound of 0 and an upper bound of 7. The final array, X, has a lower bound of –10 and an upper bound of –1. Hence it has ten elements.

Whenever an array is dimensioned with a lower and upper dimension bound, the array name must be used with a subscript value that falls within the bounds. Thus, in the example above we could use A(7) in the program but not A(3) since 3 is less than the lower dimension bound for the array A. Similarly, K(0), K(7), X(-3), and X(-1) are valid but K(-2), K(8), X(-12), and X(0) are invalid.

When processing an array in a DO loop, we often use an initial value and a test value that correspond with the dimension bounds. For example, to total the elements of the array X we can write the following:

```
            TOTAL=0.0
            DO 100 I=-10,-1
               TOTAL=TOTAL+X(I)
        100 CONTINUE
```

(Recall from Chapter 6 that this form of the DO statement is valid in some versions of FORTRAN.) Notice in this example that the DO-variable, I, is incremented from –10 to –1 which corresponds with the dimension bounds of the array X.

Finally, note that if a lower dimension bound is not included in the DIMENSION statement then it is assumed to be one. This is equivalent to the DIMENSION statement discussed earlier in this section.

10-2. INPUT AND OUTPUT OF ARRAY DATA

The most straightforward technique for input and output of array data is to list each array element name in the READ or WRITE statement. For example, assume that B is the name of a five-element array. The following statements cause the data from a punched card to be read and assigned to the array elements:

```
        READ(5,11) B(1),B(2),B(3),B(4),B(5)
     11 FORMAT(5F8.2)
```

Similarly, the array data may be printed with the following statements:

```
    WRITE(6,21) B(1),B(2),B(3),B(4),B(5)
 21 FORMAT(1X,5F8.2)
```

The problem with this technique is that if the array is very large, the READ or WRITE statement list is quite long and tiresome to code. This section presents a number of other approaches to the input and output of array data.

The "Short-List" Technique

An array name may be used in a READ or WRITE statement list without a subscript. When this is done, it specifies that *all* of the data for the array is to be read or written. For example, the following statement has the same effect as the previous READ statement:

```
    READ(5,11) B
```

Similarly, the previous WRITE statement may be coded as follows:

```
    WRITE(6,21) B
```

In both examples, the presence of the array name indicates that data for *all* elements in the array is to be read or written. This approach is sometimes called the "short-list" technique because the input or output list is short in comparison to a list of all array element names.

The "short-list" technique may be used only for the input or output of an entire array. If only part of an array is to be read or written some other approach must be used. For example, assume that only the first three elements of the array are to be read. Then the following statements may be used:

```
    READ(5,12) B(1),B(2),B(3)
 12 FORMAT(3F8.2)
```

If array elements are to be read or written in any order other than in sequence of ascending subscripts, then the "short-list" technique cannot be used. For example, assume that array elements are to be printed in reverse order. Then the following statements may be used:

```
    WRITE(6,22) B(5),B(4),B(3),B(2),B(1)
 22 FORMAT(1X,5F8.2)
```

Another case where the "short-list" technique cannot be used is when other data is to be read or written between the elements of an array. For example, assume that M and N are the names of two 3-element arrays. The data for M and N is punched in alternating fields in a card. Thus, the first field contains the value of M(1), the second field contains N(1), the third field contains M(2), and so forth. If the READ statement is coded as

```
READ(5,13) M,N
```

then all elements of M are read before the elements of N. To read the data in the indicated order, the array element names must be listed alternately as in the following READ statement:

```
READ(5,13) M(1),N(1),M(2),N(2),M(3),N(3)
```

A common use of arrays and the "short-list" technique is for the input and output of character data using numeric variables and the A-format code. Recall from Section 7-3 that the field width is limited when A-format is used. Assuming a maximum field width of four characters, a 20-character item may be broken into five 4-character fields and a variable name assigned to each field. By using a 5-element array, the same effect can be accomplished. For example, the following statements cause the first 20 columns of a card to be read and printed:

```
    DIMENSION W(5)
    READ(5,10) W
10  FORMAT(5A4)
    WRITE(6,20) W
20  FORMAT(1X,5A4)
```

In this example, the "short-list" technique is used to simplify the coding of the READ and WRITE statements.

Multiple Records

Assume that the data for the five elements of the array named B are punched in five cards. One approach to reading this data is to use a slash in the FORMAT statement to indicate a new record. For example, the following statements may be used to read the data:

```
    READ(5,14) B(1),B(2),B(3),B(4),B(5)
14  FORMAT (F8.2/F8.2/F8.2/F8.2/F8.2)
```

Since the entire array is read in the normal order in this example, the "short-list" technique may be used with the same FORMAT statement. For output, this approach may be used to print the array data on separate lines. For example, the following statements print the elements of the array B on five lines:

```
    WRITE(6,24) B
 24 FORMAT(1X,F8.2/1X,F8.2/1X,F8.2/1X,F8.2/1X,F8.2)
```

Notice that the "short-list" technique is used in this example. If only part of the array is to be printed or if the array data is to be printed in a nonsequential order, then the array element names must be coded individually in the READ statement list.

In cases such as those illustrated above, the programmer can take advantage of the technique of overloading the I/O list which was discussed in Chapter 7. In this approach there are more entries in the input or output list than there are format codes in the FORMAT statement. When additional format codes are needed, control returns to the beginning of the last major group or, if no group repetition exists, to the beginning of the format codes. Then a new record is begun, and the same format codes are used again. For example, data for the array named B may be read from five cards with the following statements:

```
    READ(5,15) B(1),B(2),B(3),B(4),B(5)
 15 FORMAT(F8.2)
```

The value of B(1) is read from the first card. Then since there are no more entries in the input list, control returns to the beginning of the FORMAT statement and the value of B(2) is read from a second card. This continues until data for all names in the input list have been read.

This approach, coupled with a "short-list," makes an extremely powerful yet easy to code technique. For example, the following statements have the same effect as the previous example:

```
    READ(5,15) B
 15 FORMAT(F8.2)
```

Although it appears that only the data for a single variable name is to be read, the fact that B is a 5-element array (as indicated by a DIMENSION statement) causes five values to be read.

Looping Techniques

Another approach to the problem of reading or writing multiple records is to use a loop to control the input or output operation. For example, the following sequence of statements uses a DO loop to control the number of records that are read:

```
DO 50 I=1,5
   READ(5,160) B(I)
50 CONTINUE
160 FORMAT(F8.2)
```

The DO-variable is used as a subscript of the array element name. With each execution of the loop, the READ statement is executed and a new record is read. Thus, with the first execution of the loop, the value of B(1) is read. Then the DO-variable is incremented and the value of B(2) is read during the second execution of the loop. This continues until the loop is terminated. This looping technique also can be used for output. For example, the following statements cause the data in array B to be printed on five lines:

```
DO 60 I=1,5
   WRITE(6,260) B(I)
60 CONTINUE
260 FORMAT(1X,F8.2)
```

Using a loop to control the input and output of array data is most useful for large arrays when the array data is to be read or written in an unusual order. For example, assume that the first 100 elements of the array M5 are punched with two elements per card. The data can be read by using a DO loop that is executed 50 times as illustrated by the following statements:

```
DO 70 J=1,99,2
   READ(5,170) M5(J),M5(J+1)
70 CONTINUE
170 FORMAT(2I6)
```

With each execution of the DO loop, two elements of the array are read. The use of the DO-variable in the subscripts J and J+1 causes the data to be assigned to the proper array element names.

As another example of the use of the looping technique, consider the problem of printing two arrays in adjacent columns. Assume that X and Y are the names of two 20-element arrays. The following statements cause the data in the arrays to be printed in columns along with another column for the value of the DO-variable:

```
     DO 80 L=1,20
        WRITE(6,280) L,X(L),Y(L)
  80 CONTINUE
 280 FORMAT(1X,I3,2F8.2)
```

If array data is to be read until a trailer value is detected, a looping technique must be used. For example, assume that the array named N has at most 150 elements. Each element is punched in a separate card. The last card in the data deck is a trailer card with zero punched in the field for the array element. To read the data, a loop must be used with a test for the trailer value included in the loop. The following statements accomplish this:

```
     DIMENSION N(151)
     J=1
  90 READ(5,190) N(J)
     IF(N(J).EQ.0) GO TO 95
     J=J+1
     GO TO 90
  95 (next statement)
 190 FORMAT(I5)
```

Notice in this example that N is dimensioned with 151 elements. This is because there can be at most 150 elements read for N plus the trailer value. When the loop is terminated, J will be equal to the number of elements read plus one for the trailer value. Hence, to find the actual number of data values in the array, J must be decreased by one.

Implied-DO lists

For input or output of partial or whole arrays a DO loop may be implied in a READ or WRITE statement list. This is called an *implied-DO list*. For example, the input list in the following statement consists of an implied-DO list:

```
     READ(5,31) (B(I),I=1,4,1)
```

The entire specification of an implied-DO list must be enclosed in parentheses. Within the parentheses is a list of variable and array element names separated by commas with a comma following the last name. In this example, there is one name, B(I), in the list. Following this, the DO-variable and parameters are specified as in a DO statement. In this example, the DO-variable is the variable named I, the intial value of the DO-variable is 1, the test value is 4, and the increment is 1. As in a DO statement the increment may be omitted when it is 1. The keyword DO and the terminal statement number are not included in an implied-DO list. The range is the list of variable and array element names. The function of the parameters is the same as in a DO loop. Thus, this example has the effect of causing the values of B(1), B(2), B(3), and B(4) to be read in that order.

The parameters of an implied-DO list may be any positive integer constants or variable names within the appropriate limits. For example, consider the following WRITE statement:

```
WRITE(6,41) (AMT(J),J=10,LIM,2)
```

In this statement the initial value of the DO-variable is 10, the test value is the value of the variable named LIM, and the increment is 2. If LIM is 18, this statement causes the values of AMT(10), AMT(12), AMT(14), AMT(16), and AMT(18) to be printed. It is important to insure that the value of a subscript for an array element name does not become zero or negative, or exceed the number of elements in the array. In this example, if AMT is the name of a 25-element array, then a test value greater than 25 results in an error.

An implied-DO list does not necessarily cause data to be read or written in the same manner as a regular DO loop. This depends on the way in which the FORMAT statement is coded. For example, consider the following sequence of statements:

```
      DO 20 I=1,4
         READ(5,33) B(I)
   20 CONTINUE
   33 FORMAT(F8.2)
```

In this case, four cards are read and the data assigned to the first four elements of the array named B. The same effect can be accomplished using an implied-DO list as follows:

```
      READ(5,33) (B(I),I=1,4)
   33 FORMAT(F8.2)
```

In this case, the input list is over-loaded since four values are to be read but the FORMAT statement contains only one format code. Thus, the data is read from four cards. If all four values are punched on one card, the following statements may be used:

```
     READ(5,34) (B(I),I=1,4)
  34 FORMAT(4F8.2)
```

The same effect cannot be accomplished with a regular DO loop because each execution of the DO loop's range causes a new card to be read.

A READ or WRITE statement list may contain several implied-DO lists as well as other variable and array names. For example, consider the following READ statement:

```
  READ(5,32) ID,SN,(N(J),J=1,10),(A(J),J=1,5)
```

With this statement a total of 17 values are read.

More than one variable or array element name may be included in the list of an implied-DO list. For example, the following statements cause values for the first 50 elements of the array M5 to be read:

```
     READ(5,17) (M5(J),M5(J+1),J=1,49,2)
  17 FORMAT(2I6)
```

Because the input list is overloaded, two values are read from each input card. As another example, consider the following statements:

```
     WRITE(6,28) (L,X(L),Y(L),L=1,20)
  28 FORMAT(1X,I5,2F8.2)
```

In this example, variable name L is included in the implied-DO list. Since this is also the DO-variable of the loop, the output consists of three columns, one listing the value of L, the other two giving the values of arrays X and Y.

The implied-DO list is a versatile approach to the input and output of array data. However, in situations where an entire array is to be read or written in sequence, the "short-list" technique is more efficient. The implied-DO list is most useful for the input or output of partial arrays or several alternating arrays. It is preferred over a regular DO loop when it can be used. In some situations neither the "short-list" technique nor an implied-DO list can be used. For example, if data is to be printed in reverse order or a test for a trailer value is needed in an input routine, then a regular loop must be used.

10-3. INITIALIZING ARRAYS IN A DATA STATEMENT

Array elements may be initialized in a DATA statement by indicating the array element name. For example, the following statement assigns the value 0.0 to each of the first three elements of the array named AMT:

DATA AMT(1),AMT(2),AMT(3)/3*0.0/

Although some versions of FORTRAN do not allow an array name to appear in a DATA statement without a subscript, most versions of the language do allow this. The effect of such a specification is to cause the entire array to be initialized to the indicated values. For example, consider the following:

DATA AMT/25*0.0/,K/10*0,5*1/

Here it is assumed that AMT is the name of a 25-element array and that array K contains 15 elements. The effect of this DATA statement is to initialize all elements of the array named AMT to 0.0 and to assign 0 to the first 10 elements of K and 1 to the remaining five elements.

Some versions of FORTRAN allow implied-DO lists in the DATA statement. For example, consider the following statement:

DATA (X(I),I=2,20,2)/10*1.0/

This statement causes X(2), X(4), X(6), and so forth up to X(20) to be each initialized to 1.0. As another example, consider the following statement:

DATA A,B,(K(J),M(J),J=1,10)/2.5,3.5,20*0/

This statement initializes A and B to 2.5 and 3.5 respectively and initializes the first ten elements of K and M to 0.

10-4. ARRAY PROCESSING TECHNIQUES

The use of arrays is one of the most powerful features of the FORTRAN programming language. With the proper use of loops and subscripts, extensive processing can be accomplished with just a few

statements. This section illustrates a number of array processing techniques. While many of the examples may seem simple, the techniques
illustrated appear often in complex array processing programs. For
the examples, we assume that the arrays named X, Y, and Z have 20
elements each.

Often it is necessary to set each element of an array to an initial
value. For example, assume that the elements of array X must be
initialized to zero, and the elements of Y and Z are each to be given
an initial value of one. Then the three arrays may be initialized in one
loop as follows:

```
        DO 110 I=1,20
          X(I)=0.0
          Y(I)=1.0
          Z(I)=1.0
    110 CONTINUE
```

After the data has been read for an array it is sometimes necessary
to copy the data into another array. As a result, the original data can be
saved in one array while it is manipulated or modified in the other. For
example, assume that data has been read for array X. Then the data is
copied into array Y by the following statements:

```
        DO 120 J=1,20
          Y(J)=X(J)
    120 CONTINUE
```

Sometimes a copy of the array data is necessary with the elements
in reverse order. In other words, the first element of one array is
assigned to the last element of another array, the second element of
the first array is assigned to the next-to-last element of the other array,
and so forth until the last element of the first array is assigned to the
first element of the other array. To accomplish this, the subscript of
the first array must be incremented from 1 to the maximum, while
the subscript of the second array is decremented from the maximum to
1. The following statements accomplish this for arrays X and Y:

```
        J=20
        DO 130 I=1,20
          Y(J)=X(I)
          J=J-1
    130 CONTINUE
```

Notice that the integer variable named J is initialized to 20 and then
decreased by 1 with each execution of the DO loop. Thus, with the

first execution of the DO loop, X(1) is assigned to Y(20). Then the value of the DO-variable is incremented to 2 while the value of J is decremented to 19. The second execution of the loop causes the value of X(2) to be assigned to Y(19). This continues until the last execution of the loop when the value of X(20) is assigned to Y(1).

Array elements are often processed arithmetically. For example, the following statements add the corresponding elements of the arrays X and Y and assign the results to the array Z:

```
     DO 140 K=1,20
       Z(K)=X(K)+Y(K)
 140 CONTINUE
```

On occasion it is necessary to determine how many times a particular value occurs in an array. For example, we may wish to know the number of elements of Y that are zero. The following statements accomplish this:

```
      NUM=0
      DO 150 I=1,20
        IF(Y(I).EQ.0.0) NUM=NUM+1
  150 CONTINUE
```

At the end of execution of this sequence, the variable named NUM will be equal to the number of elements of Y that are equal to zero. A similar situation occurs when we want to know the number of elements in two arrays that are equal. For example, we may want to know how many elements of X and Z are the same. The following statements accomplish this:

```
      NUM=0
      DO 160 J=1,20
        IF(X(J).EQ.Z(J)) NUM=NUM+1
  160 CONTINUE
```

Often it is necessary to locate the largest or smallest element in the array. For example, assume that it is necessary to find the smallest element in the array X. The following statements accomplish this:

```
      SMALL=X(1)
      DO 170 L=2,20
        IF(X(L).LT.SMALL) SMALL=X(L)
  170 CONTINUE
```

Initially we assume that the first element of the array is the smallest and its value is assigned to the variable named SMALL. Then this value is compared with each succeeding element to determine if there is one smaller. If an element is smaller, its value is assigned to SMALL, replacing the previous value. If an element is not smaller than the current value of SMALL, then this assignment is bypassed. At the end of the execution of the loop the value of the variable named SMALL is the smallest element of the array.

Searching

A common problem is to search an array for a specific value. In the simplest case, a value is given and the first occurrence of an equivalent value is to be located in an array. For example, the following statements search the array X for the first element whose value is equal to that of V:

```
      I=1
   10 IF(X(I).EQ.V) GO TO 20
      I=I+1
      GO TO 10
   20 WRITE(6,300) I
  300 FORMAT(24H VALUE FOUND AT ELEMENT ,I2)
```

In this sequence, I is used as a subscript. Initially I is one and each time through the loop I is increased by one. The loop is terminated when X(I) is equal to V. The value of I at this time is the number of the first element in X that has a value equal to V. This value of I is written when the loop is terminated.

The problem with this sequence of statements is that it does not take into account the case where the value of V is not in the array. However, we can modify the statements to print an error message if the value is not found. The following sequence of statements accomplishes this:

```
      I=1
   10 IF((X(I).EQ.V).OR.(I.EQ.20)) GO TO 20
      I=I+1
      GO TO 10
   20 IF(X(I).EQ.V) GO TO 30
      WRITE(6,310)
      GO TO 40
   30 WRITE(6,300) I
   40 (next statement)
  300 FORMAT(24H VALUE FOUND AT ELEMENT ,I2)
  310 FORMAT(16H VALUE NOT FOUND)
```

In this sequence the loop is terminated when X(I) equals V *or* when I equals 20. The latter case occurs when we reach the end of the array. After branching out of the loop, we must test to see if the value was actually found or if the loop was terminated without finding the value. In the former case, we write the corresponding array element number. If X(I) is not equal to V when the loop is terminated, then the value must not have been found and we write an appropriate error message.

Many times we need to search one array and retrieve the corresponding element of another array. For example, we may wish to search array X for value V and write the corresponding value of array Y when V is found. The only modification in the previous sequence of statements that is necessary is that Y(I) is written instead of I.

To illustrate the use of searching in an actual program consider the problem of locating the price of an item in a table. For example, Fig. 10-3 shows a table of item numbers and prices. Our problem is to store the pricing table in two arrays, one for the item numbers and one for the prices. Then we must read an item number and a value that represents the quantity of the item purchased, locate the item's price in the table, and compute the cost by multiplying the price by the quantity. Figure 10-4 shows the program that accomplishes this.

After reading the input data this program searches the item number array, ITNUM, for an element that is equal to INUM. The program assumes that the item numbers are in increasing order in the array and branches out of the searching loop when ITNUM(I) is either equal to INUM or greater than INUM. This latter case occurs when we have gone beyond the value of INUM in the array. (If the item numbers are not in increasing order, then the greater than or equal to condition would have to be changed to an equal to condition.) The loop is also terminated if we reach the end of the array without finding INUM (that is, when I is equal to 10). After leaving the loop, we check to see if INUM equals ITNUM(I). If this condition is true we multiply QTY by PRICE(I) to

Item Number	Unit Price
1001	$2.95
1023	$3.64
1045	$2.25
1172	$0.75
1185	$1.50
1201	$1.95
1235	$4.85
1278	$9.95
1384	$6.28
1400	$4.75

FIGURE 10-3. A pricing table.

```
      DIMENSION ITNUM(10),PRICE(10)
      DO 100 I=1,10
        READ(5,300) ITNUM(I),PRICE(I)
  100 CONTINUE
  200 READ(5,310) INUM,QTY
      IF(INUM.EQ.9999) GO TO 250
      I=1
  210 IF((ITNUM(I).GE.INUM).OR.(I.EQ.10)) GO TO 220
      I=I+1
      GO TO 210
  220 IF(INUM.EQ.ITNUM(I)) GO TO 230
      WRITE(6,400) INUM
      GO TO 240
  230 COST=PRICE(I)*QTY
      WRITE(6,410) INUM,COST
  240 GO TO 200
  250 STOP
  300 FORMAT(I4,F4.2)
  310 FORMAT(I4,F3.0)
  400 FORMAT(6H ITEM ,I4,10H NOT FOUND)
  410 FORMAT(6H ITEM ,I4,6H COST ,F7.2)
      END
```

FIGURE 10-4. A pricing program with a sequential
search.

get the cost and print the result. Otherwise, we write an error message
before repeating the input loop.

The example illustrates a common algorithm for "table look-up,"
the process of looking something up in a table. (Recall from Chapter 8
that an algorithm is a sequence of instructions that solves a problem.) In
this algorithm we search through the array elements in sequence. This
approach is called a *sequential search.* In a sequential search we begin
by looking at the first element of the array, then the second element is
examined, then the third, and so forth until the desired element is
found or until we can determine that the item is not in the array.

Another algorithm for searching for an element in an array is called
a *binary search.* In a binary search the array elements *must* be in ascending or descending order. We will assume that the elements of the
array to be searched are in ascending order. Then with a binary search
we first look at the *middle* element of the array and determine if this is
the desired element. If we have not found the element that we want
then we determine if it is located before or after the middle one. We
then search the appropriate half of the array by examining the middle

element of that half. Again we determine whether the element is the one we want or whether we should search above or below the middle element. We continue to search by examining the middle of smaller and smaller sections of the array until the desired element is found or until we can determine that the element is not in the array.

To illustrate this algorithm, assume that the twenty elements of the array X are in ascending order. We wish to use a binary search to locate the element with a value equal to V. The following sequence of statements accomplishes this:

```
    NBOT=1
    NTOP=20
10  MID=(NBOT+NTOP)/2
    IF((X(MID).EQ.V).OR.(NBOT.GT.NTOP)) GO TO 40
    IF(V.LT.X(MID)) GO TO 20
    NBOT=MID+1
    GO TO 30
20  NTOP=MID-1
30  GO TO 10
40  IF(V.EQ.X(MID)) GO TO 50
    WRITE(6,310)
    GO TO 60
50  WRITE(6,300) MID
60  (next statement)
300 FORMAT(24H VALUE FOUND AT ELEMENT ,I2)
310 FORMAT(16H VALUE NOT FOUND)
```

In this sequence NBOT equals the number of the bottom element of the array being searched and NTOP equals the number of the top element. Initially these are 1 and 20 respectively. The number of the middle element of the part of the array being searched is computed and assigned to MID. Each time through the loop we check to see if X(MID) equals V and branch out of the loop if this is the case. If V is not found then we check to see if V is less than X(MID). If this is the case, then we let NTOP be one less than MID. If V is greater than X(MID) then NBOT is MID plus 1. Then we compute a new MID and repeat the process. The loop terminates either when we find the desired element or when NBOT is greater than NTOP in which case the element is not in the array. Figure 10-5 shows how a binary search compares with a sequential search.

We can use a binary search algorithm in the pricing table program. Figure 10-6 shows the complete program. Notice that after the appropriate item is found, the cost is determined by multiplying QTY by PRICE(MID).

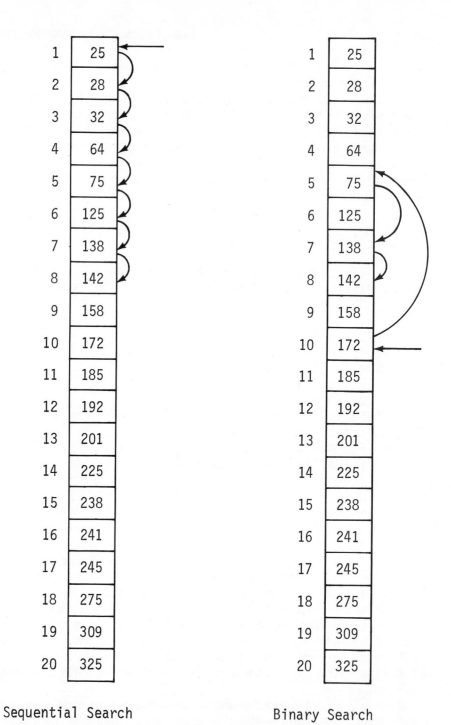

FIGURE 10-5. Sequential vs. binary search.

```
      DIMENSION ITNUM(10),PRICE(10)
      DO 100 I=1,10
        READ(5,300) ITNUM(I),PRICE(I)
100   CONTINUE
200   READ(5,310) INUM,QTY
      IF(INUM.EQ.9999) GO TO 250
      NBOT=1
      NTOP=10
210   MID=(NBOT+NTOP)/2
      IF((ITNUM(MID).EQ.INUM).OR.(NBOT.GT.NTOP)) GO TO 225
      IF(INUM.LT.ITNUM(MID)) GO TO 215
      NBOT=MID+1
      GO TO 220
215   NTOP=MID-1
220   GO TO 210
225   IF(INUM.EQ.ITNUM(MID)) GO TO 230
      WRITE(6,400) INUM
      GO TO 240
230   COST=PRICE(MID)*QTY
      WRITE(6,410) INUM,COST
240   GO TO 200
250   STOP
300   FORMAT(I4,F4.2)
310   FORMAT(I4,F3.0)
400   FORMAT(6H ITEM ,I4,10H NOT FOUND)
410   FORMAT(6H ITEM ,I4,6H COST ,F7.2)
      END
```

FIGURE 10-6. A pricing program with a binary search.

For large arrays, a binary search is much faster than a sequential search. For example, if an array contains 1000 elements then on the average a sequential search will require about 1000/2 or 500 repetitions of the loop. However, for a binary search the loop will be repeated no more than $\log_2 1000$ or 10 times. Clearly for large arrays, the extra complexity required to program a binary search results in considerable savings in execution time of the program.

Sorting

Sorting is the process of rearranging a set of data into a particular order. For example, given a list of numbers we may wish to sort the numbers into ascending or descending order. There are many times when sorted data is needed. For example, we may want to produce a list of students in a class in order by student identification number. This requires sorting if the data is not already in order. In the last subsection we saw that an array must be in ascending or descending order if the binary search algorithm is to be used. If the array is not in the appropriate order, then it must be sorted before it can be searched.

There are many algorithms for sorting. In this subsection we discuss *bubble* sorting. (This type of sorting is also called *pushdown* sorting, *interchange* sorting, and *exchange* sorting.) As we will see, bubble sorting gets its name from the fact that data "bubbles" to the top of the array.

The basic principle of bubble sorting is to compare adjacent elements of the array to be sorted. If any two adjacent elements are found to be out of order with respect to each other, then they are interchanged (that is, their values are switched). For example, assume that the array B has five elements that are to be sorted into ascending order. Then the following loop will pass through the array once, exchanging elements that are not in the proper order:

```
      DO 10 I=1,4
        IF(B(I).LE.B(I+1)) GO TO 10
        T=B(I)
        B(I)=B(I+1)
        B(I+1)=T
   10 CONTINUE
```

Notice that the loop is repeated *four* times. Each time through the loop B(I) is compared with B(I+1). Thus the first time through the loop B(1) is compared with B(2). Then B(2) is compared with B(3). Next B(3) and B(4) are compared. Finally B(4) and B(5) are compared. If any two adjacent elements are not in ascending order, then they are switched. (See Section 8–4 for a discussion of switching the values of two variables.) Figure 10–7 shows what takes place for a particular set of data.

This loop will cause the largest element of the array to be "pushed down" to the last position in the array. At the same time, smaller elements start to "bubble up" to the top of the array. We now must repeat the loop to cause the next largest elements to be pushed to the next-to-last position in the array. Then the loop must be repeated for the next-to-next largest element, and so forth. In all, this loop must be repeated four times. The last time, the smallest element will automatically end up in the first position of the array. This repeated execution of the loop can be accomplished by nested DO loops as follows:

```
      DO 20 J=1,4
        DO 10 I=1,4
          IF(B(I).LE.B(I+1)) GO TO 10
```

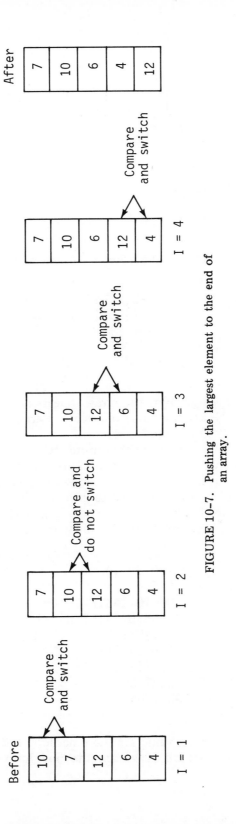

FIGURE 10-7. Pushing the largest element to the end of an array.

303

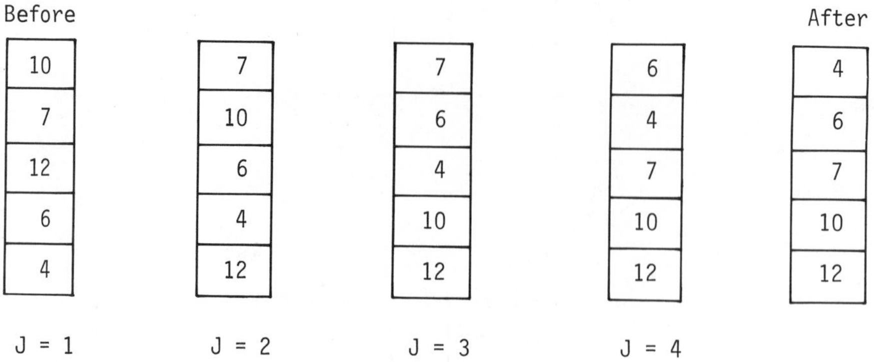

Before   After

J = 1   J = 2   J = 3   J = 4

FIGURE 10-8.   Sorting a five-element array.

```
         T=B(I)
         B(I)=B(I+1)
         B(I+1)=T
   10    CONTINUE
   20 CONTINUE
```

Figure 10-8 shows how the array appears after each execution of the outer loop. Notice that large values in the array are "pushed down" and small values "bubble up."

We can make the algorithm more efficient by recognizing that with each successive "pass" through the inner loop one less comparison is required. This is because once the largest element has been pushed to the end of the array we don't need to include it in any subsequent comparisons. The same holds true for the next largest element and so forth. The following sequence of statements includes this modification:

```
      DO 20 J=1,4
         K=5-J
         DO 10 I=1,K
            IF(B(I).LE.B(I+1)) GO TO 10
            T=B(I)
            B(I)=B(I+1)
            B(I+1)=T
   10    CONTINUE
   20 CONTINUE
```

Notice that the test value for the inner loop is the value of the variable named K. When J is 1, K is 4 and the inner loop is executed four times.

```
      DO 160 J=1,19
        K=20-J
        DO 150 I=1,K
          IF(ITNUM(I).LE.ITNUM(I+1)) GO TO 150
          ITEMP=ITNUM(I)
          ITNUM(I)=ITNUM(I+1)
          ITNUM(I+1)=ITEMP
          TEMP=PRICE(I)
          PRICE(I)=PRICE(I+1)
          PRICE(I+1)=TEMP
150     CONTINUE
160 CONTINUE
```

FIGURE 10-9. Sorting a pricing table.

When J becomes 2, K is 3 and the inner loop is only done three times. We can see that K is one less for each successive time through the inner loop. Hence, one fewer comparison is done with each repetition of the loop.

We can use bubble sorting to sort the pricing table used in the examples in the previous subsection. This would be required if a search is to be done and the table is not read in ascending order by item number. The only modification that is necessary is that each time two item numbers are found out of sequence and switched, the corresponding prices must be switched. This is so that the relationship between the item numbers and prices is maintained. The sequence of statements to accomplish this is shown in Fig. 10-9. These statements would be included in the program in Fig. 10-4 or the one in Fig. 10-6 between statements 100 and 200.

The examples so far demonstrate *ascending* order sorts. To sort an array into descending order the less than or equal to condition in the IF statement must be changed to a greater than or equal to condition. The effect then is that the smaller elements are pushed to the end of the array and the larger elements "bubble up" to the beginning of the array.

Bubble sorting is just one of many ways to sort an array. There are a number of algorithms that are considerably faster than bubble sorting for large arrays. However, these algorithms are also more difficult to program. As the programmer finds more situations where sorting is required, other techniques should be explored.[†]

[†]Most text books on data structures include sections on sorting. A very complete reference is by Donald Knuth entitled *The Art of Computer Programming, Vol. 3, Sorting and Searching*, published by Addison-Wesley.

10-5. LOGICAL DATA ARRAYS

In Section 9-3 the LOGICAL type statement was used to declare logical variable names. This statement is also used to describe the dimension of arrays that contain logical data. For example, the following statement declares that the name LA identifies a twenty-element array of logical data:

```
LOGICAL LA(20)
```

A logical array name may be subscripted like any other array name to identify an element of an array. For example, LA(1) is the name of the first element in the logical array LA. Similarly, LA(I) identifies the "Ith" element. A logical array element name may be used in a logical expression in the same manner as a logical variable name. For example, the following are valid statements that use logical array element names:

```
IF(LA(3).AND.LA(4)) GO TO 100
LA(5)=LA(6)
WRITE(6,200) LA(I),LA(I+1)
LA(1)=.NOT.LA(2).AND.LA(3).OR.LA(4)
```

As an example of a program using logical arrays consider the problem of analyzing the results of a true-false questionnaire. Assume that the questionnaire contains 50 questions and the answer to each question is punched as a T or F in the first 50 columns of a card. The program in Fig. 10-10 reads the questionnaire answers by using the "short-list" technique, counts the number of true answers (with the IF statement), and prints the result.

```
      LOGICAL ANS(50)
      READ(5,100) ANS
      KOUNT=0
      DO 10 I=1,50
         IF(ANS(I)) KOUNT=KOUNT+1
   10 CONTINUE
      WRITE(6,200) KOUNT
      STOP
  100 FORMAT(50L1)
  200 FORMAT(1X,I3)
      END
```

FIGURE 10-10. A program to analyze a true-false questionnaire.

306

10-6. CHARACTER DATA ARRAYS

An array may contain character data if it is declared in a CHARACTER statement. For example, the following statement specifies a character data array with 20 elements:

$$\text{CHARACTER CA(20)}$$

Recall from Section 7–3 that the CHARACTER statement not only indicates that a variable refers to character data but also gives the length of the character variable. With an array of character data each element in the array has the same length. In the above example, since an explicit length is not given, each element is assumed to have a length of one. When a length specification is given it may appear after the word CHARACTER or after the dimension of the array. For example, consider the following statement:

$$\text{CHARACTER*10 CB(30),CC(100)*20}$$

This statement specifies two character arrays. The first, CB, has thirty elements each of length ten. The second array, CC, contains 100 elements each with a length of twenty.

A character array element name is subscripted just like a numeric array element name. For example, CB(5) refers to the fifth element of the character array named CB. Similarly, CB(J) identifies the "Jth" element. When a substring name is used, the position of the substring follows the subscript. For example, CB(15)(3:8) refers to the third through eighth characters of the fifteenth element of the array CB.

A subscripted character array name or substring name may be used in a character expression just like a character variable name. For example, the following statements use character array element names:

```
CB(5)=CB(4)
IF(CB(30)(1:3).EQ.'END') GO TO 100
WRITE(6,200) (CB(I),I=1,10)
CC(I)=CB(I)//CB(I+1)
```

To illustrate the use of character arrays in a program, assume that on each of fifty cards is punched the name of a state and its population. This data must be stored in two arrays, one for the state names and one for the populations, to create a population table. Next a card must be read with any state's name. Then the population table has to be searched to find and print the state's population. Figure 10–11 shows a program to accomplish this.

```
      CHARACTER*12 STATE(50),STA
      DIMENSION IPOP(50)
      DO 100 I=1,50
        READ(5,300) STATE(I),IPOP(I)
100   CONTINUE
200   READ(5,310) STA
      IF(STA.EQ.' ') GO TO 250
      I=1
210   IF((STA.EQ.STATE(I).OR.(I.EQ.50)) GO TO 220
      I=I+1
      GO TO 210
220   IF(STA.EQ.STATE(I)) GO TO 230
      WRITE(6,400) STA
      GO TO 240
230   WRITE(6,410) STA,IPOP(I)
240   GO TO 200
250   STOP
300   FORMAT(A12,I8)
310   FORMAT(A12)
400   FORMAT(' ',A12,' IS AN INVALID STATE NAME')
410   FORMAT(' ',A12,' HAS A POPULATION OF ',I8)
      END
```

FIGURE 10-11. A character data array processing program.

PROGRAMMING PROBLEMS

1. Write a FORTRAN program that reads hourly temperatures for a
day into a twenty-four element array. The first element of the array
gives the temperature at 1:00 A.M., the second element is the temperature at 2:00 A.M., and so forth. Note that the thirteenth element is the
temperature at 1:00 P.M. Then search the array for the maximum and
minimum temperatures. Print these temperatures along with the times
that they occur. Supply appropriate input data to test the program.

2. An inventory table contains information about the quantity of
inventory on hand for each item stocked. Assume that there are fifteen
items in the inventory. The inventory data is punched in fifteen cards
with each card containing an item number and the quantity of the item
that is in stock. The data is in increasing order by item number.

Write a FORTRAN program to do the following:

(a) Read the inventory table into two arrays, one for the item numbers and one for the quantities. Then print the inventory data in columns below appropriate headings.
(b) Read a card containing an item number, an amount received, and an amount sold. Search the inventory table for the corresponding item using either a sequential search or a binary search. Then update the quantity on hand by adding the amount received to the amount from the table and subtracting the amount sold. Repeat this step until 9999 is read for an item number. Be sure to account for the case where the item is not in the table.
(c) After all items have been updated print the inventory data in columns below appropriate headings.

Use the following data for the inventory table:

Item Number	Quantity On Hand
1102	100
1113	25
1147	37
1158	95
1196	225
1230	150
1237	15
1239	105
1245	84
1275	97
1276	350
1284	82
1289	125
1351	138
1362	64

Use the following data to update the inventory table:

Item Number	Quantity Received	Quantity Sold
1230	25	100
1113	0	15
1255	16	42
1289	50	0
1405	26	5
1102	100	75
1239	25	25

3. The following tax rate schedule is used to compute tax for a single taxpayer:

SCHEDULE X—Single Taxpayers Not Qualifying for Rates in Schedule Y or Z

Use this schedule if you checked **Box 1** on Form 1040—

If the amount on Schedule TC, Part I, line 3, is:

Enter on Schedule TC, Part I, line 4:

Not over $2,200............ —0—

Over—	But not over—		of the amount over—
$2,200	$2,700	14%	$2,200
$2,700	$3,200	$70+15%	$2,700
$3,200	$3,700	$145+16%	$3,200
$3,700	$4,200	$225+17%	$3,700
$4,200	$6,200	$310+19%	$4,200
$6,200	$8,200	$690+21%	$6,200
$8,200	$10,200	$1,110+24%	$8,200
$10,200	$12,200	$1,590+25%	$10,200
$12,200	$14,200	$2,090+27%	$12,200
$14,200	$16,200	$2,630+29%	$14,200
$16,200	$18,200	$3,210+31%	$16,200
$18,200	$20,200	$3,830+34%	$18,200
$20,200	$22,200	$4,510+36%	$20,200
$22,200	$24,200	$5,230+38%	$22,200
$24,200	$28,200	$5,990+40%	$24,200
$28,200	$34,200	$7,590+45%	$28,200
$34,200	$40,200	$10,290+50%	$34,200
$40,200	$46,200	$13,290+55%	$40,200
$46,200	$52,200	$16,590+60%	$46,200
$52,200	$62,200	$20,190+62%	$52,200
$62,200	$72,200	$26,390+64%	$62,200
$72,200	$82,200	$32,790+66%	$72,200
$82,200	$92,200	$39,390+68%	$82,200
$92,200	$102,200	$46,190+69%	$92,200
$102,200	....	$53,090+70%	$102,200

The tax is based on the individual's taxable income. For example, if the taxable income is $17,500, then the income tax is $3210 plus 31% of the difference between $17,500 and $16,200, or $3613.00.

Write a FORTRAN program that reads the tax rate schedule into several arrays. One approach is to use three arrays, one for the first column, and two for the third column. Then the program should read a taxpayer identification number and taxable income, compute the income tax, and print the results.

Use the following data to test the program:

Taxpayer Number	Taxable Income
1234	$ 17,500
1332	6,200
1424	10,201
2134	1,500
2432	47,300
3144	154,000
3223	23,350

4. The results of a random survey of the households in an area of a city have been punched in cards. Each card contains information about one household in the area. An identification number, the annual income of the head of the household, and the number of people living in the household is punched in each card. The last card in the data deck is punched with 9999 in the identification number field. Write a FORTRAN program to analyze these data according to the following specifications:

(a) Read the survey results into three arrays, one for the identification numbers, one for the annual incomes, and one for the number of people living in the households. Assume that there are no more than 50 households in the survey and dimension all arrays accordingly. However, there may be fewer than 50 data cards, so a count of the number of cards must be kept as data are read. Finally, print the array data in columns below appropriate headings.

(b) Calculate the average income and average number of people for all households. Print the results with appropriate headings.

(c) Print the identification number and annual income of all households whose income is below the average.

(d) Determine the percent of the households in the area that have incomes below the poverty level. The poverty level depends on the number of people living in the household. If there is one person, the poverty level income is $3500. If there are two people, the poverty level is $4500. For a household with more than two people, the poverty level is $4500 plus $750 for each additional person.

Use the following to test the program:

Identification Number	Annual Income	Number of People
1011	$ 8,750	3
1020	3,250	2
1083	6,000	5
1141	6,500	1
1157	12,300	4
1235	7,000	6
1347	8,350	7
1508	2,350	1
1512	4,900	3
1513	5,600	4
1584	6,385	2
1631	4,300	2
1690	15,200	4
1742	13,350	5
1755	3,700	1
1759	6,300	3
1763	5,250	8
1809	8,250	1
1853	10,500	2
1899	12,000	6
1903	1,500	1
1952	3,250	3
9999 (trailer card)		

5. This problem involves analyzing product sales information. Input consists of the identification number and quantity sold for each of 25 products. Write a FORTRAN program to do the following:

(a) Read the identification numbers and quantities into two arrays. After all data is read print the arrays in columns below appropriate headings.

(b) Calculate and print the average of the quantities sold.

(c) Determine the number of products whose sales fall into each of the following categories:

500 or more
250 to 499
100 to 249
  0 to 99

Print the results with appropriate headings.

(d) Sort the quantity array into descending order (largest to smallest) using the bubble sort algorithm. Note that there are two arrays although only the quantity array is to be sorted. However, whenever two elements of the quantity array are out of order and need to be switched, the corresponding identification numbers must be switched. After the array is sorted, print the two arrays in columns with appropriate headings.

(e) Sort the identification number array into ascending order (smallest to largest). Again note that any exchange of elements in one array must be accompanied by an exchange of corresponding elements in the other array. After the array is sorted, print the two arrays in columns below appropriate headings.

Use the following data to test the program:

Identification Number	Quantity Sold
208	295
137	152
485	825
217	100
945	250
607	435
642	500
735	36
300	163
299	255
435	501
116	75
189	0
218	63
830	617
695	825
708	416
325	99
339	249
418	237
225	712
180	328
925	499
455	240
347	378

6. Two important applications of computers in statistics are tabulation of data and calculation of the mean. Tabulation involves counting the number of items in a set of data that fall into various categories. For example, given a set of test scores, we may wish to count the number of scores that fall between 90 and 100, between 80 and 89, between 70 and 79, and so forth.

The mean is merely the average of the data. For example, given a set of test scores the mean is calculated by adding the scores and dividing by the number of tests.

Write a FORTRAN program to read student test score data into an array, calculate the mean of the test scores, tabulate the test scores, and sort the test scores into descending order.

Test scores are punched one per card along with a student identification number for each test score. There is an unknown number of data cards. However the last card of the data deck does not contain a test score but is punched with 999 in the student identification number field. Use this trailer card to control the input process. Assume that there are no more than 99 test scores and dimension any arrays accordingly.

Prepare a program according to the following specifications:

(a) Read the identification numbers and the test scores into two separate arrays. It is necessary to count the cards as they are read to get a count of the number of test scores to be processed. Finally, list below appropriate headings the data in the identification number and test score arrays. At the end, print a statement of the number of test scores in the data.

(b) Accumulate and print the total of the test scores. Calculate and print the mean of the test scores.

(c) Determine the number of scores that fall into each of the following categories:

90–100
80– 89
70– 79
60– 69
 0– 59

Print the results with appropriate titles.

(d) Sort the test scores into descending order (largest to smallest). Print a list of the identification numbers and the test scores in descending order. Use the bubble sort algorithm to sort the test score data. Note that there are two arrays, although only the test score array is to be sorted. However, when two elements of the test score array are out of order and need to be switched, the corresponding identification numbers must be switched.

(e) Determine and print the median of the test scores. The median is the middle value of a set of data. Fifty percent of the data values are greater than or equal to the median and fifty percent are less than or equal to the median. In order to determine the median, the data must first be sorted into ascending or descending order. Then the median is the middle value of the sorted data when there is an odd number of values or the average of two middle values when there is an even number of items. Be sure to make the program sufficiently general to handle both cases.

Use the following input data to test the program:

Identification Number	Test Score	Identification Number	Test Score	Identification Number	Test Score
282	99	283	83	240	73
115	75	116	72	145	74
124	76	123	71	267	74
215	77	114	74	294	91
275	69	287	96	232	75
208	78	201	79	206	75
225	85	242	71	150	76
113	77	119	63	133	83
205	76	142	78	255	70
122	89	219	84	250	77
137	78	248	72	210	70
185	75	173	79	233	80
235	100	261	85	166	71
138	74	265	71	202	61
298	74	281	72	176	81
217	62	139	55	257	72
104	82	141	73	256	14
108	73	266	65	230	73
191	79	110	81	129	89

7. A 25-question true-false test needs to be scored. The answers to the questions are punched in the first 25 columns of a header card. Following this is one card for each student with the student's number in columns 1 to 5 and his or her answers in columns 6 to 30. Write a FORTRAN program to correct each student's answers. The program should print the student's number at the top of the page. Below this should be listed in adjacent columns the correct answers, the student's answers, and an X opposite any incorrect answers. At the end of this the program should print the percent of the answers that are correct.

Use the following data to test the program:

Correct answers: FTTTFFTFTTTFTFFFTFTTFFTFFT

Student's Number	Student's Answers
11301	FTTFTFTFTTTFTFFTFTTFFFTFT
11302	FFTTTTFFTTFTTFFFTFTFFFTFFF
11303	FTTTFFTFTTTFFFFTFTTFFTFFT
11304	TFTTFFTFTTTFFFFFFTTFTTFTT
11305	TTTTFFFFTTFTFFFTFTFFFTFFT
11306	FFFFFFTFTTTTFFFTFFTFTFFF
11307	TTTFFFFTTTFTFFFTTFTFTTFFT
11308	FTFTFTFTFTFTFTFTFTFTFTFTF
11309	TFTFTFTFTFTFTFTFTFTFTFTFT
11310	TTTTTTTTTTTTTTTTTTTTTTTTT
11311	FFFFFFFFFFFFFFFFFFFFFFFFF
11399 (trailer card)	

8. Using the data in problem 7, write a program that determines the percent of the students in the class that got each question correct. That is, determine and print the percent of the students that got the first question correct, the percent that got the second question correct, and so forth.

9. Each state has a two-letter abbreviation authorized by the U.S. Postal Service. For example, the abbreviation for California is CA; the abbreviation for New York is NY. (See a Zip Code directory for a complete list.)

Write a FORTRAN program that reads a complete table of state abbreviations and corresponding state names. Use one array for the abbreviations and another array for the names. Then print the arrays below appropriate headings. Next, read a state abbreviation and search the table for the corresponding state's name. Print the abbreviation and the name. Repeat this part of the program until an abbreviation of XX is read. Supply appropriate input data to test the program.

10. Write a FORTRAN program that reads an array of twenty names and sorts them into alphabetical order. Each name is punched in the first eighteen columns of a card and consists of the last name followed by a comma, and then the first name. It will be necessary to separate the names into two arrays before doing the sorting and then to reconstruct the names in the appropriate format after the sorting is completed. Print the sorted array of names. Supply an appropriate list of twenty names to test the program.

Chapter 11

MULTIDIMENSIONAL ARRAYS

The type of array that we described in Chapter 10 is called a *one-dimensional array*. This is because we think of the data in the array as being organized in one direction, such as a column. (See Fig. 10-1.) FORTRAN also allows two-, three-, and even higher dimensional arrays. (The maximum number of dimensions depends on the version of FORTRAN.) In this chapter we examine multidimensional arrays and their use in FORTRAN.

11-1. TWO-DIMENSIONAL ARRAYS

A *two-dimensional array* is often thought of as a table of data organized into rows and columns. Figure 11-1 shows a two-dimensional array of four rows and three columns. In an actual case this data may represent the test scores of four students on three different exams. For example, the data in row one represents the three test scores of student number 1. The score on the first test for this student is 91; this score is found in column 1 of row 1. In row 1, column 2, is the score of this student on the second test (78). The third test score for this student is found in row 1, column 3. Similarly, test scores for the other students are found in the other rows.

As with one-dimensional arrays, a two-dimensional array is given a name that refers to the whole array. To locate an element in a two-dimensional array, both the row number and column number of the element must be given. An array element name is formed from the array name and *two* subscripts; the subscripts are separated by commas

Column Numbers

	1	2	3
1	91	78	85
2	95	90	96
3	85	100	89
4	69	75	68

Row Numbers

FIGURE 11-1.   A two-dimensional array.

and enclosed in parentheses. The first subscript is the row number of the element; the second subscript is the column number. For example, assume that the array of Fig. 11–1 is named SCR. Then the element in row 1, column 2, is named SCR(1,2). The name of the element in row 3, column 1, is SCR(3,1). Figure 11–2 shows the names of all elements in this two-dimensional array.

Each two-dimensional array used in a program must be declared in a DIMENSION statement by indicating the maximum value of each subscript. For example, the test-score array illustrated previously is specified as follows:

DIMENSION SCR(4,3)

The first number in parentheses gives the number of rows; the second number indicates the number of columns. Such an array is said to be a "four-by-three" array.

Both one- and two-dimensional arrays may be specified in the same DIMENSION statement. For example, the following statement describes the dimension of three arrays:

DIMENSION S(10,10),LIST(12,2),X(20)

Column Numbers

	1	2	3
1	SCR(1,1)	SCR(1,2)	SCR(1,3)
2	SCR(2,1)	SCR(2,2)	SCR(2,3)
3	SCR(3,1)	SCR(3,2)	SCR(3,3)
4	SCR(4,1)	SCR(4,2)	SCR(4,3)

Row Numbers

FIGURE 11-2.   Element names for a two-dimensional array.

The first two arrays specified in this statement are two-dimensional while the last array is one-dimensional. Type statements also may be used to declare the dimension of two-dimensional arrays. For example, the following statements specify two-dimensional arrays of integer, real, double precision, logical, and character type:

```
INTEGER A(5,5)
REAL L(6,3)
DOUBLE PRECISION VALUE(8,12)
LOGICAL ANS(20,3)
CHARACTER*10 NAME(20,2)
```

If lower dimension bounds are allowed, then these may be given for each dimension. For example, the following statement declares a two-dimensional array with lower dimension bounds:

```
DIMENSION B(5:10,0:8)
```

This array contains six rows numbered 5, 6, . . . , 10, and nine columns numbered 0, 1, . . ., 8.

Subscripts for two-dimensional arrays must follow the rules for one-dimensional array subscripts. The only restriction is that there must be two subscripts instead of one. Thus, two-dimensional array subscripts may be integer constants, variable names, and certain simple arithmetic expressions. For example, the name SCR(I,J) indicates the element in the "Ith" row and "Jth" column. The value of a subscript must never be less than 1 (unless lower dimension bounds are allowed) or greater than the maximum allowable value for the subscript as specified in the DIMENSION statement.

Processing Two-Dimensional Arrays

A two-dimensional array is often processed by using a nest of two DO loops. The DO-variable of the outer loop is used as one subscript of the array element name, and the DO-variable of the inner loop is used for the other subscript. With appropriate parameters for each loop, part or all of the array can be processed. For example, assume that it is necessary to initialize all of the elements of the test score array to zero. The following statements accomplish this:

```
      DO 110 I=1,4
        DO 100 J=1,3
          SCR(I,J)=0.0
100     CONTINUE
110 CONTINUE
```

In this example the DO-variable of the outer loop is used in the array element name to indicate the row number. The outer loop is executed with the DO-variable incremented from one to the maximum number of rows in the array. The DO-variable of the inner loop indicates the column number. It is incremented from one to the maximum number of columns. Thus, in this example, for each execution of the outer loop the inner loop causes the elements in one row to be set to zero.

To average the test scores for each student, the total of the elements in each row must be determined. This can be accomplished most easily by using a one-dimensional array of four elements where each element is used to accumulate the total of a row. Assume that this array is called ROW and has been properly declared in a DIMENSION statement. Since this array is used to accumulate totals, it must first be initialized to zero. Then the elements in each row of the test score array are successively added to the appropriate element of the row total array. The following statements show how this is done:

```
      DO 200 I=1,4
        ROW(I)=0.0
  200 CONTINUE
      DO 220 I=1,4
        DO 210 J=1,3
          ROW(I)=ROW(I)+SCR(I,J)
  210   CONTINUE
  220 CONTINUE
```

When execution of this sequence of statements is completed, the elements of the array named ROW will contain the totals of the elements in each row of the test-score array.

A similar approach may be used to calculate the total of the elements of each column of the test-score array. Assume that the name COL has been specified in a DIMENSION statement as a three-element array. After setting the elements of COL to zero, the following sequence of statements accumulates the total of each column of the test-score array and assigns the results to elements of the array named COL:

```
      DO 300 J=1,3
        COL(J)=0.0
  300 CONTINUE
      DO 320 J=1,3
        DO 310 I=1,4
          COL(J)=COL(J)+SCR(I,J)
  310   CONTINUE
  320 CONTINUE
```

Notice in this example that the outer loop of the nested DO loops controls the column number. The inner loop controls the row number and is executed four times for each execution of the outer loop. At the end of the execution of this sequence of statements, the elements of the COL array contain the correct column totals.

In searching a two-dimensional array for a specific value, we include a test for the value in the nested DO loops. For example, assume that it is necessary to determine the student number and test number for any student who got a score of 90 or greater on any test. The following statements accomplish this:

```
        DO 410 I=1,4
          DO 400 J=1,3
            IF(SCR(I,J).GE.90.0) WRITE (6,910) I,J
    400   CONTINUE
    410 CONTINUE
```

In this example, the WRITE statement is executed only if the student's test score is 90 or more. The current values of the DO-variables for each DO loop are printed and indicate the student number and test number.

Many times when we search a two-dimensional array we search one column (or row) for a specific value and use the information from the other columns (or rows). For example, assume that we wish to calculate and print the average of the second and third test scores for each student that got 90 or above on the first test. Then the following statements accomplish this:

```
        DO 500 I=1,4
          IF(SCR(I,1).LT.90.0) GO TO 500
          AVE=(SCR(I,2)+SCR(I,3))/2.0
          WRITE(6,920) I,AVE
      500 CONTINUE
```

In the IF statement, SCR(I,1) refers to the Ith element in the first column of the array. Hence, each time through the loop we check the first score to see if it is less than 90. If this is not the case then we average the other two scores for that student and print the student number and average.

We can sort the elements in one row or column of a two-dimensional array. If it is necessary to maintain the correspondence between elements in a row or column during the sorting process, then any time two elements in one column (or row) are switched, the corresponding elements in the other columns (or rows) must be switched. For example, the following sequence of statements sorts the first column of the test score array into descending order:

```
DO 620 L=1,3
  K=4-L
  DO 610 I=1,K
    IF(SCR(I,1).GE.SCR(I+1,1)) GO TO 610
    DO 600 J=1,3
      T=SCR(I,J)
      SCR(I,J)=SCR(I+1,J)
      SCR(I+1,J)=T
600     CONTINUE
610   CONTINUE
620 CONTINUE
```

The sorting is done on the first column since the second subscript of the array element names in the IF statement is one. The inner-most loop is used to switch all elements of two rows if the elements in the first column are out of order with respect to each other.

Input and Output of Two-dimensional Array Data

The technique that is used to read or write data for a two-dimensional array depends on the format of the input data or the way in which the output is to be arranged. As a first example, assume that data for the test score array is punched with one card for each test score. The cards are not in any particular order, but the student number and test number are included on each card. The data must be read and the test score must be assigned to the proper array element. This may be accomplished with the following sequence of statements:

```
100 READ(5,800) NSTU,NTEST,SCORE
    IF(NSTU.EQ.99) GO TO 110
    SCR(NSTU,NTEST)=SCORE
    GO TO 100
110 (next statement)
800 FORMAT(2I2,F3.0)
```

After the student number, test number, and test score are read, a test is made for a trailer card. In this example, we assume that the trailer card contains 99 in the student number field. If the trailer card is not detected, then the test score is assigned to the appropriate array element and the process is repeated.

When the array data is available in order of increasing subscripts, or when the array is to be printed in such an order, looping techniques may be used. For example, assume that the entire test score array is punched in four cards with the three elements of each row on a separate card. Then the following sequence of statements may be used to read the array data:

```
      DO 120 I=1,4
         READ(5,810) (SCR(I,J),J=1,3)
  120 CONTINUE
  810 FORMAT(3F3.0)
```

This input sequence involves an implied-DO list in a READ statement that is within a regular DO loop. With each execution of the regular loop, the READ statement causes one row of the array to be read. This is accomplished by using the DO-variable of the regular DO loop as the row number of the array element name and the DO-variable of the implied-DO list as the column number. This same approach may be used to write the data with one row of the array printed on each line. The following statements accomplish this:

```
      DO 130 I=1,4
         WRITE(6,930) (SCR(I,J),J=1,3)
  130 CONTINUE
  930 FORMAT(1X,3F5.0)
```

The problem of reading or writing a two-dimensional array also may be solved by using two implied-DO lists, where one list is within the other. Such a situation is called a *nested implied-DO list*. For example, the following statements cause the test score data to be read in the same format as described above:

```
      READ(5,800) ((SCR(I,J),J=1,3),I=1,4)
  800 FORMAT(3F3.0)
```

The outer list of the nest uses the variable named I as the DO-variable. It is executed four times. The inner list is

$$(SCR(I,J),J=1,3)$$

It is completely executed for each execution of the outer list. In other words, each time that the DO-variable of the outer list is incremented, the inner list causes three values to be read and assigned to the elements in a row in the array. The row number is specified by the DO-variable of the outer list; the column number is given by the DO-variable of the inner list.

In the previous examples we assumed that the array data was to be read or written by rows; that is, that each input record contained one row of the array, or that a row from the array was written for each output record. Sometimes the data is to be read or written by columns. For example, assume that each column of the test-score array is punched in one card. Thus, there are three input cards with four fields on each card. To read these data a looping technique may be used. For example, the following READ statement uses nested implied-DO lists:

```
      READ(5,820) ((SCR(I,J),I=1,4),J=1,3)
820 FORMAT(4F3.0)
```

Notice here that the inner list controls the row number, while the outer list indicates the column number. Thus, with each execution of the outer list, one column is read. This technique also may be used to print array data by columns as illustrated by the following statements:

```
      WRITE(6,940) ((SCR(I,J),I=1,4),J=1,3)
940 FORMAT(1X,4F5.0)
```

The "short-list" technique may be used for input and output of two-dimensional arrays only if array data is arranged by *columns*. This is because the data is stored in order by columns in the computer's internal storage. (See Fig. 11–3.) Thus, the previous READ and WRITE statements may be coded as follows:

```
      READ(5,820) SCR
      WRITE(6,940) SCR
820 FORMAT(4F3.0)
940 FORMAT(1X,4F5.0)
```

Note, however, that the "short-list" technique cannot be used if the data is to be read or written by rows. In this case, a looping technique must be used. In addition, the "short-list" technique can be applied only if the entire array is to be read or written. Input and output of partial arrays must be accomplished by some other approach.

Initializing Two-dimensional Arrays in a DATA Statement

A DATA statement may be used to initialize the elements of a two-dimensional array. Depending on the version of FORTRAN, different techniques are possible. If the version of FORTRAN requires that an array name must be subscripted in a DATA statement, then

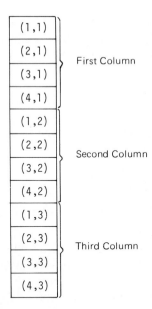

FIGURE 11-3. Order in storage of the elements of a 4-row, 3-column array.

each element must be initialized separately. For example, the following statement sets each element of the two-row, three-column array named X to zero:

```
DATA X(1,1),X(1,2),X(1,3),X(2,1),X(2,2),X(2,3)/6*0.0/
```

If the array name may be used without a subscript, then we can initialize the entire array X to zero as follows:

```
DATA X/6*0.0/
```

However, when this technique is permissible, the array is intitialized in order by columns (the same order that is used for the "short-list" technique). Because of this, we may have to be careful in coding the DATA statement. For example, if we wished to set the elements of the first row of the array X to zero and the second row to one, we would use the following statement:

```
DATA X/0.0,1.0,0.0,1.0,0.0,1.0/
```

The alternating zeros and ones are necessary to properly initialize the array.

When implied-DO lists are allowed in a DATA statement, then we usually nest the lists to get the desired effect. For example, the following statement initializes the elements of the first row of X to zero and the second row to one:

$$\text{DATA } ((X(I,J),J=1,3),I=1,2)/3*0.0,3*1.0/$$

In this statement the outer list controls the row number and the inner list controls the column number.

11-2. THREE-DIMENSIONAL ARRAYS

A *three-dimensional array* may be thought of as a group of data organized into levels, where the data in each level is arranged in rows and columns. These levels may be imagined as planes or pages, where each page contains a two-dimensional array. Figure 11–4 shows a three-

FIGURE 11–4.   A three-dimensional array.

dimensional array of four rows, three columns, and three levels. This data may represent test scores for four students (rows) on three tests (columns) in each of three different classes (levels). Thus, the element 85 in the third row and first column of the second level represents the test score of student number three on the first exam in the second class.

Each element of a three-dimensional array is identified by three subscripts, separated by commas, and enclosed in parentheses, following the array name. The subscripts represent the number of the row, column, and level respectively. For example, assume that the array shown in Fig. 11-4 is named TS. Then the element in row three, column one, level two is named TS(3,1,2). Figure 11-5 shows the names of all elements in this three-dimensional array.

Subscripts for a three-dimensional array must follow the rules for one- and two-dimensional array subscripts, except that there always must be three subscripts. Thus, subscripts may be integer constants, variable names, or certain simple arithmetic expressions. For example, the array element name TS(I,J,K) indicates the element in the "Ith" row, "Jth" column, and "Kth" level. The value of a subscript must not

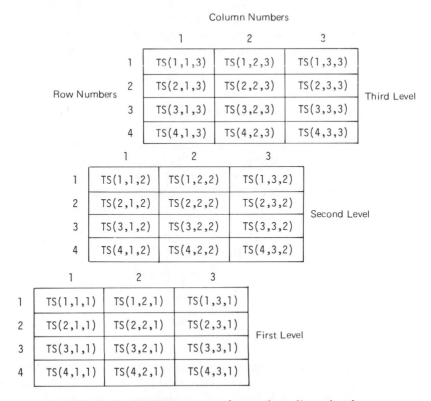

FIGURE 11-5. Element names for a three-dimensional array.

be less than 1 or greater than the maximum allowable value for the subscript.

Any array used in a program must be specified in a DIMENSION statement (or a type statement) by giving the maximum value of each subscript. For example, the following statement specifies the dimension of the array described above:

$$DIMENSION\ TS(4,3,3)$$

The entry in parentheses gives the number of rows, columns, and levels respectively in the array. This array is said to be a "four-by-three-by-three" array. (If allowable, lower dimension bounds may be specified.)

When using large arrays in a program it is possible to exceed the computer's internal storage capacity. For example, consider the arrays specified by the following DIMENSION statement:

$$DIMENSION\ D(200,200),A(1000),M(10,100,100)$$

The first array contains 40,000 elements (200 × 200), the second array has 1000 elements, and the third array contains 100,000 elements (10 × 100 × 100). Thus, these three arrays contain a total of 141,000 elements. This exceeds the capacity of the internal storage of many computers.

Processing Three-dimensional Arrays

As with arrays of two dimensions, three-dimensional arrays are usually processed by using nested DO loops. However, in this case, three loops are required, one to control each subscript. For example, the following sequence of statements uses three nested DO loops to initialize the elements of the test score array to zero:

```
      DO 120 I=1,4
        DO 110 J=1,3
          DO 100 K=1,3
            TS(I,J,K)=0.0
100         CONTINUE
110       CONTINUE
120 CONTINUE
```

The DO-variable of the inner loop is used in the array element name to indicate the level number. The DO-variables of the intermediate and outer loops specify the column and row numbers, respectively.

To accumulate the total score for each student in each class, a two-dimensional array may be used. The subscripts of this array indicate the student number and class number. Assume that STOT is the name of a two-dimensional array of four rows and three columns. The following sequence of statements first initializes the elements of STOT to zero and then accumulates the total for each student in each class, assigning the result to the appropriate element of STOT:

```
      DO 210 I=1,4
        DO 200 K=1,3
          STOT(I,K)=0.0
200     CONTINUE
210   CONTINUE
      DO 240 I=1,4
        DO 230 K=1,3
          DO 220 J=1,3
            STOT(I,K)=STOT(I,K)+TS(I,J,K)
220       CONTINUE
230     CONTINUE
240   CONTINUE
```

In the second nest of DO loops in this example, the inner loop controls the column number while the intermediate and outer loops control the level and row numbers, respectively. Thus, with each complete execution of the inner loop, the total of the elements in one row of one level is accumulated.

If the total of all test scores for each class is needed, a one-dimensional array may be used to store the results. For example, assume that CTOT has been specified as the name of a three-element, one-dimensional array. The following statements set the elements of CTOT to zero and then accumulate the total for each class, assigning the result to the appropriate element of CTOT:

```
      DO 300 K=1,3
        CTOT(K)=0.0
300   CONTINUE
      DO 330 K=1,3
        DO 320 I=1,4
          DO 310 J=1,3
            CTOT(K)=CTOT(K)+TS(I,J,K)
310       CONTINUE
320     CONTINUE
330   CONTINUE
```

In this sequence of statements, the outer loop of the nest of DO loops controls the level number. The intermediate and inner loops control the row and column numbers, respectively. Thus, with each complete execution of the intermediate and inner loops, the total of the elements in one level is accumulated.

To search a three-dimensional array for a specific value we test for the value within the nested DO loops. For example, the following statements select any student who received a score of 90 or above on any test in any class:

```
    DO 420 I=1,4
        DO 410 J=1,3
            DO 400 K=1,3
                IF(TS(I,J,K).GE.90.0) WRITE(6,900) I,J,K
    400     CONTINUE
    410     CONTINUE
    420 CONTINUE
```

In this example, the current values of the three DO-variables are printed if the test score is greater than or equal to 90. The DO-variables represent the student number, test number, and class number.

Input and Output of Three-dimensional Array Data

Input and output of the data for a three-dimensional array may be accomplished in a number of ways. For example, assume that the data for the test score array is punched in cards with the elements for one row on each card. The first four cards contain the data for the first level, the next four cards have the second level's data, and the last four cards contain the third level's data. To read this data, a nest of two DO loops and an implied-DO list may be used as follows:

```
    DO 110 K=1,3
        DO 100 I=1,4
            READ(5,800) (TS(I,J,K),J=1,3)
    100     CONTINUE
    110 CONTINUE
    800 FORMAT(3F10.0)
```

The implied-DO list in the READ statement controls the column number for the array element name. The inner loop of the nested DO loops controls the row number and the outer loop indicates the level number. With each execution of the READ statement, one card is read and the data assigned to the elements in one row of the three-dimensional array. A total of 12 cards is read because the READ statement is executed 12 times. This approach also may be used to write three-dimensional array data. For example, the following statements print the test score array with one row on each line:

```
     DO 210 K=1,3
       DO 200 I=1,4
         WRITE(6,900) (TS(I,J,K),J=1,3)
200    CONTINUE
210 CONTINUE
900 FORMAT(1X,3F5.0)
```

Three nested implied-DO lists also may be used to read or write data for a three-dimensional array. The following statements use this approach to read the test score data in the same format as described above:

```
     READ(5,800) (((TS(I,J,K),J=1,3),I=1,4),K=1,3)
800 FORMAT(3F3.0)
```

The outer implied-DO list uses the DO-variable K to control the level number. The intermediate list uses the DO-variable I for the row number. The inner implied-DO list causes three values to be read and assigned to the elements in one row of the array.

If the data to be read are punched in cards so that each column of the array is punched in one card, then the order of the loops is different. Assume that the input data consist of nine punched cards. The first three cards each contain one column from the first level. The next three cards contain the data from the second level, and the third level's data is contained on the last three cards. The following statements read the data in the specified order:

```
     READ(5,810) (((TS(I,J,K),I=1,4),J=1,3),K=1,3)
810 FORMAT(4F3.0)
```

Notice that the innermost implied-DO list now controls the row number while the intermediate list indicates the column number. Thus, each execution of the inner list causes the data for one column to be read.

If the data is arranged by columns within levels as described in the previous paragraph, the "short-list" technique may be used. For example, the following statements have the same effect as the previous example:

```
     READ(5,810) TS
810 FORMAT(4F3.0)
```

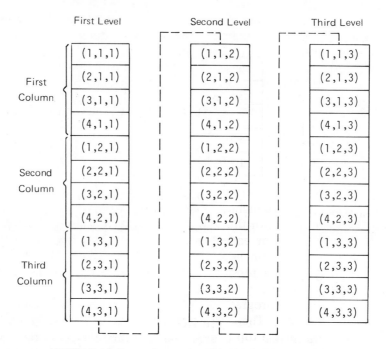

FIGURE 11-6.   Order in storage of the elements of a 4-
            row; 3-column, 3-level array.

In general, when the "short-list" technique is applied, the data is read
or written in an order such that the first subscript is incremented
through its values before the second subscript which, in turn, is incremented before the third subscript. Thus, the data for a three-dimensional array is read by columns within each level. The arrangement of
the data in the computer's internal storage is shown in Fig. 11-6.

Higher Dimensional Arrays

Some versions of FORTRAN allow arrays of more than three dimensions. For example, four-, five-, or even higher dimensional arrays
are sometimes permissible. While we normally can't visualize an array
with more than three dimensions, the computer can store such an array.
Although we have only examined two- and three-dimensional arrays in
this chapter, all of the principles apply to arrays of greater dimension.

PROGRAMMING PROBLEMS

1. A company sells five products with four models for each product.
The following table gives the unit price of each model of each product:

Model Number

	1	2	3	4
1	10.50	16.25	21.00	23.75
2	4.95	5.95	6.50	6.95
3	.38	.47	.59	.62
4	8.75	8.95	9.10	9.22
5	1.52	1.75	1.95	2.25

Product number labels rows 1–5.

The pricing table is punched in the first five cards of a data deck. Each card has the prices for the four models of one product. Following this table is one card for each sale made during the week with the customer number, the item number, and the quantity sold. The first digit of the item number represents the product number; the second digit is the model number.

Write a FORTRAN program to read the pricing table and store it in a two-dimensional array. Then print the pricing table with appropriate headings beginning at the top of a new page. Next, calculate the sales amount for each customer by multiplying the unit price from the table by the quantity sold. Starting at the top of a new page, list below appropriate headings the customer number, item number, quantity sold, unit price, and sales amount.

To test the program use the data in the pricing table above and the following sales data:

Customer Number	Item Number	Quantity
10113	21	10
11305	54	35
11412	11	100
22516	23	125
11603	42	75
11625	41	65
11735	33	50
11895	13	130
11899	24	20
11907	52	82
00000 (trailer card)		

2. Data for problem 6 of Chapter 10 consists of one card for each student in a class punched with the student's number and his or her score on a test. The first digit of the student's number indicates his or her year in school (1=freshman, 2=sophomore). A tabulation of test

scores by score category for each year is needed. The score categories are 90 to 100, 80 to 89, 70 to 79, 60 to 69, and 0 to 59.

Create a two-dimensional array of five rows and two columns where the rows represent the score categories and the columns indicate the year in school. That is, the array should appear as follows:

	Freshman	Sophomore
90–100		
80–89		
70–79		
60–69		
0–59		

Tabulate the number of scores that fall into each classification. Print the results of the tabulation with appropriate headings. After the data has been tabulated, determine the total number of freshmen and the total number of sophomores who took the test. Print the result.

Use the data for problem 6 of Chapter 10 to test the program.

3. Write a FORTRAN program to create a two-dimensional table of the number of freshman, sophomore, junior, and senior students in each major field. Also accumulate the totals for each year in school, the totals for each major field, and the total number of students. Print the table in the following format:

| | Year in School | | | | |
Major Field	Freshman	Sophomore	Junior	Senior	Totals
Business					
Social Science					
Humanities					
Physical Science					
Engineering					
TOTALS					

Input for the program is one or more cards for each department with the department number punched in columns 1 to 3, and digits ranging from 1 to 4 punched in columns 6 to 80. Department numbers are as follows:

101   Business
102   Social Science
103   Humanities
104   Physical Science
105   Engineering

Each column between 6 and 80 is punched with one student's year in school. Use the digits 1, 2, 3, and 4 to represent freshman, sophomore, junior, and senior, respectively. There may be more than one card for any department. If data for less than 75 students is punched in a card, remaining fields are filled with zeros. Data cards are in no particular order; however, a trailer card with 999 in columns 1 to 3 terminates the data deck.

To test the program, punch data with at least two cards for each department. Some cards should not be entirely filled with the digits 1, 2, 3, or 4 but should have 0's in the last 10 to 20 columns.

4. The data gathered from scouting a football team may be analyzed by a computer. In a simple system, assume that four characteristics of each offensive play are recorded by the scout. The characteristics are the down, the yards to go for a first down, the type of play (where 0 identifies a pass and 1 indicates a run), and the number of yards gained or lost (where a negative value indicates lost yardage). The information for each play is punched in a separate card. In all, 25 plays are to be analyzed.

Write a FORTRAN program to read the scouting data and store it in a two-dimensional array of twenty-five rows and four columns. Each column represents one of the characteristics of the play. Print the data in columns with appropriate headings beginning at the top of a new page. Then find and print the answers to the following questions:

(a) What was the average yards gained per play?
(b) What was the average yards gained per running play?
(c) Of all running plays, what percent gained yardage, what percent lost yardage, and what percent gained zero yardage?
(d) What was the average yards gained per passing play?
(e) What percent of the plays were passes?
(f) What percent of first-down plays were passes?
(g) What percent of second-down plays were passes?
(h) What percent of third-down plays were passes?
(i) Of third-down plays with less than five yards to go, what percent were passes?

Use the following data to test the program:

Down	Yards to Go	Play	Gain (+) or Loss (-)
1	10	Run	+4
2	6	Pass	0
3	6	Pass	+8
1	10	Run	-3
2	13	Run	+8
1	10	Run	0
2	10	Pass	+8
3	2	Pass	+15
1	10	Pass	+12
1	10	Run	-15
2	25	Pass	+5
3	20	Pass	0
1	10	Run	+2
2	8	Run	+4
3	4	Run	+1
1	10	Pass	0
2	10	Run	+6
3	4	Pass	+12
1	10	Pass	0
2	10	Run	+6
3	4	Run	+2
1	10	Pass	-3
2	13	Run	-5
1	10	Run	+2
2	10	Run	-16

5. The equation of a straight line is $y = mx + b$, where m is the slope and b is the y-intercept. A graph of this line can be easily created by calculating y for different values of x and plotting the resulting pairs of numbers. For example, if the slope of a line is 1 and the y-intercept is -2, then the equation of the line is $y = 1x - 2$. Starting with x equal to 1 and increasing x by 1, each time calculating y from the equation, the following pairs of numbers result:

x	1	2	3	4	5	6	7	8
y	-1	0	1	2	3	4	5	6

These pairs are plotted on graph paper to get the plot of the line.

One way of representing a graph by means of a computer is to use a two-dimensional array of integer values. Initially, the array should contain all zeros. Then, if y equals some value j when x equals i, the (j, i)th element of the array is set equal to 1. Through proper manipulation of output a digitalized graph is printed. For example, the equation $y = 1x - 2$ would appear as follows:

```
GRAPH OF THE LINE Y = 1X - 2

Y-VALUES

     8    0  0  0  0  0  0  0  0

     7    0  0  0  0  0  0  0  0

     6    0  0  0  0  0  0  0  1

     5    0  0  0  0  0  0  1  0

     4    0  0  0  0  0  1  0  0

     3    0  0  0  0  1  0  0  0

     2    0  0  0  1  0  0  0  0

     1    0  0  1  0  0  0  0  0

          1  2  3  4  5  6  7  8

                 X-VALUES
```

Prepare a FORTRAN program to plot a graph using this technique. Input for the program is one card for each equation to be plotted with the slope and intercept punched in two three-column fields. Use a card with 9 punched in column 80 as a trailer card.

Print each graph on a separate page. Supply headings and x and y values, as in the example, with the exception that x and y should continue to 20. Thus, a two-dimensional array of dimension (20, 20) is needed. Note that only positive x and y values are used. If a resulting pair contains a nonpositive value or a value that exceeds 20, no attempt should be made to plot it.

Test the program with the following equations:

$$y = -2x + 16$$
$$y = 1x - 5$$

A modification of this problem is to include negative x and y values in the graph. Use an array of dimension (31, 31). Thus, the element (16, 16) is the origin of the graph.

A further modification is to use blanks instead of zeros, and asterisks or some other symbol instead of the digit 1.

6. A two-dimensional array is a computer representation of the general mathematical concept of a matrix. A matrix is an ordered set of data arranged in rows and columns. If a matrix has m rows and n columns then we say it is an $m \times n$ matrix (pronounced "m by n"). For example, the following is the representation of a general 2×3 matrix.

$$A = \begin{bmatrix} a_{11} & a_{12} & a_{13} \\ a_{21} & a_{22} & a_{23} \end{bmatrix}$$

The following properties of matrices are used in this problem:
(a) Two matrices of the same size (i.e., the same number of rows and columns) are equal if and only if corresponding elements of the two matrices are equal. That is, given an $m \times n$ matrix A and an $m \times n$ matrix B, then $A = B$ if and only if $a_{ij} = b_{ij}$ for all i between 1 and m and all j between 1 and n.
(b) The product of a matrix and a constant (called a scalar) is a new matrix each of whose elements is the product of the constant and the corresponding element of the original matrix. That is, given an $m \times n$ matrix A and a constant c then a new matrix B equal to c times A is defined as $b_{ij} = c \cdot a_{ij}$ for all i and j.
(c) The sum of two matrices of the same size is a new matrix each of whose elements is the sum of the two corresponding elements of the original matrices. That is, given an $m \times n$ matrix A and an $m \times n$ matrix B, then a new $m \times n$ matrix $C = A + B$ is defined as $c_{ij} = a_{ij} + b_{ij}$ for all i and j.

Prepare a FORTRAN program that reads two matrices and determines whether they are equal. If they are equal, an appropriate message should be printed, one of the matrices should be multiplied by 2, and the result printed. If they are not equal, a message should be printed, the matrices should be added, and the result printed. The program should then repeat the process for a new pair of matrices.

Assume that no matrix has more than 10 rows or 8 columns and dimension all arrays accordingly. Record each row of a matrix on a separate card. The first card of each set of data should contain the size of the matrices to be processed (rows and columns) in integer form. Following this card should be the data for two matrices.

Use the following sets of data to test the program:

I. $A = \begin{bmatrix} 8.35 & 6.24 \\ 7.91 & -5.32 \end{bmatrix}$ $B = \begin{bmatrix} 8.35 & 6.24 \\ 7.91 & -5.32 \end{bmatrix}$

II.

$$A = \begin{bmatrix} 1.62 & 4.35 & -2.13 & 7.62 \\ -8.35 & -12.72 & 6.51 & 8.39 \\ -1.82 & 4.21 & 7.83 & -0.71 \end{bmatrix}$$

$$B = \begin{bmatrix} -4.71 & 5.63 & 7.81 & -1.22 \\ 17.39 & 8.42 & 5.61 & -2.22 \\ -5.81 & 3.92 & 8.35 & 1.11 \end{bmatrix}$$

7. An airline flies between six cities. Whether or not there is a direct flight from one city to another is indicated in the following table:

		To:					
		1	2	3	4	5	6
	1	F	T	T	F	F	T
	2	T	F	T	F	F	T
From:	3	F	F	F	T	F	F
	4	F	T	F	F	T	F
	5	F	T	F	T	F	F
	6	F	T	F	F	T	F

On the left and across the top are the numbers of the cities. If there is a T at the intersection of a row and column, then there is a direct flight from the city marked on the left to the city indicated at the top. An F indicates that there is no direct flight between the two cities.

The information for this table is punched in the first six cards of a data deck. Punched in each card is the data for one row of the table. Following the table data is one card for each customer with the customer's number and his or her request for a flight pattern. The flight pattern indicates the cities between which the customer wishes to fly. For example, a pattern of 13426 indicates that the customer wishes to fly from city 1 to city 3, then from city 3 to city 4, then to city 2, and finally to city 6. The maximum number of cities in a flight pattern is five. If the customer has less than five cities in his or her pattern, then the remaining fields are filled with zeros. Thus, a pattern of 62000 indicates that the customer wishes to fly from city 6 to city 2 and does not wish to continue beyond that.

Write a FORTRAN program to read the data for the flight table. Print the table at the top of a new page with appropriate headings. Then determine if each customer's requested flight pattern is possible. Print the customer's number, his or her requested flight pattern, and a statement of whether or not a ticket may be issued for the desired pattern.

To test the program use the data in the previous flight table and the following customer data:

Customer Number	Flight Pattern
10123	13426
11305	62000
13427	42320
18211	52500
19006	34212
20831	65426
21475	32000
22138	43621
24105	13424
24216	65231
25009	34250
00000 (trailer card)	

8. In the data processing department of a particular organization there are three basic job functions—Systems Analysis, Programming, and Operations. For each function there are four levels—Manager, Senior, Junior, and Trainee. Write a FORTRAN program that reads the job functions into a three-element, one-dimensional array, and the levels into a four-element, one-dimensional array. Then create from these arrays a job category array of three rows and four columns containing all possible combinations of functions and levels. For example, element (1,1) in the array should contain the following:

Systems Analysis—Manager

Finally, print the table in an appropriate format.

9. A telephone company charges varying rates for a long distance call between two cities. The rate charged depends on the time of day the call is made and how the call is placed. There is a fixed charge for the first three minutes and a charge for each additional minute or fraction thereof. The following table outlines the rate structure:

	Time of Day			
How Placed	Day	Evening	Night	Weekend
Direct-dialed	.79	.58	.52	.49
	.26	.23	.21	.15
Station-to-station— operator assisted	.95	.73	.64	.57
	.30	.25	.24	.21
Person-to- person	1.55	1.55	1.55	1.55
	.52	.52	.52	.52

For any given time of day and method of placing the call, two figures are shown. The top figure represents the charge for the first three minutes or fraction thereof; the bottom figure represents the charge for each additional minute or fraction thereof. For example, a night call that is station-to-station, operator-assisted is charged $.64 for the first three minutes, and $.24 for each additional minute.

The rate table is punched in six cards. Each card contains four 5-column fields with the charge for a different time of day in each field. The first three cards contain the basic three-minute charges for the different ways of placing the call. The second three cards contain the charges for additional time. Following the rate table is one card for each customer with the following format:

Card Columns	Field
4–7	Customer number
8	"how placed" code
9	"time of call" code
10–14	length of call in minutes and fraction of minutes

The "how placed" code is:

1 direct-dialed

2 station-to-station, operator-assisted

3 person-to-person

The "time of call" code is:

1 Day

2 Evening

3 Night

4 Weekend

Write a FORTRAN program to read and print the rate table. Use a three-dimensional array. Supply appropriate descriptive headings for the table output. Then determine the charge for each customer. Print the customer's number, the length of the call, and the charge with appropriate headings.

To test the program, use the data in the preceding rate table and the following customer data:

Customer Number	"How Placed"	"Time of Call"	Length
9606	1	1	3.84
2160	3	4	2.50
6100	2	2	3.00
1820	3	3	4.00
9215	2	1	8.50
2111	1	3	6.32
1452	2	3	2.15
6658	1	2	1.05
1138	3	2	9.72
6886	2	4	6.35
3552	3	1	3.51
7111	1	4	5.75
9999 (trailer card)			

10. Data on the age, sex, and marital status of students in the freshman class of a small college are punched in cards in the following format:

Card Columns	Field
1–4	Student number
23–24	Age
25	Sex (1 = male, 2 = female)
26	Marital status (1 = single, 2 = married)

A tabulation of the number of students in different age groups for each sex and marital status is needed. The results are to be presented in the following form:

Age	Single		Married	
	Male	Female	Male	Female
18 and under				
19 or 20				
21 and over				

Write a FORTRAN program to create a three-dimensional array to store the tabulated data. The array should have three rows, two columns, and two levels. The subscript of an array element should indicate age group, sex, and marital status, respectively. Print the results of the tabulation in the form shown above.

From the three-dimensional array create a two-dimensional array of the number of students in each age group for each sex. Print the data in the array in an appropriate format.

Finally, from the two-dimensional array create a one-dimensional array of the number of students in each age group. Print this array data with appropriate headings.

Use the following data to test the program:

Student Number	Age	Sex	Marital Status	Student Number	Age	Sex	Marital Status
1001	19	1	1	1021	19	1	2
1002	17	2	1	1022	26	2	2
1003	18	2	1	1023	23	2	2
1004	22	1	2	1024	17	1	1
1005	20	2	2	1025	18	1	1
1006	18	1	1	1026	21	1	2
1007	27	2	1	1027	26	2	1\
1008	17	2	1	1028	25	1	2
1009	17	1	1	1029	28	2	2
1010	18	2	1	1030	21	1	1
1011	19	1	2	1031	25	2	1
1012	20	2	2	1032	20	2	1
1013	17	1	1	1033	19	1	1
1014	18	1	2	1034	18	1	1
1015	18	1	1	1035	17	1	1
1016	20	2	1	1036	16	2	1
1017	23	1	1	1037	23	2	2
1018	20	2	1	1038	24	2	2
1019	25	2	2	1039	20	1	1
1020	17	2	1	9999 (trailer card)			

Chapter 12

SUBPROGRAMS

The types of programs that we have examined so far are called *main programs*. Another type of program is called a subprogram. A *subprogram* is a separate program that is executed along with a main program. In this chapter we discuss the programming and use of subprograms.

12-1. SUBPROGRAM CONCEPTS

Often while a main program is being prepared a set of computations must be performed at various points with different data at each point. For example, assume that it is necessary to find the maximum of three real values at several points in a main program. The first time, the maximum of the values of A, B, and C is needed. Later in the program the maximum of the values of X, Y, and Z is required. Perhaps at another time the maximum of three other real values is needed. To find the maximum of three values requires several statements in FORTRAN. Each time that a maximum needs to be found, the statements must be coded in the program. The statements are basically the same at each point, only the variable names for the data change. It would simplify the preparation of the program if the necessary statements could be coded once and then referred to each time that the computation is needed. The effect of referring to the statements would be the same as if the statements were placed in the program at the point of reference.

This is the idea of a subprogram. A subprogram is a set of FOR-

TRAN statements that can be referred to by another program. The program that refers to a subprogram is known as the *calling program*. The calling program may be a main program or another subprogram. When a subprogram is referred to it is said to be *called* by the calling program. The effect of calling a subprogram is the same as if the statements in the subprogram were coded into the calling program at the point where the subprogram is called.

Figure 12-1 illustrates these concepts. In this illustration the main program calls the first subprogram three times. Each time that the subprogram is called, the main program branches to the subprogram, the instructions in the subprogram are executed, then the subprogram branches back to the main program at the point where it was called. The second subprogram in Fig. 12-1 is called by the first subprogram. Thus, the first subprogram is not only called by the main program but serves also as the calling program for the second subprogram.

Usually a subprogram requires that data to be used for computations in the subprogram be supplied by the calling program. Such data are said to be *passed* to the subprogram by the calling program. For example, if a subprogram is used to find the maximum of three values, then the data passed to the subprogram must be three values. In Fig. 12-1 the first subprogram is called at three points, hence data must be passed to it three times. After a subprogram completes its computations, the results are usually passed to the calling program *before* the subprogram branches back. Such data are said to be *returned* to the calling program. For example, in a subprogram that finds the maximum of three values, the value returned to the calling program is the maximum.

A subprogram cannot be executed by itself. It can be executed only

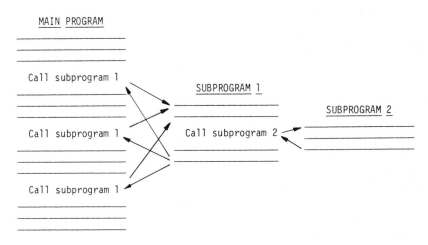

FIGURE 12-1. Subprogram concepts.

as the result of a call from another program. Although the calling program need not be a main program, there must be a main program that began the calling of subprograms. Thus, although the first subprogram in Fig. 12-1 calls the second subprogram, the first cannot be executed without being called by another program — in this case by the main program. In FORTRAN an *executable program* consists of one main program plus any number, including none, of subprograms.

There are a number of advantages to using subprograms. Where a set of computations needs to be repeated several times, the use of a subprogram saves internal storage. A subprogram appears only once in internal storage, even though it may be called several times. Coding effort is also saved by using subprograms, since statements in the subprogram are written only once by the programmer. Finally, large programs are often prepared as an assembly of subprograms. Each subprogram is coded and tested separately. Then the subprograms are linked together by a main program that calls each subprogram in turn. This simplifies the development of large programs.

There are two basic types of subprograms in FORTRAN — functions and subroutines. Their primary difference, besides the way in which they are coded, is the number of values that may be returned from the subprogram to the calling program. *Function subprograms*, or simply *functions*, return *one* value to the calling program. For example, a function subprogram that finds the maximum of three veal values returns one value, the maximum, to the calling program. In Chapter 4 a number of FORTRAN-supplied functions were discussed. SQRT, IFIX, and FLOAT are functions because each supplies the calling program with only one value. Appendix B contains a complete list of FORTRAN-supplied functions.

With a *subroutine subprogram*, or simply *subroutine*, more than one value can be returned to the calling program. For example, a subprogram may be prepared to find the largest and the smallest values from a set of three real values. In this case two values are returned to the calling program; hence a subroutine must be used. In another situation we may wish to use a subroutine to arrange data in an array of 50 elements in ascending numerical sequence. The entire array must then be returned to the calling program. Sometimes a subroutine does not return any values to the calling program. For example, a subroutine may be used to print the data of an array in a special format. In this case, the array data is passed to the subroutine, but no values are returned to the calling program. In any situation where there is one and *only* one value to be supplied to the calling program, a function or subroutine may be used. However, if no values, or if more than one value, are to be returned to the calling program, a subroutine must be used.

12-2. FUNCTION SUBPROGRAMS

The general form of a function subprogram is as follows:

> FUNCTION *name* (*a*1,*a*2,*a*3, . . . ,*an*)
> .
> .
> .
> (FORTRAN statements)
> .
> .
> .
> RETURN
> .
> .
> .
> END

The first statement in a function subprogram is a FUNCTION statement. Among other things, this statement gives the name of the function. The name must follow the rules of FORTRAN variable names and must indicate the type of data to be returned to the calling program. If the value to be returned is real, the name must be real; if the data is integer, the name must be integer. The function name may be typed implicitly by the first letter of the name. That is, I through N indicates an integer function name; any other letter specifies a real function. For example, the name of the function that finds the maximum of three real values may be RMAX for "real maximum". The name MAX could not be used because the value to be returned by the function is real. If the function is to find the maximum of three *integer* values, the name MAX is acceptable. In any case, the name of the function immediately follows the key word FUNCTION as in the following example:

> FUNCTION RMAX

This typing convention is used with the FORTRAN-supplied functions. For example, IFIX converts a real value to its integer equivalent and thus returns an integer value to the calling program. The function SQRT finds the square root of a real value. Therefore, the value returned by this function is real.

If implicit typing is not satisfactory, or if the value to be supplied to the calling program is double precision, logical, or character type, then explicit typing of the function name may be used in most versions of FORTRAN. In this case, the data type is indicated by a type specification in the FUNCTION statement. The key word FUNCTION is preceded by a key word indicating the data type. For example, if the name MAX is to be used for a function that finds the maximum of three real values, then the first part of the function statement appears as follows:

```
REAL FUNCTION MAX
```

Similarly, if a double precision value is to be returned to the calling program by a function named DMAX, the function statement must begin as follows:

```
DOUBLE PRECISION FUNCTION DMAX
```

Whenever explicit typing is used for a function name, the name must also be specified in a type statement in the calling program. Thus, if both of the functions described above are called by a program, the following statements must be included in the calling program:

```
REAL MAX
DOUBLE PRECISION DMAX
```

The same approach must be used for integer function names that are typed explicitly and for functions that return logical values and character values to the calling program. (Character type functions are not permitted in all versions of FORTRAN that allow character data.)

In addition to the name of the function, the FUNCTION statement must include a list of variable and array names, separated by commas and enclosed in parentheses. These are called the *dummy arguments* of the function. They indicate the names used in the subprogram for the data passed by the calling program. For example, in the function that finds the maximum of three real values (RMAX), the dummy arguments specify the variable names used in the function for the real data. If the variable names used are A, B, and C, then the complete FUNCTION statement is coded as follows:

```
FUNCTION RMAX(A,B,C)
```

As another example, consider the function MAX that finds the maximum of three integer values. Then the dummy arguments must be three integer variable names. If the names used are I1, I2, and I3, then the FUNCTION statement appears as follows:

```
FUNCTION MAX(I1,I2,I3)
```

Notice that the dummy arguments indicate what type of data is to be supplied by the calling program. In the first example above, the arguments are all real variable names, while the arguments are integer in the second example. In addition, the arguments indicate how many values are needed. In both examples, three arguments are used since both functions find the maximum of three values.

In order to understand the role of dummy arguments better, it is necessary to examine the way that a function subprogram is called. In a calling program, a function is used by specifying its name and values for its arguments in an arithmetic expression. Assume that it is necessary to assign the maximum of the value of X, the value of Y, and 25.0 to the variable named T. Using the RMAX function, this may be accomplished with the following arithmetic assignment statement:

$$T=RMAX(X,Y,25.0)$$

The name of the function is followed by a list of *actual arguments*, which are enclosed in parentheses and separated by commas. The actual arguments must correspond in number and type with the dummy arguments. Since there are three dummy arguments for the RMAX function (number), there must be three actual arguments. Since the dummy arguments are real (type), the actual arguments must be real. The actual arguments must be assigned values before the function is called.

When a function is called, the values of the actual arguments are assigned to the dummy arguments, and control is transferred to the function. Thus, for the example above, the value of X is assigned to the variable named A, the value of Y is assigned to B, and 25.0 is assigned to C. This has the effect of passing data to the subprogram. The program then branches to the function, and the statements in the function are executed by using the dummy arguments to refer to the data. After the execution of the function's statements, control returns to the calling program at the point where the function is called. The function returns a value to the calling program, which is used to complete the expression in which the function is called. Execution of the program then continues in its normal sequence. In the case of the RMAX function, the value returned is the maximum of the argument values. The arithmetic assignment statement in which the RMAX function is called is completed before going on to the next statement in the calling program. Figure 12-2 summarizes the effect of calling a function subprogram.

Any FORTRAN statement except another FUNCTION statement (or SUBROUTINE statement to be considered later) may appear in a function subprogram. However, the function must contain at least one statement that uses the name of the function as a variable name in such a way that a value is assigned to the name. This is because the name of

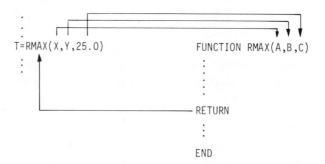

FIGURE 12-2.   Calling a function subprogram.

the function is used to return a value to the calling program. The value to be returned must be assigned to the function name at some point in the function. In the RMAX function, the maximum value of the three arguments must be assigned to the name RMAX. In this case, an arithmetic assignment statement is used to supply a value for the function name. In other functions the name may be assigned a value through a READ statement or as the left-hand side of a logical or character assignment statement.

Two other statements are required in a function subprogram. These are the RETURN and END statements. There must be at least one RETURN statement in the function. This is a control statement that, when executed, causes the computer to branch from the function to that point in the calling program where the function is called. In addition, the value assigned to the function name is returned to the calling program. The RETURN statement is coded as the keyword RETURN, with or without a statement number.

Finally, the last statement in a function must be an END statement. This statement signals the physical end of that function subprogram. When a function is prepared for processing on a computer it is compiled separately from the main program or other subprograms. The compiler must be able to recognize the end of the subprogram; this is the purpose of the END statement. After compilation, each subprogram occupies a separate part of the computer's internal storage. There is no connection between various programs in internal storage until one program calls another.

With the addition of the statements described above, the RMAX function can be completed. It is shown in Fig. 12–3. The technique used in this function assumes that the value of A is the largest. This value is assigned to the variable named BIG. The value of BIG is then compared to the values of B and C. If either is larger than the current value of BIG, the larger value is assigned to BIG. Finally, the value of BIG is assigned to the name of the function, RMAX. The RETURN statement then causes control to return to the calling program.

```
FUNCTION RMAX(A,B,C)
BIG=A
IF(B.GT.BIG) BIG=B
IF(C.GT.BIG) BIG=C
RMAX=BIG
RETURN
END
```

FIGURE 12-3. The RMAX function.

A way of simplifying this function is to substitute RMAX for the variable named BIG. The resulting function is shown in Fig. 12-4. This function satisfies the requirement that the name of the function must be assigned a value before the function returns to the calling program.

The first statement of a function subprogram is always a FUNCTION statement and the last is always an END statement. The RETURN statement may appear anywhere in the function and there may be more than one RETURN statement depending on the logic of the function.

Statement numbers and variable names used in the function have no relation to the statement numbers and variable names in other subprograms or the main program. Since all programs are stored in separate sections of the computer's internal storage, there is no connection between them. Thus, a statement numbered 10 in a function has no relation to a similarly numbered statement in another subprogram or a main program. The statement

$$GO\ TO\ 10$$

in a program means branch to the statement numbered 10 in that program, irrespective of any statement with the same number in another program. Similarly, the same variable names may be used in several programs without any confusion between the programs.

The dummy arguments of a function may be any variable or array names. Typing of names may be done implicitly, or, if this is unsatisfactory or if double precision, logical, or character type arguments are needed, explicit typing may be used. In explicit typing, the type state-

```
FUNCTION RMAX(A,B,C)
RMAX=A
IF(B.GT.RMAX) RMAX=B
IF(C.GT.RMAX) RMAX=C
RETURN
END
```

FIGURE 12-4. A variation on the RMAX function.

ments follow the FUNCTION statement and precede the first executable statement in the function. For example, the following incomplete function uses five dummy arguments:

```
FUNCTION FUN1(M,A,B,L1,L2,CC)
REAL M
DOUBLE PRECISION A,B
LOGICAL L1,L2
CHARACTER CC*20
     .
     .
     .
RETURN
     .
     .
     .
END
```

The first argument is real, the second two arguments are double precision, and the remaining arguments are logical and character type.

Actual arguments may be variable names, array or array element names, constants, or expressions. The only restriction is that the actual arguments correspond in number, order, and type to the dummy arguments. In other words, the number of actual arguments must be the same as the number of dummy arguments, the actual arguments must be in the same order as the dummy arguments, and corresponding actual and dummy arguments must be of the same type. For example, consider the following FUNCTION statement:

```
FUNCTION FUN2(I,J,X,Y)
```

This function uses four dummy arguments. The first two arguments are integer, and the second two are real. Whenever this function is called, the actual arguments must correspond to the dummy arguments. They need not be the same variable names; they may be other variable names, constants, array element names, or arithmetic expressions. But they must correspond in type, order, and number to the dummy arguments. Thus, this function may be called by the following statement:

```
X=FUN2(I,K+5,A(3),7.6)
```

With this function call, the value of I in the calling program is assigned to I in the function; the value of K+5 is calculated in the calling program and assigned to J in the function; the value of A(3) is assigned to X; and 7.6 is assigned to Y. Notice that the variable and array names in the calling program are not necessarily related to identical names in the subprograms.

Within a calling program, explicit typing of actual arguments may be used and is required for double precision, and logical and character names. For example, consider the function FUN1 described previously. The first argument of this function is real, the next two arguments are double precision, the next two arguments are logical, and the last argument is character type. In calling this function, the same types must be used for the actual arguments. Thus, the following statements may be used in a program that calls the function:

```
DOUBLE PRECISION X,Y,Z
LOGICAL A
CHARACTER NAME*20
    .
    .
    .
Z=FUN1(C,X*Z,Y,.TRUE.,A,NAME)
```

In this example, the variable names X, Y, and Z all refer to double precision data; the name A identifies logical data; C is implicitly typed as real; and NAME is of character type. A logical constant is also used in this example. An actual argument may be any type of constant — integer, real, double precision, logical, or character — as long as it corresponds with the type of the dummy argument.

When an array name is used as a dummy argument, the corresponding actual argument should also be an array name. (There are exceptions to this that are beyond the scope of this text.) The effect of calling a function with an array name as an argument is to cause the entire array to be made available to the function. The array name that is used as a dummy argument must be specified in a DIMENSION statement (or type statement) in the function, and the dimension of the actual argument must be given in the calling program. The dimensions of the arguments should normally be the same. For example, the function in Fig. 12-5(a) finds the smallest element of a 20-element array. (The programming technique used in this function is discussed in Chapter 10.) Notice that the array name is used as a dummy argument, and that its dimension is declared in the function before the first executable statement. The function name, SMALL, is assigned the value of the smallest element of the array. To call this function, the dimension of the actual argument is declared in the calling program. For example, the main program in Fig. 12-5(b) calls the function SMALL twice to find the smallest element in each of two arrays. Notice that the actual argument used each time that the function is called is an array name of the same dimension as the dummy argument.

```
FUNCTION SMALL(X)
DIMENSION X(20)
SMALL=X(1)
DO 100 L=2,20
   IF(X(L).LT.SMALL) SMALL=X(L)
100 CONTINUE
RETURN
END
```

(a)

```
DIMENSION X(20),Y(20)
READ(5,100) X
SX=SMALL(X)
READ(5,100) Y
SY=SMALL(Y)
WRITE(6,200) SX,SY
STOP
100 FORMAT(10F8.2)
200 FORMAT(1X,2F10.2)
END
```

(b)

FIGURE 12-5. The SMALL function and a main program; (a) the function; (b) the main
program.

In most versions of FORTRAN the dimension of an array used as an argument of a function need not be precisely specified in the DIMENSION statement. Instead, the dimension may be passed to the subprogram by one of the arguments (or by several arguments if a multidimensional array is used). This is known as an *adjustable dimension.* When this technique is used, the dummy argument that represents the array's dimension must be an integer variable name. The same name must be used in place of the dimension information for the array in the DIMENSION statement in the function. For example, the function SMALL may be modified to find the smallest element of an array of unknown size as shown in Fig. 12-6. Notice in this function that the array name and an integer variable name representing the array's dimension are used as dummy arguments. The same integer variable name is used in the DIMENSION statement to declare the array's dimension.

In the calling program the dimension of the actual array must be stated precisely. The actual argument that corresponds to the dummy argument representing the array's dimension must have a value equal to the array's dimension. For example, the function in Fig. 12-6 may

```
        FUNCTION SMALL(X,N)
        DIMENSION X(N)
        SMALL=X(1)
        DO 100 L=2,N
          IF(X(L).LT.SMALL) SMALL=X(L)
    100 CONTINUE
        RETURN
        END
```

FIGURE 12-6. The function SMALL with an adjustable array dimension.

be used to find the smallest element of a 50-element array named A.
The calling program would contain the following statements:

```
        DIMENSION A(50)
            .
            .
            .
        SA=SMALL(A,50)
            .
            .
            .
```

Notice that array A is specified as having 50 elements and that this
information is passed to the function as one of the arguments.

A function may be called only as part of an expression. The expression may include simply the function reference, or it may include other
operations or function references. The expression may be used as part
of an assignment statement or an IF statement. For example, assume
that functions FUN3 and FUN4 have been properly coded. Each requires two real arguments. The following are valid examples of the use
of these functions:

```
        X=FUN3(X,Y)+FUN4(A,B)
        IF(FUN3(C,D).GE.7.5) GO TO 10
        A1=A2+FUN4(A3,FUN3(A4,A5))
        IF(2.5*FUN3(P,Q).LT.1.0) GO TO 20
```

12-3. SUBROUTINE SUBPROGRAMS

In many ways a subroutine subprogram is similar to a function. Like a
function, a subroutine requires a name to identify it, a list of dummy
arguments, a RETURN statement, and an END statement. In addition,

a subroutine is compiled as a unique program and is therefore stored separately from other programs in internal storage. It is called by supplying actual arguments and branching to the subroutine. Upon completion of the statements in the subroutine, control returns to the calling program.

However, a subroutine differs from a function in the way in which the values are returned to the calling program. Whereas a function returns a value through the name of the function, a subroutine uses arguments to return values. Since there may be several arguments, more than one value may be returned.

The general form of a subroutine subprogram is as follows:

    SUBROUTINE *name*(a1,a2,a3, . . . ,an)
      .
      .
      .

    (FORTRAN statement)
      .
      .
      .

    RETURN
      .
      .
      .

    END

The first statement in a subroutine subprogram consists of the key word SUBROUTINE followed by a name and a list of dummy arguments. The name of a subroutine must follow the rules of variable names. However, there is no data type associated with the name since the name is not used to return a value to the calling program. The arguments may be variable or array names. If explicit typing is used, type statements must be included in the subroutine. In addition, if any arguments are arrays, their dimensions must be specified in a DIMENSION statement (or type statement).

Any FORTRAN statement except another SUBROUTINE statement or a FUNCTION statement may appear in a subroutine. Unlike a function, the name of the subroutine must *not* be used as a variable name within the subroutine. Arguments that are used to return values to the calling program must be assigned those values within the subroutine. This may be accomplished through an assignment statement or a READ statement. As with a function, there must be at least one RETURN statement to cause the subroutine to branch back to the calling program. Finally, the last statement in a subroutine must be an END statement.

```
SUBROUTINE CALC(A,B,SUM,DIF)
SUM=A+B
DIF=A-B
RETURN
END
```

FIGURE 12-7.   A simple subroutine.

Figure 12-7 shows an example of a simple subroutine. This subroutine finds the sum and difference of two real values. The name of the subroutine is CALC. The arguments are the real values to be used in the calculations, A and B, and the sum and difference, SUM and DIF. Notice that the first two arguments are used to send values to the subroutine and the other two arguments are used to return data to the calling program. Within the subroutine the sum and difference are calculated and assigned to the arguments. Then control returns to the calling program.

In order to call a subroutine subprogram a CALL statement is used. This is a control statement that supplies actual arguments and branches to a subroutine. The general form of the CALL statement is:

CALL *name(a1,a2,a3, . . .,an)*

where *name* is the name of a subroutine.

a1,a2,a3, . . .,an are actual arguments that correspond in number, order, and type to the dummy arguments of the called subroutine.

As an example of a CALL statement, assume that a program must calculate the sum and difference of the values of X and Y, and then assign the results to S and D respectively. The following CALL statement may be used to call subroutine CALC:

```
CALL CALC(X,Y,S,D)
```

The effect of this statement is to assign the values of the actual arguments to the dummy arguments. The values of *all* arguments are passed to the subroutine, even though some arguments may have meaningless values in the calling program. Thus, in this example, the value of X in the calling program is assigned to A in the subroutine; the value of Y is assigned to B; and the values of S and D are assigned to SUM and DIF. Then control transfers to the first executable statement of the subroutine. This process is summarized in Fig. 12-8. Upon execution of a RETURN statement within the subroutine, the values of the dummy arguments are assigned to the actual arguments, and

```
CALL CALC(X,Y,S,D)            SUBROUTINE CALC(A,B,SUM,DIF)

(next statement)              SUM=A+B

                              DIF=A-B

                              RETURN

                              END
```

FIGURE 12-8. Calling a subroutine subprogram.

```
CALL CALC (X,Y,S,D)           SUBROUTINE CALC(A,B,SUM,DIF)

(next statement)              SUM=A+B

                              DIF=A-B

                              RETURN

                              END
```

FIGURE 12-9. Returning to a calling program from a subroutine subprogram.

```
      SUBROUTINE CALCA(AA,BA,SUMA,DIFA)
      DIMENSION AA(50),BA(50),SUMA(50),DIFA(50)
      DO 100 I=1,50
        SUMA(I)=AA(I)+BA(I)
        DIFA(I)=AA(I)-BA(I)
100 CONTINUE
      RETURN
      END
```

FIGURE 12-10. A subroutine with arrays as arguments.

358

control returns to the calling program at the next statement following the CALL statement. (See Fig. 12-9.)

The actual arguments used when a subroutine is called may be variable names, array or array element names, constants, or expressions. As with functions, the only requirement is that they agree in number, order, and type with the dummy arguments. Explicit typing may be used and is required for double precision, logical, and character names. If an array is used as a dummy argument, its dimension must be declared in the subroutine and the dimension of the corresponding actual argument must be given in the calling program. For example, the previous subroutine can be modified to find the sum and difference of corresponding elements of two 50-element arrays. This subroutine is shown in Fig. 12-10. The calling program requires similar dimensions for the actual arguments. Thus, the following statements might appear in the calling program:

```
DIMENSION XA(50),YA(50),SA(50),DA(50)
    .
    .
    .
CALL CALCA(XA,YA,SA,DA)
    .
    .
    .
```

As with functions, adjustable dimensions may be used for arrays that are arguments of subroutines.

12-4. THE COMMON STATEMENT

The use of arguments is one way of passing data between a subprogram and a calling program. Another approach is to declare a common area in the computer's internal storage that is used by both the calling program and the subprogram. The variable and array names used in the subprogram are related to the corresponding names in the calling program because they refer to the same storage locations. In order to specify a common area, the COMMON statement is used both in the calling program and in the subprogram. This is a specification statement that must precede the first executable statement in any program.

The area that is created in storage by the COMMON statement is known as the *common block*. Within the block may be storage for any type of data—integer, real, double precision, logical, or character. In most versions of FORTRAN, a common block may be given a name. This is known as *named* or *labeled common*. In some versions of FORTRAN only *blank* or *unlabeled common* is allowed.

Blank Common

The general form of the COMMON statement for blank common is as follows:

COMMON *list*

where *list* is a list of variable and array names separated by commas.

For example, the following COMMON statement may be used in subroutine CALC (Fig. 12-7) that finds the sum and difference of two real values:

COMMON A,B,SUM,DIF

The effect of this statement is to cause the variable names specified to refer to the first four storage areas in the common block. In the calling program there must be a similar COMMON statement listing the variable names used for the actual data. For example, the following COMMON statement might appear in the program that calls CALC:

COMMON X,Y,S,D

The effect of this statement in the calling program is to cause the variable names to refer to the same four storage locations as the names listed in the COMMON statement in the subroutine. Thus, these two COMMON statements, the first in the subroutine and the second in the calling program, cause variable names X and A to refer to the same storage location, the names Y and B to refer to the same location, the names S and SUM to identify the same location, and the names D and DIF to identify the same location. This is summarized in Figure 12-11.

Note that the order in which the variable names are coded in the COMMON statements specifies which names correspond. Assume that the COMMON statement in the calling program for this example is coded as follows:

COMMON Y,X,S,D

Then the correspondence of variable names in the calling program and subprogram is not the same as before. In this case, Y and A refer to the

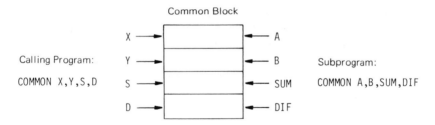

FIGURE 12-11. Correspondence of variable names in a common block.

same storage location, X and B identify the same location, and S, D, SUM, and DIF are as before. This may or may not be correct, depending on what the programmer wishes to accomplish.

Any variable or array name specified in a COMMON statement must not appear in the argument list of a subprogram. In the examples above, since all of the arguments are in the common block, no argument list is used. Thus, subroutine CALC is coded as shown in Fig. 12-12. The program that calls this subroutine requires the following statements:

```
COMMON X,Y,S,D
    .
    .
    .
CALL CALC
    .
    .
    .
```

In effect, the data is passed between the subprogram and the calling program by means of the common block.

There are two main advantages in using a common block: the amount of storage required for the object program is reduced, and the speed with which the program is executed is increased. Both of these result from the fact that no special instructions are needed to pass

```
SUBROUTINE CALC
COMMON A,B,SUM,DIF
SUM=A+B
DIF=A-B
RETURN
END
```

FIGURE 12-12. A simple subroutine with a COMMON statement.

data between the calling program and the subprogram. When using an argument list, the object program includes instructions that make the actual arguments available to the subprogram. These instructions require storage space and must be executed each time the subprogram is called. When a common block is used, these instructions are not needed. Hence, the program as a whole requires less storage and executes faster.

When using a common block, it is important that corresponding variable names are of the same type. For example, assume that the following COMMON statement appears in a main program:

$$\text{COMMON M,N,W,X}$$

In this example, the first two locations in the common block contain integer data, and the next two locations contain real data. Any COMMON statement in a subprogram called by this program must specify the same types of variable names in the same order.

A common block may be used with several subprograms. In this case the main program must assign names to all areas in the common block. Each subprogram requires a COMMON statement with a list of the names that it uses, plus additional names if necessary to align the data in the common block. To illustrate, assume that a main program calls two subroutines, SUB1 and SUB2. The first subroutine requires three real values from the main program and the second uses two integer values. If no argument lists are used, then the variable names for all values must be specified in the COMMON statement in the main program. For example, the following COMMON statement may be used in the main program:

$$\text{COMMON A,B,C,I,J}$$

Subroutine SUB1 requires a COMMON statement with names for the real values. Since these occupy the first three locations of the common block, no additional names are needed. Hence, the following COMMON statement could be used in SUB1:

$$\text{COMMON X,Y,Z}$$

However, subroutine SUB2 must be able to refer to the two integer values in the common block. Therefore, three real variable names must be specified so that the integer names used in the subroutine are properly aligned with the integer data in common. That is, a COMMON statement of the following form would be used in SUB2:

$$\text{COMMON R,S,T,K,L}$$

This is summarized in Fig. 12-13.

If an array name is specified in a COMMON statement, the entire array is stored in the common block. The size of the array in the subprogram must be the same size as the corresponding array in the calling program. For example, assume that the following statements appeared in a subprogram:

```
DIMENSION C(5),D(5)
COMMON C,D
```

The effect of these statements is to assign the elements of array C to the first five locations in the common block and the elements of array D to the next five locations. In a calling program, the dimensions of the corresponding arrays must be similarly specified. The following statements may appear in the calling program:

```
DIMENSION W(5),X(5)
COMMON W,X
```

The correspondence between the array elements is shown in Fig. 12-14. Notice that if the dimensions of the arrays are not correctly specified, correspondence of array elements is affected. For example, assume that the DIMENSION and COMMON statements in the main program are coded as follows:

```
DIMENSION W(7),X(5)
COMMON W,X
```

Then the correspondence between the array elements in the calling program and the subprogram is as shown in Fig. 12-15.

If adjustable dimensions are used, an argument list is required.

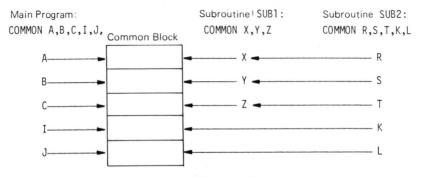

FIGURE 12-13. Correspondence of variable names in a common block referred to by two subprograms.

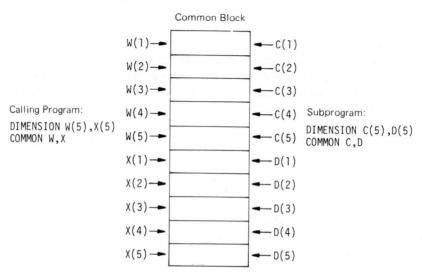

FIGURE 12-14. Correspondence of array elements in a common block.

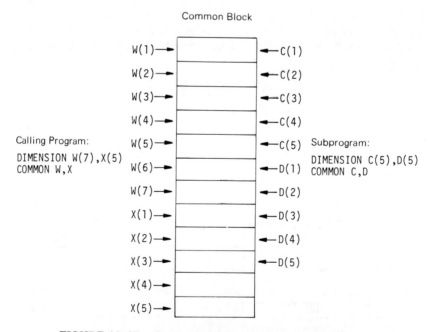

FIGURE 12-15. Correspondence of array elements in a common block where the array dimensions do not agree.

An array with an adjustable dimension cannot be specified with a COMMON statement.

In most versions of FORTRAN the dimension of arrays that are stored in a common block may be declared in the COMMON statement. For example, the arrays named C and D, each with five elements, may be specified as follows:

```
COMMON C(5),D(5)
```

This eliminates the need for a DIMENSION statement for arrays in a common block.

Named Common

In most versions of FORTRAN a common block may be given a name or label. Although only one blank or unlabeled common block is allowed, there may be any number of named blocks. A block name must follow the rules for variable names. In the COMMON statement the block name is enclosed in slashes and precedes the list of variable and array names that refer to data in the block. For example, the following COMMON statement specifies two named common blocks:

```
COMMON /B1/A,B,C/B2/I,J
```

The first block, named B1, contains locations for three real values. The values are identified by variable names A, B, and C. The block named B2 contains two locations for the integer data. The variable names I and J identify these data.

The advantage of using named common is that a subprogram need only specify variable and array names for the data in the named blocks that are used by the subprogram. For example, assume that the previous COMMON statement is contained in a main program that calls two subroutines. The first subroutine requires three real values from the main program. These values are contained in the block named B1. In this subroutine the COMMON statement need only specify names for the data in the B1 common block. Thus, the following COMMON statement may be used:

```
COMMON /B1/X,Y,Z
```

Notice that the block name must be the same as the name used in the calling program but the variable names may be different.

The second subroutine uses the integer data found in the block

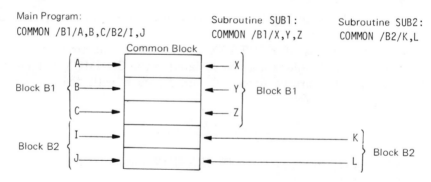

FIGURE 12-16.   Correspondence of variable names in a
named common block.

named B2. This may be declared in the subroutine by the following
COMMON statement:

COMMON /B2/K,L

The correspondence of variable names in named common blocks
is summarized in Fig. 12-16.

If both blank and named common are required, the blank common
is declared first in the COMMON statement. For example, consider the
following statement:

COMMON M,PL,N(10)/RES/AMT(100)/DAT/IM,W

This statement declares that blank common contains storage for the
variable names M and PL and for the 10-element array named N. In
addition, the common block named RES contains a 100-element array
named AMT, and the block named DAT contains storage for data
named IM and W.

12-5. STATEMENT FUNCTIONS

Functions and subroutines are the most commonly used types of
subprograms. Another type of subprogram that is often useful is the
statement function. Statement functions differ from other subprograms
in that a statement function is only one statement long and is coded as
part of the calling program. No FUNCTION statement is used; no
RETURN or END statement is required. Instead, each function consists
of one statement-function-defining statement.

The general form of a statement function is as follows:

name (a1,a2,a3, . . . ,an)=expression

where *name* is the function's name.

a1,a2,a3, . . . ,an are dummy arguments.

expression is an arithmetic, logical, or character expression.

The name of a statement function must represent the type of data to be returned to the calling program. If explicit typing is used, the name must have been declared previously in an appropriate type statement. The dummy arguments may be any variable names. Array names are not allowed as dummy arguments in a statement function. The expression must agree with the function's name. An integer, real, or double precision function requires an arithmetic expression. A logical expression may be used only with a logical function name. A character type function name requires a character expression.

A statement function is coded in the program that calls the function. All statement functions used in a program must appear after the specification statements and before the first executable statement. A statement function is called in the same way that a function subprogram is called. The statement function's name is used in an expression and actual arguments are supplied. As with function subprograms the actual arguments must agree in order, number, and type with the dummy arguments. The actual arguments may be variable and array element names, constants, and expressions, but may not be array names. After execution of the expression in the statement function, the resulting value is assigned to the name of the function, and control returns to the point where the function is called.

As an example of a statement function, assume that a program is being prepared that at a number of points needs to calculate the average of three test scores. If a function is not used, then each time that the average is to be calculated the appropriate formula must be coded in the program. A function subprogram may be prepared and called when needed, but this requires coding a complete function containing only one calculation. If a statement function is used, the advantages of a function subprogram are gained without expending effort to code a complete function.

The following statement function may be used to average three test scores:

```
AVE(TS1,TS2,TS3)=(TS1+TS2+TS3)/3.0
```

The name of the function is AVE. The dummy arguments are TS1, TS2, and TS3. They represent the test scores to be averaged. The arithmetic expression uses the dummy arguments to perform the necessary calculations.

In order to call the statement function, actual arguments must be supplied when the function is used. For example, if the three test scores to be averaged are named T1, T2, and T3, then a statement like the following may be used to find their average:

$$A1=AVE(T1,T2,T3)$$

The effect of this statement is to execute the statement function with the values of T1, T2, and T3 substituted for TS1, TS2, and TS3, respectively. As another example, assume that six test scores need to be averaged. The scores are referred to by the names S1, S2, S3, S4, S5, and S6. To accomplish this, the following statement may be used :

$$A2=(AVE(S1,S2,S3)+AVE(S4,S5,S6))/2.0$$

Here, the statement function is called twice. First, the average of S1, S2, and S3 is calculated. Then S4, S5, and S6 are averaged. The two averages are added and the result is divided by two to get the average of all six scores.

12-6. PROGRAM DEVELOPMENT REVISITED

In Chapter 8 we discussed a number of aspects of program development. These included program structure, style, and understandability, and the activities in the programming process. We saw that following the guidelines in Chapter 8 resulted in programs that were well structured, easily understood, and correct.

As programs become larger, their development becomes more complex. In Chapter 8 we introduced the idea of modular programming in which a large program is divided into sections or modules. Each module performs some function related to the overall processing of the program. The modules for a program can be developed separately and then brought together to form a complete program after all modules are finished. With subprograms we have a convenient mechanism for modularizing a program. The approach is to code each module as a separate subprogram. Then the main program is composed of a series of calls to the subprograms.

To illustrate this approach consider the problem of updating a pricing table. In an example in Section 10-4 we showed a table that consisted of two ten-element arrays, one for item numbers and one for the corresponding unit prices (see Fig. 10-3). Assume now that the pricing table is considerably larger, containing item numbers and prices for 100 items. The problem is that a number of prices have changed. We need a program to make the appropriate modifications in the table. In addition we want a printed copy of the table before and after the changes are made.

We can see that the program must basically do the following:

1. Read the pricing table.
2. Print the pricing table.
3. Update the pricing table.
4. Print the updated table.

Following our approach of using subroutines to modularize the program we can code each of these steps as a separate subroutine. However, since the second and fourth steps just involve printing the pricing table, we only need three subroutines — one to read the pricing table, one to print the table, and one to update the table. Then the main program calls these three subroutines in order and then calls the printing subroutine again to print the updated table.

Assume that we have coded the three subroutines and called them TABIN, TABOUT, and UPDATE respectively. Each subroutine requires two, 100-element arrays as arguments — one for the item numbers and one for the prices. Then the main program to call these subroutines in the proper sequence is shown in Fig. 12-17. Notice the simplicity of this program; it is just a sequence of four CALL statements with the necessary arguments.

The input and output subroutines can be coded fairly easily. Each involves a loop to read or write the elements of the two arrays. The subroutines are shown in Fig. 12-18. Notice that we have used the same names for the arrays in the main program and the subroutines, although this is not necessary. However, it is necessary that the arrays be dimensioned in the subroutines.

The updating process has not been fully defined. Assume that new

```
C
C     THIS PROGRAM UPDATES THE UNIT PRICING TABLE.
C
      DIMENSION ITNUM(100),PRICE(100)
      CALL TABIN(ITNUM,PRICE)
      CALL TABOUT(ITNUM,PRICE)
      CALL UPDATE(ITNUM,PRICE)
      CALL TABOUT(ITNUM,PRICE)
      STOP
      END
```

FIGURE 12-17. The main program for the table updating problem.

```
      SUBROUTINE TABIN(ITNUM,PRICE)
C
C     THIS SUBROUTINE READS THE PRICING TABLE.
C
      DIMENSION ITNUM(100),PRICE(100)
      DO 10 I=1,100
        READ(5,100) ITNUM(I),PRICE(I)
   10 CONTINUE
      RETURN
  100 FORMAT(I4,F4.2)
      END



      SUBROUTINE TABOUT(ITNUM,PRICE)
C
C     THIS SUBROUTINE PRINTS THE PRICING TABLE BELOW APPROPRIATE HEADINGS.
C     THE TABLE IS PRINTED ON ONE PAGE IN FOUR COLUMNS.
C
      DIMENSION ITNUM(100),PRICE(100)
      WRITE(6,100)
      DO 10 I=1,50
        WRITE(6,110) ITNUM(I),PRICE(I),ITNUM(I+50),PRICE(I+50)
   10 CONTINUE
      RETURN
  100 FORMAT(1H1,19X,18HUNIT PRICING TABLE/
     1        1H0,11HITEM NUMBER,4X,10HUNIT PRICE,6X,
     2            11HITEM NUMBER,4X,10HUNIT PRICE/)
  110 FORMAT(1H ,3X,I4,10X,F5.2,12X,I4,10X,F5.2)
      END
```

FIGURE 12-18.   The TABIN and TABOUT subroutines.

prices along with corresponding item numbers are recorded on a series of input records. There are any number of changes that need to be made and the input data is not in any particular order. However, the last input record contains 9999, in the item number field.

The updating subroutine must do the following until there is no more input data:

1. Read an item number and new price.
2. Find the corresponding item in the pricing table.
3. Make the necesssary change in the pricing table.

Assume that we have a function named LOCTN that returns the location (that is, the element number) of a given value in a 100-element array of integers. The arguments of the function are the value to be found and the name of the array. If the value is found, then the function returns its location; otherwise it returns a value of zero.

We can use this function in the UPDATE subroutine as shown in Fig. 12-19. First, an input record is read with an item number and new price. Then the check for the trailer value is made. Next, the LOCTN function is called and the returned value is assigned to LOC. We then test LOC to see if it is zero. If it is, then an error message is printed; otherwise the new price is assigned to PRICE(LOC) thus modifying the pricing table.

The only thing that remains to complete the program is to develop the LOCTN function. This function searches a 100-element array for a given value. We could use a sequential search, or a binary search could be used if the array is in ascending order. We will assume that this is not necessarily the case and search sequentially. The complete function is shown in Fig. 12-20. Notice that the name of the function, LOCTN, is assigned the subscript of the matching element if the number is found in the table; otherwise it is assigned a value of zero.

The main program in Fig. 12-17 together with the subprograms in

```
      SUBROUTINE UPDATE(ITNUM,PRICE)
C
C     THIS SUBROUTINE READS NEW PRICE DATA, LOCATES THE ITEM
C     IN THE PRICING TABLE, AND MODIFIES THE PRICE.
C
      DIMENSION ITNUM(100),PRICE(100)
      WRITE(6,200)
   10 READ(5,100) INUM,PRIX
      IF(INUM.EQ.9999) GO TO 40
      LOC=LOCTN(INUM,ITNUM)
      IF(LOC.EQ.0) GO TO 20
      PRICE(LOC)=PRIX
      GO TO 30
   20 WRITE(6,210) INUM
   30 GO TO 10
   40 RETURN
  100 FORMAT(I4,F4.2)
  200 FORMAT(1H1)
  210 FORMAT(1H0,12HITEM NUMBER ,I4,27H NOT FOUND IN PRICING TABLE)
      END
```

FIGURE 12-19. The UPDATE subroutine.

```
      FUNCTION LOCTN(NUM,ITAB)
C
C     THIS FUNCTION RETURNS THE LOCATION OF NUM IN ITAB.
C     IF NUM CANNOT BE FOUND, ZERO IS RETURNED.
C
      DIMENSION ITAB(100)
      I=1
   10 IF((ITAB(I).EQ.NUM).OR.(I.EQ.100)) GO TO 20
      I=I+1
      GO TO 10
   20 IF(NUM.EQ.ITAB(I)) GO TO 30
      LOCTN=0
      GO TO 40
   30 LOCTN=I
   40 RETURN
      END
```

FIGURE 12-20.   The LOCTN function.

Figs. 12-18, 12-19, and 12-20 make a complete program to update the pricing table. In processing these on a computer, the main program would be entered first followed by the subprograms in any order. After successful compilation of all programs, execution would begin with the first statement in the main program.

We can see from this example a number of advantages of using subprograms to modularize a program. For one, this approach allows us to develop the program in a *top-down* fashion. This is similar to the idea of stepwise program refinement that we discussed in Section 8-4. We start by designing the overall logic of the program. Each basic function that the program is to perform becomes a subprogram. The main program contains a series of calls to the subprograms. (There may be other statements in the main program besides those that call subprograms. For example, loop control or decision-making statements may be needed to control the order of execution of the subprograms.) We then design each subprogram in a similar top-down fashion. Eventually we reach the point where the basic operations of the program can be coded.

One way of displaying the top-down design of a program is to draw a diagram that shows the relationship between the main program and the subprograms. Figure 12-21 shows such a diagram for the table-updating program. The box at the top represents the main program. Each box below signifies a subprogram. A line connects two programs if one program calls the other. Thus, Fig. 12-21 shows that

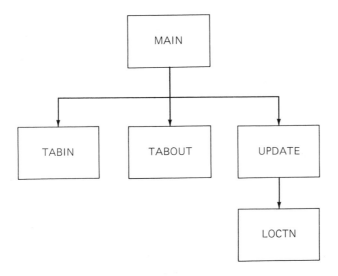

FIGURE 12-21. The calling hierarchy for the table updating program.

the main program calls TABIN, TABOUT, and UPDATE, and that UPDATE calls LOCTN.

This diagram also shows how we can think of the program in terms of *levels*. At the highest level we can think of the program as the sequence of activities that take place in the main program. If we wish we can just understand the program at this level. Then we do not have to examine any of the subprograms. However, if we wish to understand the program at a deeper level, then we can look at the subprograms that are called by the main program. Even deeper, we can examine the next level of subprograms, and so forth until we reach the bottom of the diagram.

Besides designing the program in a top-down fashion we can also follow a *top-down coding* and *testing* pattern. In this approach, we code the main program first. Then for each subprogram called by the main program we code a "dummy" subprogram (sometimes referred to as a *stub*) that simulates, but does not actually perform, the function of the subprogram. We can then run the main program with the non-functioning subprograms to make sure the logic of the main program is correct. Next we follow the same procedure for the first subprogram, coding stubs for any subprograms that it calls. We then test the main program with the completed first subprogram. This process is repeated for all subprograms until the complete program is coded and tested.

An alternative testing strategy is called *bottom-up testing.* In this approach we design the program in a top-down fashion but then start coding and testing with the lowest level subprograms. This requires writing main programs (sometimes called *exercisers*) to call and test the subprograms. We build the program from the bottom up until we finally reach the top level which is the main program.

A final advantage of using subprograms to modularize a program is that the subprograms may often be used in other programs. For example, assume that we need a program that computes the cost of various items by multiplying the quantity purchased times the price. Since we already have a subroutine to read the pricing table and one to locate an item in the table, we can use these in a pricing program. The main program to do this is shown in Fig. 12-22. The program first reads the pricing table using the TABIN subroutine. It then reads an item number and quantity and checks for a trailer value. Next the program uses the LOCTN function to find the location of the desired item in the table. The returned value is then checked to see if the item was found. If it was, then the price for the item is multiplied by the quantity to get the cost and the output is printed. If the item was not found then an error message is printed. This main program, together with the TABIN and LOCTN subprograms, forms a complete pricing program.

```
C
C     THIS PROGRAM COMPUTES TOTAL COST GIVEN THE QUANTITY PURCHASED.
C
      DIMENSION ITNUM(100),PRICE(100)
      CALL TABIN(ITNUM,PRICE)
   10 READ(5,100) INUM,QTY
      IF(INUM.EQ.9999) GO TO 40
      LOC=LOCTN(INUM,ITNUM)
      IF(LOC.EQ.0) GO TO 20
      COST=PRICE(LOC)*QTY
      WRITE(6,200) INUM,COST
      GO TO 30
   20 WRITE(6,210) INUM
   30 GO TO 10
   40 STOP
  100 FORMAT(I4,F3.0)
  200 FORMAT(6H ITEM ,I4,6H COST ,F7.2)
  210 FORMAT(6H ITEM ,I4,10H NOT FOUND)
      END
```

FIGURE 12-22. The main program for the pricing program.

We can see from these examples a number of advantages of using subprograms. In fact, most large programs are developed in the manner described here. For any complex program, the programmer should consider using the techniques in this section.

PROGRAMMING PROBLEMS

1. Write a function subprogram that finds the balance in a bank account given the initial balance, the interest rate, and the number of years since the initial amount was deposited. Assume that interest is compounded annually. Write a main program that reads the initial balance, interest rate, and number of years, calls the function, and prints the balance computed by the function. Test the program with several sets of input data.

2. Write a function subprogram to find the Nth Fibonacci number. (See problem 6 in Chapter 6 for a description of Fibonacci numbers.) Write a main program that reads a value of N, calls the function, and prints the result. Test the program with N equal to 5, 12, 1, 25, 2, 8, and 3.

3. Write a function subprogram to find e^x using the series given in problem 11 of Chapter 6. Prepare a main program that reads a value of x, computes e^x using the function, and prints the result. Test the program with several values of x.

4. Problem 2 in Chapter 9 gives the requirements for a student to be on the Dean's list of a college based on the student's year in school and his or her GPA. Write a function subprogram that accepts the student's year and GPA, and returns the logical value TRUE if the student should be placed on the Dean's list and the value FALSE if the student should not be on the list. Write a main program to read the data given in problem 2 of Chapter 9, call the function, and print a message indicating whether or not the student should be on the Dean's list.

5. Write a function subprogram that returns the logical value TRUE if a given character string is a palindrome and FALSE if the string is not a palindrome. (See problem 12 in Chapter 9 for a description of palindromes.) Write a main program that reads a character string, calls the function to determine if the string is a palindrome, and prints the string and a statement as to whether or not it is a palindrome. Use the data in problem 12 of Chapter 9 to test the program.

6. Problem 4 in Chapter 8 describes an algorithm for finding the day of the week given any date in the twentieth century. Code this algorithm as a function subprogram. The arguments of the function are the month, day, and year. The function should return a character string that gives the corresponding day of the week. Write a main program that reads a date, calls the function, and prints the day of the week. Use the data in problem 4 of Chapter 8 to test the function.

7. The tuition charged a student at a small private college is based on the number of units that the student takes during a quarter. The tuition charge is $200 plus $25 per unit for each of the first eight units and $32.50 per unit for all units taken over eight. Write a function subprogram to determine the tuition charge, given the number of units.

Prepare a main program that reads student data in the following format:

Card Columns	Field
1–4	Student number
23–26	Units taken — fall quarter
27–30	Units taken — winter quarter
31–34	Units taken — spring quarter

Using the function described in the previous paragraph, calculate the tuition for each quarter. Also calculate the total tuition for the year. Print these results along with the student number. Supply appropriate headings for the output data.

Use the following input data to test the program:

Student Number	Units Taken		
	Fall Quarter	Winter Quarter	Spring Quarter
1018	7.0	18.0	15.0
1205	15.0	12.5	6.0
1214	15.5	15.5	15.5
1218	8.0	7.0	5.0
1293	8.5	7.5	4.0
1304	6.0	6.0	6.0
1351	10.5	18.5	0.0
1354	0.0	15.0	6.0
9999 (trailer card)			

8. Prepare a function subprogram to determine the expected population of a group in ten years given the current population and the annual growth rate. Prepare a main program that reads population data for two socio-economic groups in each area of a city. The input format is as follows:

Card Columns	Field
1–4	Area number
11–17	Current population — group A
18–20	Growth rate — group A
21–27	Current population — group B
28–30	Growth rate — group B

Using the function subprogram described above, calculate the expected population of each group in ten years. Print the area number, the expected population of each group, and the total expected population for the area.

Use the following data to test the program:

Area Number	Group A		Group B	
	Current Pop.	Growth Rate	Current Pop.	Growth Rate
001	14,500	3.5%	6,300	4.1%
002	18,251	2.3%	2,215	2.9%
003	6,205	4.0%	8,132	3.9%
004	3,738	5.4%	12,730	2.7%
005	12,100	3.0%	10,150	3.0%
000 (trailer card)				

9. Prepare a subroutine subprogram that finds the total and average of up to four test scores. The subroutine receives the number of test scores (1 to 4) and the scores from the calling program and returns the total and average of the scores.

This subroutine is to be used in a program that analyzes the results of a psychological experiement. Each subject in the experiment is given two series of tests with up to four tests in each series. The results of the tests were punched in cards in the following format:

Card Columns	Field
1–3	Subject identification code
4	Number of tests in first series
5–6 7–8 9–10 11–12	Test scores in first series
13	Number of tests in second series
14–15 16–17 18–19 20–21	Test scores in second series

Prepare a main program that reads the test-score data and uses the subroutine described above to find the total and average of the test scores in each series. This requires two calls of the subroutine. Then find the total and average of all test scores in the two series with a third call of the subroutine. Print all results with appropriate headings.

Use the following input data shown to test the program:

Identification Code	First Series		Second Series	
	Number of Tests	Test Scores	Number of Tests	Test Scores
408	3	17,16,21	2	22,24
519	1	24	3	17,23,16
523	2	14,18	4	25,14,17,19
584	4	22,16,17,14	4	18,17,17,21
601	1	12	2	11,9
677	3	25,23,24	1	25
701	4	17,18,21,15	2	21,13
713	2	13,12	3	18,18,12
999 (trailer card)				

10. Adding amounts of time expressed in hours and minutes requires special manipulation because there are 60 minutes in an hour. Write a subroutine subprogram that accepts two amounts of time and determines their sum. For each time accepted by the subroutine and for their sum, two arguments are needed — one for the hours and the other for the minutes. Thus, this subroutine requires six arguments in all.

Prepare a main program that reads the time that an employee worked on each day of the week in the following format:

Card Columns	Field
1–5	Employee number
6–9	Time worked on Monday
10–13	Time worked on Tuesday
14–17	Time worked on Wednesday
18–21	Time worked on Thursday
22–25	Time worked on Friday

The first two columns of each time field contain the hours; the next two columns give the minutes. Using the subroutine described in the previous paragraph, calculate the total time worked by the employee for the week. This requires four calls of the subroutine. Print all input data and the total of the times with appropriate headings.

Use the following data to test the program:

| | Time Worked | | | | |
Employee Number	Monday	Tuesday	Wednesday	Thursday	Friday
10011	0800	0730	0800	0730	0730
10105	0745	0755	0630	0500	0845
10287	1000	0805	0625	0800	0715
10289	0945	0800	0610	0830	0000
10304	0000	0000	0800	0825	0745
10455	0635	0840	0000	0000	1155
00000 (trailer card)					

11. Prepare the following subprograms:

   (a) CHRG(THERM). This is a function subprogram that determines the total gas utility charge based on the number of gas
   therms used (THERM). (Gas consumption is measured in
   therms.) The charge is 9¢ per therm for the first 200 therms,
   8¢ per therm for the next 300 therms, 7¢ per therm for the
   next 500 therms, and 6½¢ per therm for all gas used over 1000
   therms. The value returned to the calling program should be
   the total charge.

   (b) OUTPT(KUSNO,THERM,CHARG). This is a subroutine subprogram that prints with appropriate headings the customer
   number, the gas used in therms, and the charge for one month.

Prepare a main program that reads the customer number and the
gas consumed for three separate months. The input format is as follows:

Card Columns	Field
1-5	Customer number
6-15	Therms used 1st month
16-25	Therms used 2nd month
26-35	Therms used 3rd month

Then, through three separate calls of the function CHRG, calculate the
charge for each of the three months. Print the results for each month
using three calls of the subroutine OUTPT.

   Use the following data to test the program:

| | Therms Used | | |
Customer Number	1st Month	2nd Month	3rd Month
11825	425	172	253
13972	665	892	1283
14821	45	572	313
19213	1562	973	865
28416	200	500	1000
31082	0	300	600
99999 (Trailer card)			

12. Many introductory calculus text books describe a technique for numerical integration of a function in which the area under the curve is divided into a number of rectangles. Then the total area of all rectangles is an approximation of the definite integral of the function. Write a FORTRAN function subprogram that uses this rectangular method to find:

$$\int_a^b x^2 \, dx$$

The arguments of the function are the limits of integration (a and b) and the number of rectangles that are to be used in the approximation.

Write a main program that uses the subprogram to repeatedly integrate the function between the limits $a = 0$ and $b = 3$. Start with two rectangles, then use four, then eight, and so forth each time doubling the previous number until 8192 are used. For each case, print the number of rectangles, the definite integral, and the error, that is, the difference between the correct integral (which is 9) and the computed value.

Finally, use the function to find

$$\int_{-2}^{1} x^2 \, dx + \int_{.75}^{1.25} x^2 \, dx$$

Use 256 rectangles. All output should be through the main program, not the subprogram.

13. Assume that F, G, and H are polynomials defined as follows:

```
F(X)=A(1)+A(2)*X+A(3)*X**2+...+A(N+1)*X**N
G(X)=B(1)+B(2)*X+B(3)*X**2+...+B(M+1)*X**M
H(X)=C(1)+C(2)*X+C(3)*X**2+...+C(L+1)*X**L
```

Note that the degrees of these polynomials are N, M, and L respectively. Assume a maximum of 20 for each of these and dimension any arrays accordingly. Note also that the coefficient of X**I has subscript I+1.

Prepare the following subprograms:

(a) INPUT(A,N). This is a subroutine to read an array A of the coefficients of a polynomial of degree N. Input data should include a card with the degree of the polynomial followed by a card or cards with the coefficients. Note that a polynomial of degree N has N+1 coefficients.

(b) OUTPUT(A,N). This is a subroutine to print the array A of the coefficients of a polynomial of degree N. The coefficients should be neatly arranged and labeled.

(c) SCALM(A,N,D,C). This is a subroutine to multiply a polynomial of degree N with array A of coefficients by the constant D returning a polynomial of degree N with array C of coefficients.

(d) ADDP(A,N,B,M,C,L). This is a subroutine to add a polynomial of degree N with coefficient array A and a polynomial of degree M with coefficient array B returning a polynomial with coefficient array C and its degree L.

Prepare a main program that uses these subroutines to do the following:

Read F(X)
Print F(X)
Read G(X)
Print G(X)
Compute H(X) = F(X) + 2*G(X)
Print H(X)
Compute a new F(X) = 3*H(X)
Print the new F(X)

Use the following data to test your program:

Polynomial F(X) N = 5	Polynomial G(X) M = 2
A(1) = 1.0	B(1) = -7.0
A(2) = 17.6	B(2) = 3.1
A(3) = 0.0	B(3) = -1.0
A(4) = 2.0	
A(5) = -3.6	
A(6) = 1.0	

14. Problem 6 in Chapter 10 involves writing a program to process student test score data. Rewrite this program as the following series of subprograms:

(a) IN(ID,TEST,KOUNT). This is a subroutine that reads identification numbers and test scores into two arrays named ID and TEST respectively. The subroutine must count the data as it is read to get a count of the number of test scores to be processed (KOUNT). Note that the value of KOUNT should not include the trailer card.

(b) OUT(ID,TEST,KOUNT). This is a subroutine that prints in columns below appropriate headings the array of identification numbers and test scores.

(c) RMEAN(TEST,KOUNT). This is a function that calculates the mean of the test scores. The mean is simply the average.

(d) TAB(TEST,KOUNT,K1,K2,K3,K4,K5). This is a subroutine that tabulates (that is, counts) the number of test scores in various categories. The subroutine should determine the number of scores in each of the following categories:

90–100
80–89
70–79
60–69
 0–59

K1 returns the number of scores in the first category (90–100), K2 returns the number of scores in the second category, and so forth through K5.

(e) SORTT(ID,TEST,KOUNT). This is a subroutine that sorts the *test score array* into descending order (largest to smallest). Be sure that the correspondence between the identification number array and the test score array is maintained during the sorting.

(f) RMED(TEST,KOUNT). This is a function that determines the median of the test scores. The function should handle both the case where there is an even number of test scores and the case where the number of scores is odd.

In addition to the subprograms, prepare a main program that uses the subprograms to process the test score data. The main program should call the subprograms in the following order:

IN
OUT
RMEAN
TAB
SORTT
OUT
RMED

Notice that after sorting, the arrays are printed using the OUT subroutine. The main program also requires other output operations. The mean must be printed by the main program after RMEAN is called. The tabulated data must be printed after TAB is called. The median must be printed after RMED is used. All output should be printed with appropriate headings or descriptive comments. Use the data in problem 6 of Chapter 10 to test the program.

15. Code the IN and OUT subroutines described in problem 14 above. Then code the following subprograms:

(a) SORTI(ID,TEST,KOUNT). This is a subroutine that sorts the *identification number array* into ascending order. Note that as the ID array is rearranged the TEST array must also be rearranged to keep the correspondence between the two arrays.

(b) SEARCH(ID1,TEST1,FOUND,ID,TEST,KOUNT). This is a subroutine that searches the ID array for the element that corresponds with ID1. It then sets TEST1 equal to the corresponding element of TEST. If ID1 is found in ID, then the logical variable FOUND is set equal to TRUE. Otherwise, FOUND is set equal to FALSE. This subroutine may use a binary search or a sequential search. Assume in either case that the ID array has previously been sorted into ascending order.

Prepare a main program that calls the subprograms in the following order:

    IN
    OUT
    SORTI
    OUT
    SEARCH

The SEARCH subprogram should be called within an input loop that reads an identification number, calls SEARCH, and then prints either the corresponding test score or a message indicating that the identification number was not found. This loop should terminate when an identification number equal to 999 is read. (If all of problem 14 was completed, these subroutines can be added to those from problem 14 and the main program can be extended to meet the additional requirements.)

To test the program use the identification numbers and test scores in problem 6 of Chapter 10. This data should terminate with a trailer card. Following this should be data to test the SEARCH subroutine terminated with another trailer card. Use the following identification numbers for this:

    202
    137
    195
    298
    248
    104
    173
    101
    150
    299
    233
    138

16. Problem 6 in Chapter 11 describes some operations using matrices (i.e., two-dimensional arrays). Refer to this problem and prepare the following subprograms:

(a) GET(A,M,N). This is a subroutine that reads a matrix A with M rows and N columns.

(b) PUT(A,M,N). This is a subroutine that prints the M×N matrix named A in an appropriate format.

(c) EQUAL(A,B,M,N). This is a function that returns the truth value TRUE if the M×N matrices A and B are equal and returns FALSE if they are not equal.

(d) SCMLT(C,A,M,N). This is a subroutine that multiplies the M×N matrix A by C.

(e) ADDM(A,B,C,M,N). This is a subroutine that adds the M×N matrices A and B, assigning the sum to the M×N matrix C.

Prepare a main program that uses these subprograms to process two matrices according to the requirements in problem 6 of Chapter 11. Use the data in that problem to test the program.

Chapter 13

INTERNAL
DATA REPRESENTATION

To program in FORTRAN, little knowledge of the internal organization of the computer is needed. If fact, in Chapter 1 we discussed only briefly the physical components of a computer before going on to programming concepts. However, some understanding of the internal structure of the computer helps explain some of the characteristics of FORTRAN. In particular, it is useful to understand the way data is represented in the internal storage of the computer. In this chapter we discuss internal data representation and its relationship to FORTRAN.

13-1. DATA REPRESENTATION

Humans usually represent data by using *characters*. In the Western world the character set consists of the *alphabetic characters* (A,B, . . . , Z), the *numeric characters* (0,1, . . . ,9), and a number of *special characters* ($, + / etc.). Computers, however, cannot use human characters to represent data. A computer's internal storage is composed of a large number of electromagnetic circuits where each circuit has only two states — "on" and "off". An example of a common electronic circuit that has only two states is a light bulb. Like a circuit in a computer, a light bulb can be only on or off. There are 50 to 60 common characters used by humans to represent data. If a single circuit in a computer were used to represent any character, then that circuit would have to have 50 to 60 different states. However, because a computer's circuit is a two-state device it is not possible to represent any human character with a single circuit.

How, then, do computers store data? The answer is that computers use a series of electromagnetic circuits in a particular pattern of on/off states to represent data. A computer processes data (that is, characters) by converting the data to its two-state representation. For output, the computer converts the results of its processing from the two-state internal representation to human characters.

Data represented in this two-state manner is said to be in the *binary mode*. For ease of presenting data in the binary mode on paper, the digit "1" is used to represent the "on" state and the digit "0" is used for the "off" state. The characters "1" and "0" are called the *binary digits* or *bits*. Internally, all data is stored as bits.

13-2. NUMBER SYSTEMS

In order to understand how data is represented in the binary mode it is necessary first to consider number systems. A *number system* is a way of expressing quantities. Most humans use the *decimal number system*. However, most computers express quantities by using the *binary number system*.

The Decimal Number System

Consider the decimal number 285. What does this number really mean? We can think of 285 as 200 plus 80 plus 5. But 200 is 2 times 100, 80 is 8 times 10, and 5 is 5 times 1. Finally, 100 is 10 times 10 or 10^2, 10 is 10^1, and 1 is 10^0. Thus 285 can be interpreted as follows:

$$285 = 200 + 80 + 5$$
$$= (2 \times 100) + (8 \times 10) + (5 \times 1)$$
$$= (2 \times 10^2) + (8 \times 10^1) + (5 \times 10^0)$$

[It is appropriate at this time to review briefly the concept of raising a number to a power. Any number raised to a power means multiply the number by itself the number of times specified in the power; that is, use the number as a factor the number of times given by the power. For example, 6^4 means use 6 as a factor 4 times:

$$6^4 = 6 \times 6 \times 6 \times 6 = 1296$$

As other examples consider the following:

$$10^2 = 10 \times 10 = 100$$
$$10^3 = 10 \times 10 \times 10 = 1000$$
$$10^4 = 10 \times 10 \times 10 \times 10 = 10,000$$
$$2^2 = 2 \times 2 = 4$$
$$2^3 = 2 \times 2 \times 2 = 8$$
$$2^4 = 2 \times 2 \times 2 \times 2 = 16$$
$$2^5 = 2 \times 2 \times 2 \times 2 \times 2 = 32$$

A number raised to the first power is just that number. For example, 6^1 is 6, 10^1 is 10, and 2^1 is 2. Finally, a number raised to the zero power is one. This is true for any number except zero. (0^0 is indeterminate.) For example, 6^0 is 1, 10^0 is 1, and 2^0 is 1.]

As another example of a decimal number, consider 4096:

$$4096 = 4000 + 000 + 90 + 6$$
$$= (4 \times 1000) + (0 \times 100) + (9 \times 10) + (6 \times 1)$$
$$= (4 \times 10^3) + (0 \times 10^2) + (9 \times 10^1) + (6 \times 10^0)$$

Notice how the digit zero can be used to hold a place in the number without adding value to the number. In this example zero holds the 100's place. But since zero times any number is zero, it does not increase the value of the number.

These examples illustrate the basic concepts of a number system. A number system is composed of a set of *digits*. In the decimal number system the digits are 0, 1, 2, 3, 4, 5, 6, 7, 8, and 9. The number of digits is called the *base* of the number system. There are ten digits in the decimal number system because the base of the system is ten. A *number* is a quantity that is represented by a *numeral* composed of a string of digits. For example, the decimal numeral 285 is composed of digits that are acceptable in the decimal number system. This numeral represents the number two-hundred eighty-five. The digits in a numeral occupy positions that have value. The *position values* (also called *place values*) of a number system are successive powers of the base. Considering only whole numbers, the right-most position has a value of the base to the zero power, the next position to the left has a value of the base to the first power, the next position has a value of the base to the second power, and so forth. Thus, the position values for the decimal number system are as follows:

$$\ldots 10^5 \quad 10^4 \quad 10^3 \quad 10^2 \quad 10^1 \quad 10^0$$

A numeral is interpreted in a number system as the sum of the products of the digits in the numeral and their corresponding position values. Thus, 285 is interpreted as a decimal number as follows:

Digits:	2	8	5
Position values:	10^2	10^1	10^0
Interpretation:	$(2 \times 10^2) + (8 \times 10^1) + (5 \times 10^0)$		

The interpretation of the numeral is found by multiplying the digits in the numeral by their corresponding position values and then adding the results. Notice that the right-most digit occupies the 10^0 position and the position values increase to the left.

As another example, consider 4096:

Digits:	4	0	9	6
Position values:	10^3	10^2	10^1	10^0
Interpretation:	$(4 \times 10^3) + (0 \times 10^2) + (9 \times 10^1) + (6 \times 10^0)$			

Note how the digit zero serves the purpose of holding a place in the numeral without adding value to the number.

In summary, a number system is composed of a set of digits. The base of the system is the number of digits that are acceptable in the system. The position values are successive powers of the base. A numeral is a string of digits that represents a number or quantity. A numeral can be interpreted as the sum of the products of the numeral's digits and their position values.

Although we have made a distinction here between a numeral and a number, the distinction is rarely made in practice. Most often we use the word "number" whether we mean "quantity" or the representation of the quantity by a "numeral." We will follow this practice in the remainder of this chapter. The meaning of the term should be evident from the context in which it is used.

The Binary Number System

Computers do not use the decimal number system to express quantities. Since a computer uses two-state electronic circuits, it requires a number system that has only two digits. Such a system is the *binary number system.*

The base of the binary number system is two. The digits of the binary number system are 1 and 0. These are the binary digits or bits that correspond to the "on" and "off" states of a computer's circuits. The position values are successive powers of the base:

$$\ldots 2^5 \quad 2^4 \quad 2^3 \quad 2^2 \quad 2^1 \quad 2^0$$

A number in any number system can be composed only of digits acceptable to the system. Thus, a binary number can be composed only of the digits 1 and 0. For example, 10011 is a binary number (read "one-zero-zero-one-one"). To interpret a binary number, each digit is multiplied by its corresponding position value and the results are totaled. Thus, the binary number 10011 can be interpreted as follows:

Digits: 1   0   0   1   1

Position values: 2^4 2^3 2^2 2^1 2^0

Interpretation: $(1 \times 2^4) + (0 \times 2^3) + (0 \times 2^2) + (1 \times 2^1) + (1 \times 2^0)$

Since the position values are expressed in the decimal system, such an interpretation results in converting the binary number to its equivalent in the decimal number system:

$$10011 = (1 \times 2^4) + (0 \times 2^3) + (0 \times 2^2) + (1 \times 2^1) + (1 \times 2^0)$$
$$= (1 \times 16) + (0 \times 8) + (0 \times 4) + (1 \times 2) + (1 \times 1)$$
$$= 16 + 0 + 0 + 2 + 1$$
$$= 19$$

Thus, 10011 in the binary system is equivalent to 19 in the decimal number system.

A special notation is sometimes used to distinguish numbers in different number systems. In this notation the base of the number system is written as a subscript immediately following the number. Thus, 10011_2 is a base 2 or binary number and 19_{10} is a base 10 or decimal number. This notation, while not required, is important when there may be confusion about the base of the number. For example, consider the number 10. This may represent a decimal number ("ten") or a binary number ("one-zero"). However, 10_{10} is not equivalent to 10_2 ($10_2 = (1 \times 2^1) + (0 \times 2^0) = 2_{10}$). Therefore, to avoid confusion this special notation is used to indicate what type of number is being expressed.

As a final example, consider the binary number 110101. This number can be interpreted as follows:

Digits: 1   1   0   1   0   1

Position values: 2^5 2^4 2^3 2^2 2^1 2^0

Interpretation: $(1 \times 2^5) + (1 \times 2^4) + (0 \times 2^3) + (1 \times 2^2) + (0 \times 2^1) + (1 \times 2^0)$

$= (1 \times 32) + (1 \times 16) + (0 \times 8) + (1 \times 4) + (0 \times 2) + (1 \times 1)$

$= 32 + 16 + 0 + 4 + 0 + 1$

$= 53$

Thus, 110101_2 is equivalent to 53_{10}.

Decimal to Binary Conversion

So far, we have only shown how to convert a binary number to its decimal equivalent. The inverse, that of converting a decimal number to its binary equivalent, is only slightly more complex. There are a number of quick techniques for this. The technique discussed here, while not the fastest, is based on the underlying nature of number systems.

To convert a decimal number to its binary equivalent, the largest power of two that is less than or equal to the decimal number is first found. Then the maximum significant position value in the binary equivalent of the decimal number is that power of two. Working backwards toward 2^0, the next significant position value is found. This value is the next power of two that is less than or equal to the original decimal number minus the position value that has already been used. This continues until the 2^0 position is reached, or until the remainder from subtracting significant position values from the original number is zero.

For example, consider the decimal number 21. The largest power of two that is less than or equal to 21 is 2^4 or 16. Thus, there is 1×2^4 in 21. Subtracting 2^4 from 21 leaves 5. The largest power of two that is less than or equal to 5 is 2^2 or 4; there is 1×2^2 in 5. Subtracting 2^2 from 5 leaves 1. The largest power of two that is less than or equal to 1 is 2^0 or 1; there is 1×2^0 in 1. Subtracting 1 from 1 leaves 0 and there are no more significant position values. Thus, in 21 there is 1×2^4, 1×2^2, and 1×2^0. The intermediate position values (2^3 and 2^1) are held by the digit 0. Therefore, the binary equivalent of 21_{10} is 10101_2. These calculations can be summarized as follows:

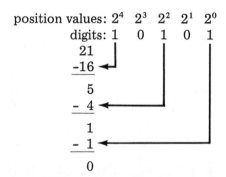

As another example, consider the decimal number 54. The largest power of two that is less than or equal to 54 is 2^5 or 32. Working backwards from 2^5 to 2^0, the following is obtained:

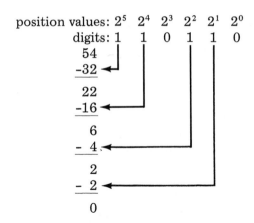

Thus, 54_{10} is equivalent to 110110_2.

It is useful to be able to convert to and from binary numbers easily. Following the techniques described here, it is a simple matter to convert a binary number to its decimal equivalent or vice versa. Figure 13-1 lists the binary equivalents of the first sixteen decimal numbers.

Fractions

So far we have only described how whole numbers (integers) are represented in the binary number system. However, as we know, computers can process numbers with fractional parts. Thus, we need some way of expressing fractions as binary numbers.

Decimal	Binary
0	0
1	1
2	10
3	11
4	100
5	101
6	110
7	111
8	1000
9	1001
10	1010
11	1011
12	1100
13	1101
14	1110
15	1111

FIGURE 13-1.   Binary-decimal equivalence.

In the decimal number system, the position values of the digits to the *right* of the decimal point are *negative* powers of ten. That is, the position values of the fractional part are as follows:

$$10^{-1} \quad 10^{-2} \quad 10^{-3} \quad 10^{-4} \quad 10^{-5} \ldots$$

(A number to a negative power is one over the number to the absolute value of the power. Thus, 10^{-3} is $1/10^3$ or $1/1000$ or .001.) To illustrate the use of these position values, consider the decimal number 5.625. This number is interpreted as follows:

Digits:	5	6	2	5
Position values:	10^0	10^{-1}	10^{-2}	10^{-3}

Interpretation: $(5 \times 10^0) + (6 \times 10^{-1}) + (2 \times 10^{-2}) + (5 \times 10^{-3})$

With the binary number system the position values of the bits to the right of the *binary point* (which is the equivalent of the decimal point in the binary system) are negative powers of the base two. That is, the position values of the right-hand bits are as follows:

$$2^{-1} \quad 2^{-2} \quad 2^{-3} \quad 2^{-4} \quad 2^{-5} \ldots$$

These correspond to the following values:

$$2^{-1} = \tfrac{1}{2} = .5$$
$$2^{-2} = \tfrac{1}{4} = .25$$
$$2^{-3} = \tfrac{1}{8} = .125$$
$$2^{-4} = \tfrac{1}{16} = .0625$$
$$2^{-5} = \tfrac{1}{32} = .03125$$

To interpret a binary number with a fractional part we follow the usual approach. For example, the binary number 101.101 is interpreted as follows:

Digits:	1	0	1	1	0	1
Position values:	2^2	2^1	2^0	2^{-1}	2^{-2}	2^{-3}

Interpretation: $(1 \times 2^2) + (0 \times 2^1) + (1 \times 2^0) + (1 \times 2^{-1}) + (0 \times 2^{-2}) + (1 \times 2^{-3})$
$= (1 \times 4) \ + (0 \times 2) \ + (1 \times 1) \ + (1 \times .5) \ + (0 \times .25) + (1 \times .125)$
$= \quad 4 \quad + \quad 0 \quad + \quad 1 \quad + \quad .5 \quad + \quad 0 \quad + \quad .125$
$= \quad 5.625$

Thus, 101.101_2 is equivalent to 5.625_{10}.

To convert a decimal number with a fractional part to its binary equivalent, we follow the procedure of finding the largest power of two as described earlier. For example, the following summarizes the conversion of 3.3125 to a binary number:

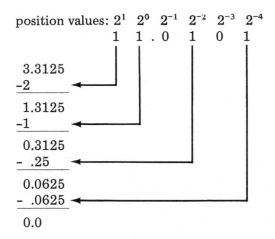

position values: 2^1 2^0 2^{-1} 2^{-2} 2^{-3} 2^{-4}

```
                  1   1  .  0   1   0   1

     3.3125
    -2
     1.3125
    -1
     0.3125
    -  .25
     0.0625
    -  .0625
     0.0
```

Thus, 3.3125_{10} is equivalent to 11.0101_2.

One problem with decimal to binary conversion where a fractional part is involved is that there is not always an exact equivalent of the decimal fraction in the binary number system. For example, consider the decimal number 0.2. If we try to convert this number to binary we get the following:

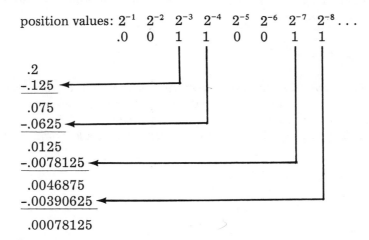

position values: 2^{-1} 2^{-2} 2^{-3} 2^{-4} 2^{-5} 2^{-6} 2^{-7} 2^{-8} ...

```
              .0   0   1   1   0   0   1   1

     .2
    -.125
     .075
    -.0625
     .0125
    -.0078125
     .0046875
    -.00390625
     .00078125
```

We can see that although we have carried out the conversion process to eight bits we still do not have an exact binary equivalent of 0.2. In fact, we can continue this process as long as we want and never get an exact equivalent. The binary number that we come up with will always be slightly less than 0.2.

There are many decimal fractions for which there is not an exact binary equivalent. However, decimal integers can always be represented exactly in the binary number system. In the next section we will see how this relates to the internal data representation of integers and reals.

13-3. INTERNAL DATA REPRESENTATION

Computers use the binary number system or some variation of it to represent data in their internal storage. In general, a computer's internal storage is composed of a large number of electromagnetic circuits. The individual circuits are grouped to form *storage locations.* Each storage location is a group of several computer circuits. By setting the circuits in a storage location to a particular pattern of on/off states, a value can be stored. Later, the computer can examine the pattern of on/off states to determine what value is stored at the storage location.

As a simple analogy consider a sequence of four light bulbs. In Fig. 13-2 the light bulbs are shown in the pattern on-off-off-on. Using binary digits this represents 1001 or the decimal number 9. A different pattern of on/off states (i.e. bits) represents different data. Of course computers don't use light bulbs for their internal storage, but the idea is the same; a pattern of bits, stored in a series of computer circuits, is used to represent data.

Types of Data

As we have seen in previous chapters, computers can process a variety of types of data. However, there are two basic categories of data that are processed. *Numeric data* consists of numbers that are manipulated arithmetically. For example, a student's grade point average is

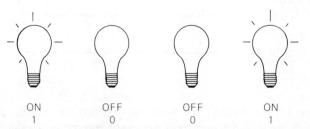

FIGURE 13-2. Internal data representation—the light bulb analogy.

numeric data because it results from arithmetic processing and may be used in further calculations. *Nonnumeric data* consists of data that cannot be processed arithmetically. For example, a student's address is nonnumeric. An address usually consists of numbers, letters, and special characters. However, the numbers in an address are not normally used in arithmetic calculations. Therefore, an address, even though it may contain numbers, is considered nonnumeric data.

In FORTRAN there are two basic types of numeric data. *Integer data* is represented in a program without a decimal point. *Real data* has a fractional part and therefore has a decimal point when coded in a program.

Nonnumeric data in FORTRAN includes character data and logical data. *Character data* is represented in a program as a group of characters enclosed in apostrophes or as a Hollerith constant (see Section 9-4). *Logical data* consists of truth values (see Section 9-3).

Internally, computers represent different types of data in different ways. In order to process a FORTRAN program, a computer must be able to store numeric and nonnumeric data. This section examines how these types of data are stored in a computer. The system that is used varies with different types of computers. This section only considers the internal data representation used by the IBM System/370 and related computers. However, the basic principles can be extended to almost all computers.

Character Data

Character data consists of alphabetic, numeric, and special characters. In the IBM computers a character is stored as a sequence of eight bits. That is, each character is assigned a unique eight-bit code that represents the character. For example, the letter A is represented by the code 11000001; the letter K is represented by 11010010; the number 5 is 11110101; the decimal point is represented by 01001011. There is a unique eight-bit pattern for each alphanumeric character.

This code is called the Extended Binary Coded Decimal Interchange Code or EBCDIC. It is a standard code that has been adopted by many computer manufacturers. There are a total of 256 different configurations of eight bits but not all are used in the EBCDIC code. However, all of the characters used in FORTRAN have a unique representation in this code.

Although the EBCDIC code uses binary digits to represent characters the computer does not confuse a character with a true binary number. For example, if the computer is told that 11000001 represents a character in the EBCDIC code, it interprets it as the letter A. If this pattern of eight bits is interpreted as a true binary number, it is equivalent to the decimal number 193. This is especially important when considering the numeric characters. For example, 5 is represented in the EBCDIC code as 11110101. However, if this pattern is interpreted as a true binary number, it is equivalent to the decimal number 245. Thus, the way in which a series of bits is interpreted depends on whether the bits are supposed to represent character data or numeric data.

In IBM computers, each storage location is composed of eight bits. An eight-bit storage location is often referred to as a *byte.* Bytes are the basic building blocks of internal storage and each byte is given a separate *address.* The computer locates data in storage by specifying the address of the byte or bytes where the data is stored. The internal storage capacity is measured in terms of the number of bytes that can be stored. For example, one common model of the IBM System/370 has a capacity of about 512,000 bytes.

Integer Data

Integer data (also called *fixed-point data*) is the simplest type of numeric data. Internally, integers are represented in the binary number system. Each integer is stored in a fixed number of bits. In IBM computers each integer is stored in 32 bits. For example, the decimal number 25 is 11001 in binary. As a 32-bit binary number, 25 is represented as follows:

00000000000000000000000000011001

Note that when a binary number does not use all 32 bit positions, leading positions are filled with zeros.

A configuration of a fixed number of bits used to represent numeric value is called a *word.* In IBM computers each word is 32 bits. Since internal storage is composed of eight-bit bytes, four consecutive bytes are required to form a word. Thus, integer data is stored as a true binary number in a four-byte word.

The difference between numeric and nonnumeric data can be understood more clearly at this point. As a 32-bit binary number, 25 is represented as shown previously. As character data, however, 25 appears as follows:

11110010 11110101

The first byte represents 2; the second byte is 5. In this form, the data cannot be used in arithmetic calculations. It only can be stored in the computer's internal storage and retrieved when needed. However, as a binary number the data can be used in arithmetic processing.

An integer value can be either positive or negative. As a 32-bit binary number, the sign is represented by the first bit. If the first bit is 0, then the number is positive; if the first bit is 1, then the sign is negative. In fact, negative numbers are stored in a special manner known as *two's complement form*. To form the two's complement of a binary number, the number is first inverted (that is, all of the 1-bits are changed to 0's and all of the 0-bits are changed to 1's) and then 1 is added. The result is the negative of the original number in two's complement form. For example, -25 is formed as follows:

00000000000000000000000000011001 (+25 as a true binary)
11111111111111111111111111100110 (invert the number)
<u>   +1</u> (add 1)

11111111111111111111111111100111 (-25 in two's
                                  complement)

Note that the first bit (the sign bit) is a 1, indicating a negative number in two's complement form. Internally, all negative integer numbers are represented in two's complement form.

Since the sign bit for a positive number is 0, the maximum integer that can be stored is:

01111111111111111111111111111111

This corresponds to the decimal number +2,147,483,647. The minimum negative number in two's complement form is:

10000000000000000000000000000000

This corresponds to the decimal number -2,147,483,648.

Real Data

Real data (also called *floating-point data*) is represented internally in a different form than integer data. This form, known as *floating-point notation*, involves rewriting the number as a fraction times some power of ten. For example, 27305.85 is written as .2730585 $\times$ 10^5. Similarly, .00008356902 is written as .8356902 $\times$ 10^{-4}. In writing a number in this way, the decimal point is shifted to the right or left until it is just to the left of the first nonzero digit in the number. Then the exponent for the power of ten is equal to the number of places that the decimal point is shifted. If the decimal point is shifted to the left, then the exponent is positive; if it is shifted to the right then the exponent is negative.

In floating-point notation a number is represented by its fraction and exponent. The decimal point, the multiplication symbol, and the number 10 are not necessary since it is assumed that the decimal point is always just to the left of the fraction and that the number is the fraction times ten to the power of the exponent. Thus, in floating-point notation, if the fraction is given as 2730585 and the exponent is 5, then the number is .2730585 $\times$ 10^5 or 27305.85. Similarly, if the fraction is 8356902 and the exponent is –4, then the number is .8356902 $\times$ 10^{-4} or .00008356902.

Any real value can be expressed in floating-point notation. It is in this form that real data is stored in the computer's internal storage. The computer converts the number to floating-point notation and stores the fraction and the exponent in the binary mode. In IBM computers, data is stored in a 32-bit word as shown in Fig. 13–3. The sign of the number occupies the first bit of the word. The exponent occupies the next seven bits. The last 24 bits of the word are reserved for the fraction. Note that the point to the left of the fraction is called a decimal point only in the decimal number system; in the binary number system it is called a *binary point* and in general it is referred to as the *radix point*.

Because of this representation of real numbers, limitations on the size of numbers are expressed in terms of maxima and minima for the fraction and the exponent. For IBM computers the maximum exponent is approximately 75 and the minimum is –78. These values express the range of *magnitude* of the number; real numbers must have a magnitude between 10^{-78} and 10^{75}. The fraction is limited to a maximum of approximately seven decimal digits. This gives the maximum *precision* of the number. Thus, there can be a very large number in magnitude (up to 10^{75}) but with only seven digits.

Limitations on the magnitude and precision of a real number as

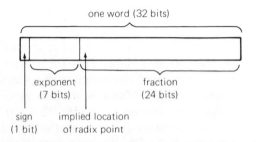

FIGURE 13–3.   Internal representation of real data.

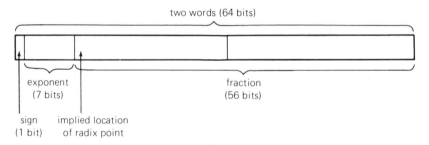

FIGURE 13-4. Internal representation of double- precision data.

stated here are approximate because they are expressed as decimal numbers. Precise limitations are in terms of binary digits, and their interpretation is beyond the scope of this book; however, the values stated here are sufficiently accurate for programming purposes.

It is possible to extend the precision but not the magnitude of real data. For IBM computers, two words can be linked together and real data stored in *double precision form.* (See Fig. 13-4.) The sign of the real number occupies the first bit of the first word. The next seven bits are reserved for the exponent. The fraction occupies the remaining 24 bits of the first word and all 32 bits of the second word. For double precision data the size of the exponent is the same as for the standard real data form. Therefore, the range of magnitude is the same. However, the amount of storage allocated to the fraction increases substantially. In the double precision form the computer can store real numbers up to approximately sixteen decimal digits.

Because real data may contain a fractional part its representation in floating-point notation may not be exact. In the last section we saw that some decimal fractions do not have an exact equivalent in the binary number system. Hence, in converting a real number to its internal data representation, some accuracy may be lost. However, because integers do not have fractional parts, the conversion of an integer to a binary number is always exact.

Logical Data

Logical data consists of truth values; that is, *true* and *false*. In IBM computers, each logical value is stored in a 32-bit word (four bytes). However, only the first byte is used for the truth value and the remaining three bytes are ignored. If the value is *true* then this first byte contains all 1's. However, if the value is *false*, then the first byte is all 0's.

13-4. RELATIONSHIP OF INTERNAL DATA REPRESENTATION TO FORTRAN

Data to be processed by a FORTRAN program is stored in the computer's internal storage in one of the forms discussed above. Character, integer, real, double precision, and logical data each has its own internal representation. Within a FORTRAN program we use constants and variable names to identify data. The internal representation of the data is indicated by the type of the constant or variable name.

A numeric constant may be coded in a FORTRAN program with or without a decimal point. When a constant is written without a decimal point it is stored in the computer's internal storage as a true binary number; that is, it is stored as integer data. When a constant is coded with a decimal point, it is converted to floating-point notation and stored as real data. A real constant is stored in the standard real data form (also called *single precision form*). A double precision constant is coded in a program using the exponential form discussed in Appendix D. Such a constant is stored in double precision, floating-point form.

When a variable name is used in a FORTRAN program, a storage location (or perhaps several locations) is reserved for the data to which the name refers. Each time the variable name is used in the program the computer locates the same storage location. If the variable name is integer (either typed implicitly or explicitly) then storage is reserved for integer data. Any time a value is assigned to the variable name by an assignment statement or by an input statement the value is stored in integer form. If an integer variable name is used in an arithmetic expression or an output statement, then the value retrieved from storage is integer.

When a variable name is real (either because of implicit or explicit typing), storage is reserved for real data. If a value is assigned to the variable name, then the value is stored in single precision, floating-point form. When a real variable name is used in an arithmetic expression or an output statement, then the computer retrieves a real value from storage.

A double precision variable name is declared in a DOUBLE PRECISION statement. When this statement is used it causes extra storage to be reserved for all variable names specified. Any data assigned to a double precision variable name is stored in double precision form.

A character constant is written in a FORTRAN program as a group of characters enclosed in apostrophes. Each character in such a constant is converted to the appropriate binary code. The entire constant is stored as a sequence of such codes in a group of storage locations. A character variable name is declared in a CHARACTER statement. Such a name identifies a group of storage locations each containing a character in the appropriate code. The length is given in the CHARACTER statement. Any use of a character variable name retrieves all of the characters to which the name refers.

In Section 7–3 we discussed the use of A-format code for input of character data using numeric variable names. When used with an IBM computer the maximum width of the input field is four columns. The reason for this is that the computer reserves one word for each variable name in the I/O list. Since a word in the IBM computers is four bytes and since one byte is required for each character in the EBCDIC code, a maximum of four characters can be stored in a word. Thus, a separate variable name must be used for each four-column field of alphanumeric data. However, if the variable name is double precision the computer reserves two words (eight bytes), and the character input field can be as many as eight columns wide. The same restrictions apply to Hollerith constants.

A logical constant is coded as .TRUE. or .FALSE. in a FORTRAN program. Such a constant is stored in a storage location in the appropriate logical data form. Any variable name declared in a LOGICAL statement refers to a storage location containing logical data.

In summary, we have shown in this chapter how different types of data are represented in the computer's internal storage. Character, integer, real, double precision, and logical data each have their own internal data representation. The type of data that a constant or variable name refers to in a FORTRAN program is determined by how the constant is coded or the variable name is typed. An understanding of the internal data representation for the computer being used helps the programmer understand and use FORTRAN.

REVIEW QUESTIONS

1. What is meant by a "two-state" representation of data?

2. What three things are needed to describe a number system?

3. What is meant by the *position values* of a number system?

4. Show how the decimal number 3208 is interpreted as the sum of the products of the number's digits and their position values.

5. What is the difference between a *number* and a *numeral?*

6. What are the base, digits, and position values of the binary number system?

7. What is the equivalent in the decimal number system of each of the following binary numbers?

(a) 110   (f) 101.11
(b) 1001   (g) 111.0101
(c) 1010   (h) 110.0011
(d) 10111   (i) 100.1001
(e) 101001   (j) 10000.00001

8. What is the equivalent in the binary number system of each of the following decimal numbers?

(a) 5   (f) 3.25
(b) 8   (g) 5.125
(c) 14   (h) 18.375
(d) 27   (i) 21.5625
(e) 52   (j) 10.10

9. What is meant by a *storage location* in a computer's internal storage?

10. How is character data represented in a computer's internal storage?

11. What is a *byte?*

12. How is integer data represented in a computer's internal storage?

13. What is meant by a computer *word?*

14. Write each of the following real numbers in floating-point notation. (Remember that in floating-point notation a number is represented by only a fraction and an exponent.)

(a) 38.35
(b) .0048
(c) −1528.0
(d) .897
(e) .000000062

15. How is real data represented in a computer's internal storage?

COMPUTER EXERCISE

Investigate the internal data representation of the computer that is used to process programs that you prepare. What is the size (number of bits) of each storage location? How many storage locations are there in the computer's internal storage? What coding system is used to represent character data? How many bits are required for each integer? each real? each double precision value? What are the real and double precision floating-point formats? What is the maximum and minimum integer that can be stored in the computer? What is the range of magnitude and the maximum precision of real and double precision data? How is logical data stored?

Appendix A

FORTRAN VERSION DIFFERENCES

The first version of FORTRAN was developed in the mid 1950's by researchers at the IBM Corporation. It became available for use with the IBM 704 computer early in 1957. Since that time FORTRAN has undergone several modifications and improvements. In 1958 a version called FORTRAN II became available. In 1962, FORTRAN IV was developed. (For a more complete discussion of the early history of FORTRAN see Jean Sammet's book, *Programming Languages: History and Fundamentals*, published by Prentice-Hall, Inc., in 1969.)

Although these early versions of FORTRAN had many common characteristics, they were sufficiently different that a program written in one version could not ordinarily be processed as if it were another version. For example, a program written in FORTRAN IV could not normally be run as a FORTRAN II program. A further problem was that each computer manufacturer usually made modifications in the language for use with the computers developed by the company. For example, the version of FORTRAN IV used on computer A might have some characteristics different from the version of FORTRAN IV used with computer B. Thus, although a program was written in what was supposed to be a common language, it usually could not be used on different computers without some modification.

In an attempt to overcome this problem of incompatibility between different versions of FORTRAN, the American National Standards Institute (or ANSI) developed American National Standard (ANS) FORTRAN in 1966. This standard version of FORTRAN brought together the most commonly used characteristics of FORTRAN IV. The objective was to have each computer manufacturer implement precisely the ANSI version of FORTRAN so that programs written in this version could be used on any computer without modification

ANSI also developed a subset of ANS FORTRAN called ANS Basic FORTRAN. This version is similar to FORTRAN II and was designed to be used with computers that were too small to implement the full ANS FORTRAN. However, all of ANS Basic FORTRAN is contained in the full ANS FORTRAN so that a program written in the basic version can be processed as a full FORTRAN program (but not necessarily conversely).

Subsequent to the development of these ANSI versions of FORTRAN, in 1966, most computer manufacturers implemented one or both of these. However, even though these were standardized languages, computer manufacturers still made small modifications in their form of FORTRAN. Hence, not all implementations of ANS FORTRAN or ANS Basic FORTRAN are entirely compatible.

In 1978 ANSI published a revised standard FORTRAN known as FORTRAN 77 (since the development of the language was completed in 1977). In addition, a subset of the language, known as Subset FORTRAN 77, was published. These versions contain a number of features not available in the 1966 ANSI languages. At the time that this is being written, few computer manufacturers have implemented FORTRAN 77 or Subset FORTRAN 77. However, we can expect that these versions will become quite common in the next few years.

One commonly used implementation of FORTRAN was developed at the University of Waterloo in Canada. It is called WATFIV for WATerloo Fortran IV. WATFIV is actually a modification of a previous version called WATFOR (for WATerloo FORtran). Although WATFIV is similar to the 1966 ANS FORTRAN, it includes special features that are useful for beginning students of programming. The most recent version of WATFIV is called WATFIV-S. It includes all of the features of WATFIV plus a number of control structures and other elements not usually found in FORTRAN. (Some of the features of WATFIV-S are included in FORTRAN 77.)

In this book we describe the most common and useful characteristics of FORTRAN. We present mainly those features that are compatible with both the 1966 version of ANS FORTRAN and FORTRAN 77 as well as some additional features found in WATFIV-S. However, not all elements of FORTRAN described in the text are found in all versions of FORTRAN.

The purpose of the tables in this appendix is to summarize the differences between several versions of FORTRAN. Specifically, we list differences between the following versions of FORTRAN:

ANS FORTRAN 77
ANS Subset FORTRAN 77

ANS FORTRAN, 1966 Version
ANS Basic FORTRAN, 1966 Version
WATFIV-S

Differences are listed by the chapter in which reference to the FOR-TRAN characteristic is first made. In the tables, "YES" means the feature or characteristic is included or required in the version of FOR-TRAN, "NO" means the element is not included or required, and "N.A." means "not applicable".

The following publications can be consulted for further details about these versions of FORTRAN:

American National Standard Programming Language FORTRAN, X3.9–1978. New York: American National Standards Institute, Inc., 1978. This publication describes both FORTRAN 77 and Subset FORTRAN 77.

American National Standard FORTRAN, X3.9–1966. New York: American National Standards Institute, Inc., 1966.

American National Standard Basic FORTRAN, X3.10–1966. New York: American National Standards Institute, Inc., 1966.

WATFIV Implementation and User's Guide. Waterloo, Ontario: University of Waterloo, 1969.

FORTRAN VERSION DIFFERENCES

	Full FORTRAN-77	Subset FORTRAN-77	Full FORTRAN (66)	Basic FORTRAN (66)	WATFIV-S
Chapter 2: Introduction to FORTRAN					
Character set contains:					
Currency symbol ($)	YES	NO	YES	NO	YES
Apostrophe (')	YES	YES	NO	NO	YES
Colon (:)	YES	NO	NO	NO	NO
Maximum continuation lines	19	9	19	5	Varies
Maximum statement number	99999	99999	99999	9999	99999
Chapter 3: Basic Input and Output Programming					
Maximum number of characters in a variable name	6	6	6	5	6
Format-free I/O	YES	NO	NO	NO	YES
Asterisk required in format-free READ and PRINT statements	YES	N.A.	N.A.	N.A.	NO
Excess fractional digits rounded on output	YES	YES	YES	NO	YES
Chapter 4: Arithmetic Programming					
Mixed mode arithmetic expressions	YES	YES	NO	NO	YES
Chapter 5: Programming for Decisions					
Logical IF statement	YES	YES	YES	NO	YES
Relational expressions	YES	YES	YES	NO	YES
Mixed mode in relational expressions	YES	YES	NO	N.A.	YES
Block IF statements	YES	YES	NO	NO	YES
Computed GO TO statement:					
Out of range value allowed	YES	YES	NO	NO	YES
Expressions allowed	YES	NO	NO	NO	NO
Comma optional	YES	YES	NO	NO	NO
Chapter 6: Programming for Repetition					
WHILE loop	NO	NO	NO	NO	YES
DO loop:					
Nonpositive parameters	YES	YES	NO	NO	NO
Noninteger DO-variable and parameters	YES	NO	NO	NO	NO
Expressions for parameters	YES	NO	NO	NO	NO
Pre-test/post-test	Pre	Pre	Post	Post	Post
Chapter 7: Programming for Nonnumeric Input and Output					
Format-free nonnumeric output	YES	NO	NO	NO	YES
Use of apostrophes instead of H-format	YES	YES	NO	NO	YES
Carriage control	YES	YES	YES	NO	YES
Character variables	YES	YES	NO	NO	YES
Character I/O:					
Format-free	YES	NO	NO	NO	YES
Formatted with character variables	YES	YES	NO	NO	YES

FORTRAN VERSION DIFFERENCES — *Cont.*

	Full FORTRAN-77	Subset FORTRAN-77	Full FORTRAN (66)	Basic FORTRAN (66)	WATFIV-S
Formatted with numeric variables	NO	NO	YES	NO	YES
End-of-file specifier	YES	YES	NO	NO	YES
Nested group repetition	YES	YES	YES	NO	YES
Chapter 9: Data Types					
INTEGER and REAL statements	YES	YES	YES	NO	YES
DOUBLE PRECISION statement	YES	NO	YES	NO	YES
DATA statement	YES	YES	YES	NO	YES
Placement of DATA statement before executable statements required	NO	YES	NO	N.A.	NO
Logical expressions	YES	YES	YES	NO	YES
Logical constants and variable names	YES	YES	YES	NO	YES
LOGICAL statement	YES	YES	YES	NO	YES
Logical assignment statement	YES	YES	YES	NO	YES
L-format code	YES	YES	YES	NO	YES
Character data type	YES	YES	NO	NO	YES
Character assignment statement	YES	YES	N.A.	N.A.	YES
Character data in DATA statement	YES	YES	N.A.	N.A.	YES
Substrings	YES	NO	N.A.	N.A.	NO
Concatenation	YES	NO	N.A.	N.A.	NO
String comparison	YES	YES	N.A.	N.A.	YES
Hollerith constants	NO	NO	YES	NO	YES
Chapter 10: Arrays					
Generalized integer subscript expressions	YES	YES	NO	NO	YES
Lower dimension bound	YES	NO	NO	NO	NO
Non-subscripted array name in DATA statement	YES	YES	NO	N.A.	YES
Implied-DO list in DATA statement	YES	NO	NO	N.A.	YES
Chapter 11: Multi-dimensional Arrays					
Maximum number of dimensions	7	3	3	2	7
Chapter 12: Subprograms					
Explicit typing of function names	YES	YES	YES	NO	YES
Character type functions	YES	NO	N.A.	N.A.	NO
Adjustable dimensions	YES	YES	YES	NO	YES
Named common	YES	YES	YES	NO	YES
Array dimension specified in COMMON statement	YES	YES	YES	NO	YES
Appendix D: Exponential Form and Input/Output					
Integer constant allowed in exponential form	YES	YES	YES	NO	YES
Double precision constant (exponential form)	YES	NO	YES	NO	YES
D-format code	YES	NO	YES	NO	YES

Appendix B

FORTRAN-SUPPLIED FUNCTIONS

FORTRAN-SUPPLIED FUNCTIONS

General Function	Definition	Name	Number of Arguments	Type of Arguments	Type of Value Returned	Full FORTRAN 77	Subset FORTRAN 77	Full FORTRAN (66)	Basic FORTRAN (66)	WATFIV-S
Square Root	Square root of argument	SQRT[1]	1	Real	Real	X	X	X	X	X
		DSQRT	1	Double	Double	X		X		X
		CSQRT	1	Complex	Complex	X		X		X
Integer Conversion	Convert argument to integer	IFIX[1]	1	Real	Integer	X	X	X	X	X
		INT[1]	1	Real	Integer	X	X	X		X
		IDINT	1	Double	Integer	X		X		X
Real Conversion	Convert argument to real	FLOAT	1	Integer	Real	X	X	X	X	X
		SNGL	1	Double	Real	X		X		X
		REAL[1,2]	1	Complex	Real	X		X		X
Double Precision Conversion	Convert argument to double precision	DBLE[1]	1	Real	Double	X		X		X
Complex Conversion	Convert argument to complex	CMPLX[1]	1 or 2[3]	Real	Complex	X		X		X
Absolute Value	Absolute value of argument	IABS	1	Integer	Integer	X	X	X	X	X
		ABS[1]	1	Real	Real	X	X	X	X	X
		DABS	1	Double	Double	X		X		X
		CABS[4]	1	Complex	Real	X		X		X
Maximum	Maximum value of arguments	MAX0[5]	≥ 2	Integer	Integer	X	X	X		X
		AMAX1	≥ 2	Real	Real	X	X	X		X
		DMAX1	≥ 2	Double	Double	X		X		X
		AMAX0	≥ 2	Integer	Real	X		X		X
		MAX1	≥ 2	Real	Integer	X		X		X
Minimum	Minimum value of arguments	MIN0[6]	≥ 2	Integer	Integer	X	X	X		X
		AMIN1	≥ 2	Real	Real	X	X	X		X
		DMIN1	≥ 2	Double	Double	X		X		X
		AMIN0	≥ 2	Integer	Real	X		X		X
		MIN1	≥ 2	Real	Integer	X		X		X
Truncation	Truncate fractional part of argument	AINT[1]	1	Real	Real	X	X	X		X
		DINT	1	Double	Double	X				
Transfer of Sign	Sign of argument 2 times absolute value of argument 1	ISIGN	2	Integer	Integer	X	X	X	X	X
		SIGN[1]	2	Real	Real	X	X	X	X	X
		DSIGN	2	Double	Double	X		X		X

(continued)

FORTRAN-SUPPLIED FUNCTIONS — Cont.

General Function	Definition	Name	Number of Arguments	Type of Arguments	Type of Value Returned	Full FORTRAN 77	Subset FORTRAN 77	Full FORTRAN (66)	Basic FORTRAN (66)	WATFIV-S
Remaindering	Remainder of argument 1 divided by argument 2	MOD[1]	2	Integer	Integer	X	X	X		X
		AMOD	2	Real	Real	X	X	X		X
		DMOD	2	Double	Double	X		X		X
Positive Difference	Argument 1 minus minimum of arguments 1 and 2	IDIM	2	Integer	Integer	X	X	X		X
		DIM[1]	2	Real	Real	X	X	X		X
		DDIM	2	Double	Double	X	X			
Nearest Whole Number	Round to nearest whole number	ANINT[1]	1	Real	Real	X	X			
		DNINT	1	Double	Double	X				
Nearest Integer	Round to nearest integer	NINT[2]	1	Real	Integer	X	X			
		IDNINT	1	Double	Integer	X				
Double Precision Product	Product of arguments	DPROD	2	Real	Double	X				
Imaginary Part of Complex Argument	Obtain imaginary part of complex argument	AIMAG	1	Complex	Real	X		X		X
Conjugate of a Complex Argument	Obtain conjugate of a complex argument	CONJG	1	Complex	Complex	X		X		X
Length	Length of a character string	LEN	1	Character	Integer	X				
Convert to Character	Character equivalent of integer	CHAR	1	Integer	Character	X				
Convert to Integer	Integer equivalent of character	ICHAR	1	Character	Integer	X	X			
Index of Substring	Location of substring argument 1 in string argument 2	INDEX	2	Character	Integer	X				
Lexically Greater Than or Equal	Argument 1 $\geq$ argument 2[7]	LGE	2	Character	Logical	X	X			
Lexically Greater Than	Argument 1 $>$ argument 2[7]	LGT	2	Character	Logical	X	X			

Function	Definition	Symbolic Name	Number of Arguments	Type of Argument	Type of Function					
Lexically Less Than or Equal	Argument 1 $\leq$ argument 2[7]	LLE	2	Character	Logical	X	X		X	X
Lexically Less Than	Argument 1 $<$ argument 2[7]	LLT	2	Character	Logical	X	X		X	X
Sine	sin(argument)	SIN[1]	1	Real	Real	X	X	X	X	X
		DSIN	1	Double	Double	X	X			X
		CSIN	1	Complex	Complex	X	X			X
Cosine	cos(argument)	COS[1]	1	Real	Real	X	X	X	X	X
		DCOS	1	Double	Double	X	X			X
		CCOS	1	Complex	Complex	X	X			X
Tangent	tan(argument)	TAN[1]	1	Real	Real	X	X	X	X	
		DTAN	1	Double	Double	X	X			
Arcsine	arcsin(argument)	ASIN[1]	1	Real	Real	X	X	X	X	
		DASIN	1	Double	Double	X	X			
Arccosine	arccos(argument)	ACOS[1]	1	Real	Real	X	X	X	X	
		DACOS	1	Double	Double	X	X			
Arctangent	arctan(argument)	ATAN[1]	1	Real	Real	X	X	X	X	X
		DATAN	1	Double	Double	X	X			X
	arctan(argument 1 / argument 2)	ATAN2[1]	2	Real	Real	X	X			X
		DATAN2	2	Double	Double	X	X			X
Hyperbolic Sine	sinh(argument)	SINH[1]	1	Real	Real	X	X	X		
		DSINH	1	Double	Double	X	X			
Hyperbolic Cosine	cosh(argument)	COSH[1]	1	Real	Real	X	X	X		
		DCOSH	1	Double	Double	X	X			
Hyperbolic Tangent	tanh(argument)	TANH[1]	1	Real	Real	X	X	X	X	X
		DTANH	1	Double	Double	X	X			
Exponential	e^{argument}	EXP[1]	1	Real	Real	X	X	X	X	X
		DEXP	1	Double	Double	X	X			X
		CEXP	1	Complex	Complex	X	X			X
Natural Logarithm	$\log_e(\text{argument})$	ALOG[8]	1	Real	Real	X	X	X	X	X
		DLOG	1	Double	Double	X	X			X
		CLOG	1	Complex	Complex	X	X			X
Common Logarithm	$\log_{10}(\text{argument})$	ALOG10[1]	1	Real	Real	X	X	X	X	X
		DLOG10	1	Double	Double	X	X			X

Notes

1. In Full FORTRAN 77 these names are *generic names*. A generic name may be used with any type of argument that is consistent with the function. For example, SQRT is a generic function name and may be used for the square root of a real, double precision, or complex argument. Generic names are only available in Full FORTRAN 77.

2. REAL returns the real part of a complex argument.

3. If CMPLX has two arguments, the result is argument 1 plus argument 2 times $\sqrt{-1}$. With Full FORTRAN 77 one argument may be used. In this case, the result is argument 1 plus zero times $\sqrt{-1}$.

4. CABS returns $\sqrt{(\text{real part})^2 + (\text{imaginary part})^2}$

5. The generic function name is MAX. It may be used to find the maximum of integer, real, or double precision arguments, returning the same type value as the arguments.

6. The generic function name is MIN. It may be used to find the minimum of integer, real, or double precision arguments, returning the same type value as the arguments.

7. The lexical order is determined from the ASCII code.

8. The generic function name is LOG.

Appendix C

KEYPUNCH OPERATION

A keypunch is operated in much the same manner as a typewriter —
one character is recorded with each depression of a key. However,
special operating procedures are needed to move the cards through
the machine and to perform other functions. This appendix describes
the main features of the IBM 29 keypunch and the procedures for
its operation. A more detailed description of this machine may be
found in the IBM publication *Reference Manual IBM 29 Card Punch*
(A24-3332).

General Features

The main features of the keypunch are: (See Fig. C–1)

MAIN LINE SWITCH: The main line switch turns on the power for
the keypunch. The machine may be used immediately once the switch
is turned on. When all punching is finished, the switch should be turned
off.

CARD HOPPER: Blank cards are placed in the card hopper, face
forward, with the 9-edge down. A pressure plate holds the cards in
place. The cards are fed from the front of the deck, down to the card
bed.

PUNCH STATION: Punching is performed at the punch station as
the card moves from right to left.

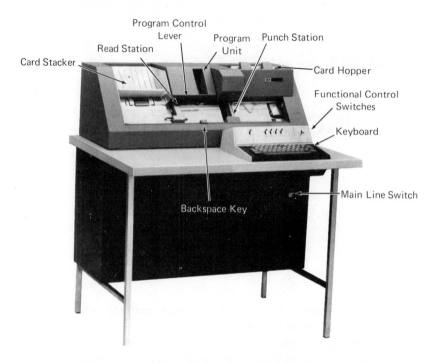

FIGURE C-1.   The IBM 29 keypunch. (Courtesy of IBM
             Corp.)

READ STATION: After a card leaves the punch station it passes
through the read station. If a card is in the read station and another is
in the punch station then the two cards move simultaneously. Data
may be duplicated from the first card to the second. (See discussion of
the DUP key.)

CARD STACKER: After a card leaves the read station it is fed
into the card stacker. If the stacker becomes full, a switch is operated
that locks the machine. Removing excess cards from the stacker releases
the switch.

BACKSPACE KEY: The backspace key causes the cards at the
read and punch stations to be moved back as long as the key is held
down.

PROGRAM UNIT: The program unit controls certain automatic
features of the machine. The unit is accessed by lifting the back of the
cover over the unit. Since punching can be performed without the use
of the program unit, no further discussion of it is included here. See

the IBM reference manual mentioned above for a complete description of program unit use and operation.

PROGRAM CONTROL LEVER: The program control lever is located above the card bed between the read station and the punch station. The normal position for this lever for punching without the use of the program unit is depressed to the right.

COLUMN INDICATOR: The column indicator is located at the bottom of the program unit. It shows the number of the column that is ready to be punched.

PRESSURE-ROLL RELEASE LEVER: The pressure-roll release lever is at the right of the column indicator. Pressing this lever releases cards at the read and punch stations. This is used when it is necessary to remove a card manually.

Keyboard

The keyboard consists of a set of punching keys, a space bar, and a number of functional keys. (See Fig. C-2.) Each depression of a punching key causes one character to be punched and the card to advance

FIGURE C-2. Keyboard elements for IBM 29 keypunch.
(Courtesy of IBM Corp.)

one column. Depression of the space bar causes the card to advance one column without a character being punched. The important functional keys are:

NUMERIC (Numeric Shift): When this key is pressed, the keyboard is shifted into numeric shift. As long as this key is held down, depression of a punching key causes the upper character on the key to be punched. With the numeric shift key released, the lower character on the punching key is punched.

MULT PCH (Multiple Punch): When this key is pressed, the keyboard is in numeric shift and depression of a punching key does not cause the card to advance. This feature may be used to punch a unique code in a column.

DUP (Duplicate): When this key is held down, the data in the card in the read station is duplicated in the card in the punch station. This is accomplished column-for-column and may be stopped by releasing the DUP key.

REL (Release): When this key is pressed, the cards at the read and punch stations are released and moved to the next station.

FEED: When this key is pressed, one card moves from the hopper down to the card bed just before the punch station. A second depression of this FEED key causes the card to be moved into the punch station and another card to come down from the hopper.

REG (Register): When this key is pressed, the card that is next to enter the punch station is moved into the punch station. Similarly, any card that is just before the read station is moved into the read station. An additional card is not fed from the card hopper when this key is pressed.

Functional Control Switches

The important functional control switches located above the keyboard are (see Fig. C-2):

AUTO FEED: When this switch is on and a card is released by depression of the REL key, another card is fed automatically from the card hopper.

PRINT: When this switch is on, any character that is punched is also printed above the column in which it is punched.

CLEAR: When this switch is activated, all cards in the card bed are cleared and stacked. No additional cards are fed from the card hopper.

Operating Procedures — Batch Punching

When a group of cards is to be punched, blank cards are placed in the card hopper and fed automatically. Make sure the auto feed switch is on. The procedure is:

1. Place a group of blank cards in the card hopper.
2. Press the feed key twice.
3. Punch the first card.
4. Press the release key.
5. Repeat Steps 3 and 4 for each succeeding card.
6. After all punching is completed remove all cards from the stacker and the hopper and turn off the main line switch.

Operating Procedures — Punching a Single Card

Sometimes it is necessary just to punch one card when there are no cards in the keypunch. To do this, insert a blank card at the right of the punch station. Make sure the card lays flat on the card bed after it is inserted. Then press the register key. The card may now be punched. After punching, the card can be released with the clear switch.

Operating Procedures — Correcting a Card

If an error is made while punching a card, the entire card must be repunched. A simple procedure for correcting a card is:

1. Note the column or columns where the erroneous characters are punched.
2. Remove all cards from the keypunch.
3. Insert the erroneous card to the right of the punch station.
4. Press the register key and then the release key. This moves the card to the read station.
5. Insert a blank card to the right of the punch station.
6. Press the register key.
7. Pressing the duplicate key and watching the column indicator, duplicate the correct information from the first card into the second.

8. When a column that contains an error is reached, release the duplicate key and key in the correct information.

9. Repeat steps 7 and 8 until the entire card is duplicated or corrected.

Removing Jammed Cards

Sometimes a card jams at the read or punch station. When this happens, push the pressure-roll release lever with one hand while gently pulling the jammed card with the other hand. If small torn pieces are caught at either station, push them out with another card or blow them away.

Appendix D

EXPONENTIAL FORM
AND INPUT/OUTPUT

In Chapter 3 the input and output of real data was described, and in Chapter 4 real constants were discussed. With both topics we dealt with real data where the magnitude or size of the data was not very large or very small. When real data used in a program is extremely large or small, the approaches described in Chapters 3 and 4 become cumbersome. This appendix examines another way of coding real constants and another approach to the input and output of real data.

Exponential Form for Real Constants

Assume that we need the following real constant in a program:

$$5863000000000000.0$$

Although this is an acceptable way of coding this value, it is rather cumbersome. Another approach is to write the value as a real constant times some power of 10. To indicate the power, the letter E is used followed by an exponent. For example, the previous constant may be coded as:

$$5.863E15$$

This means "5.863 times 10 to the fifteenth power." This is equivalent to the previous value and may be used in a program in exactly the same manner as any other real constant.

In general, this form requires a basic real constant followed by the letter E and a signed or unsigned integer exponent. For example, the following are valid real constants in this form:

5.8E2	$(5.8 \times 10^2$ or 580.)
+.051E13	$(.051 \times 10^{13})$
-.39E+7	$(-.39 \times 10^7)$
789.E-25	$(789. \times 10^{-25})$
-6.0E-8	(-6.0×10^{-8})
21.3E+05	(21.3×10^5)

With the exponential form, the exponent must not be of such magnitude that the constant exceeds the maximum real value of the computer. For example, the following constant is too large for the IBM System/370:

$$3.72E85$$

In most versions of FORTRAN a real constant may be coded in exponential form as an integer constant followed by an exponent as described above. For example, the following are valid real constants in some versions of FORTRAN:

75E+10	(75×10^{10})
-138E3	$(-138 \times 10^3$ or -138000)
+6E-35	(6×10^{-35})

Double Precision Constants

In Chapter 9 we examined double precision data and how variable names that refer to such data are declared. Sometimes it is necessary to use a constant to describe double precision data. To code a double precision constant the exponential form described above is employed except that the letter D is used instead of the letter E. For example, the following are valid double precision constants:

25.3D7 (25.3×10^7)

1.23456789012D-16 $(1.23456789012 \times 10^{-16})$

-40D+21 (-40×10^{21})

.83260547012D27 $(.83260547012 \times 10^{27})$

5.6204D-08 (5.6204×10^{-8})

Double precision constants are not available in all versions of FORTRAN.

E-Format Code

Input and output of real data of large magnitude may be accomplished with the E-format code. The general form of this code is as follows:

> $Ew.d$
> where w is the field width.
> d is the number of decimal positions.

For input, this code may be used to describe data in the same format as the F-format code or the input data may be in an exponential form. For example, consider the following statements:

```
     READ(5,10) X,Y
 10 FORMAT(E10.2,E12.4)
```

The two input fields described by the E-format codes in the FORMAT statement are 10 and 12 columns in length respectively. The first field has two positions to the right of the decimal point, and the second field has four decimal positions. The input data may be punched in an exponential form consisting of an integer or real value followed optionally by the letter E and a signed or unsigned integer exponent. For example, assume that the values to be read for the fields are 5.62×10^8 and $-.0321 \times 10^{-25}$. Then the input card may be punched

123456789...............

5.62E8   -.0321E-25

The letter E may be left out of the field, in which case the exponent *must* be preceded by a sign. Thus, the following is another way of punching the data for the previous example:

```
123456789...............
```

	5.62+8	-.0321-25

It is not valid, however, merely to leave a blank in front of the exponent without a sign or the letter E.

The exponent may be any integer constant within the limits of the computer. It is important to right-justify the exponent since any trailing blanks in the field are interpreted as zeros.

If the decimal point is left out of the field, then the computer uses the number of decimal positions specified in the format code to determine its position. The number of decimal positions are counted, beginning with the first digit left of the exponent. Thus, the previous example may be punched as follows with the same result:

```
123456789...............
```

	562+8	-0321-25

When a decimal point is included in the field, its position overrides the position specified in the format code.

For output, the E-format code always specifies a field to be printed in a standardized exponential format. In this format the output data is arranged so that the decimal point appears at the left of the first non-zero digit in the output. Ahead of the decimal point a zero is printed and, if necessary, a negative sign. The exponent occupies the last four positions of the field. It begins with the letter E followed by a negative sign if the exponent is negative or a blank if it is positive. Following this is a two-digit exponent. For example, consider the following statements:

```
        WRITE(6,20) X,Y
    20 FORMAT(1X,E10.2,E12.4)
```

If the values of X and Y are as in the previous example, then the data is printed as follows:

```
123456789...............
```

0.56E 09	-0.3210E-26

Notice in both of the output fields that the exponent has been modified to reflect the shift in the decimal point to the left of the first nonzero digit. In addition, because of this shift and because of the number of decimal positions specified in the format code, the last digit of the first field is not printed and a zero is added to the second field.

When using the E-format code for output, the field must be sufficiently large to accommodate the output data. In general, the field width should be at least seven positions larger than the number of decimal positions. Seven positions are necessary to print the sign, the lead zero, the decimal point, and the four-position exponent.

D-Format Code

The input or output format for double precision data is specified by the D-format code. The general form of this code is as follows:

> Dw.d
> where w is the field width.
> d is the number of decimal positions.

For input, the D-format code may describe data in the same format as the F-format code or in exponential format. The exponential format may use the letter E, the letter D, or just a sign to specify the exponent. For example, consider this sequence of statements:

```
      DOUBLE PRECISION A,B
      READ(5,30) A,B
   30 FORMAT(2D12.4)
```

In this example, two 12-column fields are specified, each with four positions to the right of the decimal point. If the values 53.8721×10^{-8} and 4.3601×10^{25} are to be read and assigned to variable names A and B respectively, then the input data may be punched as follows:

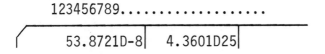

When used for output, the D-format code describes a field in the same format as an E-format code except that the letter D is printed instead of the letter E. For example, assume that the values of A and

B are printed with the following statements:

```
      WRITE(6,40) A,B
   40 FORMAT(1X,D13.6,D12.5)
```

Then the output appears as follows:

```
    123456789...................

  | 0.538721D-06| 0.43601D 26|
```

D-format code is not available in all versions of FORTRAN.

Appendix E

FLOWCHARTING

A tool that is often used to help design a computer program and also to document a program is a *program flowchart*. A flowchart is a diagram of the logic in a computer program. Figure E–1 shows a flowchart of the sample program discussed in Chapter 2 (see Fig. 2-7). This program reads three test scores, calculates the total and average of the scores, and prints the results. Notice that the flowchart depicts this sequence of steps. The flowchart is drawn by using special symbols connected by lines. Within each symbol is written a phrase that describes the activity at that step. The lines connecting the symbols show the sequence in which the steps take place.

During the program-designing activity the programmer may prepare rough flowcharts of how he or she thinks the program should work. Sometimes several flowcharts are drawn so that different designs can be compared. After the program logic is worked out with the rough diagrams, a final flowchart is drawn. Then the programmer can code the program directly from the flowchart.

When the program is being tested, errors may be detected in the logic. Then changes need to be made not only in the program but also in the flowchart. The final flowchart should depict precisely the logic in the completed program. This flowchart serves as documentation so that other programmers will be able to understand the program's logic more easily.

Flowchart Symbols

In a flowchart, the shape of the symbol indicates the type of activity that is to take place. Figure E–2 shows the standard program

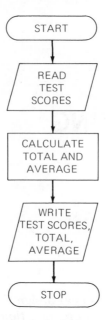

FIGURE E-1.   Flowchart of a test score averaging program.

flowchart symbols adopted by the American National Standards Institute (ANSI). The *process symbol* is used to represent any general processing activity such as an arithmetic calculation or data manipulation but not input/output, decision making, or preparation. For these other activities, special symbols are provided. The *input/output symbol* is used for any step that involves input or output data. The *decision symbol* is used whenever a decision is made in the program. For a step that involves setting up some part of the program, the *preparation symbol* is used. The *terminal point symbol* appears at the beginning and end of the flowchart. The *connector symbol* is used to connect parts of a flowchart. *Flowlines* show the direction of the flow of logic in the flowchart. The normal direction is from top to bottom and left to right. Arrowheads on the lines are optional (but usually used) if the normal flow is followed and required if the direction of flow is other than normal. Finally, the *annotation symbol* is used for additional comments or notes. This symbol may be open on either the right or left with the dashed line extending to the symbol that requires comment.

Simple Flowcharts

Figure E-1 illustrates a simple flowchart using some of these symbols. The terminal point symbol is used to mark the point where the flowchart logic starts and where it stops. The input/output symbol

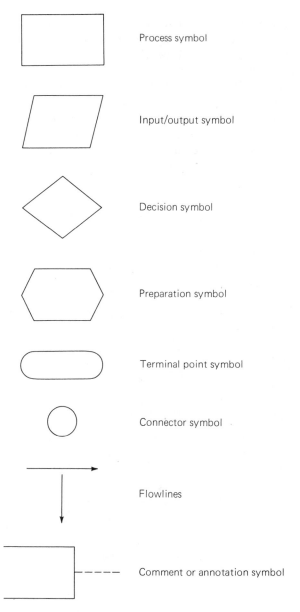

Process symbol

Input/output symbol

Decision symbol

Preparation symbol

Terminal point symbol

Connector symbol

Flowlines

Comment or annotation symbol

FIGURE E-2.   ANSI flowchart symbols.

shows where the input data is read and the output is printed. The process symbol is used for the calculation step. Notice that the flowchart symbols do not necessarily correspond directly with individual instructions in the program. For example, the process symbol in the flowchart in Fig. E-1 corresponds to two arithmetic calculations in the program. However, the *sequence* of symbols does follow exactly the sequence of instructions in the program. By beginning with the symbol marked START and following the flowlines through the flowchart to the STOP symbol, the logic of the program can be understood.

Another example of a simple flowchart is shown in Fig. E–3. This is the flowchart for the payroll calculation program discussed in Chapter 4 (see Fig. 4–3). In this flowchart, each calculation is shown as a separate step. Notice that the order of these steps corresponds to the order of the arithmetic assignment statements in the program.

This figure also demonstrates how a loop is represented in a flow-

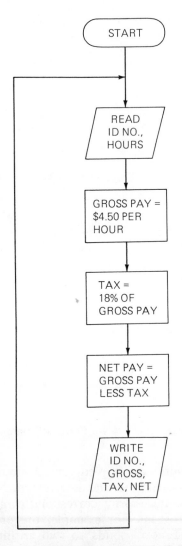

FIGURE E–3.   Flowchart of a payroll calculation program.

chart. A loop is shown by a flowline that goes from the end of the loop to its beginning. Notice that there is not a separate symbol for a GO TO statement; branching from one point to another is simply indicated by a flowline. Also in this flowchart there is no symbol that shows where the flowchart logic ends. The loop in this flowchart does not contain any step that automatically stops the repetition.

Flowcharting Decisions

The flowchart in Fig. E-4 shows the logic in the tuition calculation program discussed in Chapter 5 (see Fig. 5-1). This flowchart uses the decision symbol to show the test of whether the number of units is

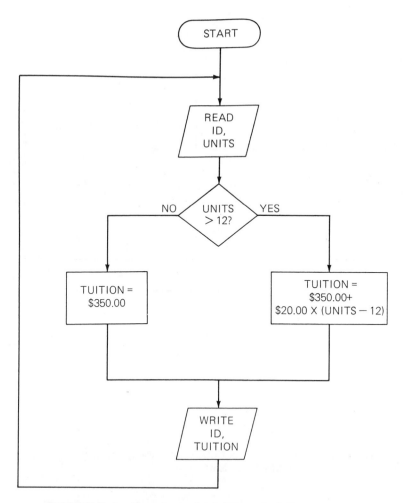

FIGURE E-4. Flowchart of a tuition calculation program.

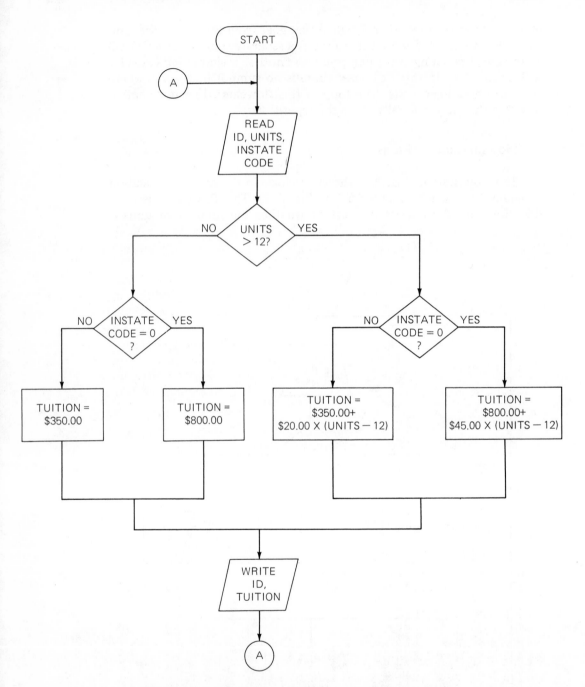

FIGURE E-5. Flowchart of a tuition calculation program
with nested decisions.

greater than twelve. Whenever a decision symbol is used, two or more flowlines *must* leave the symbol. These lines represent the possible answers to the questions asked in the symbol. The flowlines leaving a decision symbol *must* be labeled with the possible answers. The decision symbol in Fig. E-4 asks whether the number of units is greater than twelve and the possible answers — yes and no — are written above the flowlines leaving the symbol.

This flowchart depicts the basic decision logic discussed in Chapter 5. If a condition is true, then one thing is done, otherwise something else is done. After doing the necessary processing the logical flow comes together to continue on to the next step.

A nested decision can be depicted in a flowchart. Figure E-5 shows a flowchart for the tuition calculation program with a nested decision (see Fig. 5-9). Notice that after the first decision is made, a second decision is required. The nesting of the decisions shows up very clearly in the flowchart.

This flowchart also shows the use of the connector symbol. This symbol is used when it is necessary but inconvenient to connect distant parts of a flowchart with a flowline or when it is necessary to continue a flowchart on to another page. When the connector symbol is used, it appears once where the flow logic leaves one part of the chart and again where the logic enters the other part. Within each set of connectors is placed an identifying letter or number. In Fig. E-5, the letter A identifies the pair of connectors. If another set of connector symbols is needed for another part of the flowchart, a different letter or symbol such as B is used.

Selection can be indicated in a flowchart by a series of nested decisions. When the selection is done by a computed GO TO statement a single decision symbol with multiple flowlines is used. Figure E-6 shows how this is done. This is a flowchart for the payroll calculation program where the payrate is based on a shift code (see Fig. 5-12). Notice that the decision symbol indicates the variable that determines the flow path and that each line leaving the symbol is labeled with a possible value of this variable.

Flowcharting Loop Control

When a loop is controlled by any of the techniques discussed in Section 6-1, the condition that determines when the loop is to be terminated is indicated by a decision within the loop. For example, Fig. E-7 shows the flowchart for the tuition calculation program with the input controlled by a trailer value (see Fig. 6-2). The first step after the input operation is to check for the trailer value. If the

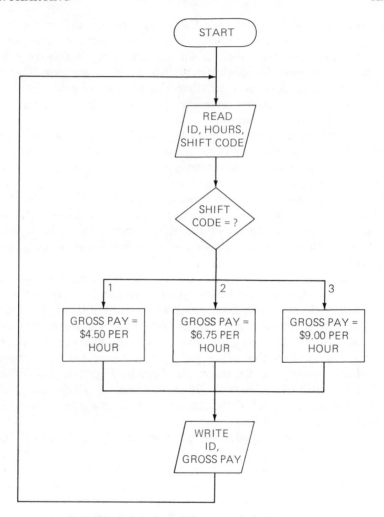

FIGURE E-6.   Flowchart of a payroll program.

ID is 9999, then the processing stops. This step is shown in the flow-chart by a decision symbol.

Figure E–8 shows the flowchart for the interest calculation program with a processing loop (see Fig. 6–3). In this program the loop ter-minates when the bank balance becomes greater than or equal to $2000. This is shown in the flowchart by the decision step at the beginning of the loop. Notice also that the balance and year are ini-tialized before the loop is entered.

When a program includes a counting loop, the corresponding flow-chart must show the steps that initialize the counter, modify the counter, and test the counter. Figure E–9 is a flowchart of the program

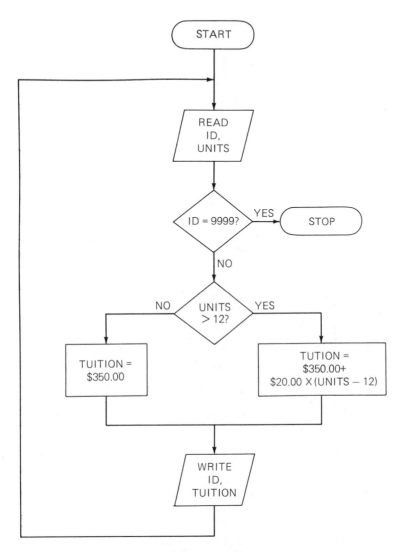

FIGURE E-7.   Flowchart of a tuition calculation program
with input loop control.

that finds the total and average of fifty test scores (see Fig. 6–5). The
loop is executed exactly fifty times. The counter is initialized to one
before the loop is entered. Each time through the loop the counter is
increased by one and tested to determine if it is still less than or equal
to fifty.

A modification of this program is to read the number of data cards

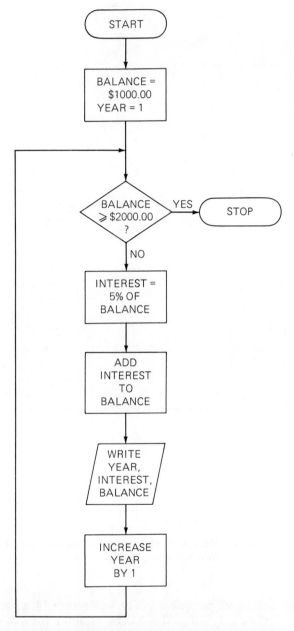

FIGURE E-8. Flowchart of an interest calculation program.

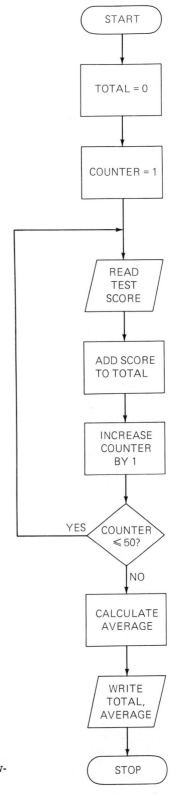

FIGURE E-9. Flowchart of a program to total and average fifty test scores.

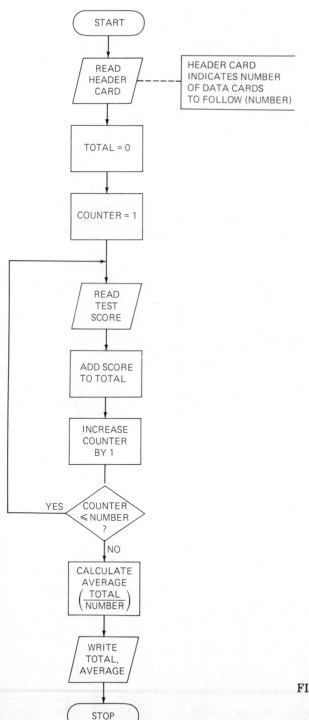

FIGURE E-10. Flowchart of a program to total and average a given number of test scores.

from a header card (see Fig. 6-6). The flowchart in Fig. E-10 includes this modification. This flowchart also shows the use of the comment or annotation symbol. This symbol is used to add clarifying comments to another symbol. The dotted line extends to the symbol that requires clarification.

A WHILE loop can be flowcharted with a decision symbol for the condition that determines whether the loop should be repeated. For example, Fig. E-11 shows a flowchart of the tuition calculation program with a WHILE loop (see Fig. 6-11). Notice that the loop is repeated as long as the condition is true.

There is no standard way of flowcharting a DO loop. The DO statement alone implies all of the operations necessary to control a counting loop. One approach is to show the initialization, modification, and testing of the DO-variable explicitly in the flowchart. However, this can be cumbersome when many loops are involved. Another approach is shown in Fig. E-12 which is the flowchart of the program to total and average fifty test scores using a DO loop (see Fig. 6-16). In this flowchart the preparation symbol is used to specify the DO-variable and its initial value, test value, and increment. The end of the loop is indicated by a connector symbol which can be thought of as corresponding to a CONTINUE statement. Repetition of the loop is shown by a flowline from the connector symbol to the beginning of the loop. When the loop has been executed the required number of times, the logic flows through the connector symbol at the end to the next step after the loop.

Nested DO loops may be flowcharted as illustrated in Fig. E-13. This is the flowchart of the program that finds the total and average of five groups of fifty test scores each (see Fig. 6-22). Notice that each DO loop is set off by a preparation symbol to set up the loop and a connector symbol at the end of the loop.

Flowcharting Subprograms

When subprograms are used, a separate flowchart is prepared for every subprogram. The terminal point symbol is used to show the entry and exit points of the subprogram's logic. The name of the subprogram is written in the entry point symbol. The exit point symbol may be left blank or the word RETURN may be used. Between these terminal point symbols, the subprogram's logic is shown using standard flowchart conversions.

Figure E-14 shows the flowchart for the RMAX function described in Chapter 12 (see Fig. 12-3). Notice that the logic of the function is

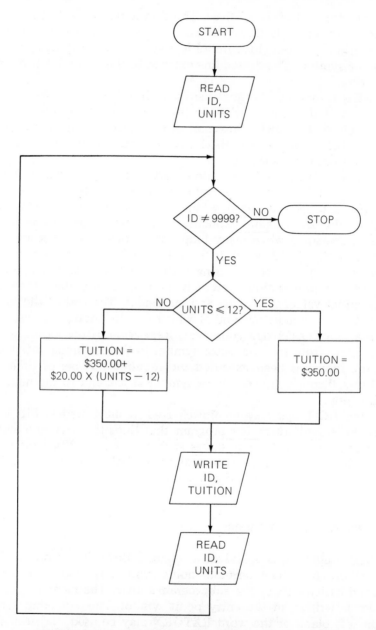

FIGURE E-11. Flowchart of a tuition calculation program with a WHILE loop.

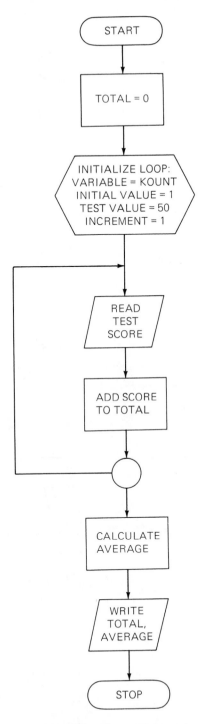

FIGURE E-12. Flowchart of a program to total and average fifty test scores with a DO loop.

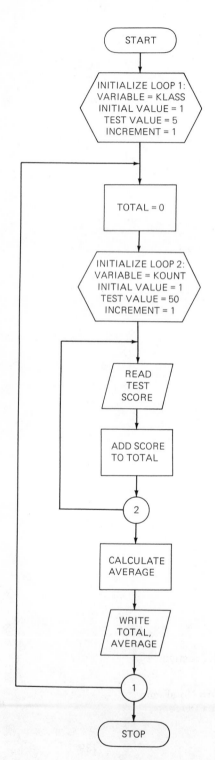

FIGURE E-13. Flowchart of a program with nested DO loops.

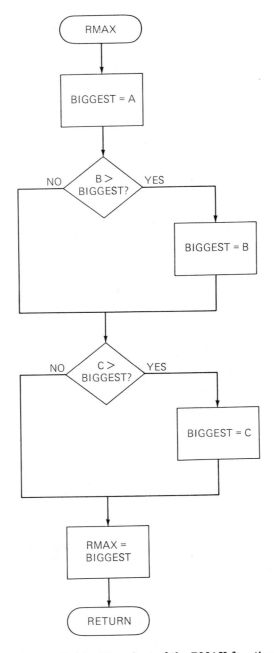

FIGURE E–14. Flowchart of the RMAX function.

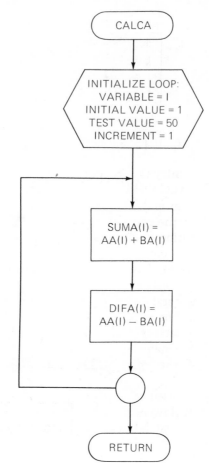

FIGURE E-15. Flowchart of the subroutine CALCA.

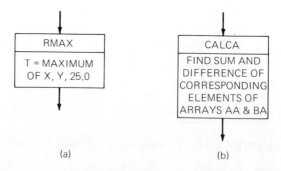

(a)   (b)

FIGURE E-16. Striped symbols used in the flowchart of
a calling program: (a) calling the function
RMAX; (b) calling the subroutine CALCA.

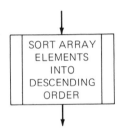

FIGURE E-17.   Use of the predefined process symbol.

displayed between the entry point and exit point symbols. In Fig. E-15 the flowchart of the CALCA subroutine is shown (see Fig. 12-10). This subroutine finds the sum and difference of corresponding elements of two arrays. Notice that the conventions are the same whether the flowchart represents a subroutine or a function.

In the flowchart of a calling program, reference to a subprogram is shown by a flowchart symbol with a horizontal line drawn near the top. This is called a *striped symbol*. The name of the subprogram is entered above the line, and a general description of the process to be performed by the subprogram may be written below the line. Figure E-16 shows two examples of this technique for the subprograms illustrated previously. Notice that the name used above the line is the same as the name that appears in the entry point symbol of the subprogram's flowchart.

A striped symbol is used when the flowchart of the subprogram is part of the same set of flowcharts as that of the calling program. Sometimes the subprogram used is a standard routine, previously prepared by another programmer. Its logic appears in a flowchart that is not part of the set of flowcharts that shows reference to the subprogram. In this case, the *predefined process* symbol is used in the flowchart. This symbol is a process symbol with a vertical line near each side. Within the symbol, reference is made to the appropriate subprogram. For example, assume that a standard subprogram is available for sorting the elements of an array into descending numerical sequence. This subprogram is general enough to be used in many programs and its logic is shown in a separate flowchart. In the flowchart of a program that calls this subprogram the predefined process symbol is used as in Fig. E-17.

INDEX